In Quest of the Dates of the Vedas

Comprehensive Study of the Vedic and the Indo-European Flora, Fauna and Climate in Light of the Information Emerging from the Disciplines of Archaeology, Archaeo-botany, Geology, Genetics and Linguistics for the Last 10,000 Years

Premendra Priyadarshi

PARTRIDGE
A Penguin Random House Company

ISBN:	Softcover	978-1-4828-3425-3
	eBook	978-1-4828-3424-6

To order additional copies of this book, contact
Partridge India
000 800 10062 62
orders.india@partridgepublishing.com

www.partridgepublishing.com/india

Contents

Preface

There has been a perpetual debate about the dates of the Vedas and the origin of the Indo-European speaking people. "Paradigms, especially old ones, die harder than Bruce Willis." said James Adovasio.[1] There have been explosively new findings in archaeology and genetics, and also in the field of linguistics, having the capacity to rewrite an entirely different history of mankind. But the history as stated in the books and preserved in the minds of the authors has not changed the least.

There is a lot of information in the Vedas which pose the time limits for each of the four Vedic *Samhitas*. The *Rig-Veda* does not have wheat, rice, millets, lentil, date-palm (*Phoenix*). These appear in the *Yajur-Veda*. From archaeology, we know that wheat and rice both were well cultivated in the Ghaghar-Hakra culture in the fifth millennium BC (Shinde). Thus *Rig-Veda* must be before that time. Lentil was domesticated in West Asia, but it arrived in India in the Bronze Age. Its absence from the *Rig-Veda* and presence in the *Yajur-Veda* speaks a lot about the dates of the two texts. Date-palm arrived in the region in the mid sixth millennium (Costantini). Its absence from the *Rig-Veda* fixes the date of this text to before the sixth millennium BC.

---

1 My friend Stephen Oppenheimer had once cited this, and I owe this quote to him.

The finger millet, which came from Africa to India in the late second millennium BC (Fuller) is absent from all the Vedas, clearly indicating that all the Vedas had been edited finally before this time. Contrasting this, the foxtail millet (*priyaṅgu*), which arrived in India from China during the early Bronze Age has been mentioned in the *Yajur-Veda*, and not mentioned in the *Rig-Veda*. This finding would fix the date of the *Rig-Veda* before the Bronze Age and that of the *Yajur-Veda* contemporary with the Bronze Age.

The *Yajur-Veda* corresponds to the wet and warm mid-Holocene (5,500-2500 BC). And this is the reason why we generally get mention of those animals in the *Yajur-Veda* which lived only in the wet and warm climates, but cannot live in cold dry climates. Such animals are crocodile, tortoise, beaver, rhinoceros etc which are completely absent from the *Rig-Veda*. Rhinoceros, beaver and crocodile become absent again in the *Atharva-Veda* indicating change to the dry climate, and placing the *Athava-Veda* after 1900 BC. However the domestic animals are present in all the periods indicating early domestication of the cow, buffalo, camel and horse.

The period of the *Sama-Veda* comes to 6000-5,500 BC, which was the transition period between cold-dry Early Holocene and the wet and warm mid-Holocene. The *Rig-Veda* gets placed in the cold and dry Early Holocene (8000-6000 BC) when the Sarasvati was connected with the Himalayan glaciers.

The DNA of the humans have revealed that once evolved in East Africa, man used the Arabian southern coast as a land-bridge to reach India and then all further human expansion and dispersal took place from there. This has been proved again and again that this was the sole route out of Africa. That the man came out from Africa through the Sinai land-bridge has been ruled out by an infinite number of DNA studies. Yet most of the authors, including even many of the geneticists refer to the out of Africa route as through Sinai to Middle East, and then trifurcating the way one leading to Europe, other to Central Asia and the third to Iran!

The human DNA studies have not been covered in this book, because I have already dwelt on that topic in my previous book *The First Civilization of the World*. Nor have I discussed here in this book the DNA studies of most of the domestic animals and plants, as they too have been discussed and analyzed in my earlier book as well as some of my journal articles. The conclusion of these DNA studies is that domestic mouse (*Mus musculus*), black rat (*Rattus rattus*), Shrew, cow (*Bos indicus*), pig, buffalo, sheep and goat were domesticated first in India, and then they migrated to the rest of the world. Some of these have been mentioned in this book.

The most powerful blow to the Aryan Invasion Theory came not from the study of the human DNA but from the studies of the horse DNA. The theory had rested on the hypothesis that the steppe was the home of the wild caballus horse Przewalskii, which was domesticated there and with the help of this domesticated horse the countries to the west (Europe) and to the south (India, Iran) were conquered by the Aryans of the steppe. However the DNA examinations of the horses have contradicted this view. They have revealed that the Przewalskii was not a member of the caballus horse species at all, but it was an independent species with two chromosomes more than the true horse--*Equus caballus* (or *Equus ferus f. caballus*). Other studies came out with the conclusion that the DNAs recovered from the archaeological remains of the domestic horse found in Central Asia and western steppe were all of the horses originating in China or anywhere else but not in the steppe itself. Frachetti demonstrated that the domestic horse and riding became features of Central Asian nomads in the Common Era, and not before that. Levine clarified that the horse bones recoverd from the steppe and Central Asia belonged to the hunted horses, not the domestic horses.

There is enough evidence generated in literature about origin of the light race horses from the Indian *Sivalensis* (*q.v.*). Nearly all of such evidence had been generated by the benevolent generation of the English and other Western scholarship which lived before the Second World War. Current generation of scholars, whether Indian or Western, is more interested in popularity and important positions, and concern for the truth has become uncommon. Thus, whenever DNAs of the domestic horses (or even sheep, goat and camel) of the world have been compared, the Indian samples have been left out.

As such, there is no sound evidence of the origin of the domestic horse from the steppe. Thompson found that either the European wild horse Tarpan or the Mongolian wild horse Przewalskii was the ancestor of the heavier built daft type horse of Europe, and that the lighter race horses of the south like the Arabian horse originated from the *Sivalensis*. By this time it has become clear that the Tarpan was the ancestor of the European daft horse, not the Przewalskii.

The DNA studies of the living as well as the archaeological horses found that there were centres of local horse domestication in Europe older than the supposed presence of the domestic horse in the steppe. Another development was the collapse of David Anthony's Dereivka horse of 4200 BC. The claim was retracted by the author himself after the radiocarbon dating of the Dereivka horse's skull proved him wrong.

The reason why there was a sharp decline in the number of horses after 6000 BC in India is climatic. The mid-Holocene wet climate converted the Indus-Sarasvati region from grassland to a dense forest region making it inhospitable to the wild horse and camel, as well as the ostrich and giraffe. Hence the Indian wild horse *Sivalensis* became extinct from the wild existence soon after 6000 BC. The regional wild horses either died or migrated to the Thar region in India and also to Iran and South Central Asia (Turkmenistan, Tajikistan). Some of the light Indian horses which had adapted to the high altitudes of the Himalayas too survived this period. But over the time their mares were captured and assimilated into the domestic stock, and they too became extinct from the wild.

During 6000 BC to 2000 BC, and even after that, the Indus-Sarasvati region had only domestic horses, which dwindled greatly in number because of the Vedic ritualistic slaughter of the horse. This is the why we get so less horse bones in the Indus Valley Civilization. But Kazanas pointed out in his lecture delivered in the Patna University in April 2013 that the horse bones do not increase in Indian archaeology even up to 800 BC; and there is no archaeological evidence of any increase in the number of the horse bones in Indian archaeology at about 1500 BC or any time in the second millennium BC. The animal got strongly associated with the burial-ritual and its graphic depiction probably became a taboo. This could be one of the reasons for its not having been depicted in the Indus seals.

When the DNA studies ruled out any human migration from Europe, Central Asia or West Asia to have arrived into India between 8,000 BC and 1000 BC, it was expected that the Aryan Invasion hypothesis would be retracted. However, it did not happen. The argument was changed from "invasion" to "language-conversion". The languages of North India and Iran were changed under the powerful rule of a handful of invading Aryans who have not left any mark of their genes on India, yet were able to convert the whole of North India into Indo-European speaking within a couple of centuries, at a time when there was no mass media, a very low literacy rate and very restrictive travelling conditions. This is a very far-fetched imagination. This type of language change did not happen in north India during the 600 years of rule by the Persian speaking elite Muslims in India. Nor did it happen in Europe during the period of the Roman Empire or in Spain during the long Arab rule in the country.

Often self-contradictory stands have been taken by people when it comes to the history of India. Thus, Peter Bellwood wrote that the elite-dominance leading to language change cannot operate over a very large population. However when the issue related with India, he supported the hypothesis that the Aryans from Turkey arrived into India with farming, and changed the language of the northern part of India under their dominating farming skills.

There was the need to produce a robust multi-disciplinary work to clarify the confusions, false beliefs and wrong impressions prevailing in the field of Indo-European history. For the purpose, I persuaded and talked with a large number of learned people in India. Failing in my effort, I decided to do the team work alone. By this I mean, I had to myself study the basics of all the disciplines involved and make in-depth examination of the available facts, arguments and possibilities.

The whole philology of the animal and plants having bearing on the homeland issue has been re-examined in this book. It has been established in this book on the basis of philological examination that lion, tiger, mongoose, camel, crab, oyster, conch-snails, carp (fish), snakes (including even the python), frog, tortoise, chameleon and lizard lived in the original home of the Indo-Europeans. These animals are characteristically Indian or southern in distribution and presence of the Indo-European name for these animals proves that the Indo-Europeans lived at a place where these animals were found.

The Lachs Theory of Thieme (1951) has been examined here and it has been found that words *lachs* etc for "salmon" are actually words from the substrate language of Europe and Central Asia and the cognates are distributed up to Japanese and even North Amerindian languages. Hence, these words are certainly not Indo-European, and the Lachs Theory should not have been launched in the first place. Thus the Lachs Theory can be discarded now onwards in the Indo-European studies.

That the plants mulberry, opium, *Calotropis*, lotus, *Acacia* and rose-apple (Indian plum) grew in the homeland has been made evident by the philological survey done in this book. These are typically Indian plants. However there are some European plants which have been claimed by Witzel and the other authors to have been part of the philologically deciphered Indo-European flora. The examination of such claims reveals that there was gross manipulation of facts for achieving such conclusions. The sections on beech and oak demonstrate how scholars have concocted and lied. However attempt has been made in this book to identify the Vedic names of those plants and animals which existed in India in the Early Holocene dry and cold climate but became extinct once the region became wetter and warmer, and are not found in India toady except some of them in the Himalayas.

I have tried not to repeat the arguments of the earlier authors like Nicholas Kazanas, B.B. Lal, S.P. Gupta and Koenraad Elst. However if anything in the argument needed to be explored further that has been done. The fundamental bases of some of the arguments of Parpola, Witzel, Thieme etc have been examined and found to be wrong. Copper toy-chariots have been found from the Indus Valley Civilization (Mackay, Vats), although denied by these authors. There is enormous genetic and cultural evidence of dispersal of Indians in all direction during the Bronze Age, which cannot be accounted for by the hypotheses of the AIT authors.

Although the language used in the Veads is nearly the same, the content covers information of periods separated by thousands of years. Obviously it will have to be accepted that the same contents were given new language as the time changed. Thus the texts were regularly edited for the language change taking place with time within the northwest India's Indo-European linguistic stock. However it is possible that no further editing has been done after 1300 BC, the date of the last of all the Vedas (*Atharva-Veda*).

It is easier and better to accept that the language of the texts were changed with time, rather than to say that the two thirds of such a large and populous sub-continent as India changed its language at 1500-1300 BC. Both are assumptions, but which one could have happened more easily is the deciding point—language change of the entire population or the gradual language editing of the sacred texts as time passed. After all it was an oral tradition in which the language changes take place even without being discernible to the speakers.

In this entire book the word "Veda" has been used to imply the respective *samhita* portions of the four Vedas only. The flora, fauna and climate of the four Vedas are all entirely different from each other as if they describe or pertain to four entirely different periods of time. Such information needed to be correlated with that available from the recent studies in archaeo-biology and geology.

Geology has recently clarified that the Sarasvati River lost her connection with the Himalayan glaciers at about 8900 BP or about 6950 BC. This problem can be only resolved if we date the *Rig-Veda* to about 6000 to 8000 BC. That was the time when no tiger lived in that region although the lion lived because it was a grassland ecosystem. Consistent with this information we find that there is no mention of the tiger in the *Rig-Veda*. Historians have ignored the Vedic texts completely while writing about the history of the Vedic period. The *Rig-Veda* depicts all three modes of life, hunter-gatherer, pastoral and farming. This pertains to the dawn of the Neolithic period.

The reports of the presence or absence of the pollens of the various trees have come out in the last ten years in many scientific journals. They have been thoroughly exhausted here to provide a picture of the different trees or types of ecosystems present during the various eras of the Holocene in India, Iran, Central Asia, the steppe and North and South Europe. This picture explains why some names of certain plants and animals survived in either North Europe or South Europe but not in both.

The survival of the names of the plants and animals depended on the presences of such animals or plants throughout the route of migration as well as at the source and the destination. Such climatic conditions were present in which millennium has been determined in this book on the basis of the recent palynological reports. That gives us the precise date of migration to any particular country or region. This method has been utilized for the first time in this book.

Attempt has been made to identify the some of the animals and plants mentioned in the *Rig-Veda* or in the later Vedas but which no more exist in India. Or if at all they exist, they exist in the high reaches of the Himalayas and have slipped out of the popular memory. Such plants include the *soma, suparṇā, kadru, kuṣṭha, devadāru* etc. Such identifications will help the medical field as many of such plants have been mentioned in the Vedas as the cure of some serious diseases like tuberculosis.

Although I believe that the word Aryan has been abused too much, and the phrase 'original Indo-European speakers' should be used instead, yet I have used it often because of its brevity and handyness. I do suppose that that was an original language for all mankind, and its relic evidence is printed on all the languages of the world (Bengston and Ruhlen). Thus the family tree of the languages will also emerge parallel to the DNA family trees. Matrilineal trees (mtDNA) would reflect more exactly the language tree. There was a language which was ancestral to all the Indo-European languages, although it was not the same as the suggested PIE forms, but in many ways similar. It cannot be the same because of the limitations of the human minds to visualize the truth. But this language did not come in isolation from the heaven, and it resembled the other languages in its neighbourhood, like the Proto-Munda, Proto-Dravidian etc. In this book, the word Veda has been used to denote the respective *Samhita* portions only.

To err is human. One, who fears too much from making any mistake, does very few good things either. I am sure there may be many mistakes of facts and their interpretation in this book because of sheer lacuna in my knowledge. I will welcome any such issue noted by the valued readers to be pointed out to me by my email id. The thing will be gratefully acknowledge in the next edition if found true.

I am grateful to many people for their help, guidance and moral support. They Include Prof. Nikolas Kazanas (Athens), Er Ram Naresh Sharma (Patna), Dr Madhusudan Mishra (Delhi), K.N. Dikshit (Delhi), Shri Raghunath Prasad Sinha (Patna), Prof Jayashri Mishra (Patna), Dr Avinash Jha (Magadh University), Shri S. Kalyanaraman (Chennai), Shri A.K. Joshi (Chennai) etc. I am also thankful to Jireh Ingod, Anne Minoza and other staff of the Partridge Publications who were always encouraging and warm. Dr Ravi Kirti (Patna), Shri Shailendra

Shubhadarshi (Patna) and many others helped me by time to time suggestions. I thank them all. I am specially thankful to my daughter Sneha and wife Alka for bearing all troubles and who maintained the moral support and helped me survive during the worst financial nightmare which this project imposed on to the family.

P.P.
New Delhi
11 June 2014.
email: premendrap@gmail.com

Section I

Ecology and Climate Change

Chapter 1

Human Migration at the end of Glacial Period: The DNA studies

It has been clear from the DNA as well as the archaeological studies that the earliest humans lived in Africa, India, Southeast Asia and Australia only (Dennel and Porr 2014). Recent DNA studies have thrown remarkable light on the human migration history over the last 15,000 years. It has revealed that not only man, but animals dependant on man like the domestic mouse, rat, shrew, cow, goat and sheep too have migrated out from India over the last 15,000 years (Priyadarshi 2011, 2012, 2013). No evidence of human arrival into India through the northwest corridor between 13,000 BC and 1,000 BC could be detected from the DNA studies (Sahoo 2006:847). In another study, the only signal of any ancient immigration from the West to India over the last 4000 years was that of the Greek arrival in the first millennium BCE leaving traces on the genetic record of the Swat Valley (Hellenthal 2014).

The Last Glacial Maximum (LGM, 20,000 BC-16,000 BC) was the time when the earth saw a four thousand years long freeze of the northern temperate regions. Human life remained restricted to the tropical regions like India, Southeast Asia and tropical Africa. Beyond this, man survived in the cold refugia in some places. Some population survived in Southeast Tibet, some parts of China, Franco-Cantabrian refugia, the Balkans, north east of the Black Sea and eastern Central Asia. Thus most of Europe and Asia had become denuded of human population, except the southern regions of Eurasia.

Between 16,000 BC and 14,000 BC, climate started improving and human population increased. Better climate promoted better growth of vegetations which constituted the food for man and herbivores both. Rise in herbivore population cased increased availability of pray for hunting, and that too increased the food availability leading to increase in the human population in India just following the LGM (Priyadarshi 2011:137-43).

This population growth of India resulted in a pressure on land resulting in early experiments with food production, ultimately leading to the development of farming (Priyadarshi2011:66-90). However, capturing the animals live and keeping them for future food requirement must have started before the onset of the LGM. In India we get the concrete evidence of cattle, goat and sheep rearing since the end of the Last Glacial Maximum (Priyadarshi 2013).

Because of all these factors, Indian population soon got saturated after the LGM and a migration was forced by ecological constraints. The first emigrants out of India through the northwest corridor of India have been identified to have carried with them the Y-Chromosomal haplogroup R1a1a and J2b (Underhill 2009; Sahoo 2006; Sengupta 2006; Priyadarshi 2011:91-105; 2012:336-42, 337-Table 1). The J2b seems to have started earlier then the R1a1. It followed a south route and reached Anatolia (Turkey) and from there to Europe. However an important section of these preferred to venture through the sea from the eastern coasts of the Mediterranean Sea. The R1a1 started from the Gujarat region at about 14,000 BC, yet its expansion suddenly ceased because of another short 1000 year long mini-glacial period which we know today as the Tardiglacial (Underhill 2009: Fig 1 inset).

The process was however interrupted or rather reversed for some time when the Late Glacial period (Younger Dryas; Tardiglacial) came in for a couple of millennia from 11,000 BC to 9500 BC. Most of the northern/temperate human populations vanished or survived in a few refugia. There were only two small human refugia in Europe in the Iberian and Balkan Peninsulae. However in India, Southeast Asia and tropical Africa, human population survived well with the help of domestic goat, sheep and their wool, which had been domesticate several millennia before this period in India.

Once this cold period passed, there was an unprecedented growth of human population resulting in the relative scarcity of the hunted animals necessitating the live capture of animals and keeping them as stock for future food. This necessity for increasing the food supply forced pastoralism and later farming which is evident from the archaeology of Mehrgarh and the Ganga Valley (Priyadarshi2011:66-90). Necessity is the mother of invention applied to the invention of pastoralism and farming too. Farming further led to availability of more food and faster population growth. Once the population approached the carrying capacity, migration out from the northwest and northest corridors became essential.

In northwest India, the first farming started during the Early Holocene when the rainfall was less yet the rivers were full from the water coming down from the melting Himalayan glaciers. The landscape was semi-arid grasslands and open forest. There were no burnt bricks or pottery at Mehrgarh at this time although pottery was present at that very time in the Ganga Valley Neolithic, which is older than the northwest India Neolithic.

After 6000 BC, the monsoonal change led to conversion of the region into a high rainfall area by 5500 BC. The fauna and flora changed to accommodate to the new climate. Atmospheric temperature increased too. This is the time when we get the spread of farming to the other regions within India. This period is called Early Harappa and is represented by the archaeology of Rakhigarhi and Bhirrana. Mehrgarh Period-II belongs to this time. The Harappa culture evolved and developed against this background maturing fully by 2500 BC. The food production and industrial production reached record high. There was again a population growth resulting from the industrialization of the region which causeed some human migration out from India during the period we know today as the Bronze Age.

After 3000 BC, the climate changed again gradually converting to the arid ecology by 1900 BC. Between 2200 and 1900 BC, there were large-scale famines, resulting in death, disease, degradation of the culture and finally abandonment of the Indus Valley Civilization.

The migrations also took place to Southeast Asia and Australia at this time. However all these regions had been well populated much before as the results of the earlier migrations. Hence the Bronze Age migrations out of India did not result in language spread or language change, but yet influenced the vocabularies of the host countries and there was transmission of the Indian Bronze Age culture too as a consequence of these migrations.

Chapter 2

Climate Change during the Early Post Glacial Period

> *"yās cedam upaśṛṇvanti yās ca dūram parāgatāḥ"*
> "All Plants that hear this speech and those that have departed far away"
>
> *Rig-Veda* 10.97.21.

This mantra from the *Rig-Veda* is evidence of its authors' awareness of the fact that by the time of the last phase of the *Rig-Veda* (the tenth *mandala*) many plants had already become extinct from the Indus-Sarasvati region and had receded to the Himalayas or even more distant locations. This mantra is evidence of the climatic and ecological change taking place during the very period of the *Rig-Veda*.

When the climate changed, the flora changed and fauna changed too. But the words--the names of the plants and animals --often stayed, after having been applied to the new species of plants and animals inhabiting the newer climate. Bloomfield rightly mentioned in his introduction to the translation of the *Atharva-Veda* that the meanings of the Vedic mantras are generally altered as per the requirements of the changed environments with time:

> "Not infrequently a stanza has to be rendered in some measure of harmony with its connection, when, in fact, a more original meaning, not at all applicable to its present environment, is but scantily covered up by the 'secondary modifications of the text. This garbled tradition of the ancient texts partakes of the character of popular etymology in the course of the transmission of words. New meaning is read into the mantras, and any little stubbornness on their part is met with modifications of their wording. The critic encounters here a very difficult situation: searching investigation of the remaining Vedic collections is necessary before a bridge can be built from the more original meaning to the meaning implied and required by the situation in a given *Atharvan* hymn." (Bloomfield 1897: Introduction).

The *Rig-Vedic* descriptions of the Northwest Indian climate encompass a long period spread over several millennia and the varied shades of environments and climates changing with time possibly transmitted as oral tradition and later recollected from the folk memories and edited into the hymns as we get them today. Thus the language of the hymns is of a much later time, yet the content remaind the recollection of the northwest Indian past covering several thousand years. That the language and grammar was changed several times over the ages has been made out as the result of the in depth study by the Indologists like Arnold, Thomson and Slocum, Van Nooten and Holland etc.

Bloomfield may be right in his assessment that "The entire Vedic tradition, the *Rig-Veda* not excepted, presents rather the conclusion than the beginning of a long period of literary activity" (Bloomfield 1897: Introduction). And in this recollection we find the reflections and the glimpses going back up to the Late Glacial and the early Holocene times and the descriptions of the climate, plants, trees and mountains pertaining to those periods.

The *Rig* and the other Vedas mention the presence of such trees in the northwest India which grow today only in the temperate regions of Europe, Siberia and in the Himalayas (Bhargava 1964). This prompted many authors to suggest that the Vedas, particularly the *Rig-* was composed somewhere to the north of India. Witzel proposed Bactria. However, no other evidence suggesting the composition of the *Rig-Veda* outside India has ever been produced, and the geography described in the text is that of India. Clearly the objective impression should be that a colder climate prevailed in India at the time of composing the *Rig-Veda*, and not that the Veda was written somewhere in the temperate region of the modern world.

Studies of the fossil pollen of northwest India have revealed that northwest India was a colder place soon after the Last glacial period. Trees of the colder climate like willow, juniper, oak, pine etc grew there in the Kachi plain. This type of flora lasted up to 4000 BC (Costantini 2008); and could have well continued up to the fourth millennium (J.-F. Jarrige, 2008). However the date 1500 BC, which has been claimed to be the date of the arrival and subsequent settlement of the Aryans in northwest India, was climatically quite hot and dry and no 'cold climate' tree could have survived there. Hence the date of the *Rig-Veda* (as 1200 BC) needs to be revised.

The type of vegetation changed everywhere during the Holocene. The western coasts of the Black sea, where we get forest today, were steppe lands up to 5000 BC (Wright 2003:133). East of the Black Sea in the Caucasus region, the climate changed from the steppe to the woodland at 3000 BC (*ibid*: 133-4). In the Altai region at the junction of Kazakhstan, Russia, Mongolia and China, the steppe changed into conifer forest at about 6,000 BC (*ibid*: 134). The "western steppe" to the north of the Black Sea was unforested until a much later date than all these.

Immediately after the end of the glacial period, about 8,000 BC, the birch forests expanded in north India, Central Asia and Europe. Soon after the expansion of the birch, a warmer period conducive to the growth of oak arrived. The period 6000 BC to 3000 BC is called the "Mid-Holocene Thermal Maximum" or the "Mid-Holocene Climate Optimum" for the temperate zones. However, the climate change was not uniform for all the regions of Asia. Siberia and other northern latitudinal regions experienced warming during this period. No such dramatic warming was experienced in the tropical regions (Battarbee and Binney 2009) where temperature rise was only about 1 degree centigrade on the average. Hence up to 3000 BC the temperature of northwest India remained cold, although warmer than the early Holocene.

The studies done by the different groups of authors have said more or less the same thing. Some difference of 500 years to 1000 years, however, can be noted between the dates given by the different authors. Thus, in contrast to what it is today, Central Asia was a moist place with dense forest cover during the mid-Holocene, i.e. 3000 BC (Harris 2011:25). During the glacial period (ending 9500 BC), the Central Asia was a dry desert steppe, which transformed into forest by about 8,000 BC. The lake level rose up in the Aral Sea between 7000 and 5000 BC. In Pamir Mountains, early Holocene glacial advance took place about 6750 BC. In north Kazakhstan, lake levels show the rising trend between 6500 and 5500 BC. However the region became dry again slowly. Central Asia converted back to steppe after 2000 BC (Zhou 2008, cited by Chen F. 2009:3). The northern steppes which had become forest during this Climatic Optimum reverted back to steppe ecosytem by 5,000 BC (Zhao 2009:249; Jiang 2006).

Although only a few fossil pollen studies have been published for the Holocene Central India, yet from the world-wide general trends we can say that north India up to the Vindhyas, particularly the colder regions of the belt like Chotanagpur and Mount Abu, must have received snowfalls until 6000 BC, and therefore should have had birch up to that time. Only scanty pollen studies for the early and mid-Holocene India have been done so far. Ones by Costantini at Mehrgarh and by Saraswat in the Punjab throw light over the climate of northwest India during early and mid- Holocene.

Chapter 3

The Climate of the *Rig-Veda*

While the *Rig-* and the *Sama- Veda* (*SV* 2.6.3.9.1) mention the river Sarasvati as the river, the *Yajur-Veda* generally mentions her as Goddess, particularly of the speech, and at only one place the meaning 'river' is implied (*TS* 1.8.18.1). We do not find the mention of the Sarasvati as a river at all in the *Atharva-Veda* which describes the Sarasvati only as the powerful goddess. In our reconstruction of the dates, we find that the *Yajur-Veda* is contemporary with that stage of the Sarasvati River when it had lost connection with the Himalayan glaciers and was surviving only as a monsoon-fed river, and that the *Atharva-Veda* was composed after the Sarasvati River had dried up complete. We know that the river had started drying at about 3500 BC and dried up fully by 1900 (Giosan 2012; Francfort 1992).

The good monsoons came, brought by *Indra* and *Varuṇa*, ending the drought and desert like state of the region (*RV* 7.82.3).[2] From 6,000 BC a less dry period starts. When the dry environment improved, the *Rig-Vedic* people started experimenting with early farming (*RV* 4.57.1-8; 10.117.7). By 5,500 BC the region got transformed into a wet-humid

---

2 ***Varuṇa*** in this mantra represents the southwest monsoon (from the Arabian Sea), because the abode of the God ***Varuṇa*** has been said to be in the ocean in the southwest direction from India

region because of changes in monsoon (Polanski 2012). And this is the time we find described in the *Yajur-Veda* lasting up to the mature Harappa culture.

As per the *Rig-Vedic* description, in the earliest phase, only scanty water was flowing in the Northwest Indian river-beds, as if waters had been stolen and were encapsulated or hoarded inside the glaciers at the mountain tops (*vṛtrasya jaṭhareṣu parvataḥ, RV* 1.54.10). This description of the climate is consistent with the hydrology of the dry-cold climate of the region during the Late Glacial Peak (11,000-9,500 BC) when lot of water had been trapped in the glaciers, and represents the folk memory of the period of drought and aridity recollected at the time of composition of the *Rig-Veda* at 8000-6000 BC.

The picturesque breaking and falling of the glaciers releasing the flow of the waters resulting in floods as described in the *Rig-Veda* is consistent with the fluvial phase (about 9,500 BC) when the glaciers melted releasing great amounts of water. Wherever the discussion of *Vṛtra* takes place the *Rig Veda* always speaks in the 'remote past' tense. The *Vṛtra* spread over the mountains like a huge snake, holding waters of the rivers, describes the *Rig-Veda*. This is how the glaciers spreading over the mountain tops look from a distance. *Indra* (the lord of water, rain or monsoon) broke the forts of this serpent, killed the *Vṛtra*, and thereby released waters into the seven rivers resulting into the floods (*RV* 1.32.1-11; 4.28.1; 4.19.1-8). It is a picturesque metaphorical description of glaciers' melting and streams coming out in between the breaking ice-rocks ("thou hast let loose to flow the Seven Rivers", *RV* 1.32.12). This description must be a recollection of the breaking of the glaciers and ensuing floods from the melting ice about 9,500 to 9,000 BC.

At the end of the glacier period ice melted in huge quantities, and the rivers got flooded with cold water. The first section of the *Rig-Veda* describes this release of the rivers as floods from the mountains running through the plains and finally meeting the ocean. The theme recurs again and again in the *Veda* (*e.g. RV* 1.130.5).

We may somewhat agree with the Monier-Williams' interpretation of *Vṛtra* as the "Vedic personification of an imaginary malignant influence or demon of darkness and drought, supposed to take possession of the clouds causing them to obstruct the clearness of the sky and keep back the waters" (p. 1007). *Vṛtra* is certainly a product of mythological symbolism and not an individual. Monier-Williams gives the etymology of the *Vṛtra* from '*vṛ*' meaning to cover (MWD).

Vṛtra is a personification of natural phenomenon, no doubt. But it is difficult to restrain water in the clouds for too long, therefore Monier-Williams' this part of assumption is not correct. In fact the water was 'covered' inside the glaciers, which indeed lay over the Himalayan Mountains. That the abode of *Vṛtra* was on the mountains has been explicitly mentioned in the Veda (*RV* 1.32.2). *Vṛtra* has been understood and explained more appropriately by Bhagwan Singh (1987) as the glaciers and the sheets of ice covering mountains the lakes which started melting as the floods when the warmer period came. We know that below the sheets of ice, water exists in liquid form in bodies of water in the freezing cold regions. The epithet *Purandara* used for the water-god *Indra* has confused the authors for two centuries, and they have thought that it means "the breaker of the forts". This conception of the *Purandara* is wrong. *Pura* means any 'human settlement larger than about three kilometres' (MWD) and *dara* means 'stream' (MWD). *Indra* being the god of waters is the *Purandara* or the source of the water coming to the human settlements. In fact the current of the rivers of the region, particularly the Sarasvati was so strong that it destroyed the human settlements located on the banks of the rivers of the region during the early Holocene and the larger townships like Mehrgarh could develop only at some distance from the Indus-Sarasvati (*vide infra*).

The scenario surrounding northwest India and the plants, trees, animals and rivers of the region did not remain the same always. With time, the climate changed from dry-cold to slightly warmer but that happened slowly and the overall weather remained cool and dry, with a marked increase in the cold and aridity at 6250 BC (or 8,200

BP; Staubwasser and Weiss 2006:1). This phase, the 8.2 Kilo event, corresponds to the *Rig-Vedic* description of the period of drought when the king *Atithigva Divodasa* was not able to show appropriate hospitality to his guests because of his own poverty caused by the drought caused by the demon *śuṣṇa* (etymology from *śuṣ-* to dry; see MWD). Many people died and many habitation sites were abandoned. We find archaeological evidence of the sudden decline in Hakra Wares sites in Sarasvati Delta, Cholistan and Kot Diji areas and other regions in India, and also in Levant in West Asia corresponding to this 8.2 Kilo event draught (Possehl 1997, also 2002:63; Staubwasser and Weiss 2006).

The *Rig-Vedic* demon *śuṣṇa*, which caused the drought at that time is the personification of aridity (*śuṣ-* to dry; see MWD). It has been called the "foe of harvest" (*RV* 4.16.12). His life was ended by *Indra* (*i.e.* Rain-God) implying that the improvement in the monsoon led to amelioration of the dry climate. His friend was another demon *kuyava i.e.* "one which causes the bad harvest" or damages the crops (*RV* 1.103.8, 7.19.2). This event chronologically heralds the beginning of the mid-Holocene Optimum. This time is the composition of the *Sama-Veda* and since 5,500 BC we can consider the period of good monsoons and the *Yajur-Veda.*

However we find that the rivers were all full or flooded during the *Rig-Vedic* period, and noria or simple water-wheel was used by people to fetch water from the wells. Presence of noria (water-wheel) in the *Rig-Veda* (*RV* 10.101.7) indicates that the underground water level in the wells was quite high i.e. shallow.[3] This was possible from the everflooded glacier-fed rivers of the Indus-Sarasvati region at the *Rig-Vedic* period. *Rig-Veda* (10.101.7) says, "Pour forth the well with stone wheel, wooden buckets, the drink of heroes, with the trough for armour." (Griffith Translation). The *Rig-Vedic* region was often flooded, as we find from the several mentions of the floods, yet these floods

---

3 Griffith Translation : *Rig-Veda* 10.101.7, "Pour forth the well with stone wheel, wooden buckets, the drink of heroes, with the trough for armour."

generally came from the Himalayan Rivers as has been explicitly mentioned in the text, and rarely from any torrential rain.

The *Rig-Veda* does not explicitly mention the animal *babhru* (beaver, *Castor sp.*), although it is an animal which can live even in the less than zero degree Celsius temperatures. They also cannot live in the streams and rivers which have high flow or gradients (Meuller-Schwarze 2003:107), which unfortunately for this animal, all the seven Vedic rivers had at that time because of the fast melting glaciers of the early Holocene.

Another reason why we do not find the beaver in the *Rig-Veda* is that the beavers construct their own island-hut in a self constructed artificial lake, which they make by logging trees in such a way as to make small dams and later the rains or the flooding riverwaters fill them up. Northwest India had plenty of glacier-fed cold-water rivers no doubt during the early Holocene, yet it was principally a grass-land ecosystem, something like the patches of the Western description of prairies, steppe and savannah and it had scanty rainfall and the trees were far and few between. Hence the region was inhospitable to the beavers. Beavers eat wood. Forest, particularly the one with poplar and aspen trees, is essential for the survival of the beaver, as they need them for food as well as for making the dams. This is precisely the reason for the absence of the beaver from the *Rig-Vedic* text.

Thus we can say that the dry grassland stage of northwest India was not hospitable to the beavers and they did not live in that region during the *Rig-Vedic* age before 6000 BC. However the beaver appears in the *Yajur-Veda*. Archaeologically the poplar, aspen and other trees grew into dense forest only after the region's climate changed to the humid one. Beavers should be expected only then. Beaver was found in India, and became extinct when northwest India became dry. The last remains of beaver have been dated 2000 BC and 1200 BC at Burzahom and Gufkral in Kashmir (Misra 2001:507; U. Singh:114; IAR 1962) and the poplar and other forests too became extinct from the region about the same time BC owing to aridity.

The early Holocene was dry because of the scanty rainfall and the cold air temperature, although the rivers were full with water from the melting Himalayan glaciers. The ecosystem was most suited to the pastoral economy which the *Rig-Vedic* people mainly pursued. However they did pursue the hunting-gathering economy too. Yet the early experimenting with farming must have started during the *Rig-Vedic* period itself by 6000 BC. The dry weather of the early Holocene northwest India is not liked by the buffalo. Yet buffalo has been often mentioned in the *Rig-Veda*, and also in the other three Vedas. Buffalo being a domestic animal could have survived even the adverse climates with the human assistance and under care. This is the reason why buffalo, although an animal of wet regions and swamps was found in northwest India throughout all the Vedas. The fact correlates well with archaeology. The beast was found in all the the archaeological periods in the Holocene of northwest India starting from Mehrgarh Period 1 to the Harappa Civilization (J.-F. Jarrige 2008:143). The early Holocene presence of the domesticated buffalo in Northwest India has been confirmed in the Mehrgarh excavations (J.-F. Jarrige 2008:143; Bellwood 2004: 84).

Northwest India is not the natural range of the wild buffalo. This animal loves wet monsoonal climates and the natural range of the animal has been restricted to the south and east portion of Central India, East India, Southeast Asia and South China (Kumar 2007; Groves 1995). Presence of buffalo at Mehrgarh indicates its domestic status in Northwest India at least since 8,000 BC. Prof. Bokonyi (1969:219) found if any animal is found at a site far removed from its natural range, it should be considered 'domesticated' (cited by Crabtree and Champana 1989:6, and also by Rissman 1989:16). For this reason the buffaloes of Mehrgarh and *Rig-Veda* both must be considered domestic.

The *Rig-Veda* (10.75.8) describes the *Sindhu* (Indus) river as one which has good horses, good cars, good dwelling places, which has *sīlamā* grass and which has plenty of wool. This description applies to the colder period of the early Holocene when wool was the preferred garment material.

Possibly some later hymns of the *Rig-Vedic* text were composed during the early part of the mid-Holocene Optimum--when the rains arrived into the desert and the the torrential rains flooded the desert (*RV* 1.38.7-8). Such heavy rainfall in the desert in fact heralds the end of the generally dry post-glacial and early Holocene semi-arid or cold semi-desert type climate. Thus this particular event of heavy rainfall can be conveniently dated sometime between 6000 BC and 5,500 BC. The *Sarasvati* River passed through the Thar which was a desert during the Early Holocene. The *Rig-Vedic* people located at the banks of the *Sarasvati* were aware of the ecological changes taking place in the adjoining desert, and their environmental descriptions can be considered the actual representation of the environment of their times.

There were water filled playas, called *saras* in the *Rig-Veda*, after which the river Sarasvati got her name. There is archaeological evidence of such playas located within the Thar region in the period between 13,000 BC and 3000 BC. Deotare demonstrated that the playas had the Lake-Full Phase between 6000 BC and 5000 BC (2004a:20, Table 1; 2004b). Before 6000 BC, water in the playas remained shallow and seasonal, generally drying duing the summer. At 6000 BC this region, the western margin of the Thar adjoining the river Sarasvati, shows evidence of beginning of better rainfall and that of the Mesolithic or pastoral human activity (Deotare 2004a:Abstract). The playas were ephemeral between 13,000 BC and 6,000 BC when they got dried in the summar (*ibid*:20, Table 1), and as the *Rig-Veda* notes, the frogs hibernated in the dry mud in the bottom of the playas (*śuṣkam sarasī śayānam*, *RV* 7.103.2).

Hence the *Rig-Vedic* hymn 7.103 probably pertains to the time about 6,000 BC to 5800 BC, when although the monsoonal optimum was in the process of arriving yet it was overall a dry period and the playas were getting dry durieg the summer and the lake-full stage had not arrived. The hymn also declares that the year started with the first showers of the rains. Such calendric condition *i.e.* the start of the year with the onset of the rainy season existed at about the same time.[4] *Sama-Veda*, contemporary with the end part of the *Rig-Vedic* times too reports floods caused by the rains (*SV* 5.2.15).

However, at least one incidence of flood described in the *Rig-Veda* had originated from the glaciers of the mountain as a result of an earthquake taking place in the Himalayan mountains, which shook the mountains and the glaciers over it. The resulting flood swept the Thar Desert (*RV* 4.17.2). This should be understood as the description of a massive earthquake taking place in the source region of the Sutlej River, which was then a tributary of the Sarasvati. Reference to the desert makes it clear that the flood was in the Sarasvati which passed across the Thar Desert region.

We find that the flood came from the mountain into the desert. Hence we can infer that the *Rig-Vedic Sarasvati* River was connected with the Himalayan glaciers at the time of this particular event. We know from the latest geological research that the Sarasvati River lost her connection with the glaciers about 6,500 BC (Giosan 2012). Giosan tells us the cause why Mehrgarh was located not on the banks of any river but quite away from that: "Wild, untamed rivers once slashed through the heart of the Indus plains. They were so unpredictable and dangerous that no city could take root on their banks." (cited by Nuwer 2012). Usually human habitats were located on the banks of the rivers. However during the early post-glacial or early Holocene period, the Himalayan rivers destroyed the human habitations by the torrential flow of water, hence human habitations were kept away from the river.

This is the precise reason why the water-god Indra has been considered the *purandara* or the 'destroyer of the villages'. It may be noted here that contrary to the general claims that the *pura* means 'fort', the word is an Indo-European word and always means 'village' in the Indian and

4 I owe this verse and its interpretation to Madhusudan Mishra, who communicated this to me in a private conversation.

Iranian languages. "As the centuries passed, however, the monsoons became less frequent and the floods less intense, creating stable conditions for agriculture and settlement." (Nuwer). Other geological studies of the region too show that the river lost her connection with the Himalayan glaciers during the early Holocene. Hence the *Rig-Veda* must be dated to the early Holocene (references in Goisan 2012 and Gupta 2001).

Purely on the basis of the vegetation (and climate) we can date the *Rig-Veda* to a much colder and drier period of Early Holocene northwest India, and the *Yajur-Veda* to the moist and less cold period of the mid-Holocene. Kazanas (2009:1) noted, on the basis of the cultural features described in the *Rig-Veda*, that a date earlier than 4500 BC to 7000 BC should be assigned to the early Indo-Aryans which in our view were the Vedic people. This reconciles with the archaeology well and any later date is not possible.

There is no mention of the seals, statues, paintings, writing, burnt brick, potter's wheel, cotton, urban citadel culture etc in the *Rig-Veda*, which are so common in the Harappa Culture (3500-1800 BC) and which continued to persist in northwest India even until 1000 BC. Had the *Rig-Veda* been composed after 1500 BC, such objects must have had mention in the *Rig-Vedic* text itself (Kazanas 2009). There are no words for pen, reading, writing and inscriptions or any other material associated with writing in the *Rig-Veda* (Kenoyer 2005a:45; Dandekar 1947, cited by Kenoyer 2005a). Since writing is well attested from Harappa and later periods, the *Rig-Veda* must belong to a much earlier time.

On this ground we can infer that the *Rig-Vedic* period ended sometime between 6,000 BC and 5,500 BC. One of the reasons for the end of that stage of culture and development of the next stage of civilization evolution was the change of weather from dry-cold to warm-wet. This must have influenced the dwelling pattern and subsistence and promoted specialization of the arts and crafts.

Chapter 4

Periodization of the *Rig* and *Yajur* Vedas on the basis of some other features

One possible explanation for the absence of the burnt bricks from the *Rig-Veda* (Kazanas 2009:23) and the *Sama-Veda*, and their extensive use in the *Yajur-Veda* (*TS* 1.5.8.2 etc) could too lie in the climatology, *Rig-Veda* belonging to a drier period having the least rainfall and the *Yajur-Veda* to the heavy monsoonal mid-Holocene period. Probably the *Rig-Vedic* people did not very much need the burnt brick. They were rural and pastoral. There were no public drains and artificial ponds and tanks at that time. The culture was not urban, and population was small in the semi-arid economy.

However, just following the *Rig-Veda*'s time, the *Taittiriya Samhita* and *Vajasaneyi Samhita* both the volumes of the *Yajur-Veda* report extensive use of the burnt bricks for lining waste-water drains, embankments of the rivers, wells, ponds and tanks etc (*TS* 3.4.3.1) and in the construction of the human dwellings, which were intended for "protection and prosperity" (*TS* 3.4.3.6). Dwellings made with the burnt bricks protected from the rains and had defence purpose too as they helped "endure the battle for cattle" (*TS* 4.4.4.1). The *Taittitira Samhita* explicitly mentions the "rain-winning bricks" (*TS* 5.3.10.1). These utilities resulted in the need for the burnt bricks as the result of increasing population, economic growth, urbanization and specialization of trades and crafts. Such economic change ultimately led to the growth and development of the mature Harappa Civilization of the Indian archaeology. Marshall noted the same usage and utility of the burnt bricks in the Harappa Civilization (cited by Possehl 2002:9, 15).

The *Yajur-Veda* (*TS* 4.5.7) pays homage to the different classes of manual labours, because of their valuable services to the society. In that list the hymn mentions the sewar workers and cleaners etc. employed to take care of streams, pavements, drainage pipes, pools, lakes and tanks. Obviously these structures were further departures from the *Rig-Vedic* days and involved construction with the burn bricks. These structures and pukka houses have been found from the Harappa culture indicating a possible link between Harappa and the *Yajur-Veda.*

Brick is one of the the most adored object in the two volumes of the *Yajur-Veda* text. Hence the dwellings of at least the rich people of the region must have been made of the burn bricks for the protection from rain-waters and the burglars. This finding suggests that the *Yajur-Veda* was contemporary with the Harappa Civilization, possibly from its earliest period i.e. 5000 BC as dated by Dikshit and Mani (2013) for the early Harappan period at Bhirrana. Archaeological findings report that the Mehrgarh Period I (about 8000-5500 BC) did not have the burnt bricks, which appears at the Mehrgarh Period II starting about 5500 BC and becoming common still later (Jarrige 2008). Hence Mehrgarh Period-I, which had no burnt brick, should be considered pre-*Yajur-Veda* and contemporary with the *Rig-Veda.* The date of the *Rig-Veda* as determined by Kazanas (2009) is consistent with our dates.

Harappa was contemporaneous with the *Yajur-Veda.* Amulet (*pratisara*), so common in the Harappa culture (McIntosh 2008:246, 260, 291), has been mentioned nowhere in the *Rig-Veda*, although once in the *Yajur-Veda* (*TS* 4.5.6.1) and at several places in the *Atharva-Veda.* Amulets have not been found from Mehrgarh, while a large number of amulets have been recovered from the later Harappan sites and later Indian archaeology. This finding too indicates that the *Rig-Veda* was pre-Harappa chronologically.

Writing, which emerges in a large scale in Harappa at about 2500 BC, was not known in the *Rig-Veda*, although we get the mention of the earliest writing in the *Yajur-Veda* (5.1.3.4), and much more of it in the *Atharva-Veda*. There was no writing at Mehrgarh. This fact supports the conclusion that the Harappa civilization is in all likelihood the contemporary of the *Yajur-Veda*, and the *Rig-Veda* is earlier than Harappa, comtemporary with early Mehrgarh.

Cotton has not been mentioned in the *Rig-Veda*, although it mentions 'wool' for the dress material, and on this basis we can say that the cotton was not exploited for dress-making during the *Rig-Vedic* period (Kazanas 2009). However, as the time passes, we get the mention of the cotton tree in the *Yajur-Veda* (*TS* 7.4.12.1). The earliest spun cotton thread recovered from northwest India is from Mehrgarh Period 2 (6,000 BC; Moulherat 2002; Mithen 2006), however in the Indus Valley Civilization, we get evidence of cotton cloth (McIntosh 2008:115; Marshall 1931: 585-6). Its use for dress must have increased only when the climate became warmer requiring the abandonment of wool, and wetter making larger cultivation of cotton possible, i.e. in the mid-Holocene Optimum.

Cold climate is perhaps the reason why cotton dress was not popular during the *Rig-Vedic* times, and wool and animal hide were the preferred dress material. Pre-eminence of the Fire-God (*Agni*) and the routine fire sacrifices several times a day too point to the climate being cold at the *Rig-Vedic* times. The further continuation of the fire sacrifice in the later *Vedas* was probably the atavistic continuation of the older practice coming down from the glacial and early Holocene period of Indian northwest.

The *Rig-Veda* and *Avesta* do not mention the potter's wheel, and the pottery was in all probability handmade during the *Rig-Vedic* period (Kuz'mina and Mallory 2007: 313 and 370, and the references therein).

Potter's wheel appears for the first time in the *Yajur-Veda* (*TS* 4.5.4; also see Bryant 2001:211). In northwest Indian archaeology, the potter's wheel appears in the Mehrgarh Period-II, at about 5,500 BC (Possehl 2002:90). This finding helps us place the *Rig-Veda* before 5500 BC and the *Yajur-Veda* after that.

Wilhelm Rau found that although the potter's wheel was known at the time of the *Yajur-Veda* and was used for the commercial production of pottery, it was the hand-made pottery which was still used for the ritual purposes. He suggested that in the *Yajur-Veda* "the more primitive technique persisted in the ritual sphere while in secuar life more advanced methods of potting had already been adopted" (Rau 1974:141, as quoted by Bryant 2001:211). This fact too proves that the *Rig-Veda* was composed when there was not wheel-turned pottery and the pottery was was only hand made. It is difficult to find such a location in the entire Eurasia at 1500 BC or 1200 BC where no wheel-made pottery existed. Hence such late dating of the *Rig-Veda* is wrong.

Rau, on the basis of his philological investigations, found the charecteristics of the oldest *Rig-Vedic* pottery as, "that it was made of clay mixed with various materials, some of them organic, resulting in porous pots. These pots were poorly fired and ranged in size from about 0.24 m to 1.0 m in diameter at opening and 0.24 m to 0.40 m in height. Furthermore, they showed the lack of plastic decoration and were unpainted" (Rau:142, as cited by Bryant 2001:211). He also discovered that the firing was accomplished by the covered baking method between two layers of raw bricks in a simple open pit (*ibid*). Hand-made pottery made somewhat later was red in colour, Rau found.

Both the features of the earliest Vedic pottery described by Rau were found at Mehrgarh, where we get the earliest pottery of northwest India in the Period IIA ending by 6000 BC. This earliest pottery was found as hand-made crude pot-shreds with heavy chaff temper (Jarrige 2008:149, 151). Following this we get the fine red pottery between 6000 BC and 5800 BC (*ibid*), which again is as per the Rau's findings. We can say with enough confidence that this Mehrgarh pottery was the pottery of the *Rig-Vedic* description. However Eurocentricity forced some scholars to look for such pottery outside India, and they could not get them anywhere, except in Andronovo in East Russia/Southwest Siberia dating about 1600 BC (Bryant 2001:211). In our study, we find that this Indo-Aryan culture of Andronovo was the product of the late Bronze Age migration i.e. the second migration out of India, during the *Yajur-Veda* period. Central Indian pottery of Koldihwa and Lahuradewa predated the Mehrgrh pottery by about two millennia.

In the Sarasvati region, the handmade Hakra Ware was the oldest pottery. Chronologically it was before Early Harappa, hence called Pre-Early Harappa Culture. Radiocarbon dates have been received only recently. Oldest samples found at the Bhirrana site sates from 7380 BC to 6201 BC (Dikshit and Mani 2013:49). At about 6250 BC, there was a cold episode named as the 8.2 Kilo Event, which caused severe reduction in the farming communities in West Asia (Weninger 2006), and the same seems to hold true for the Sarasvati Basin too. Possehl too notes that in the vicinity of the inland delta of the Sarasvati (Ghagghar-Hakra) river, near the Port Derawar, there were 82 Hakra Wares sites, which were suddenly reduced to 20 at Early Harappa. Then at mature Harappa such archeological sites increases to 140 in number (Possehl 2002:63). Thus the 8.2 Kilo cold event may have been responsible for the break in the continuity of the civilization and the Hakra Wares pottery. From our study, this period, *i.e.* the seventh and eighth millennium BC is the time of the *Rig-Veda* too, which too had the hand-made crude pottery. Chronologically and typologically, the Hakra Ware Culture of the Sarasvati basin fits in the description of the *Rig-Vedic* culture.

Copper was present in the *Rig-Veda* (*RV* 4.27.1) period as well as is in the Mehgarh Period I (Moulherat 2002) and it was known by the name *ayas*. There is no mention of the 'black-metal' or iron in the *Rig-Veda* (Bryant 2001:247), and the entity occurs for the first time in the *Yajur-Veda*. The word *ayas* means only the copper in the *Rig-Veda* and not iron, forcing us to place this text before the oldest recorded evidence of iron in northwest India. The presence of copper (*ayas*) in the *Rig-Veda* is not inconsistent with the placing of this text before 6000 BC.

However Bryant thinks, on the basis of the resemblance between the languages used in the *Rig-* and the *Atharva-* Vedas that the two texts were nearly contemporary, wherein the latter text shows the awareness of the black metal iron. On this ground, Bryant thinks that the *Rig-Vedic* people too knew iron although they have not mentioned it. This argument is wrong. All the Vedic texts were converted into the understandable language of the age. This was always the practice adopted for the very old texts, and the practice was followed until recent times for many texts. For example the *Rama-charit Manas*, a rendering of the ancient text *Ramayana* or the epic of the king Rama, written in the sixteenth century by Tulasidasa, is in the language of the sixteenth century AD North India. Clearly the language of the Vedas was updated in the second millennium BC. Possibly each Vedic *Samhita* took about a hundred years time for its final rendering/editing. Thus the language of the *Rig-* and the other Vedas follows the language of second millennium BC northwest India, when the linguistic editing was done for the last time although the material content belongs to the much older days.

Iron appears in the *Yajur-Veda* (*śyāmam*; *TS* 4.7.5.1). The same verse of the *Yajur-Veda* also mentions lead (*sīsam*), tin, gold, bronze and copper. Iron being highly perishable in the warm humid climate of the early Bronze Age, its artefacts from the wet mid-Holocene Optimum dating between 5000 BC and 2500 BC (or the *Yajur-Vedic* period in our study) cannot be expected to have survived till today. Yet some early pieces of iron have been found from the Bronze Age of the Indus Valley Civilization, particularly from Mundigak, Said Qala Tepe, Deh Morasi, Ghundai, Ahar, Chanhu Daro and Lothal (Possehl 2002:93-94) and date back to third millennium calBC after calibration (*vide infra*; see uncalibrated dates in Agrawal 1965, Agrawal 1963; calibration can be done through calpal web site). On the bank of the Kala rivulet near Taxila some early Bronze Age graves bear iron objects like finger-rings and 'paste bracelet' fragments although the other features of the grave are those of the Kot Diji graves (Dani and Masson 1992:401). Hence the date of the Indian Iron-Age goes back to 2500 BC if we caliberate the dates.

The acquisition of iron technology took place at least a thousand year before the onset of the Iron Age in India (Lahiri 2009:6). Lahiri noted "Among other things, what is now reasonably clear is the presence of chronological distinctions between the advent of iron technology and beginning of what is described as the Iron Age, the first distinct phase in the development of a technology capable of producing iron in the Indian subcontinent coinsides with Chalcolithic cultures of the third and second millennium BC." In our study such capability was acquired probably about in the middle of the fourth millennium BC, a thousand year before the caliberated date for Iron-Age in India.

These pure metallic iron artifacts could have been either smelted iron or meteoric, Possehl postulated (Possehl, quoted by Bryant 2001:247). The meteoric iron and other metals are the pure metals brought to the surface of earth by the falling meteors. However, unfortunately, authors like Bryant opted to reject these items dubbing them as ones made of iron-ore (2001:247). Iron ores are not malleable and are stones. Nothing can be made of them except the stone-axe etc. No body can confuse them for iron, and the iron-ore idea should not have crept into this discussion at all. The iron artefacts and items recovered from the Bronze Age Indus Valley date to 2700 BC uncalibrated (Bryant:247; Possehl and Gullapalli 1999:161), i.e. about 3400 calBC, precise within our considered time frame for the *Yajur-Veda.*

In fact the Harappa Civilization people "regularly worked with copper, tin, arsenic, lead, silver, gold and electrum. The documentation of metal begins in a burial at Mehrgarh Period I with native copper in it. The story of Indus metallurgy is one of gradual change, in both technology and the scope of the metals commonly worked." (Possehl 2002:93). Thus we can say that the Indus Valley Civilization's metallurgy is comparable with the described metallurgy in the *Yajur-Veda*. While the *Rig-Vedic* Civilization as well as the Mehrgarh had only copper, the later cultures had many other metals too fixing the time of the *Yajur-Veda* to the Bronze Age north-west India.

It has been noted that the earliest inhabitants of the Hakra Ware Culture settlements lived in the pit-dwellings (Shinde 2008: 103, 156; Dikshit and Mani:51; U. Singh 2008:109). This period has been dated only recently by the radio-carbon mehod and goes up to 7400 BC for the Sarasvati Valley Civilization (Mani 2013:45). We are aware that after 5,500 BC, strong monsoons took over the northwest India region and no one could survive in the pit-dwellings because the pits would have got filled with water. Hence the pit-dwellings can be considered only appropriate in the dry cold climatic set up. Hence the timing of the pit-dwellings before 6,000 BC in the Sarasvati Valley archaeology is consistent with the climatic condition of the region for the period.

Philology adds to our insight into the lives of the *Rig-Vedic* people. The Hindi words *gaḍḍhā*, *gaḍhā* (large pit), *gaḍha* (house, building) and *gaṚā* (buried; past participle of 'to bury') are all cognates of the Sanskrit word *gṛha* (home) and *gaḍa* (ditch). In the *Rig-Veda* this word *gṛha* had the meaning "underground house" (*mṛṇmaya gṛha*, *RV* 7.89.1), and Monier-Williams thinks that the "underground house" mentioned in the hymn meant "grave" by implication (see under *gṛha* in the MWD). However literally it is a house located in the pits in the earth. Most likely the people did not like to live inside the pit-dwellings unless the weather became very harsh. That is why the author of the the hymn prays to the Lord Varuṇa not to bring the harsh and torrential weather which would force him to enter into and hibernate in his pit-dwelling: *mṛnmayaṃ gṛhaṃ rājanna ahaṃ gamam*. By the time of the *Atharva-Veda* the pit-dwellings had become the things of their remote past and had been forgotton.

The above etymology is consistent and compatible with the etymology of PIE **ghrebh*[2] (to dig). OHG *grouba* and Old English *grafu* (pit, grave), OHG *graban* (to dig, bury), and OHG *grab* (grave) and English 'grave' are not far removed from the Sanskrit *garbha* (inner chamber, sleeping room, interior of anything, MWD), and these words seem to be cognates. Sanskrit *gṛha* (home, grave, underground house) claimed to be from the PIE **ghardh* (to enclose) too may actually be a cognate of this set of words. However the Sanskrit *garbha* (womb) and *guru* (heavy), English 'gravid', and 'grave (Adj.)' constitute another set of cognates and are not related etymologically to the Sanskrit *garbha* meaning the interior of the home (see Harper). The Persian word *kān* (mine, ditch), *khān* (home), and Sanskrit *khan-* (to dig), *khani* (mine) are another set of cognates which indicated that the oldest Aryan homes in the Sarasvati basin were the pit-dwellings. Another Sanskrit word *kṣiti* means 'house' in the *Rig-Veda* yet acquires the meaning 'earth' during the later times (see under *kṣiti* in MWD).

Those days (i.e. before 6000 BC) rain was scanty, and people entered their homes (pit-dwellings) generally to protect from cold. The prayer in *Rig-Veda* (7.89.1) shows someone's dislike for the rains, possibly because it caused seepage into the pit dwellings. Yet the semantic feature "subterranean" associated with the word *gṛha* had been retained in the *Atharva-Veda* where it meant "the lower world" in the *Atharva-Veda* (*AV* 2.14.2; see MWD). Thus we can say that the *Rig-Vedic* people had pit-dwellings. However supra-terranean homes too may have existed those days--made of mud-bricks as they did in Mehrgarh I. But they must have been more expensive and available to the elite alone.

In the *Rig-Veda*, God Varuna is mentioned generally together with Indra and/or Mitra. However in the *Yajur-Veda* Varuna is mentioned alone quite frequently. Although Varuna was the Supreme God in the *Rig-Veda* and the same status continued in the *Yajur-Veda*, He gained reputation more as the God of waters, and quite often the Rain-God. This was because of the increasing magnitude of the southwestern monsoon in the Indus-Sarasvati region. The part of Indian Ocean to the southwest of India became known as the abode of God Varuna. Development of the sea-trade in this period led to sailing of the large ships in the Arabian Sea—the home territory of Varuna. This further augmented the importance of God Varuna. That is why we find in the

Yajur-Veda prayer to God Varuna for the protection of the ship which is about to sail in the sea (*TS* 1.2.2.2).

As far as fauna is concerned, *Rig-Veda* had lion (*RV* 1.64.8 etc), leopard (*pṛdāku*, *RV* 8.17.15), wild horse (*RV* 8.17.15), camel, but no tiger, rhinoceros, tortoise and crocodile. This fauna is consistent with open forest environment intermingled with grass-lands. In the early Holocene, northwest India had this type of ecosystem. Presence of the wild camel, which too has been mentioned in the *Rig-Veda*, is consistent with the semi-arid climate interspersed with cold deserts prevalent in northwest India during the early Holocene.

Section II

Flora

Chapter 5

A General Account of the minor Flora of the Vedas reflecting climate

In the Vedas, particularly the *Rig-Veda*, we get description of the plants and animals most of which today are characteristically found in the colder regions of the world, particularly Europe, and most of them are not found in any part of India today including even the Himalayas, although a few continue to exist at the high cold altidues. Some authors have considered this as evidence supporting the alleged Aryan arrival into India from outside (Bhargawa). Some authors like Witzel even suggested that the *Rig-Veda* was composed outside India. However the same evidence could have been considered supporting an older date for the *Rig-Veda* when northwest India was colder and moister.

Avaka grass (*Blyxa octandra*) is a hydrophytic plant generally grows in the marshes or submerged in water. Frequently it grows along with the golden willow, with which it (*avaka*) has often been mentioned in the *Yajur-Veda* (*TS* 5.4.4.2), where it has been mentioned as the 'cream of waters'. This epthet has been attached to this plant probably because of the mucous content of its leaves, which was used for the treatment of skin-burns. In the *Yajur-Veda* this aquatic plant has been considered very important for many of the rituals like the one for the horse sacrifice (*TS* 5.7.11.1, 5.4.2.1). This implies a moist monsoon-rich climate at that time.

However this plant *Blyxa*, which is of so much ritual importance, has not been mentioned anywhere in the *Rig-Veda*. This is significant. Clearly this indicates that the plant did not exist in the region at the rime of the *Rig-Veda*. That is only possible if the *Rig-Vedic* period did not have enough logged water for this plant to grow. That implies the paucity of rains and an arid or semi-arid climate for the *Rig-Vedic* times. This is only possible if the *Rig-Veda* belonged to the Early Holocene and the *Yajur-Veda* to the mid-Holocene Optimum.

Sesame or *Sesamum indicum* is an Indian oilseed herb which is very important for the Vedic rituals. Its name does not occur in the *Rig-Veda*. It appears in the *Yajur-Veda* as a plant growing both in the wild (*TS* 5.4.3.2) as well as cultivated (*TS* 4.7.4.2). The wild variety was called *jartila* in the *Yajur-Veda*. The wild *sesamum* did not yield any oil (Dymoc, Warden and Hooper 1891:27).

That means a proper domestication process must have undergone for this oilseed only after the time of the *Rig-Veda* had passed, because the *Rig-Veda* does not mention this plant even in the wild, or its product at all. Possibly the plant arrived in the north India from South India only after the cold early Holocene had passed and the mid-Holocene optimum has arrived. The plant needs a warmer climate. The *Yajur-Veda* mentions the *jartila* (wild sesame) and *gavīdhuka* (*Coix* grass) at the same place where they have been offered to God. The seeds of the *Coix* grass are eaten in many Southeast Asian countries as millets, and probably were eaten in India too before the domestication of better cereals. Thus the wild sesame and the wild-grass offering to God seem to be reminisce of older custom when the seeds were eaten by man too. has been considered less than adequate and to compensate for the inferior quality of offering many other offerings are made in the same hymn (*TS* 5.4.3.2). But when the better offerings were available why the offerings of the inferior things were made at all?

That means the northwest India had graduated into the cultivation of crops stage by the late *Yajur-Vedic* period, and the wild poor quality food was not eaten by man by this time although was used for the sacrificial purposes as a ritual inherited from the past. Both of these items are reminisces of the facultative forager stage of life of the early *Yajur-Veda* period. Facultative foragers are those who have farming, yet this is supplemented by foraging, and when farming fails they adopt foraging as an alternate way of life.

This plant (sesame) requires hot climate for growth and is a summer crop (McIntosh:14, 110). Although it is drought resistant, its early growth requires adequate moisture. We may infer that the sesame was absent from northwest India at the time of the *Rig-Veda i.e.* the dry and cold early Holocene. As climate became warmer and moister, the wild type (*jartila*) arrived there from the soutnern India. And after a lapse of adequate time people were able to domesticate it, after which the domestic variety came to be used for the cooking purposes, but the wild one continued to be used for the rituals which had continued from the early *Yajur-Veda* stage. The *Atharva-Veda* (18.4.32) too mentions the wild variety of the *sesamum* plant (*jartila*). Absence of the *sesamum* from the *Rig-Veda* is consistent with our other findings about the climate of the *Rig-Veda*.

Charred seeds of sesame have been found from the Indus Valley Civilization dating back to 3500 BC (Bedijian and Harlan 1986: Abstract). The plant has been mentioned in the cuniform text of Bronze Age Mesopotamia where it was imported from India, and later cultivated by 2250 BC; and the Mesopotamian word for 'oil' *ellu* and the ones for oil in Europe like 'oil', *oleum*, 'olive' and the suffix meaning oil '*-ol*' etc are the borrowings from the same original word *ellu* of the Dravidian lexicon (Bedijian and Harlan; McIntosh:114).

The Dravidian word for sesame "*ellu*" was borrowed into the Sumerian, Akkadian and many West Asian languages (Witzel 1999:28). That means sesame had been domesticated in India by the early Harappa stage. Fuller suggests that it was domesticated in India before 2500

BC however his assessment is too conservative (Fuller 2006). Misra mentions the finding of sesame from the Chalcolithic remains of the Ganga Valley (Misra 2001:515). Pokharia too notes the sesame cultivation from Chalcolithic period of Senuwar in Central India (2200 BC; Pokharia 2008: 252, Table 2).

It was primarily because of the change in climate and rainfall that a large number of crops not cultivated earlier came to be cultivated in the *Yajur-Vedic* period. From the Neolithic, now the transformation to the true agriculturist society took place. They grew several types of millets, rice, barley, beans, sesame, kidney beans, vetche (*Lethyrus* species), lentils (*Lens culinaris*) and wheat (*TS* 4.7.4.2). In the *Rig-Veda*, the wild as well as the domestic rice (*nīvara* and *vrīhi*) and wheat are absent, only barley is present. Rice and wheat crops appear in the *Yajur-Veda* signifying contemporaneousness of the early *Yajur-Vedic* period with some stages of the Ghagghar-Hakra culture wherein we find the cultivation of rice and wheat both (Shinde 2008:121,122,156).

This is not because the *Rig-Vedic* people travelled down the Gangetic plains of India then composed the *Yajur-Veda* after making themselves aware of rice, as has been suggested by many, but because of the improvement in monsoon, the rice cultivation arrived into northwest India by the natural factors following the onset of the mid-Holocene Optimum.

Although there were several varieties of the cultivated rice (*vrīhayaḥ*, note the use in the plural), the wild rice *nīvāra*, which grows only in the deep stagnant waters, too was exploited as gathered food (*TS* 4.7.4.2). The *nivara* was the wild rice of the Vedic literature (Macdonell and Keith vol 2: 456) and it has been considered by the scientists to be the wild progenitor of the Indian cultivated rice. This implies heavy monsoonal rains in the Indus-Sarasvati region during the *Yajur-Vedic* times leading to water-logging in the lowlands in which even the wild *nivara* rice too could arrive from the eastern India. This type of wet climate as has been described in the *Yajur-Veda* existed in the Indus Valley region from 5500 BC to 3500 BC. The rice cultivation as mentioned in the

Yajur-Veda text corroborates well with the archaeological finding from the Hakra Wares sites, which show good evidence of rice cultivation, particularly in the water-logging regions located in the Sarasvati Basin region dating back up to the sixth millennium BC (Shinde 2008:81; to be read with, Dikshit and Mani 2013).

Shinde's excavation of the Ghagghar River basin has revealed that adequate rice was cultivated in the pre-Early Harappa period in the Sarasvati region (Shinde 2008: 121, 122, 155). We know from recent archaeological studies that the rice agriculture started about 8,000 BC in the Ganga Valley at several palces like Lahuradeva, Jhusi and Koldihwa (Tewari 2008; Dikshit 2009; G.R. Sharma 1985). When rainfall increased in the Indus-Sarasvati region during the mid-Holocene Optimum, the wild rice *nivara* invaded the water-logging regions of northwest India (Fuller 2006:46, 61), and subsequently the rice farming developed in this region too by 5,500 BC. That is why we get archaeological evidence of rice farming from the Gagghar Basin, which of course diminishes rapidly during the mature Harappa primarily because of the aridity developing in the Indus-Sarasvati region secondary to the shifts in monsoon.

Hence even before the Early Harappa, the rice was already being cultivated in the Indus-Sarasvati region. During the mature Harappa, the cultivation of rice had declined as can be inferred from the scanty archaeological records (Posselh 2002: 64; McIntosh: 85). The scholars usually quite wrongly think that the rice cultivation was minimal during mature Harappa and may have increased in the Northwest South Asia after 2000 BC. This could not have been true because the aridity increased after 2000 BC even more, further reducing the prospects of the rice cultivation in that region until it stopped completely. This poor state of rice cultivation in northwest India remained thus up to the middle of the twentieth century AD.

List of crops mentioned in the *Yajur-Veda* matches well with that of the Indus Valley Civilization people who cultivated millets, wheat, barley, pulses, sesame, cotton and rice (McIntosh:85, 89, 110). The crops cultivated by the *Yajur-Vedic* people were diverse and certainly the *Yajur-Vedic* people were cultivating multiple crops, which included the summer crops (rice, *kharif*) and the winter crops (wheat, barley, *rabi*), and often a third crop (*TS* 7.2.10.2; Gopal 2008:867). There is evidence from the Harappa culture too favouring the harvesting of two crops in the year (McIntosh:120).

The multiple crops must have led to the surplus in agriculture, thereby promoting diversification of trade, art and export, ultimately culminating in the level of economic growth visible in the Harappan Civilization. We cannot accept the second millennium BC as the time of the composition of the Vedas (particularly the *Yajur-Veda*). Because if we do so, we can neither imagine the water-intensive multiple cropping, nor the water-intensive crops like wheat and rice in the dry period that it had been. Hence to accommodate the facts mentioned in the Vedas, we need to re-date the whole chronology.

Then the too much change between the *Rig-Veda* and the *Yajur-Veda* too cannot be explained if we allow as short a time interval as one century in between the two Vedas. The absence of rice from the *Rig-Veda* and its presence in the *Yajur-Vedic* northwest India cannot be explained if we consider the time of composing the *Rig-Veda* at 1500 BC (or, 1200 BC) and that of the *Yajur-Veda* only one or two centuries afterwards.

In this time-interval no major climatic change had taken place. Nor was it a long enough interval to explain the great difference in the flora, fauna, environment, crops, dress-material, trade, hand-made vs wheel pottery, housing (mud vs burnt brick, pit dwelling) etc between the two Vedas *viz. Rig* and *Yajur.* The variations between the two Vedas are however explained only if one is placed in the early Holocene and the other in the mid-Holocene.

Wheat was an important crop in the *Yajur-Veda* (*TS* 4.7.4.2; *VS*). It was an important crop in the Gagghar Basin (Sarasvati Valley) too at about 5000 BC, when wheat farming comprised 36 percent of area under cultivation (Shinde 2008: 81). This was the time when rice, wheat and barley all were cultivated in good amount by the people of the Gagghar Basin (Shinde:121, 122). In the drier parts of the valley, barley was the main crop and in the water-logging parts, rice was the dominant crop, while wheat remained the main crop in general (*ibid*:81).

Interestingly, wheat was neither grown by nor known to the people of the *Rig-Veda* which does not mention wheat at all (B.D. Sharma 2008:126). This is quite understandable. Wheat requires more water, and it is the barley which can grow under the lesser rainfall. We have noted that the *Rig-Veda* was composed during the Early Holocene when the region was quite arid. Hence not wheat but barley alone could have been cultivated there in the Indus-Sarasvati region. Yet wild wheat ancestors were present in the region. A few grains of domestic einkorn, emmer and durum (tetraploid) types of wheats have been identified by Lorenzo Costantini from Mehrgarh Period 1 (cited by Jarrige 2008: 142).

These may have been the limited local experimentation with domestication of the wild wheat. The early wheats were not hexaploid like the later ones, and therefore were not very good to taste. Hence it had limited popularity. Possehl postulates the wheat domestication in northwest India from the wild wheat that might have existed there during early Holocene but later became extinct (Possehl 2002:28). He also noted that "the modern distribution of the wild ancestors of early domesticates may not reflect the late glacial or the early Holocene distribution of the same species. In other words, the absence of wild wheat in the Afghan-Baluch region in modern times does not mean that it was not there in the deep antiquity." (Possehl 2002:23).

It is now known that wheat was independently domesticated from the wild in India as well as West Asia (Brown 2008; Jones and Brown 2000; Renfrew 1990:190). Yet there is no evidence of significant cultivation of these grains by the Mehrgarh people (Jarrige 2008: 142). Thus it was not owing to any lack of farming skills or availability of wild wheat, but to the adverse climate that the Mehrgarh I people did not cultivate the wheat. This is consistent with the absence of wheat from the

Rig-Veda which in our study is contemporary with the early Mehrgarh. However the mutation took place and the tetraploid wheat became available in the wild. And then during the *Yajur-Veda* period the wheat was cultivated from the local wild breeds. That the Indian cultivated wheat is distinct from the West Asian one has been proven genetically.

It is also important to note that West Asia had cultivated only the einkorn wheat in northern Levant and Southeast Anatolia at the time of the Neolithic and this variety had a single grain per spike (Harris 2011:77). The definite evidence of the domestic two-grain form of einkorn is restricted to the two much later sites in northern Syria, where the grain was found in a late Neolithic or Early Chalcolithic context (*ibid*:77), and that could have been a late borrowing of the cultivated wheat from Indus-Sarasvati.

Not only Mehrgarh had the tetraploid wheat (durum-type) earlier than West Asia but southern Turkmenistan's early Neolithic (at Jeitun) too had several varieties of wheat namely one- and two- seeded einkorns and durum wheat (Harris 2011:77,162). Thus a less Eurocentric or less biased interpreter would agree that the archaeological findings support the origin of the domesticated emmer and durum wheats from northwest India, and then migration from there to south Turkmenistan (Jeitun) and from there again to the Levant. It is the tetraploid which gave rise to the hexaploid or bread-wheat after accidental hybridization with a wild wheat species *Aegilops tauschii*. which is found in the wild in India as well as Central Asia and West Asia (flowersofindia.net report).

The oldest samples of the domestic wheat in Ukraine come from the Crimean Peninsula dated 3500 BC onwards (Motuzaite-Matuzeviciute 2013). Ukraine was a forest which converted into steppe only after the mid-Holocene Optimum ended. Yet Crimea being surrounded by the Black Sea had more rainfall and its farming continued even after Ukraine became semi-arid grassland.

Thus if the *Rig-Vedic* Aryans had arrived from the steppe of Ukraine through Arkaim and Central Asia about 1500 BC, they must have known wheat. In fact Central Asia too had wheat, of course imported from south and not cultivated locally, since 2200 BC (Lawler 2012). Northwest India where the *Rig-Veda* was composed had wheat as the most important crop during the Harappa period. No evidence has so far been produced that this cereal ceased to be cultivated in the region after the Harappa period. Hence it is not evidence based to assume that the wheat was not cultivated at 1200 BC in the region, the impugned date for the *Rig-Veda*'s composition. And if it was there then why was it not eaten by the *Rig-Vedic* people? Hence the non-mention of wheat in the *Rig-Veda* implies that the text had been composed at a time when wheat was not known or popular in northwest India, Ukraine and Central Asia irrespective of whatever was the direction of migration of the Indo-Europeans. Absence of wheat from this whole region implies a date much older than the earliest presence of cultivated wheat in these regions. This date will go before 3500 BC on this account alone even if the migration had taken place from the steppe to India.

Grape-pips have been recovered from Mehrgarh and Nausharo, and later from Pirak 1 indicating exploitation of the grapes in the Kachi plain up to Harappan times (McIntosh:64; 78; 98; 114). However Constantini (2008) and also Jarrige (2008) report that the grape became extinct from most of the region following 3000 BC. In all likelihood, a larger amount of wine was consumed by the richer, urbanized and denser population of the Harappa Civilization than any time before. When grape became extinct from the wild it came to be cultivated. Gradually the cultivation of the grapes shifted to the Swat Valley in the Himalayas by 2000 BC, when the Indus Valley region became arid and completely inhospitable to the grape production. This we can say on the basis of the archaeological finding of emergence of the Swat Valley site where grape was cultivated at 2000 BC (McIntosh:98). Grape was consumed in the Central India too during the Bronze Age.

Wine came to be manufactured commercially or industrially during the mature Harappa period, in contrast to the *Rig-Vedic* times when it was made individually by the joint families. It is probably because of this reason that the wine-sieve or the "perforated jar" recovered from Harappa archaeology was invented for filtering wine. The same has been mentioned in the *Yajur-Veda*. The "hundred holed perforated jar" used as a sieve for wine in the White *Yajur-Veda* (*VS* 19.37, explained in Sayers 2008:209 fn274) is identical with the one found from the Harappa excavation. Resembling the ones described in the *Yajur-Veda* and the *Shatapatha Brahmana* (5.5.4.27) as the hundred-holed-jar to be used as sieve for the *soma* juice, the Harappan perforated jar too was in all probability used as the wine-sieve and had only a few more than a hundred holes (MacIntosh:311; picture on *ibid*:312; Kazanas 2013:10).

In our examination the Vedic *soma* was not ephedra but grape (see later). Watt thought that the Afghan grape was the real *soma* (cited by B.P. Roy 2008:567). From archaeology, we know that grape grew naturally in the Indus Sarasvati region since early Holocene until it became extinct from the region as the aridity increased. By 1500 BC grape had become restricted to the Himalayan regions of northwest India. We find mention of the *soma* as a vine and the drink being made of it in the *Rig-* and *Yajur-* Vedas, but the *Atharva-Veda* mentions the *soma* generally as the name of a god (probably moon-god) or as the divine drink used by Indra before slaying *Vṛtra* in the remote past. However in it mentions that the *soma* lives in the mountains (*AV* 3.3.3, 3.21.10). We know from the other sources that that the grape continued to grow in the Himalayas even after it became extinct from the Indus-Sarasvati plains (*e.g.* in the Swat region). In fact there is evidence that the grape was consumed in the Central India even in the first millennium BC (Vibha Tripathi 2008:357), and its continued cultivation in Himalayas and internal trade within India till quite later times is very much likely.

A reference to the *gandharvas* drinking *soma* is made in the *Atharva-Veda* (*AV* 4.34.3). It has also been mentioned that the tendril of the *soma* vine contains substances which cure the tuberculosis infection (*AV*

5.29.10-13). Vardhan demonstrated that the extract of the *Vitis* leaves kill the tuberculosis bacteria (2006:914). Experiments conducted for the other bacteria causing chest and other infectios show that *Vitis* contains valuable anti-bacterial properties (Jigna and Sumitra 2006; Abramovic *et al* 2012). Resveratrol present in the grapes is very useful in many diseases including even memory loss and cancers (see later). Hence divine status given to this plant is understandable.

Again we find that the 'bean' is absent from the *Rig-Veda* text, however it comes into existence in the *Yajur-Veda* (*TS* 4.7.4.2). Beans require rains for their growth. In the Early Holocene, it was dry or semi-arid to arid climate hence beans could not have grown in that part of India then. But when the monsoon improved, the region became hospitable to the beans.

Archaelogical evidence of use of hyacinth beans (*Dolichos lablab* or *Lablab* bean) comes from Ahar (2000 BC, Rajasthan; Dhavalikar 1984:141), Chalcolithic Inamgaon (R.P. Singh 2008:323) etc. Vishnu-Mittre noted the presence of this bean in India in the fourth millennium BC (cited in Evans 1996:79). The lablab bean is of East African origin (Fuller 2006:50). It arrived into India during the Bronze Age. Hence its absence from the *Rig-Veda* too is understandable only by placing the Veda to the earlier dates we suggest.

Lentil (*Lens esculenta, L. culinaris, masūra*) has been mentioned in the *Yajur-Veda* yet it is absent from the *Rig-Veda* and the *Atharva-Veda* (*TS* 4.7.4.2; Macdonnel and Keith vol 1:182). Its absence from the *Rig-Veda* is understandable, because this pulse-seed had been domesticated in West Asia, and it arrived in India during the Bronze Age (Fuller 2006:20). It was present in all the layers of Inamgaon (R.P. Singh:323). Earlier Harappans cultivated this pulse (at Ahar, Misra 2001:513; at Nausharo, Rojdi and Shortugai McIntosh:110; at Indus Valley about 2600 BC, Fuller and Harvey 2006:340; Fuller 2006:20). Lentils have been reported from third millennium BC Tokwa in UP (Pokharia 2008:248, 251) and Neolithic 1A period of Senuwar (V.D. Misra 2008:24-25). Allchin and Allchin report its presence in Loebnr, Tarakai Qila (early Indus) and

Navdatoli phase III (1982:115; 154; 267). At Tarakai Quila charred seeds of lentils were found (Thomas 1999) and although not radiocarbon dated so far, the associated findings belong to Pre-Harappan phase. Thus lentil seems to be an introduction in the northwest Indian economy by 3500 BC or sometime earlier. Its absence from the *Rig-Veda* indicates the older antiquity of the *Rig-Veda.*

However in the *Atharva-Veda* too the lentil is absent. This means the climate of northwest India had become dry enough by the time of the *Atharva-Veda*, and its cultivation had been abandoned in the region. It was absent from the Late Harappa site Savalda (R.P. Singh:325). Till recently the lentil was not grown in Punjab, Rajasthan and Haryana—the region identified with the Vedas. Almost 90% of lentil produced in India comes from Uttar Pradesh, Bihar and Madhya Pradesh and the rest comes from Orissa, West Bengal and Assam (Tickoo 2005). Clearly the region of lentil cultivation had shifted to the eastern parts of India by the time of the *Atharva-Veda*, concomitantly with the shift of most of the monsoonal rain from west to east in South Asia.

The *balbaja* which is a wild grass and is the ancestor of ragi (*Eleusine coaracana* or finger millet; see MWD) has been mentioned in the *Yajur-Veda* where it has been implied that it was a weed used for making ropes (*TS* 2.2.8.1-2). It was not cultivated, or in other words, not domesticated by that time. The rope made of this grass, mentioned in this context was used to fasten the arrow-head to stick.

This particular plant has been mentioned in the *Rig-Veda*, apparently as a wild grass (*RV* 8.99.3, Griffith's translation; *RV* 8.55.3 in Romanized Sanskrit version by Briggs). At one instance, it was brought from the forest by a hunter along with the skin of hunted beasts, bamboos and dogs, which shows that the grass was used for making ropes in a primarily hunter-forager economy. However consumption of grass-seeds during famines has been a common practice in India and the Early Holocene people, particularly the foragers, must have consumed the seeds of this grass for food during bad weathers.

The historians maintain that this particular grass was domesticated into the finger millet in Africa (Ethiopia) in the third millennium BC (Dogett 1991:145), and from there imported to India in the late second millennium say 1150-1000 BC (Fuller 2006:18, 37, 39, 42, 50; Fuller and Boivin 2009; Mitchell 2005:45; Engels and Hawkes 1991:29, 37). Older dates such as 2500 BC given by Possehl (1986, cited by Fuller 2006:37) for the presence of the finger millet in Gujarat has been rejected by Fuller (2006:37), who supports a late second millennium date for such event.

While the East African domestic *Eleusine species* has tetraploid chromosomes, the native Indian wild species *Eleusine indica, i.e.* the *balbaja* of the *Rig-Veda*, has diploid chromosomes. And it is from the diploid that the tetraploid is born. Hence from science we can say that it was the *Eleusine indica* which gave birth to the *Eleusine Africana* or *coracana* by a mutation causing tetraploidy. The diploid cereals have smaller grain size and lesser food value than the tetraploid ones. Clearly it indicates the early transfer of the *Eleusine indica* to Africa via sea route, where it mutated to *Eleusine Africana*, which then got domesticated and subsequently was brought to India in the Late Bronze Age. Such transfers are very much likely because India and Africa had intense relationship during the human prehistory (Kearsley 2010).

We can say from the Vedic description of the plant that by the time of composition of the *Rig-* and *Yajur-* Vedas, the *balbaja* (*Eleusine indica* plant, the wild ancestor of the finger millet) was wild and had not been domesticated, but was consumed as a part of the the gatherer (forager) mode of existence during the *Rig-Vedic* period or earlier. It has not been mentioned along with the crops particularly the several other millets listed in the *Yajur-Veda*. Nor has it been mentioned in the contexts of sacrifices. It had very small seeds which did not have much food value. Hence it was used only for making ropes when farming became widely adopted during the *Yajur-Veda*.

It will be appropriate to explain the nomenclature of the millets. Finger millet or *Eleusine coracana* is *ragi* (Sanskrit, Hindi) or *marua* (Bihari, Bangali). It was domesticated in East Africa and then came to India after the Vedic age just before 1000 BC (*vide supra*). Finger millet is black in colour, yet different from the black-millet. It has not been mentioned in any of the Vedas, although its wild form, which is Indian in origin the *balbaja* has been (*vide supra*). Dorian Fuller finds that the domesticated finger millet had not arrived into India before the late second millennium BC (Fuller 2006:39). Its complete absence from all the four Vedas means that all of them had been composed before the mid-second millennium BC and corroborates well with what Fuller says.

The black-millet is *śyāmaka* (Sanskrit) i.e. the *Panicum frumentaceum* (CDIAL 12667). It is known by the common names *sāmā* (Bihari, Bengali), *samai* (Tamil) etc. It is found only in South Asia and is believed by the scientists that it is of Indian origin. Its presence in the *Yajur-Veda* (*TS* 1.8.1.2, 2.3.2.6, 4.7.4.2 and *VS* 18.12, cited by Macdonell and Keith vol 2) and *Atharva-Veda* (*AV* 19.50.4-, 20.135.12, cited by *ibid*) is consistent with its being the millet of Indian origin.

Turner identifies another millet *śyāmā*, different from the *śyāmaka*, as the *Panicum italicum* (CDIAL 12666). This millet is also black in colour like the *śyāmaka*, and has been renamed as *Setaria italicum*. Foxtail millet is the common name given to this millet. The foxtail millet, which is of Chinese domestication, arrived in India in the early Bronze Age. This cultivar appears in the *Yajur-Veda* by the name *priyaṅgu* and is absent from the *Rig-Veda*. This fact again pushes the date of the *Rig-Veda* to before the Bronze Age.

The name 'foxtail millet' includes three millet species namely *S. italicum*, *S. verticillata* and *S. pumila*. There is lot of confusion in the names and they have been renamed several times. The foxtail millet species have been found from the third millennium BC Harappan cities Surkotada and Rojdi. The exact species have not been accurately identified beyond the genus *Setaria* level.

Monier-Williams as well as Turner (CDIAL 2605) think that the foxtail millet is the Vedic *priyaṅgu*. Khare (p. 602) also writes the same thing. However the name of the species that Turner, Monier-Williams or Macdonell and Keith (p. 52) suggest (*Panicum italicum*) is no more in use. Yet we can say that the Vedic *priyaṅgu* was the foxtail millet which arrived in India from the East during the Bronze Age and its exact species mentioned in the *Yajur-Veda* needs to be ascertained.

The foxtail millet was domesticated in China first. However it reached India and other parts of Eurasia quite early in the Bronze Age. Foxtail millet or *priyaṅgu* which has been mentioned in the *Yajur-Veda* has been found in the archaeological remains of the Harappan civilization particularly of Rojdi, Surkotada, Shikarpur, Sahghol and Daimabad, as well as from Central India (McIntosh:111, 120; P. Singh:110; V.D. Misra 2008:25 also IAR 1974-75:78, 1978- 79:108, 1990-91:103, 1992-93:123; Possehl 1989:175). This is consistent with Harappa civilization being contemporaneous with the *Yajur-Veda*. This crop is a rain-fed agriculture crop, and once the draught became severe in the Indus-Sarasvati region by 1900 BC, this could not have grown there. This is precisely the reason for the absence of the foxtail millet from the *Atharva-Veda*.

A related plant species is *aṇu* (Sanskrit) or *Panicum miliaceum* (proso millet or common millet) was known to the people of the *Yajur-Veda* in the cultivated form (*TS* 4.7.4.2; *VS* 18.12; CDIAL 192; MWD; Macdonell and Keith vol 1:14). This species could have been domesticated locally in India because its wild ancestor is native of India and is widely distributed in the rest of Asia. However it is generally believed that this millet was domesticated in Southern Central Asia (Turkmenistan) and China.

The idea of the cultivation of *Panicum miliaceum* or even the cultivated seed could have reached the Indus Valley from Shortugai (a city of Turkmenistan) during the Bronze Age is the general belief among the historians (McIntosh:112). Absence of this millet from the *Rig-Veda* and the *Atharva-Veda* tell a lot about the likely dating of the two texts.

This millet is rain-fed and its farming must have been abandoned once the Indus Valley became dry in 1900 BC. *Panicum sumatrens* (or *miliare*) is another millet species widely found within and outside India and could have been any one of the millets mentioned in the *Yajur-Veda*, not identified so far.

The period 1500 BC to roughly 1300 BC was a slightly more humid period in the whole of the second millennium BC (V. Tripathi), and it was the time when trees and animals adapted to both the dry and the wet climates could be found in the Indus-Sarasvati region in patchy distribution. This period seems to be the most appropriate time for the composing of the *Atharva-Veda*. This we can say on the basis of several findings.

The most important climatic information about the *Atharva-Veda* period is that regarding the presence in the *Atharva-Veda* of the following plants: *Ficus religiosa, F. bengalensis, F. racemosa, F. infectoria* (*vide supra*), *samī* (*Prosopis sp, AV* 6.30.2-3, 6.11.1), bottle-gourd (*alābu, AV* 8.10.29, 20.132.1), barley, rice, *śyāmaka* (black millet, *Panicum frumentaceum, AV* 20.135.12), beans (*AV* 12.2.4), *khadira* (*Acacia katechu*, 20.13.17, 5.5.5.), *dhava* (*Anogeissus latifolia, AV* 5.5.5) etc. This is a combination of both the xerophytic and mesophytic plants.

The wild grass *balbaja*, which was there in the *Rig*- and the *Yajur- Veda*s too is present in the *Atharva-Veda* for use as cushion-grass (*AV* 14.2.22). However the domestic finger millet (*ragi*) which came to India at late second millennium BC, and which is absent in the earlier Vedas, is absent from the *Atharva-Veda* text too. Apart from the *śyāmaka*, which is India's local product, and possibly *palāla* we do not get any other millet's name in the *Atharva-Veda*.

Fuller noted that sorghum had arrived into India from Africa in the early second millennium BC (Fuller 2006:39), that is, before the composition of the *Atharva-Veda*. This fact is reflected in the *Atharva-Vedic* verse (*AV* 8.6.2) where *palāla* (sorghum, *jowar* in Hindi; MWD) has been mentioned as 'something' to be avoided for the small children.

It is possible that the newly introduced sorghum millet was not well digested by the small children at that time. Or it could have been just a xenophobic expression. Whatever be the reason initially only its straw was used (MWD, *palāla*= sorghum straw), and later in the Bihari languages the meaning became "straw" (*puar, pual, pora* etc CDIAL 8800). This millet could never become a favoured food food for humans and is generally used as fodder for the cattle.

Thus from Fulle'r research we know that there was a period between about 1750 BC and 1250 BC when sorghum was cultivated in India but not the finger millet. This is exactly what the position of the two millets in the *Atharva-Veda* is. The sorghum (*palāla*) is mentioned with contempt and the finger millet is not mentioned at all. This finding fixes the date of the *Atharva-Veda* somewhere between these two limits. This, in light of the climatic study by Prasad (2013), helps us accurately define the time of *Atharva-Veda* between 1500 BC and 1300 BC.

A glance through the list of plants and trees mentioned in the *Atharva-Veda* makes it clear that some of these grow well in the arid regions while the others need much humidity or water. This situation could have been possible only between 1500 and 1300 BC, the relatively humid period of the dry second millennium BC.

The *dūrvā* grass (*Panicum dactylon*, or *Cynodon dactylon*; Hindi *doob*) has been mentioned in the *Rig-Veda* as well as the *Yajur-* and *Atharva-*Vedas (Macdonell and Keith vol 1:372). It is essential for all the Vedic rituals even today. Recently it has become clear from the germplasm studies that it is native of Pakistan, Afghanistan, Uzbekistan, Iran and Iraq, and also some parts of Turkey (Harlan, J.R. 1970). It needs good rains or otherwise it grows on the banks of pools of water or rivers. However the Indian breeds are draught resistant as well as frost resistant.

Hence during the Early Holocene, northwest India was dry and cold. Then this grass could have grown by the banks of the rivers. This grass is the favourite food of the horse. It is the reason why the horses thronged the banks of the river Sarasvati, as depicted in the *Rig-Veda*. The importance of this grass in the Vedic rituals is reminiscent of the pastoral life of the pre-Neolithic Indians who lived in the Indus-Sarasvati Valley about 8,000 BC.

Chapter 6

A General Account of the Forest Trees of the Vedas with understanding of the ecology of the respective periods

The *Acacia catechu* (Sanskrit *khadira*; Hindi *khair*) and *Dalbergia sissoo* (Sanskrit *śimśapā*) appear together in the *Rig-Veda* (3.53.19; Lal 2005b:71). From the forest ecologists, we know that the two trees grow together in the colder (*i.e.* temperate) climates even today as the *Khair-Sissoo Forest* (Singh and Lal 2006:109; *Tengberg* 2008:928). *Sissoo* tree can tolerate as low as −4 degree celcius temperature. Incidentally the woods of both the trees were used for making the *ratha* (car) during the *Rig-Vedic* times (*RV* 5.53.19). From Mehrgarh (Period 2) *sissoo* charcoal has been recovered (Thi´ebault 1992; Tengberg 2008:930-31).

Although *sissoo* is a tree of the temperate climate, yet it has been recovered from the archaeological remains from the warmer mid-Holocene Optimum. Hence we can say that the *sissoo* tree continued to be cultivated in the region. The charcoal of the *sissoo* has been recovered from the Bronze Age Mehrgarh from the layer dating the mid-third millennium where the Eupharetes poplar and tamarisk too were found (*ibid*). Hence the generalization by the botanists that the Indus Valley region is the home to the *sissoo* tree is not wrong (*Tengberg* 2008:Abstarct). Cultivation of *sissoo* must have started much earlier than the Bronze Age in northwest India, because we find its presence in the Mesopotamia about the mid-third millennium BC.

Sissoo tree did not grow in the wild in Iraq which was not its natural range. However it was brought there from India and cultivated during the Bronze Age. The recovery of very artistically made *sissoo* leaves made of gold from a burial from Ur (Tengburg *et al* 2008) should be analysed in light of the fact that the *Rig-Vedic* chariots were made of *sissoo* wood (Kazanas 2013) and the gold *sissoo*-leaves could be just the ritualistic representation of the chariot intended for the burial at Ur. The artefact dates to the mid-third millennium BC. It was probably symbolic of the Vedic *ratha* (chariot) which was made from the *sissoo* wood. DNA studies of ancient human fossils from Syria dated 2,500 BC have demonstrated that large number of northwest Indians had migrated to Mesopotamia and had settled there (Witas 2013).

Hence the cultivation of the *sissoo* tree might also have migrated with these people. In spite of being a tree of the temperate climates the *sissoo* can tolerate the warmer climates well. They naturally grow in the colder reaches of the Himalayas whereas in the rest of India they are cultivated (Champion and Seth; Singh and Lal; Singh and Bhatt 2008). They require annual rainfall of 1000-2000 mm, however below 600 mm annual rainfall they die. They also cannot tolerate water-logging and require well drained land or slopes for growth (Louppe 2008:215).

Study of the fossil pollen of northwest India has revealed that northwest India was dry and cold (semi-desert grassland) quite early in the late Pleistocene and early Holocene, following the end of the Late Glacial Period at 9,500 BC, yet the rivers of the region were full from the waters from the melting glaciers. There were ponds receiving groundwater flow or the stream-flow of the glacier-fed rivers. The blue lotus (*puṣkara*) grew in these ponds and playas as is obvious from the *Rig-Veda* (*RV* 5.78.7, 10.184.2, 7.33.11 and 6.16.13; Macdonell and Keith vol 2:9; Garzilli 2003).

The *Shorea* or *sāl* (Hindi) or *śāla* (Sanskrit) is a forest tree which provides high quality wood for house construction works, and that is why the Sanskrit word *śāla* and *śālā* also mean 'home', 'building' etc. The word *śālā* occurs in the *Atharva-Veda* (9.3.7 etc), and *śāla* and *śālā* do not occur in the *Yajur-Veda* and the *Rig-Veda*. *Shorea* grows in tropical rainforests which have good drainage of water. Thus they grow well in the hilly regions. However they can grow in sandy loams if they are well darined. Thus today they also grow in the plains of Haryana, Rajasthan and Madhya Pradesh.

It seems likely that the species invaded the Haryana and Rajasthan only after the water-logging humid phase for the region, *i.e.* after the mid-Holocene Optimum had passed and a drier climate had set in about the second millennium BC. The oldest evidence of the trees of *Shorea sp.* in Holocene north India has come from 3500 BC Himalayan foot-hills (Prasad, Khare and Agrawal 2008). The forests of this tree were established in Madhya Pradesh about 800 AD (Chauhan 1995:100). However in the pollen stage before 800 AD too, the tree grew intermittently in the region (*ibid*). Thus it appears that the tree species took time to arrive from the Himalayan foot-hills to the Madhya Pradesh from 3500 BC to 800 AD. In Rajasthan and Haryana, that is the Vedic regions, it must have arrived sometime in between 3500 BC and 800 AD and the middle point of this interval is about 1400 BC. That is the reason it appears in the *Atharva Veda* for the first time, a text which in our study pertains to the second millennium BC about 1500-1400 BC.

The trees of the genus *Ficus* require warm and humid climate, and they are distributed in the tropical countries with good rainfall (*vide infra*; **Orwa 2009; Doherty 2012:3**). *Ficus* fossils have been found in Maharashtra from Late Pleistocene up to recent times. However, from the northern India *Ficus* fossils have been recovered only from the late Holocene *e.g.* from Sirmur district of Himachal Pradesh (Prasad 2002). Obviously such trees which require heavy rainfall and warm climate for growth like the *pippala* (*Ficus religiosa*) and *nyagrodha* (*Ficus benghalensis*) could not grow in the *Rig*-Vedic times in northwest India owing to the cold arid climate of the region, and that is why this name (*nyagrodha*) does not occur in the *Rig-Veda.*

Although the words *pippala* and *aśvattha* occur in the *Rig-Veda* representing some tree/trees, these words could not have been the names of the *Ficus religiosa*, in spite of the fact that the *Ficus religiosa* tree is called *pippala* and *aśvattha* in today's Sanskrit language. This we can say because the climate of the Early Holocene was not conducive to the growth of any species of the *Ficus* trees in northwest India. The period was both cold and dry. The *Ficus* trees require warm and humid climate. It needs mean annual temperature between 16 and 35 degrees Celsius and rainfall between 50 cm and 500 cm, and prefers deep alluvial sandy loams with good drainage (Orwa 2009).

Macdonell and Keith record two *Rig-Vedic* references to *pippala* and find them "in neither case with any certain reference to the berry of the fig tree" (vol 1:531). They note the first certain use of this word for the berry of the *Ficus reliosa* in the *Brihadaranyaka Upanishad* and then in the *Atharva-Veda.* This finding is consistent with the fact that the *Ficus religiosa* is late to arrive there, and the earlier use of this word was for the medicinal plant poplar.

Although the words *pippala* and *aśvattha* have been mentioned in the *Rig-Veda*, they have been mentioned as medicinal plants (*RV* 7.101.5; 10.97.5), and possibly these were some trees other than the modern *pipal* or *Ficus religiosa.* The word *pippala* has always been mentioned with the prefix *su* in the *Rig-Veda* and the adjective *oṣadhi* has always been appended to the name of the tree. *Ficus religiosa* does not have so much important medicinal property (Khare 2007:269; API,1.1:21-22), as to warrant the epithet *oṣadhi i.e.* 'the Medicine'. The Vedic *aśvattha* tree possibly resembled with the *Ficus religiosa* tree in that they had ever-trembling leaves and that is why at one place *aśvattha* has been named the abode of the wind-god (*RV* 1.135.8).

It is probable that the words *pippala* and *aśvattha* were names of one or two different genus or species of trees than what we get today growing in India by the same names. Possibly those trees grew in northwest India then and later become extinct, however the names got applied to another tree. It is also likely that the *Ficus religiosa* did not grow there at all during the early Holocene. Pollens of poplar (Latin *populus*, German *pappel*; *c.f.* Sk. *pippala*) which includes its species aspen (English 'asp', Old High German *aspa*; ?cognate of Sanskrit *aśvattha*) have been found from that region dating back to 6000 BC (Costantini 2008). However neither pollen nor fruit of the *Ficus religiosa i.e. pipal* has been reported from those early days of northwest India.

The earliest depiction of the leaves of the *Ficus religiosa* tree on the pottery and later on the seals in Harappa Civilization can be dated back to 2500 BC (Misra 2001:501). The fruit (berry) of the tree has been recovered from the Late Harappan site Hulas dating 2000-1200 BC (McIntosh:114; Saraswat:46, BSIP) and that of Kaj and Kanjetar dating about 2000 BC (Farooqui 2013).

The *Populus* species whether poplar or aspen, are famous for their trembling leaves and thus could have been called the "abode of the wind-god" in the *Rig-Veda* (*RV* 1.135.8). Its medicinal value is also well-known because of the salicylic acid content in them. Hence the reference to the medicinal tree which is also the abode of the wind-god should be construed to be that of the poplar tree or the aspen which has similar charecters and belongs to the same genus *Populus*.

The *Ficus religiosa i.e.* the holy fig tree or *pipal* cannot grow in the hot arid regions and a minimum of 50 cm (maximum up to 500 cm) annual rainfall is required, which was not available in the second millennium BC (except during the mildly humid time window 1500-1300 BC) in the Indus-Sarasvati region. For the survival and propagation of the holy fig tree species, the *Blastophaga* and similar tiny fig-wasps are essential, and are indispensable for the pollination of the *Ficus* trees. The fig-wasps cannot tolerate aridity, and certainly could not have survived in the late second millennium BC in those regions of northwest India which had converted into semi-deserts by that time. This fact rules out the possibility of the widespread presence of the *Ficus religiosa* tree there in the late second millennium BC between 1250 BC and 1000 BC--the oft claimed time for the composition of the Vedas.

In fact the *Ficus religiosa* tree must have arrived into the Indus Valley region after the establishment of the moist mid-Holocene Optimum. The only site of the Indus-Valley where its berry has been found is Hulas, a late Harappan site (McIntosh: 114). The archaeo-botanical evidence so far has not demonstrated the presence of any *Ficus* species in northwest India as a whole before 3000 BC. The earliest trace of the *Ficus* tree (not clearly whether *bengalensis* or *religiosa*) appears only about this time in northwest India. Study by Thiebault (1988) revealed that at 3000 BC, there was no *Ficus* tree at Lal Shah and Mehrgarh. At Nausharo only three out of the 4035 samples of charcoal had any likely resemblance with *Ficus* wood, although there was no element of certainty to call it *Ficus.* It is possible that it was a time of ecological transition for the vegetations of the region, when the *Ficus* had just entered there in negligible numbers and the poplar was in the way to becoming extinct soon, as confirmed from the Costantini's study. Some trees of *Ficus religiosa* gradually penetrated the region by 3000 BC, as is evident from the charcoal study. In the Indus Valley region,

Because of the ever-trembling leaves of the similar shapes, the *Ficus religiosa* and the *Populus* trees both were probably identified by the same name *pippala* at the transition period when both the trees may have coexisted in the same region. However possibly to mark the distinction, the prefix '*su-*' was attached to the name of the *Populus* species (*supippala*), which was most of the times followed by the word *oṣadhi* too to distinguish it from the *Ficus religiosa* which was certainly present there after 3000 BC, and could have been present even since 5500 BC in some localities of the region.

Further than this, *Yajur-Veda* (*TS* 1.2.2.3) explicitly mentions that the agricultural farms were situated in between the medicinal *supippala* trees, and the trees were very tall, i.e. tall enough to watch and ward off the thieves (*sūpasthā-devo-vanaspatir-ūrdhvomā-pāhi-odṛcah*). We know that the poplar tree is usually interplanted along with other crops popularly known as agro-forestry (Nair 1993: 452), however *Ficus religiosa* cannot be interplanted with the crops. Hence this *Yajur-Vedic* reference implies the poplar tree and not the *Ficus religiosa.*

The trees were tall enough to support the sky (*TS* 1.3.6.1). *Yajur-Veda* also mentions that the *supippala* trees were planted and watered so that they grew and provided the valuable medicine for the cure of the people--*ayakṣmāya prajāyāḥ* (*TS* 4.1.2.4). The *Atharva-Veda* too mentiones that 'the medicine tree *supippala*' was cultivated, and the mantra also prays to the Goddesses *śūnā* and *sīrā* to be pleased to give adequate produce of the medicine to the cultivator (*AV* 3.17.5). This can apply only to the poplar and not to *Ficus religiosa* which cannto be interplanted with the crops. This inference would suggest that the poplar had been extinct from the wild yet it was being cultivated because of its immence medicinal value. The extinction from the wild had taken place for poplar by 3000 BC. Thus it appears that the poplar was effortfully cultivated in northwest India for about two millennia even after its extinction from the wild (Late *Yajur-Veda* and *Atharva-Veda* periods). Such features cannot accommodate *Ficus religiosa* which is not cultivated by the farmers.

Elsewhere the Veda states that the *supippala* tree had beautiful flowers (*puṣpāvatīḥ supippalāḥ*; *TS* 4.1.4.4) and fruits (*TS* 6.1.3.7). The *Ficus religiosa* tree does not have visible flowers. Its fruit, a berry, is also not at all popular. At another place it has been said that the *supippala* trees preserve (or, keep within) the gods (*devagopāḥ*; *RV* 7.101.5). This is probably because of its medicinal value. Hence the Vedic description of the *supippala* tree is only consistent with the meaning 'poplar tree' and *Ficus religiosa* is inconsistent with the details of the tree provided in the Vedas.

The *Rig-Veda* contains references to the *aśvattha* tree, a term which we take to mean the *Ficus religiosa* today. Its name is derived from *aśva* which means horse. However there is no observed association of this tree with horse, and hence the name *aśvattha* (abode of horse) cannot be justified. Its nearest philological cognate is *aspen* (asp;

Populus tremula) which has documented association with horse. In general the *Populus* trees act as tonic to the horse, and horses like it. However, the particular species *Populus tremula* or aspen is not liked by horse and it refuses to eat the leaves or bark of this tree. Thus this tree (aspen) may have been used as a horse stand by the early Vedics. Most probably *aśvattha* was the name of the aspen tree which grew in India before 3000 BC.

However, by the time of the *Atharva-Veda* the meaning 'aspen' had been lost and the meaning *Ficus religiosa* was acquired by the word *aśvattha*. This we can say because of many new descriptions of the tree *aśvattha* in the *Atharva-Veda*. The *Atharva-Veda* mentions *aśvattha* tree along with *Ficus bengalensis*, and states that the tree has tuft of hairs (*śikhaṇḍin*) (*AV* 4.37.4). This is true of *Ficus religiosa*, not of the poplar or aspen. It has also been mentioned in the *Atharva-Veda* but never before this text that the *aśvattha* grows over other trees like *Acasia* and *Prosopis* (*samī*) and often destroys them (*AV* 3.6.1, 3.6.6, 6.11.1).

We are aware that the *Ficus religiosa* trees grow over other trees as the epiphytes. The tree also grows over buildings and destroys them. By the time of the *Atharva-Veda* the tree had acquired the name *aśvattha*, the cold-adapted aspen tree having been extinct from the region long back shortly after the Early Holocene ended. However poplar being relatively warmth tolerant and a medicinal plant was still cultivated in the region and the *supippala* name was still attached to it. Hence the word *aśvattha* has been used to mean a tree which 'breaks', 'splits' or 'tears apart' *i.e.* the *Ficus religiosa*, and has been used for the magical and sorceretical purposes for destroying the enemies of the clients (*AV* 3.6.2-3, 8.8.3). We can say theat *aśvattha* was more a magical than a medicinal plant in the *Atharva-Veda*. These features have not been attributed to the *pippala* at any place in the *Atharva-Veda*.

The *Ficus bengalensis* (*nyagrodha*, *vata*, banyan), which is absent from the *Rig-Veda*, appears in the *Yajur-Veda* (*TS* 7.3.14.1; 7.4.12.1) and is present in the *Atharva-Veda* (*AV* 4.37.4, 5.5.5) too. The *Ficus racemosa* or *gular* (*udumbara*) as well as the *Ficus infectoria* (*plākṣa*) too are absent from the *Rig-Veda* and appear in the *Yajur-Veda* (*TS* 7.3.14.1; 7.4.12.1) and continue in the *Atharva-Veda* (*AV* 19.31.1, 5.5.5). This implies that the *Yajur-Veda* was composed at a wetter period when the *ficus* species could penetrate and spread into the region.

We know that the moist and warmer climate arrived after the early Holocene, and the period is known as the mid-Holocene Optimum. Riparian trees of the temperate and sub-tropical climate *e.g.* willow, juniper, oak, pine etc grew there in the Kachi plain during the mid-Holocene Optimum. This climate continued up to 4000 BC (Costantini 2008); and could have at the most continued latest up to 3000 BC (Jarrige 2008).

Costantini's soil samples from Mehrgarh were radiocarbon dated and the calibrated dates were about 7000 BC to 5000 BC (2008:171, 168). Date palm (*Phoenix dactylifera*) seeds were found from the sixth millennium BC layer (*ibid*:168). Although many wild species of the dates such as *Phoenix sylvestris* which yield smaller fruits are native of India (East and South), the particular large date *Phoenix dactylifera*, which was recovered from Mehrgarh is of West Asian origin (Iraq) and its presence in the middle of the sixth millennium BC in northwest India is the result of improved climate of the mid-Holocene Optimum favouring contacts and trade with West Asia.

The *Yajur-Veda* mentions the date-palm (*kharjūra* tree; *TS* 2.4.9). This was identified as the Indian date-palm species *Phoenix sylvestris*, which is found today in the monsoon rich forests of eastern India (Macdonell and Keith Vol 1:215). However it could have been the western species *Phoenix dactylifera* which might have reached there by 5500 BC when the region became monsoon rich and warm. The *Rig-* and the *Sama-Vedas* being older do not mention this tree. The tree cannot tolerate cold, and require warm humid climate. As the *Rig-Veda* and the *Sama-Veda* pertain to the dry and cold period of the region, it could not have grown at all in the Indus-Sarasvati region during Early Holocene (8000 BC-6000 BC). Costantini in his archaeo-botanical study of Mehrgarh found seeds of the date-palm (*Phoenix dactylifera*), which pertained to the sixth millennium BC after the cold dry period had waned (2008:168). This fruit requires heat for ripening and its presence could have been possible only in the mid-Holocene Optimum climate.

The cotton seeds (*Gossypium species*) too were found from the same date *i.e.* mid sixth millennium BC and not before (Costantini:168-9). This plant too, which is warmth adapted and needs much water for survival, is mentioned in the *Yajur-Veda* (*TS* 7.4.12.1) and not in the earlier Vedas like the *Rig-* and the *Sama*. Hence the date of the *Sama-* and the *Rig-* Vedas must be before the mid-sixth millennium BC.

The jujube (*Ziziphus jujuba*) seeds were found from the same layer (*i.e.* sixth millennium BC) and also from the earlier layer dated about 7000 BC. The date 7000 BC pertains to the *Rig-Veda*. It is highly probable that these were from the domesticated plants. Jujube was domesticated in India during the Early Holocene (Gupta 2004). Such medicinal plants were mainly domesticated by the early medicinal practitioners who practiced medicine for humans, veterinary medicine and botanical science as well, working under the divine patronage of the God of the medicinal science and botany--the *Aśvinī Kumara*-s (literally the 'twin horses').

Hence in the *Rig-Vedic* hymn dedicated to the medicinal-god *Aśvinī Kumaras* (*RV* 1.112), they have been thanked for helping the survival of *karkandhu* (*RV* 1.112.6) which is the *Rig-Vedic* name of the medicinal plant 'jujube' (Khare 2007:736). The names of some plants have been mentioned in the hymn (*RV* 1.112) as surviving unders the protection by the *Aśvinī Kumara*-s. Unfortunately these have been considered human names by Griffith and also by Monier-Williams. Surviving under the protection of the medicine-god only means carefully cultivated or horticultured plants and trees, which were used in treatment, and must have been planted by the medical physicians of the day. Declaring to be under the protection of god, creates fear and prevents theft of the plant products by the masses living around.

The view that these mentions in the *Rig-Veda* are for humans and not trees is wrong. Other names too actually pertain to the medicinal plants, for example: *Purukutsa* (?Artemisia plant; ? costus); Pṛsnigu (c.f. *prishniparni*, *Uraria*, Khare:684) etc. However most of the plants mentioned therein cannot be identified today. In general, plants have been mentioned as persons in the *Rig-Veda*. Therefore the word *karkandhu* which literally means the 'jujube' should be considered the name of the plant not person. The jujube has been mentioned in the *Yajur-Veda* too (*TS* 2.5.3.5, 5.6.11.1).

Although there was a general aridity of the region most marked after 1900 BC, yet between 1500 BC and 1310 BC there was a moister period, the Phase III, although much less moist than the mid-Holocene Optimum (Vandana Prasad 2013). After 1300 up to 700 BC, the climate was very dry. The climate improved again to some extent at 700 BC and has remained more or less same till the present, although with some fluctuations (*ibid*).

Thus the dry spell between 1900 BC and 1500 BC led to extinction of many plants and animals from the Indus-Sarasvati region. At 1500 BC when the climate became humid again, many of those plants arrived back into the region. The *Atharva-Veda* mentions that the *pippalī* plant (*Piper longum*), which requires humid climate, had been banished from the region by the demons. However it had come back to the region (*AV* 6.109.3). This statement is consistent with Pennington's finding for Patia Valley located on the tropic of Cancer in USA that the *Piper* became extinct there after 2250 BC due to climate change leading to arid conditions (Pennington and Ratter 2010:409). Most probably roughly at the same time *Piper* became extinct from the Indus-Sarasvati region too. However when the slightly better mid-second millennium came the plant came back to the region.

Chapter 7

Climatic Information Contained in the *Sama-Veda*

Recent geological studies show that the Sarasvati River dried at abour 2600 BC, and not at 1900 BC as had been earlier proposed (Clift 2012: Abstract). For the several millennia preceding that it had been not glacier-fed, but rain-fed. Giosan noted that the Yamuna River too had fed the Sarasvati system (Ghagghar-Hakra) during the Last Glacial period. The Last Glacial ended about 9,500 BC and at 8000 BC the Holocene started. Sometime in the early Holocene the Sutlej and Yamuna broke away from the Sarasvati, leaving the river dependant on the strong monsoonal rains of the mid-Holocene Optimum. This is what emerges from the more recent geological research (Clift 2012; Giosan 2012:e1690; Valdiya 2013). Earlier Francfort (1992) had found from the French satellite SPOT data that the river had started drying up at the middle of the fourth millennium, say about 3500 BC. However her previous 'the largest river' status must have come down much earlier than this date.

On the other hand the *Rig-Veda* depicts the *Sarasvati* River as the *nadītamā* (the greatest of all rivers) clearly indicating that she had more water than the other six rivers of the region (*RV* 2.41.16; 7.95.2; 6.61 etc). She has also been called the "best Mother, best of Rivers, best of Goddesses, Sarasvati," (*RV* 2.41.16) and the "mother of rivers" (*RV*

7.36.6) implying that it was the largest of all rivers of that region. This description of Sarasvati places the date of the *Rig-Veda* to the early Holocene (8000-6000 BC).

When the river lost the mighty form of the glacier fed river, she became the monsoon fed river at about 7000 BC. The monsoon fed rivers too are often perennial. In a millennium and a half the mid-Holocene Optimum arrived which was a period of torrential rains and floods. This kept the river flowing well, although the glacial might of Early Holocene must have not been equalled by the rain-fed stream. The stream became thinner over time after 3500 BC when the mid-Holocene monsoons started becoming weaker.

We find that the *Sarasvati* River is still flowing during the *Sama-Veda* (*SV* Part Second 6.3.9.1). However as time passes, *Sarasvati* becomes entirely heavenly goddess in the *Yajur-Veda*. The *Yajur-Veda* and the *Atharva-Veda* do not mention the "river" Sarasvati but at every place mention her as the heavenly Goddess. This has something to do with the loss of the earlier mighty form. Probably it meant that the earlier mighty river *Sarasvati* has returned to her heavenly abode and what was flowing on earth was only an earthly representation of the former, just like a statue represents a heavenly God or Goddess. The earlier might of the river was not allowed to be forgotten by the grateful descendants of the *Rig-Vedic* people. They maintained Sarasvati's status of the greatest Goddess and the Goddess of speech.

The *Sama-Veda* mentions wolves, but does not mention the tiger or the lion. The phenomenon needs to be examined under ecological principles. Wolves live in the regions where large ungulates live. These are generally grasslands or open forests. Lion too lives grasslands or in the forest if the forest is very sparse. Both of them work in groups, chasing the prey and killing them. Tiger on the other hand lives in dense forests and hunts singly, and strikes the prey from behind the trees and bushes. Presence of tiger is inhibitory to the wolves and the both are not generally found in the same forest, while lion and wolf often coexist, which is the case of the *Rig-Veda* where lion and wolf occur but the tiger does not occur (*RV* 1.105).

From the presence of the wolf we can safely say that the tiger was not present in the *Sama-Veda's* times. Yet lion too was not there. This means that the grasslands and sparse open forests were no more in the Indus-Sarasvati region, forcing the extinction of the lions--yet the tigers had not arrived into the forest from the more easterly regions of India. This scenario is the transition point of climates—dry and wet--and may have occurred in the sixth millennium, say about 6,000 to 5,500 BC. It is a transition period between the dry and the wet wild fauna too. Wolf continued to survive as it can manage in many types of ecological regions.

Because of the very small volume of the *Sama-Veda* text, it cannot be expected to have contained much information. However buffalo, desert-deer, elephant, falcon, bee, horse and cattle have been mentioned. Hence the time of the *Sama-Veda* was neither very cold nor very hot and neither very wet nor very dry. It was the time of transition from cold and dry to warm and humid climate, that is clearly after the cold and dry early Holocene had passed. It was the time when small water-pools (playas) were forming inside the deserts too, where wild bulls too could roam about (*SV* First-Part, 3.2.1.10).

Chapter 8

Fauna of the *Yajur-Veda* and their concordance in Harappa

The period after the early Holocene i.e. from the middle Holocene up to the onset of the historical period may be divided into two distinct periods ecologically. One is the wet mid-Holocene with plenty of rainfall in northwest India and the other is the later drier period which saw desertification of northwest India over time leading to the abandoning of the Indus-Sarasvati archaeological sites. In our study, we find that the *Yajur-Veda* was composed in the wetter period while the *Atharva-Veda* was composed in the mid-second millennium BC which was drier than the former.

De-desertification of Thar and Afforestation of NW India:

An extensive study by Deotare showed that in the Thar Desert (Rajasthan), the playas were full only during the 6000 BC to 3,500 BC period and before and after that period the rainwater accumulating therein was so small in amount that it evaporated quickly (Deotare 2004a:Abstract). Out of these the period between 5,500 BC and 4,000 BC was particularly more humid. Overall the wet period in the Thar was between 6000 BC and 3,500 BC, when it converted into grasslands and scattered open forests. There is evidence of human activity in previously non-habitable Thar, particularly of the nomads who came and lived within the Thar itself since 5000 BC (Deotare 2004a:404; 2004b:Abstract).

We do not have any stratigraphic report from the Punjab, yet from the Thar data we can say that any swamp may have existed in northwest India only during the wettest period *i.e.* between 5,500 BC and 4,000 BC which saw the highest monsoon output of the entire Holocene. During this narrow time period (5500-4000 BC), it is possible that even the whole of the Thar might have been converted into grassland and open forest in patches, as has been evidenced from some of the palynological studies. The *Yajur-Veda* mentions the clouds pouring heavy over the deserts (*TS* 2.4.8.1). This description could be possible for the Thar Desert only between 5,500 and 4,000 BC. It also mentions presence of wells in the desert (*TS* 2.5.12.4), implying settled human community within the desert. Such climatic conditions existed between 5500 BC and 4000 BC. Afforestation of the region must have led to large scale death of horses by predation from tiger and other large cats which live in denser forests.

This should be the time when the rhinoceros may have lived in the Indus-Sarasvati region some of which may have survived until 2,500 BC, the time of mature Harappa, wherein we get the seals depicting the rhinoceros (Marshall 1931: 387, 390, 391). About 2200 BC there was the onset of a particularly dry and hot epoch, known as 4.2 kilo event (Staubwasser 2003). In fact Harappa period was enough, it not too much, wet at least till 3,000 BC. And even until 2500 BC it could not be classed as dry or even semi-arid climate.

It correlates well with what Marshall noted: "We have been struck by the number of antlers and bones of the Sambur deer that have been found at Mohenjo-daro. This deer is a forest-loving animal and does not frequent the arid and/or semi-arid plains."(1931:391 fn2). This proves beyond doubt that Mohenjo-Daro was not arid but reasonable wet until 2500 BC. The Early Harappan (previously named Pre-Harappan) and

Harappan periods were the time when the *Yajur-veda* was composed in the Indus Sarasvati region.

Aquatic and semi-aquatic animals: None other but the *Yajur-Veda* alone among all the Vedas presents the climatic scenario of the wet and humid country. Its flora and fauna are those of the humid, aquatic and/or swampy climate. The animals mentioned are tortoise (*TS* 2.6.3.3, 5.2.8.4-5, 5.5.17.1, 5.7.8.2-3, 5.7.13.1), crocodile (*TS* 5.5.11.1, 5.5.13.1), rhinoceros (*TS* 5.5.21.1&5), otter (*TS* 5.5.20.1), buffalo (*TS* 6.2.7.3), dolphin (*nāktra*, Bloomfield; *TS* 5.5.13.1) and beaver (*babhru*, *TS* 1.8.8.1, 5.5.22.1, 5.6.11.1, 5.6.15.1).

Then there were animals like tiger which generally belong to the tropical rain-forests. Finally the miscellaneous forest animals like chameleon, hyena, deer (*TS* 5.5.19.1), wolf (*TS* 1.7.8.2) and ichneumon (*nakula*, *TS* 5.5.21.1, 5.6.15.1) are also present in the *yajur-Veda* period. These animals must pertain to a time well within the mid-Holocene moist climate window for the region.

Snakes:

Not only ordinary snakes (*sarpa*) which have been mentioned at several occasions, but the python (*ajagara*) too was found in the *Yajur-Vedic* northwest India (*TS* 5.5.14.1, 7.3.14.1). The *ajagara* is absent from the *Rig-Vedic* text, but is present in the *Yajur-Veda* and the *Atharva-Veda* (*AV* 11.2.25). In fact the *Rig-Veda* mentions the word '*sarpa*' (snake) only once and that too in the last *mandala* (*RV* 10.16.6), otherwise it uses the word *ahi* (snake) having the metaphorical meaning *Vṛtrāsura* in the *Rig-Veda*.

The generally used word for snake in the *Rig-Veda* is '*ahi*'. However, it has been used in the text not to name the animal 'snake' but the large Himalayan glaciers, which have been symbolized in the *Rig-Veda* as the demon *Vṛtrasura* which looked like a snake lying at the top of the mountain. Thus we can say that that there were scanty snakes if any in the *Rig-Vedic* age and no python at all at that time indicating the cold and arid climate, and that the *Yajur-Vedic* age witnessed many snakes including even the *ajagara* indicating a humid warm climate.

The word *sarpa* is present only in the languages of India, Iran and South Europe which are warmer and where snake can survive (L. *serpēns, serpent*, Gk. *herpeton*, Alb *gjarpen*). Its Indo-European status is evidence that the Indo-European homeland was not in any northern country where snakes do not live.

The word *ahi* has lost the meaning 'snake' from the north European languages. In Old High German its cognate *egala* meant 'leech', in Danish and Norwegian, *igle* means a parasite worm of the animals. This fact too is strong evidence ruling out the northern locations from being the possible homeland. Then the word *ahi* is present in some compound words in the Germanic *e.g.* OHG *egi-dehsa*, Old Sax *egi-thassa*, MLG *egi-desse*, German *Ei-dechse* (lizard) all probably from the Old India *ahi-dviṣ* which literally means 'enemey of snake', i.e. ichneumon. In fact the lizard somewhat looks like a miniature ichneumon. In the Germanic languages the words cognate to *ahi-dviṣ* lost the original meaning 'ichneumon' because the ichneumon was not found there. However they got applied to similar looking animals. To these words, when the prefix '*elle*' (red-yellow) was added, the meaning became red-yellow-ichneumon. These words which contracted or fossilized to give the words like **ill-it-wīso* (weasel or polecat; Pokorny 302-304). Its short form is iltis. Clearly no snake lived in North Europe during the colder periods, and the original must have come from the south.

Beaver and Mongoose controversy:

In the *Yajur-Veda* (*TS* 5.6.15.1) *nakula* (ichneumon or mongoose) and *babhru* both have been mentioned as distinct and different animals in the same sentence, signifying that the *Vedic babhru* was not the ichneumon or mongoose, but the beaver (*Castor*), falcifying the claims made by Neringer and Witzel etc in this regard. Identification of the

Sanskrit *babhru* with the 'beaver' is consistent with the philology too (Pokorny). The poplar and aspen trees, so much vital for the existence of the beaver, arrived into the Indus-Sarasvati region only after the post-glacial and early Holocene dry chill receded. These trees require good rainfall for growing. These trees became extinct from northwest India by 4000 BC or the latest by 3000 BC (Jarrige 2008). Thereafter the beavers must have become extinct there. However these trees probably continued to grow in Kashmir until later times. That is how we get bones of the hunted beavers from Gufkral and Burzahom sites dating back to 3100 CalBC to 1800 CalBC (Upinder Singh:114; Misra:507-8; 114; IAR 1962). It may be added that the presence in the *Avesta* of the beaver can be used to date the text to the *Yajur-Veda* period (*Avesta*: Yt 5.129, cited in Witzel's Autochthonous Aryan:52).

The other words connected with the beaver too need examination. Musk is the perfume produced by the beaver's musk-glands (castorius). The word 'musk' is a cognate word of Sanskrit *mūṣaka* (mouse), and its derivative *muṣka* (testicle, which resembles a mouse), all are from *mus*. However the original application of the word 'musk' (literally 'mouse') was probably for the beaver itself, because in some ways it resembles a large mouse. In Persian *mušk* means 'beaver'. German *muschus* (musk) and Greek *μύσχον* (*muschon*, sex-organ) are related. The Latin name of the animal "castor" is derived from Sanskrit *kastūrī* (Starostin:1662), which is again the name of an Indian perfume. Another cognate is Lithuanian *kastoras* (beaver). It is likely that the word *kastūrī* was originally the name of the beaver in Sanskrit and it was applied to name the prfume of the 'musk-deer' much later only after the beaver had become extinct from India. These words like the musk and the castor with the meaning 'beaver' travelled out of India during the Bronze Age, when lot of cultural exchange of India with the rest of the world was taking place. However the cognates of 'musk' had once earlier too travelled to parts of Europe at about 8000 BC with the migrating mice.

However absence of rhinoceros and crocodile from the *Rig-Veda* and the *Atharva-Veda* was probably because of the lack of swamps and marshes in the region during the periods of these two texts, i.e. Early Holocene and second-millennium Late Holocene respectively. Crocodile and tortoise dislike cold and they cannot live in very dry place. Hence the cold and dry *Rig-Vedic* period in Indian northwest was not congenial to the survival of these two animals. However the tortoise which entered the region continued to occupy the river banks till later times and that is why we find them in the *Atharva-Veda.*

The *Yajur-Veda* had the higher rainfall than the *Atharva-Veda, Sama-Veda* and *Rig-Veda.* This we can say because it is only in the *Yajur-Veda* that the rhinoceros has been mentiond. Thus we can say that by the time of the *Atharva-Veda*, the rhinoceros had become extinct from the Northwest India region because of loss of habitat owing to aridity. The *Rig-Veda* too, belonging to the driest period of all, does not mention the rhinoceros.

All the riverine and swampy animals listed in the *Yajur-Veda* are water-loving yet the rhinoceros needs more of water as it lives in the 'floodplain grassland' and swamp habitat. It requires huge amount of herbs daily as food. The rhinoceros could by no means survive the dry climate of Northwest India after 2000 BC, except in the foot-land of the Himalayas where they existed until few centuries back. Hence between 1500 BC and 1000 BC, the generally believed time for the composition of all the four Vedas, no rhinoceros lived in the Punjab region. Thus the *Atharva-Veda* may have been composed about 1500 BC, but the *Yajur-Veda* could not have.

Camel:

We shall discuss the camel in more detail later. Camel has been mentioned in the *Rig-Veda* as well as the *Yajur-Veda* (*TS* 5.6.21.1). In our study, the *Rig-Veda* belongs to the early Holocene which was dry hence the presence of the wild camel at that time in the region is very much expected. But presence of the camel in the *Yajur-Veda*, which in our dating belongs to the wet forest period of the Punjab and Indus Valley region, cannot be explained by ecological grounds. Presence of the desert animal camel in the midst of a forest region implies capture from the nearby Thar Desert and domestication. Camel bones have been recovered from the oldest layer of the Harappa Civilization (see later).

Crow:

Crow (which is most likely the house crow) occurs in the *Black Yajurveda* and the *Atharva-Veda* but is not there in the *Rig-Veda* and the *Sama-Veda*, signifying that the *Rig-Veda* and the *Sama-Veda* were the driest (and also the coldest) of the Vedas. The house crow needs a warm wet climate for the survival. Crow is present in the *Atharva-Veda* (11.9.9) too.

The Indus Valley Civilization, or the Harappa Civilization, flourished between 3500 BC and 1700 BC. Recent excavations at Bhirrana indicate that the Date may be 2000 years earlier than what has been generally believed for the Indus-Harappa Civilization (Dikshit 2013; Mani and Dikshit 2013). These pre- and Proto- Historical periods come under the period of the *Yajur-Veda*. Desolation of the region due to the onset of desertification had started following 2200 BC. But before 2200 BC this civilization shows features of wet ecosystem. At this very time crime, violence, starvation, disease and anarchy started growing which took the region completely within the grips after 1900 BC (Schug 2013), and the Vedic tradition of scholarship was abandoned by the masses living in this region after this, to be restarted again when better climate leading to better socio-economic life came into existence at 1500 BC.

Marshall noted, "It is a curious fact that the lion is not represented on any of the seals, the more so, as it appears repeatedly on the archaic seals from Elam and Sumer. In the early seals from Kish it was one of the most frequently portrayed animals.... On the seals of Mohenjo-daro the tiger takes the place of the lion," (1931:391).

Marshall was able to notice a very important ecological fact in these sentences. Elam, Kish and Sumer were arid regions then with plenty of open forest and grasslands—the perfect habitat for the lions. On the other hand the Indus Valley region had become a dense forest where lion could not live, however tiger preferred to live in such forests. This situation is strikingly different from the *Rig-Veda* which mentions the lion, but does not the tiger. The *Rig-Vedic* period in the early Holocene was drier--arid/semi-arid. Hence there were grasslands and open forests in the region. In such ecological niches lions live well.

Marshall further noted, "These facts are of considerable interest as they tend to show that the fauna of ancient Sind was radically different from the fauna of both Elam and Sumer. If this be granted, we can safely say that the physical nature of these countries must have been just as different. The lion and antelope, for instance, inhabit rocky and sandy wastes, and are not to be found in a country of forests. On the other hand, the tiger, the elephant, and the rhinoceros live chiefly in forest country and in high grass near water. **These facts would also argue that the climate of Sind was entirely different anciently from what it is at the present day**" (1931:391; emphasis added).

He further noted, "The Brahmanī bull, elephant, gharial, and rhinoceros are not to be found, to my knowledge, on any but the seals of the Indus Valley civilization." (1931:391). Here again Marshall underlines the difference in the climates or the ecosystems of Harappa and the West Asian civilizations.

We find that these all animals are mentioned in the *Yajur-Veda* indicating the ecological concordance of the Harappa civilization with the *Yajur-Vedic* description. Although the elephant and and the bull are present in all the Vedas, the gharial and the rihinoceros are to be found only in the *Yajur-Veda*, proving overlap of this civilization with the period of the *Yajur-Veda*. Turtle (*Trionix gangeticus*), a small tortoise, too was found only from the third-fourth millennium BC (Period VII of Mehrgarh, Jarrige and Meadow 1980), and mentioned, out of the four Vedas, only in the *Yajur-Veda* (*TS* 5.7.8.2).

Chapter 9

Athrva Veda and the arid Second Millennium BC of Indus-Sarasvati region

Among the animals the *Atharva-Veda* mentions camel (2.127.2; 20.132.13), tiger, lion and buffalo. This is again a mixed picture of the fauna of both the dry as well as the wet region—camel and lion from the dry while the buffalo and tiger from the wet one. It either means that the time of the *Atharva-Veda* was that of in between dry and wet. Or otherwise, the dry and the wet patches were intertwined in the region when the Veda was being composed. We have dated this particular Veda to 1500 BC-1300 BC period on the basis of vegitations and trees mentioned in the *Atharva-Veda* text.

Beaver mentioned on several occasions in the *Yajur-Veda* is completely absent from the *Atharva-Veda*. The latest skeleton of the beaver recovered from India (Kashmir) dates back to 1800 calBC (Gufkral and Burzahom sites; Upinder Singh:114; Misra:507-8; 114; IAR 1962). Hence the *Atharva-Veda* can be dated after that time.

Lion may have lived then in the Thar grasslands when the Indus-Sarasvati region had transformed into forest during the Harappa days. When the aridity increased, the Thar again became a desert and the Indus Valley region proper became grassland after 1900 BC. This may have caused extinction of the lions from the Thar and simultaneous arrival of the lions in the *sapta-sindhu* grasslands.

Even during the time of the *Atharva-Veda* (1500-1300 BC), which was not so dry, and not very humid either, lions may have survived in the grassy open forests located in between the denser forests in thich the tigers lived. Tiger, which lived earlier in the dense Harappan forests, may have survived in the region towards the northeast. However when the moister spell came there for two centuries, 1500 BC-1300 BC, the tigers may have moved into the newly growing patches of the thicker forests in the Indus-Sarasvati region. Thus both the lion and the tiger may have been well known to the people of the *Atharva-Veda.*

Possibly because of these ecological factors, the *Atharva-Veda* mentions both, the tiger and the lion (*AV* 4.8.7, 4.22.7, 4.36.6 etc). Wolf too is present. The carnivore fauna is almost the same as in the *Black Yajurveda*. This means during the *Atharva-Vedic* and *Yajurvedic* periods, the grassland and the forest ecosystems coexisted in adjoining areas in the northwest India, although the proportions varied. The Thar region had certainly become grassland with broken open forests at the time of the Harappa Civilization during the mid-Holocene wet period. On the other hand Baluchistan became semi-arid grassland by the end of the mid-Holocene Optimum, when the dry period arrived at the late Harappa period itself. Marshall noted this point during the archaeological study of the area. He found as to when Mohenjo-Daro was humid, wet and flourishing, Baluchistan had already become dry and deserted (Marshall:391).

Lions and wolves may coexist in the open forests and the grasslands, but the tigers live in the denser forests and it inhibits the wolves. Tigers and lions do not coexist in the same type of ecosystem because of the Gauss's Competitive Inhibition principle. Deotare (2004b:15) notes that the Thar was a grass dominated region even during the wettest period. In this region lions could have lived, whose descendants have survived in the Gir till today. But when the Thar was humid the Punjab and Sind were quite wet and and had converted into dense forests, in which lions could not have lived, but tigers could have successfully ruled as the top carnivore.

It is because of the absence of lions from the Punjab and Sind during the Harappa Civilization, that we do not find any depiction of lion in the Harappan seals. However the *Yajur-Vedic* authors located towards the Thar in the Sarasvati basin had knowledge of the lions. Hence we get the mention of the lion in the *Yajur-Veda.* However we can be sure about the fact that Harappa was surrounded by the dense forests, and had tigers (depicted on seals) and Sambar deer (bones and antlers found; Marshall), but no lion. But later after 2000 BC this region too suffered aridity and the tiger and Sambar must have become extinct in the Harappa region.

The *Atharva-Veda* pertains to the wet-in-dry period. Thus tiger and deer both have been mentioned in the *Atharva-Veda* many times because the period 1500-1300 BC was not desert but a climate moister than today's (*AV* 4.7.6,). Yet the period was not so wet as the mid-Holocene Optimum because no rhinoceros has been mentioned in the *Atharva-Veda.* Not only this, at the same time the spotted deer too were found (*AV* 2.67.4, Griffith), which live in the relatively dry open forests and grasslands, the abode of the lions.

Among the trees, *sissoo* (*Dalbergia*) dies when the climate becomes very dry or very hot. In the *Atharva-Veda* we find no mention of the tree indicating that it was not very wet. We get mention of the *sami* (*śami* or *śamī*) *i.e.* the *Prosopis cineraria* tree (CDIAL 12308) in the *Atharva-Veda* (*AV* 6.30.2; Macdonell and Keith vol 2:354), which is a desert adapted tree of the hot dry climates found from India up to Arabia. The trees of the hot and dry climate like the *śamī* (*Prosopis spicigera*) appear only in the *Atharva Veda* (6.2) and not earlier. It has been present in the Thar region adjoining the Indus Valley region since the time of the Harappan Civilizatio till today.

Although *Prosopis* has been depicted in a Mohenjo-Daro seal, possibly it did not grow then in Mohenjo-Daro, but in its neighbouring Thar region (Marshall: 390-1). After 1900 BC deserts and dry grasslands spread into the whole of the northwest India. Hence the occurrence of the semi-desert or desert region's flora and fauna in the *Atharva-Veda* is understandable, because we note that the date the *Atharva-Veda* was certainly after 1900 BC.

Saraswat found the presence of *Acacia* species with the sissoo tree in the soil layer of the Harappa period. He found that the pre-Harappan layer at Rohira (Sangrur District, Punjab) contained the pollens of "*Acacia* sp., *Capparis aphylla, Cedrela toona, Mimusops* cf. *hexandra, Tectona grandis, Tamarix* sp., *Cedrus deodara, Vitis vinifera* and *Lawsonia inermis.*"

Out of these *Cedrus deodara* needs cold climate and open forest, while others may grow in cold and hot both types of climates. On the other hand soils from the mature Harappa layer contained the pollens of *Acacia* sp., *Tamarix* sp., *Dalbergia sissoo, Nyctanthes arbarlstris* and *Vitis vinifera.* Clearly the mature Harappa shows evidence for the presence of the warmth tolerant species, however cold loving trees like *Cedrus deodara* were absent from the mature Harappa.

We find *soma* being pressed by the humans and then being offered to the gods in the *Rig-Veda* (1.2.6; 1.15.1; 1.16.4; 1.23.2). The use of the *soma* drink by humans for gaining health has been mentioned in the *Rig-Veda* (1.23.20-21; 1.30.11). But in the *Atharva Veda* (3.3.3; 3.21.10) and the *Krishna Yajurveda* (*TS* 6.1.6.1) *soma* grows only in the high mountains of the Himalayas, and humans have not been depicted as pressing the *soma* and offering it to the gods. In the *Atharva Veda soma* is no more the drink of the humans, but that of the gods. In fact *soma* itself becomes deified as god in the *Atharva Veda* (*AV* 1.20.1; 3.15.6). It is present not as the creeper, but only in the (invisible or dissolved) form in the waters of the rivers (*AV* 1.6.2). In our identification *soma* is *Vitis*, and it is certainly not the cardio-toxic drug ephedra. *Vitis* became extinct from the region after about 2000 BC.

We find the appearance of *naḍa* or the grass-reed (*Arundo or Phragmites karaka*, CDIAL 6936) in the *Atharva-Veda* (12.2.54). This is consistent with the moist spell of 1500 BC-1300 BC inside an arid setting. The *Atharva-Veda* mentions the mat made from the reed (*naḍa*) crushed by women with stones, however the mats described in the *shatapatha Brahmana* were golden in colour (Macdonell and Kieth vol 2:144).

This means the golden-mats at the time of the *Shatapatha Brahmana* were made from the golden coloured twigs of the golden willow tree, however when the willow became extinct or rare, the mats came to be made from the grass-reeds. This fact again is consistent with our dating of the *Shatapatha Brahmana* at about 3000 BC (Kak) after which the golden willow disappeared from the Indus plains. Much later after this disappearance event the *Atharva-Veda* was composed.

The *gulgulu* (bdellium) is the resin or gum product of the Indian plant *Commiphora wightii* which is a plant of the warm semi-arid to arid climates (**Orwa** *et al* 2009b). Bdellium has been mentioned in the *Atharva-Veda* as something very local (*AV* 2.36.7: "Here is the Bdellium"). *Atharva-Veda* mentions two varieties of bdellium, the indigenous coming from the *sindhu* and the one imported from the sea (*AV* 19.38.2).

This mantra signifies the local growth of the *Commiphora wightii* plant in the Indus Valley region at times of the *Atharva-Veda* indicating that that the Indus Valley had converted into a semi-desert ecosystem by the time of the *Atharva-Veda*. This time is after 1900 BC. This mantra also provides evidence that the sea-trade was taking place between the Indus Valley region and the Afro-Arabian coasts. We know from the archaeology that such trade was taking place during the Bronze Age and it became marked during the late third millennium to early second millennium BC period. This trade was an important source of the imported bdellium for the Indus-Sarasvati people.

It is not that the *Atharva-Veda* does not mention the *vetasa* (willow). It mentions the *vetasa* (golden willow) at two places. However the context indicates that they are remembrances of something extinct long back, and something considered divine by the time of the *Atharva-Veda*, and which were known from the folk memory but were no more extant by that time:

> "*Yo vetasaṃ hiranyayaṃ tiṣṭhantaṃ salile veda.*
> *sa vai guhya prajapatiḥ.*" (*AV* 10.7.41)

> "One who knows the golden willow living in the midst of floods
> He is verily the hidden Lord of the Living Beings."

[Here it is implied that the golden willow is generally not known to the people at large, but known to the God only.]

> And again,
> "*upadyāmupa vetasamsvattaro nadīnām*" (*AV* 18.3.5)
> "The rivers speed up, craving for the golden willow".

We do not find mention of the Sarasvati River in the *Atharva-Veda*, instead we find her mentioned as a powerful Goddess *Sarasvati* living in the heaven (*AV* 3.2.7 etc), "who comest with the Fathers" (*AV* 18.1.43). This could possibly be because of the drying up of the Sarasvati River after 1900 BC. However it is also possible that the people of the Vedic culture had moved to a wetter place located east and north.

There is no mention of the rhinoceros, and crocodile in the *Atharva-Veda*. Although crocodile (*gharial*) and rhinoceros depictions on the seals as well as the crocodile bones have been found from the Harappa Civilization (Marshall 1931:392, 395, 396), both the animals are absent from the *Atharva-Veda* implying that the text pertained to a relatively drier period of the region, when there would not be enough swamps for the survival of the crocodile and rhinoceros. This proves *Atharva-Veda's* status as post-Harappan. In fact the *Atharva-Veda* belongs to the Indian Iron-Age, when the use of iron had become quite widespread. This is the reason why we get the mention of the black-iron (*śyāma*) in the *Atharva-Veda* (*AV* 2.3.7).

Iron has been mentioned earlier too, as in the *Yajur-Veda* (4.7.5.1) where iron, copper and lead have been mentioned in the same sentense, implying the presence of iron in the northwest Indian Bronze Age. Archaeology confirms it. However its use was minimal, often limited the tips of the ploughs or arrowheads (Pigott 1999:161; Possehl and Gullapalli 1999:161). Iron is absent from the earlier Vedas, and the reference to 'metal' in these are not to the 'black' metal iron, but of the red metal copper.

The Humid Period of Thar:

In a study based on the Bay of Bengal data, Rashid and colleagues (2011) noted that the reduction in the Indian monsoon had initiated at 3000 BC itself (Abstract). Enzel (1999) too showed that it was at about 5250 calBC that the Thar desert abruptly became wet and the Lake Lunkaransar became full, however the lake dried up again at about 3550 calBC.

In another study Deotare noted that the lakes were full in the Thar between 6000 BC and 4,000 BC (Deotare 2004b: Abstract). Deotare noted that at about 5000 BC, hunter-gatherer people arrived in Bap-Malar, District Jodhpur (Rajasthan), and established their camps (Deotare 2004a:404). This was because of the improvedment in rainfall in the region owing to which, by this time (5000 BC), the Thar must have converted into a savannah or grassland in which hunter-gatherers could subsist. However while better monsoons changed the Thar from desert to a grassland, the amelioration of climate influenced the adjoining Punjab, Baluchistan and Sind too which changed from grasslands and open forests to closed dense forests.

Chapter 10

Evidence of the Bronze Age Migrations Out of India

The Bronze Age technological revolution resulted in a population expansion in northwest India, resulting in migrations in all directions out from India. Many scientific investigations have revealed that there were large migrations out of India in every direction, not only to Mesopotamia, but also to Indonesia and Australia, Central Asia and Arabia at this time (Pugach 2013; Karafet 2005; Hemphill 1999a; Schurr 2001; Hemphill and Mallory 2004:199).

Pugach while giving the date of Indian migration to Australia as 2,300 BC, observed: "We also detect a signal indicative of substantial gene flow between the Indian populations and Australia well before European contact, contrary to the prevailing view that there was no contact between Australia and the rest of the world. We estimate this gene flow to have occurred during the Holocene, 4,230 y ago. This is also approximately when changes in tool technology, food processing, and the dingo appear in the Australian archaeological record, suggesting that these may be related to the migration from India." (Abstract). Similarly Karafet noted in a study of the Balinease population that 12% of the population had Indian ancestry from the male lineage side (2005:94).

Indian migrations to Mesopotamia have been supported by archaeology and inscriptions. Possehl mentions, "Cuneiform documents also inform us that some people in Mesopotamia called themselves "Son of Meluhha," and there are references to Meluhhan villages and granaries.We even have the personal cylinder seal of Shu-ilishu, a translator of the Meluhhan language (*Expedition* 48(1):42-43)." (2007:41). Meluhha has been identified as the Indus-Valley region.

Possehl also described that "First, beginning in the 4th millennium BC, the people of southern Central Asia shared a pottery style called "Quetta Ware" with the people of Baluchistan far to the south. Along with female figurines and occasional compartmented seals, this style of pottery persisted until the early centuries of the 2nd millennium BC," (2007:42).

Possehl names southern Turkmenistan as "middle-Asia" and notes its rich connections with Indus. About its city Altyn Depe Possehl notes, "at Altyn Depe in Turkmenistan, the Soviets found two provincial-style Indus seals, along with much ivory (presumably from elephants), which was also apparently from India. Their discoveries were all found in correct chronological sequence dating to the second half of the 3rd millennium BC, indicating that Altyn Depe was contemporary with the Indus cities. Furthermore, this also provided evidence for Middle Asian interaction" (2007:42).

Chunxiang (2010) studied the DNA of early Bronze Age bones from Central Asia and found that all the male lineages detected belonged to R1a1a. This lineage was subsequently demonstrated by Underhill (2009) to have originated in India. In the study, about 28% of the female lineages (one M* and three R* mtDNA out of 15 studied) were of the mitochondrial DNAs of Indian ancestry (Chunxiang :6 Table3).

Bennett and Kaestle (2010) examined ancient mtDNA from Sargat Culture and adjoining Western Siberia near the steppe. They concluded that this region of Siberia had received Indo-Iranian population possibly coming all the way through the steppe in their past. Matween

(2000), on the basis of craniometric analyses, found that a significant proportion of the people of the ancient West Siberia (Sargat Culture) belonged to the Iranian population.

In another study the examination of Central Asian ancient mtDNAs by Lalueza-Fox (2004) revealed that the Central Asian ancient gene pool contained Eastern DNAs only after the Bronze Age period, but not before that. The Indian DNAs (M, particularly M* and M4) were found to be frequent in the Kazakh DNAs (Central Asia), and were included within the 'Eastern DNAs' in that study. In fact by the presence of Indian mtDNA lineage M4 in the ancient Kazakhstan, the authors arrived at a very significant conclusion: "This fact could correspond to an independent, Indo-Iranian genetic infusion into the steppes (*ibid*:945)". They also note that about 7% of modern Kazakh populations carry Indian mtDNAs (*ibid*:945). These Indian DNAs must have reached there during the prehistoric times, because there is no known movement of Indians into Kazakhstan during the historic period.

Hemphill (1999b) ruled out any arrival from the Central Asian 'Oxus region' to northern Iran during the Bronze Age. They also ruled out any possibility of people from western China (like Tarim Basin) having arrived and lived in Bactria during the Bronze Age.

Hemphill and Mallory (2004) did refined craniometric study of the Bronze Age skulls of the Tarm Basin population from the northern Central Asia in Xinjiang province of China. The results revealed that that population comprised of people who were neither from the steppe not from the Bactrian oasis nor even from the Han China (p. 214). However the population of the region after 1200 BC consisted of people arriving there from the places like Fargana and Pamir which are located on the northern frontiers of the Indian sub-continent. They thought that these could be the Shaka (p. 216, 199). Thus this evidence proves the northerly migration of the Shaka (or Saka) from the northern Indian frontiers.

They reject the Andronovo as a source of the widespread culture of the region and also as the source of migration to the other parts of Asia (p. 214). They write in conclusion, "The results of this study provide little support for the steppe hypothesis, for none of the statistical procedures yields the close phenetic distances expected between colonizers (steppe samples) and the colonized (Tarim Basin samples). Similarly, none of the analyses revealed any affinity between the Bronze Age inhabitants of the Tarim Basin and Han Chinese. Thus, it appears that neither steppe populations nor Han Chinese populations played any significant role in the establishment of those Bronze Age populations of the Tarim Basin for which samples were available." (Hemphill 2004:218).

These migrations, from India to the other regions, disseminated cultural and civilizational influence over a very vast area of the world. Yet the migrations did not lead to significant language change of the host regions. Of course the host countries borrowed many words from the Indo-Aryan, and also from the Dravidian because of the incomers, even then the languages of the host countries remained largely unchanged but for these loan-words. However, enclaves of Indo-Aryan migrants were located in the region, for which we have archaeological evidence.

This clearly indicates that most of the imaginary steppe migrants did not move out of the steppe but stayed there. On the other hand there is mtDNA evidence from the modern and ancient Ukrainian population's DNA indicating that the Eastern human lineages C and T4 from South Siberia, China and Altai region entered the north Pontic region during the mid-Holocene Bronze Age and Iron Age (Nikitin 2010, 2012; Newton 2011) bringing the cultural innovations to Ukraine.

These Bronze Age and Iron Age migrations move westward from or through Central Asia, but do not enter the South Asia. In fact these migrations from inner Asia had been initiated in response to arrival of the Bronze Age and Iron Age revolutions from northwest India. Hence the subsequent waves moved away to West after having established in inner Asia.

The Indo-Aryans migrated to West Asia too during the Bronze Age. Witas and colleagues (2013) examined the ancient DNA recovered from the teeth of several skeletons from the Bronze Age graves in Mesopotamia. They found that quite a large number of both the male and the female individuals from the Mesopotamian graves belonging to the Bronze Age had characteristically Indian mtDNAs, particularly the haplogroups M4b1, M49 and M61.

The authors felt, "it can be claimed that the studied individuals represent genetic association with the Indian subcontinent." "The fact that the studied individuals comprised both males and a female, each living in a different period and representing different haplotypes, suggests that the nature of their presence in Mesopotamia was rather long-lasting than incidental.".

The authors also noted that the two of the individuals (DNAs) found from Syria belonged to Indian gene pool and have been found from a date just after the founding of the city of Terqa about 3000 BC. They suggest that these "could fall within the population founding Terqa, the historical site constructed probably in the early Bronze Age" (2013:7).

Kenoyer and his colleagues applied a new technique to the skeletons dating back to the third millennium BC (2550-2030 BC) recovered from the Indus Valley and Ur (Mesopotamia), which involved study of strontium, carbon, and oxygen isotopes for identifying migrations of non-local grown people. The held, "it should be feasible to identify Harappans in Mesopotamia" (2013:Abstract).

There were not many skeletons made available for study from Ur. From third illennium BC Ur, only two human samples could be examined. Therefore no conclusion could be drawn about Ur. Yet Kenoyer and colleagues were able to comment: "there are many non-local objects found in the cemetery that indicate contact with the Indus valley and the Gulf region to the east. These include a circular Gulf style stamp seal with Indus style script, carnelian beads and shell cylinder seals that appear to have been made from the Indus shell species Turbinella pyrum" (*ibid*: 2291).

From the Indus Valley they, were able to examine more skeletons. They found that many people from the different parts of the Indus Valley region had arrived there after attaining adulthood, and had even married and permanently settled in the Indus cities. Some may even have come from distant countries as these cities were cosmopolitan in nature, the authors felt.

Kenoyer's results need to be read with what earlier archaeological reports had suggested, "For example, the burial of a BMAC personage at Quetta and the French excavations at Sibri, a BMAC settlement, indicate that BMAC peoples travelled in the Greater Indus Valley and even took up residence there." (Possehl 2007:42).

Chapter 11

Indian Migrations to Central Asia and the Steppe during Bronze Age: Linguistic and Archeological Considerations

After having seen the scientific evidence favouring the Indo-Aryan and Iranian migrations to Central Asia and the Steppe, we shall now examine the linguistic and archaeological evidence here.

Linguistic Evidence

There is linguistic evidence of post-Vedic Indo-Aryan presence in the steppe/Ural region and also in West Asia. Udmurt (Votyak), Kami, Mari, Moksha and Erzya languages of the Uralic family are found in the neighbourhood of the presumed Aryan homeland in the steppe. The words borrowed by the Finno-Ugric languages of the steppe region are not from any of the neighbouring branches of the Indo-European like the Slavic, but from the Post-Vedic Sanskrit located in India. From there many of such Indo-Aryan loan words have travelled into the Uralic languages of the further northwest. In the West Asian Mittani language too, post-Vedic vocabulary is found (*vide infra*).

Some examples of Indo-Aryan borrowings in the Uralic are:

i. Sanskrit *Arya* → Saami **orja* > *oarji* (southwest) (Koivulehto 2001: 248, cited by Parpola and Carpelan 2005:111-112); *ārjel* (Southerner), and Finnish *orja*, Votyak *var,* Syry. *ver* (slave) (Redei 1986: 54). Here we get a clear philological indicator to the fact that the Indo-Aryans had arrived there from the south because words for *Arya* mean the 'southerner' in many Uralic languages. This is also clear from philological analysis that the Indo-Aryans were foreigners in the steppe land. That is why their epithet '*arya*' was not used with respect, but used with contempt to mean 'slave' in some Uralic languages.
ii. Some other such borrowing noted by Burrow are: Sanskrit *martya* →Udmurt *marta* (man); Sanskrit *śata*, Hindi *sau* (hundred)→ Finn. *sata*, Lappe *coutte*, Mordv. *sado*, Zyry *so*, Voty *śu*, Vog *sāt*; Sanskrit *vārāha* → Finn. *oras* (castrated boar); Sanskrit *udara* →Finn. *utar,* Mordv. *odar* (udder); Sanskrit *hiraṇya* (gold) →Hungarian *arany* (gold); Sanskrit *śarabha* 'a large deer' →Vog. *šourp*, *šōrp* (elk); Sanskrit *setu* → Mordv. *sed'* (bridge) etc. (Burrow 2001:25).

Out of these the Uralic words for 'boar' are important. DNA studies as well as archaeology have revealed that the boar did not live in the steppe, particularly when the PIE was taking shape, and the steppe boars have not contributed to the domestic pig populations of the world today (Larsen 2005: 1619 Fig1).

Not only Uralic borrowed; the Russian, a steppe language herself, also borrowed words from the Indo-Aryan. One example of such words is the Russian *stan* (nomad, nomad camp; from Sanskrit *sthana*; Kuz'mina and Mallory:56). It implies that the arriving Indo-Aryans living in the tents and camps were considered 'nomad' or vagabound by the steppe Slavs, who had been already living there. I find that there is a large number of such words in the Slavic which belong to this category (of Indo-Aryan borrowings) so far unrecognized. Some of such words are: Russ *shakal* (jackal) from IA *śṛgāla*; Russ *omela* (mistletoe) from IE *āmlā*;[5] Russ *yabloko* (apple) from IA *jambūla-ka* (rose-apple); Russ *leemon* (lemon) from Iranian *limun* (< IA *limoo, nimbu*).

These examples are enough to prove the point that there was an Indo-Aryan/ Indo-Iranian migration from northwest India/Iran to the steppe, and there is no evidence to support the migration from the steppe to India or Iran. The AIT interpretation of these loan words is very unimpressive. The protagonists of the Aryan Invasion Theory like Witzel (2003) and Burrow (2001) think that the Indo-Iranian language originated there: "it appears probable that the seat of this primitive Indo-Iranian must have been in the region of the middle Volga and the Urals for this contact to have been possible." (Burrow 2001:26).

This recieved interpretation of the linguistic findings is Eurocentric and absurd. It implies that the entire Indo-Aryan speaking tribe migrated to north India and settle here, without leaving any trace of its speakers in the steppe. However the migration to north India actually never took place because no DNA of possibly steppe ancestry can be identified in India today (Sahoo 2006:847). In fact no evidence of even a single fossil/living- DNA material/population has been found in India by any investigator which could be traced-back to the claimed homeland *i.e.* the North Pontic region!

Thus we conclude that the claims of Witzel, Burrow, Parpola etc are simple products of ethnocentricity. Almost all of the words are clearly established Vedic and post-Vedic Indo-Aryan, and not the "primitive Indo-Iranian". In all likelihood, they are the results of migration of the Indians and East Iranians to Sintashta and the Uralic region during the Bronze Age, not the *vice-versa*. They must have made Indo-Aryan speaking enclaves in the steppe region as many Indo-Aryan speaking immigrants did in West Asia whereby the words percolated into Uralic and Slavic. The whole thing needs further examination under the light of archaeological and genetic evidence.

5 The Russian fruit mistletoe and Indian ***āmlā*** look similar.

Archaeological Evidence:

In spite of the designation of Neolithic, the Western or the Pontic-Caspian steppe was a hunter society till late. Frachetti (2012:7) noted the absence of the domestic cattle and sheep from the remains of Tentek-sor which is located to the north of Caspian in Kazakhstan: "The faunal record from the year-round settlement of Tentek-sor (4500–4000 calBC) reflects a hunting strategy of mainly Asian wild ass (*Equus hemionus kulan*; 85%) as well as antelope (*Siaga tatarica*; 5%), aurochs (5%) and a few wild horses (Barynkin and Kozin 1998:71; Kuz'mina 1988:175). Domesticated sheep and cattle were not recovered in sites of this time period."

Tentek-sor is located to the south-west of Arkaim, to the west of Sintashta and to the east of Dereivka in the steppe. This archaeological finding clearly proves the absence of the domestic horse, sheep and cattle from the steppe at 4000 calBC the claimed time of origin of the Indo-European languages in the steppe. It may be noted that the pig too was abent from the region then.

Central Asia too was actually hunter till much later times. For example Kyzyl Khak site (Uzbekistan) dated 3700-3600 calBCE exhibited the bones of saiga antelope 62%, cattle (wild) 13%, sheep 9%, horse 7%, onegar 7% (Anthony 2009:275). The steppe horse (Przewalskii) was too fast a runner to be captured or to be hunted frequently. Yet one thing is clear that the horse and the aurochs were almost at par, horse being even less than the cattle, in numbers among the hunted beasts. That means neither of the two were domestic and both were wild and hunted.

The steppe and Central Asian cultures (Kyzl-khak II, Kurpezhe-molla, and Kara Khuduk I, Botai, Tenktor-Sor) remained primarily hunting until the last part of the fourth millennium BC. Frachetti clarifies,

"Nevertheless, the low percentages of domesticated[6] animals in faunal assemblages recovered from sites in the north Caspian steppe and trans-Caucasus do not indicate a specialized mobile pastoralist economy among any communities of the western steppe during the first half of the fourth millennium BC (Kuz'mina 1988)." (Frachetti 2012:8).

Most probably the transformation of the steppe into pastoral society took place under influences coming from both directions--West and South--after about 2000 BCE. Frachetti (2012:8) argues "that interactions surrounding exchanges of commodities and resources represent a dominant catalyst for economic changes at the domestic level and an important factor for subsequent shifts in institutional organization in the western steppe at end of the third millennium BC".

The "interaction" of the western steppe was taking place with the Central Asia, but the Central Asia itself was receiving cultural inputs from northwest India, Afghanistan, the Pamir and Bactria. Clearly the arrival of the domestic sheep can be traced from northwest India through Sarazm (early fourth millennium site at Pamir, *vide infra*).

Lawler (2012:44-45) writes about Begash, "The inhabitants did not begin to use horses until well into the second millennium b.c., and the varieties of sheep and goat found here today appear to be related to the varieties first domesticated thousands of years before in western Iran...". We learn here that the sheep recovered from the Chalcolithic Central Asia were not Central Asian in origin, but had been imported. Whether the sheep and goat had been first domesticated in South Asia or Iran may be an issue for further research, but one thing is clear that the domestic animals came to the steppe from the south.

There is no doubt that the steppe did not have cow and sheep early on. The question arises as to how these animals reached there. Anthony

---

6 Given the lack of evidence for domestication (***q.v.***), the word "domesticate" should have been used instead of "domesticated" in this quote.

(2009:132) thinks that the cow and sheep reached the Western steppe from the Danube river basin after 5,000 BC. This naïve Eurocentric conjecture is however ruled out by DNA studies of the Ukrainian and the steppe cows.

The DNA study of Ukrainian cattle done by Kantanen (2009) says "The mtDNA data indicates that the Ukrainian and Central Asian regions are zones where hybrids between taurine and zebu (*B. indicus*) cattle have existed. This zebu influence appears to have subsequently spread into southern and southeastern European breeds" (Kantanen 2009: Abstract). Thus it was the spread of the zebu cattle from India to Central Asia, and from here to steppe/Ukraine to the southeast and south Europe, not the *vice-versa*.

Anthony's date too is wrong; the archaeologists working in the field do not support such an early date (like 5000 BC) for the domestic cow and sheep in the steppe or even in Central Europe (Staublei 1995:229). Nor has the arrival of sheep from Central Europe to the steppe been supported by the DNA studies. In fact the early Central European and East European Neolithics were charecterized by presence of pottery but absence of farming, as Dolukhanov observes: "There are no definite signs of widespread farming in the East European Neolithic sites, even though there is clear evidence of the interaction of those cultures with farming. This suggests yet another scenario where an advancing wave of farming is not accepted by the local huntere-gatherers, but still results in considerable demographic and cultural modifications." (2005:1457).

Recent archaeological work had found that the cereal economy was late to penetrate Central Asia and the steppe. At Begash, Lawler (2012) notes: "The grains were used ritually in a burial, and radiocarbon dating of the remains dates them to about 2200 b.c., making them the **oldest known domesticated grains in Central Asia**" (Lawler 2012: 44; emphasis added). The 2200 BC samples of wheat found at Begash is an indication of trade with the nearby Pamir people, who were in turn in trade with the Harappans (*ibid*). Begash shows no evidence of wheat agriculture or the grinding stone, therefore any wheat must have been imported (*ibid*).

Located in between Harappa and Begash, in the Pamir plateau, just north of the Hindu Kush, we get the Sarazm Chalcolithic centre, which had farming, and which was intensely related with Harappa. Frachetti writes, "Central Asians were likely in contact with urban communities across the Iranian Plateau and into the Indus Valley, as indicated by the presence of precious stones and minerals from the Pamir Mountains at Harappa by the third millennium BC (Law 2006)." (Frachetti 2012:17). Sarazm sites had large number of domestic sheep (Frachetti 2012:14), which must have reached there from the Indus Valley, because the sheep was never domesticated in Central Asia (*q.v.* in the sheep section).

Although Frachetti does not utter the phrase considered blasphemous by the Eurocentrics --"Indus to steppe movement"—yet he holds equivalent view, as Lawler narrates: "The combined finds in Uzbekistan and at Begash suggest to Frachetti that the people living in Central Asia around 2000 b.c. were part of the rapidly urbanizing world, when the great cities of Egypt, Mesopotamia, and the Indus were at their first peak, ... Frachetti maintains they had access to the wider world. And, by passing along important innovations such as grains and other goods, they had a hand in connecting far-flung civilizations. **This movement from south to north** took place centuries before the horse-riding pastoralists moved across the Eurasian steppes from west to east." (Lawler:46; my emphasis).

On the other hand, if we examine the case *vice-a-versa*, the Iranians and the Indus people had received no migration from the steppe. They traded wheat, sheep, goat and cattle in lieu of precious stones and metals. Shishlina and Hiebert noted "no steppe nomadic complex has been found on the Iranian plateau, not even evidence of indirect contact or interaction" (1998; quoted by Witzel, *The home of the Aryans*). Yet some influence of Bactria and Margian cultures has been noted to have occurred on Iran during 1900 to 1700 BC period visible in the funerary practices at two sites namely Khurab and Shahdad.

Archaeological evidence, if impartially examined, suggests that during the Chalcolithic period, the Indo-Aryan speaking Indians moved with advanced farming, domestic sheep, cow, pig and horse, urban civilization, chariot and the Chalcolithic culture out of the Indus Valley to South Central Asia (Tajikistan, Uzbekistan and Turkmenistan), and then to the northern Central Asia, and from there to the steppe. From southern Central Asia these Indo-Aryans also moved to West Asia.

These movements were not in the form of invasions but were like slow infiltration, or immigration type. The time frames of the different cultures also are consistent with this migration: Indus-Sarasvati Civilization 3,300-1,700 BCE; BMAC (Bactria-Margiana Archaeological Complex, south Central Asia) 2,300-1,700 BCE and the Andronovo Culture (Kazakhastan, Kurgan and Eastern Steppe) 2,100-1,400 BCE (dates insisted by the Russian authors; dates accepted by the west European and American archaeologists are 1600-1000 calBCE; Anthony 2009:423).

David Anthony, the main protagonist of the steppe, himself takes the year 1900 BCE for the onset of the Andronovo culture. However, all such dates are arbitrary. Lamberg-Karlowski (2005:156) points out the completely fluid or non-existent nature of the dates of the Sintashta and Andronovo cultures: "The dating of the Andronovo culture, with respect to the chronology of its geographical distribution and cultural variation is simply non-existent" (*ibid*). Obviously the AIT scholars have taken advantage of this anarchical situation.

Immediately to the northwest of Harappa was the BMAC culture, and further to the north of the latter was the Andronovo culture stretching up to the eastern steppe of the south Ural region. The BMAC was not too far from the northernmost reaches of the Harappa Civilization. Dani and Masson note the increasing influence on the southeast Turkmenistan from northwest India, Pakistan, Afghanistan and Iran during the late fourth millennium to early third millennium BC. (1999:228-229)

This was the time when the cultures of Kalibangan, Banawali, Amri-Nal and Harappa were flourishing. After comparing the terracotta figurines at Mehrgarh period I (6,000 BC) with those of the later Asian civilizations, Jarrige (2008) noted, "The pawn figurines can now be linked to a prototype from period I level 4 at Mehrgarh, as are the rounded based figurines. Striking parallels can be drawn on a peculiar type overlapping the Indus period. With a stout body, almost no head and two stumps of arms (Fig.16), this type is going to be widespread in time and space, at Jarmo and Tello, and also at Susa, Tepe Yahya, Mundigak, Nausharo IC, Shahr-i Sokhta, Tell-i Bakun, Altyn tepe, Hissar and many other sites." (Jarrige 2008:163).

The BMAC, as well as Arkaim of Andronovo, was a fortified city culture (e.g. Kelleli III; Gonur; Togolok *etc*) resembling the fortified sites of the Indus Valley Civilization like Kalibangan, Dholavira, Harappa and Mohenjo-Daro, and was very unlike the rural Vedic Civilization (Anthony 2009: 395, 424 Figure 16.4; U. Singh 2008:155 Fig 4.7, 152). We are aware from the Arkaim and other remains that the steppe Indo-Aryan civilization was fully urbanized. However, even if one assumes that the Indo-Aryan people started their journey from a pre-urban steppe to Indus, the long passage through the urbanized parts of Central Asia, particularly the BMAC, should have made the Indo-Aryans people urbanized before they reached northwest India. In that case, the *Rig-Vedic* Indo-Aryans should have exhibited the elements of city culture like the burnt-brick etc.

Aridity of the early second millennium BC which affected Harappa had affected the steppe too, and pastoralism, herding and hunting were the only ways to survive after the Sintashta period. We find mention of a crude water-wheel of noria type in the *Rig-Veda* (RV 10.101.7) which could draw water only from the shallow wells. The verse says ""Pour forth the well with stone wheel, wooden buckets, the drink of heroes, with the trough for armour." (Griffith translation) Such shallow wells do not exist in the arid climates, nor do the pastoralist-nomads use noria. If the Indo-Aryans had arrived from the arid Central Asia to the arid northwest India in the mid-second millennium BC, they should not have shown any awareness of the noria technology.

A recent investigation of the Indus Valley region for this period has revealed that there was a two century long draught in the region aused by abrupt weakening of the monsoon, resulting in disease, poverty, deprivation and crime, culminationg in dirty pathology of power ultimately ruining the civilization (Schug 2013; Dixit 2014; Cambridge 2014). It is difficult to imagine why any Aryan from the steppe should have arrived and settled in such situation when locals were deserting the place out of miseries and chaos.

Another proof from archaeology which makes the *Rig-Veda* anterior to the Andronovo comes from the pottery. The *Rig-Veda* (and *Avesta* too) does not mention the potter's wheel, and the pottery was in all probability handmade during the early Vedic period (Kuz'mina and Mallory 2007:370, and the references therein). On the other hand the hallmark of the Andronovo culture of the second millennium is the wheel-thrown grey ware. Kuz'mina and Mallory write: "The Grey Ware was made on a potter's wheel, while the Vedic texts describe the production of hand-made pottery (Rau 1972; 1974; Grantovsky 1981; Kuz'mina 1986a)" (Kuz'mina and Mallory 2007:313). Had the Indo-Aryans come through the BMAC about 1500 BCE, they surely would have shown awareness of the potter's wheel and the wheel-made pottery.

In fact the wheel made grey ware has been found in the third millennium eastern Iran (Kuz'mina and Mallory 2007:219) and Indus Valley (Dales, Kenoyer and Alcock:54, 123, 190, 222 etc) in abundance much earlier than the date of the Andronovo culture. Therefore the *Rig-Veda* and the *Avesta* of Indus region and Iran respectively, which did not have wheel-made pottery, could not have been after the third millennium. In fact they were much older than the third millennium. This fact also hints at the likelihood of the Indus-Sarasvati origin of the Andronovo culture.[7] Similarly, the much publicised characteristic pottery of Sintashta—ICW or Incised Coarse Ware—is found at many older Indian cites (Ghosh 1990:253, 254; Shirwalkar and Shinde 2008:220).

Khlopin's view on the genesis of the Andronovo culture is more consistent with the evidence. He connected the genesis of the Andronovo culture with the Anau (south Turkmenistan) culture, wherein the Andronovans were driven out and forced to move to the north where they had to adopt a primarily cattle-breeding economy. In this way they introduced agriculture, metallurgical skills and the Iranian language to native hunting populations of the steppe (Khlopin 1970c: 95, 98-99) (cited by Kuz'mina and Mallory 2007:xv).

Kuzmina and Mallory give examples of southern influence on the steppe: "The relations with the Bactria-Margiana archaeological complex (BMAC) are demonstrated by the discovery of lapis lazuli beads in Sintashta (Kuz'mina 1997), a BMAC type vessel at the settlement of Ustye (Vinogradov 1995b), and a mirror with a BMAC type handle at the Krasnoye Znamya burial mound". (*ibid*:463). Also, "The next stage of the relations is represented by the findings of imported BMAC pottery of the Namazga VI period at an Andronovo settlement of the Fedorovo type (Malyutina 1991); numerous mixed complexes of Tadjikistan and Uzbekistan combining the wheel-made ware of Namazga VI, the hand-made pottery of Fedorovo and Andronovo metal types"(*ibid*:463). However they ignore the diagnostic value of these findings.

A description of the region in the sixteenth century BC provides insight into the scenario. "By 1600 BCE all the old trading towns, cities and brick-built fortified estates of eastern Iran and the former

---

[7] I am aware that following this claim, arguments based on typological differences will be put forth. Yet one thing is common to all grey ware that they were burnt in hypoxic conditions which prevented oxidation of iron molecules present in clay to the red oxide. We conclude that this technology was invented after the ***Rig-Vedic*** times.

BMAC region in Central Asia were abandoned. Malyan, the largest city on the Iranian plateau, was reduced to a small walled compound and tower occupied within a vast ruin... Pastoral economies spread across Iran and into Baluchistan where clay images of riders on horseback appeared at Pirak about 1700 BCE[8]" (Anthony 2009:454).

This imagination implies that the Aryans came on the horseback to the drought affected abandoned places of Iran and northwest India, and the Pirak people could foresee them at least 200 years before they actually came! But why should anyone choose to come to a place which others are finding impossible to live in? Some authors may offer an earlier date (say 2000 BCE) for Indo-Aryan arrival to Indus to neutralize the Pirak argument. However such possibility is not allowed by the absence of horse in the BMAC at this time (2100-1750 BCE).

From BMAC no evidence of horse or horse related furniture has been found (Witzel 2003:7 of 12, pdf). Lamberg-Karlovsky (2002:73) noted "in Bactrian Margiana communities there is scant evidence for steppe ceramics and a complete absence of horses and their equipment or their depiction." Hence there is no question of the Pirak horse and the steppe-Aryans having arrived through the way of Bactria-Margiana in 1800 BCE.

The people doing copper-mining in the Zeravshan Valley at Tugai in 1900 BCE and tin-mining at Kurnab and Mushiston in the neighbourhood of India have been identified with the Andronovo people (Anthony 2009:452, 420). Andronovo type pottery and burial appear in the Zervshan Valley and the adjoining BMAC region just following 1800 BCE (*ibid*). These dates are much earlier than the Andronovo culture's existence in the steppe (1600 BCE). This is not the correct direction of movement and chronology.

---

8 The uncalibrated date of Pirak mounted horse figurine is 1460 ±140 BCE (Kuzmina and Mallory:434), which on calibration gives 1796, and it should be approximated to 1800 BCE.

This has to be read with the following chronological events in the steppe: "The first culture to the east of Ural was the Petrovka culture, an eastern offshoot of Sintashta dated about 1900-1750 BCE". ... "it is clear that Petrovka grew out of and was generally later than Sintashta". "Petrovka II was reoccupied by people who made classic Andronovo-horizon ceramics of both the Alakul and Fedorovo types stratified above the Petrovka layer" (*ibid*:441). Thus the chronological sequence of the cultures is Sintashta > Petrovka I > Petrovka II > Andronovo—and not the *vice-versa*. The Alakul-Andronovo settlements (where we noted the preponderance of the cattle) having the Kurgan graves have been dated 1740-1320 BCE (*ibid*:423). Thus we can note the confusion in the dates which is obvious. We may conclude, on the basis of the chronological sequence of the cultures involved that the Andronovo migration was from south to north.

A large number of the typical early Indus objects *e.g.* the flat knife without axial ribbing, metal frying pan with handle, ivory etc. have been found in the Margiana culture (Masson 1988:93). Many Proto-Indian seals including one with the *swastika* and many with the Indus pictographic inscriptions have been found at Altyn-Depe (a site within Margiana in Turkmenistan), and this has been considered by many as evidence favouring the Indus Valley ethnicity of the authors of this southern Central Asian culture (Masson 1988:118; Gupta 2005:179; also see Renfrew 2005:209). Thus we have the evidence of south to north migration of culture (*vide supra*), human beings (DNA evidence, *vide supra*) and cattle (Kantanen 2009).

Thus a synthesis consistent with reason and evidence could be as follows: Under the various influences percolating from Iran and India, BMAC civilization grew. In the Indus Civilization itself we get the source of the BMAC and Andronovo type pottery, fortified city culture, stepped-pyramid motif, swastika etc which influenced the latter civilizations in the course of time.

At 2000 BC aridity started building up in the Indus-Sarasvati region, pushing the economy of the civilization into a severe recession.

The artisans and miners, and many others were forced to abandon the Indus-Sarasvati Civilization for better financial prospects soon after. Many of them moved to the adjoining south Central Asian regions. However, the Bactria-Margiana culture too could not remain uninfluenced from the regional aridity. It became dry and abandoned by 1600 BCE.

Movement of people to the west and north from BMAC had started as early as 1900 BCE. From these regions the Indo-Aryan culture migrated to further north reaching up to Arkaim in the steppe by the sixteenth century. These were larger migrations, yet did not result in language conversion of the regions. However, loan words of the Indo-Aryan and Iranian stocks have left their imprints on the steppe region, notable till date (noted earlier). Other than these larger movements, earlier continuous low grade migrations/interactions spreading from northwest India did take place resulting in the growths of earlier cultures like Sintashta.

Chapter 12

Indian Migrations to West Asia during Bronze Age

"On the basis of this well dated bead and numerous other surface finds that appear to date the Late Harappan period, we can say that glass production in the Indus Valley is an indigenous development and slightly earlier than glass production documented in Mesopotamia and Egypt." (Kenoyer 2001: 167)

Kenoyer gives the date for the oldest finding of the synthetic glass at Harappa as 1900 BC, that at Mesopotamia as 1600 BC and that at Egypt as 1500 BC (*ibid*; also Kenoyer and Kimberley 2005b:72). This time gradient is consistent with the migration of technologies (with the migrating artisans) from the Late Harappa to West Asia, which must have taken place owing to the increasing aridity of the Harappa region. This fact helps us determine the date of the Vedic texts. "Between 1700 and 800 BC, glass production developed into a common industry and became quite widespread throughout the northern subcontinent." (Kenoyer 2005a:37).

This is the period in which the Vedas have been generally claimed to have been composed in the Northwest India region (between 1400-1000 BC). However there is no mention of glass in the *Rig-Veda* (*ibid*; Lal 1998:444). The oldest Vedic text where we find mention of glass is the

Shatapatha Brahmana. The *Shatapatha Brahmana* has been dated to 2926 BC by astronomical studies (Achar:9; Kak 1993). We can use the glass to date the *Shatapatha Brahmana* independently.

In the Harappa region, the earliest finding of the natural (non-manmade; volcanic) glass has been dated to the Kot-Diji Phase Period 2 dating 2800-2600 BC (Law 2008:167; Meadow 2001:10, Mackay 1931:546, both cited by Law:167). Clearly we have not found the very first or the oldest of such specimens of glass owned by the Kot-Dijian Harappan people, and such glass pieces must have been known to the Kot-Dijians for a few centuries by that time. This we can say because the Kot-Daji settlement was located over a site which had plenty of such volcanic glass pieces (Law). Law also lists similar findings from the same period from Monejo-Daro. This finding, being from a date just 126 years later than the *Shatapatha Brahmana,* correlates well with the first mention of the glass in this text. Clearly the *Rig-Veda* must be much older than this text, and must be dated before 3000 BC on this account alone.

We have discussed the DNA and other scientific studies attesting Indian migration to West Asia during the Bronze Age. There is abundant evidence supporting the fact that the zebu cattle too migrated from Indus Valley to West Asia at that time. That is how zebu cattle reached West Asia. From the DNA studies, it has been proved beyond doubt that all the humped bulls of the world have Indian ancestry (Chen S. 2009).

We get the statuettes of the humped bull from several archaeological sites of West Asia. Examples are: terracotta figurine of the humped bull from Arpachiyah near Mosul (North Iraq; 4000 BC, al-Ubaid Period; Mallowan & Rose 1935:164, 88, figure 48 No.13); stamped seals of the humped bulls from Neneveh (Zeuner 1963:239); the humped bull figurine from East Africa through South Arabia (Agrar, Ur, Susa, Arar) and Sumer (Epstein and Mason 1971:508); a marble amulet from Ur in the form of a zebu (Hornblower 1927:508, cited by Epstein and Mason); an ivory humped bull of three inches size made as the handle of a knife from Egypt (*ibid*) etc. The Ur items dated about 3000 BC.

The Indus bull inspired a bull cult in Assyria (Mallowan and Rose 1935: 80).Nearly the same time representations of zebu are found as figurines and painted pottery motifs at Susa in southwest Iran (Epstein 1971:508; Zeuner 1963: 239). From Mohenjo-daro zebu also reached Oman and the head of the Persian Gulf (Potts 1997: 257). A stone bowl sherd, of mid 3rd-millennium date, from Tell Agrab in the Diyala region northeast of Baghdad, shows an impressive zebu bull (Zeuner 1963: 217). Matthews (2001) presents a big list of zebu artifacts in West Asia. He notes that the role of zebu increased as the aridity of climate increased in West Asia and Iran. This is because it is relatively a draught resistant animal in comparison to the Taurine cow or ox.

Not only the humped bull but many other elements of the Indus culture also found their way to West Asia. We get the Indo-Aryan speaking people (the Mittani) in Anatolia about 1750-1500 BCE. The most likely source of these people could only have been the Margiana Indo-Aryan population.[9] However they could have come from Indus Valley directly. It has been wrongly claimed that the Mittani were Proto-Indo-Aryan, or that the Mittani Indo-Aryan language is older than the Vedic Sanskrit. Such wrong views could not have been conceived without the ignorence about the later Indo-Aryan languages.

The Mittani is later than the Vedic Sanskrit, and uses words and grammar resembling later Indo-Aryan languages like Pali, Prakrit and Magadhi *etc.* Mittani *mitta* (from Vedic *mitra*), *satta* (from Vedic *sapta*) etc are there in the Post-Vedic Indo-Aryan languages Pali and Prakrit (*mitta, satta*), and also the modern IA languages like Punjabi (*mittar, satta* etc.). Vedic language is older because the "p" in Sanskrit *sapta* is also present in the Iranian (*hafta*), Greek *hept-*, Latin *sept-*, English *seven* etc. Hence loss of "p" is later, not that the "p" was gained later into the Mittani word *satta.*[10]

---

9 For the invasionist view of the Mittani Indo-Aryan origins, see Mahindale 2005:53.

10 Some authors have claimed that presence of "p" in Vedic ***sapta*** is later, and the older form is ***satta***, but it is no longer held in the mainstream circles.

In the same way, other such allegedly "older than Vedic" Mittani words is Mittani *aika* "one"; the diaphthong *ai* is present today in Bengali *ēk* (written form; *æk* Starostin:858), which is pronounced by the laity as *oiko* (*aika>oiko* in the Bangali lay pronunciation; *a>o*). The Sanskrit *eka* (one) is derived from PIE *eĝ-* (Pokorny:281-286). Hence Sanskrit *eka* is older than Mittani *aika* (one). *e* > *ai* mutation is seen in Avestan and Armenian too which are later than the Vedic (Kazanas 2012:216-217)[11].

Some other allegedly older words are: Mittani *tera* (three), c.f. Western Hindi *tera* (three), Punjabi *tare* (three) for Vedic *tri*; Mittani *panza* (five), c.f. Punjabi *panja* for Vedic *pañca*; Mittani *Indara*, Punjabi *Indar* for Vedic *indra* etc. Another evidence favouring a post-Vedic migration of Mittani is the fact that all the Mittani kings acquired Vedic throne-names, even if they had originally Hurrian proper names: *Tus'ratta* (*Tveṣa-ratha*), *Artatama* (*Ṛta-dhāman*), *Artas's'umara* (*Ṛta-smara*), *S'attuara* (*satvara*) (Anthony 2009:49).

Thus we conclude that the Mittani Indo-Aryan language is later than the Vedic, and has been derived from the Vedic. These views about language of the Indus and its relationship with the Indo-Aryans of the Mittani kingdom are consistent with our date of the *Rig-Vedic* civilization (6,000 BCE; Kazanas 2009). The *Rig-Vedic* civilization is certainly pre-urban/ pre-Indus and the language of the *Rig-Veda* too is certainly pre-Mittani. The migrations to Bactria, Margiana-Turkmenistan and the Armenia-Kurdistan regions have been symbolically referred to in the *Baudhayana Śrautasūtra* as *Gandhara*, *Parśu* and *Aratta* (*Ararat/Urartu?*) respectively and must date to the time of the Indus Civilization (see also Kazanas 2012:224; Lal 2007).

The Chalcolithic migration from Indus to the south Central Asia (BMAC) and then to the Andronovo region follows the general rule of migration, that migration takes place as a consequence of "the population growth that follows the invention of agriculture, leading

---

11 In Avestan the cognate word is ***ae:uua-*** (Starostin:857) indicating that there was a trend of lengthening of the vowel at the period concerned.

to a steady pressure for territorial expansion, against less populous non-agricultural people." (mentioned as Renfrew's view by Trautmann 2005:205; also see Priyadarshi 2011:136-143).

Such a view of migration is held by ecologists too. In case of the Chalcolithic Indo-Aryan migration, the rule is applicable because the Chalcolithic increased the food production and consequent population growth tremendously in the Indus Valley Civilization. The Central Asians and the steppe people had been hunters till quite late, and cannot be expected to migrate in violation to this general ecological rule. This analysis collapses the theory of the Indo-Aryan invasion on India from the BMAC (see Bryant 2001 for the whole theory and Kazanas 2009).

Mittani, horse and chariot

People have doubted the AIT school's date for the onset of riding (4200 BCE) and charioteering (2100 BCE). Archaeologist Renfrew (2000:44; quoted by Drews) wrote, "The mounted warrior nomad horseman does not make his appearance until the end of the second millennium". Another prominent archaeological researcher of the subject Kuz'mina wrote "warrior-horsemen appear in the steppe not in the fourth millennium BC but at the end of the second millennium BC" (2000:122, quoted by Drews:132). And we know it was impossible to cross the Hindu Kush ranges by chariots. This makes the theory of arrival of the Aryans in chariots from Sintashta (South Ural) to the Northwest India at 1500 BCE impossible.

The historians have constantly denied the existence of chariot in India before 1500 BCE. A re-examination of the excavation (1920-21 and 1933-34) report of Harappa published by the British Government of India in 1940 reveals that the chariot appears in India at 3000 BCE at Harappa (Vats 1940:452). The matter was well publicized in the academic circles and a book review too was published in the *Current Science* (A.A. 1940). It was likely that the chariot-toys of copper may have been made for the first time at Harappa itself. Many chariot toys including a covered copper chariot model were found from that date. The real-size uncovered chariot must have been made at least a thousand years earlier. We should not doubt India had chariots even before 4,000 BC. However no physical remain should be expected to have survived because of the ephimeral nature of the material with which they had been made. Later another copper chariot from 2300 BCE layer was found from Daimabad in Maharashtra (Sali 1986:477-479). It is only after this time that the chariot appears in many civilizations simultaneously at about 2000 BCE (Egypt, Mesopotamia, Sintashta etc). The spoked wheel too is attested in the Indus seals. Mackay found that the Harappan chariots were of more "primitive pattern than those found at either Kish or at Ur" (page 555 in Vats 1940). That means the Indian chariots were older or ancestral. Primitiveness is the sign of ancestrality. About the bird chariots, Mackay opined that the concept went to China from India (Mackay 1940:561).

Thus the chariot and horse appearing in the Mittani Indo-Aryan culture is clearly due to the migration from India. This is clear from a piece of literature written by someone named Kikkuli from the land of Mittani at about 1500 BCE for the Hittite rulers. This treatise uses typical Indo-Aryan words for horse-breeding, charioteering and horse-training (Kuz'mina and Mallory :xi). This has been taken as a strong piece of evidence by many scholars favouring the dispersal of the art of the horse-breeding and the chariots by the ancient Indians to the West Asia (D'yakonov 1956; Kammenhuber 1961; Myerhofer:1966, 1974; Salonen:1955-1956; Theime:1960; Ivanov:1968; all these references quoted and cited by Kuz'mina and Mallory: xi.). In our view, this event took place at the time of late Harappa Civilization.

The Light Race Horse of Swat

Azzaroli (1985:94; also see Azzaroli 1975) noted that the domestic caballus horse remains found from the second millennium BCE horse burials at Katelai (Swat, Pakistan) belonged to the eastern breed which was different "from the Bronze and Iron Age horses of Eastern and Central Europe and recalls some horses from Etruscan tombs: presumably it belongs to some **oriental strain**." The Etruscan region is in Italy. Kuz'mina and Mair express their agreement with this view (2008:59). Yet they give their own meaning to the Oriental Strain as the 'steppe horse', which is unfair as this term is applied to a specific group of horse breeds originating from the southern regions like Iran, Arabia and India.

The oriental horse is different from Central Asian, steppe and European horses. It is the horse which has developed from inter-breeding of the horses from India, Iran and Turkmenistan and the Barber (north African) after the Arab conquest of these regions (Louise Firouz, cited by Hendrick 1995:325-328). Kuz'mina and Mair (2008:59) have construed the term "oriental horse" as the "eastern breed from Central Asia" or the steppe, a meaning which is not permissible because "oriental horse" is a specific term applied to some specific or particular breeds of horse. It certainly does not include the zebrine Mongolian Przewalskii horse or the heavy daft type Kazakh breeds.

More than this, Azzaroli found that this horse (Indian Swat type) was entirely different from the Central and East European horses. The latter two too in the Kuz'mina's belief had derived from the steppe horse, and thus should have been indistinguishable from the Swat horse, which is not the case at all here. The European horse was heavy, short and stout draught type.

In fact we find that the Central Asian and the steppe breeds of horses, if they have not reached there from south, are all stout and heavy with shorter limbs indicating their arrival from the colder regions of Europe and/or north China. Examples are the Vyatka and Kazakh breeds of horse. The light long legged southern Central Asian horse from Turkmenistan adjoining Iran is the Akhal Teke, and this is not of the Central Asian or Kazakhstani origin. This in fact can be grouped with Indian, Arab, Iranian and north African horses on the basis of its anatomical features.

Thus the steppe horse and the European horse could not have been the ancestors of the Swat horse of India. Contrary to the general belief that the *sivalensis* was a small horse looking like a zebra (zebrine), the reality is that the the *sivalensis* was light, tall, slender racehorse, with long neck and long face (Osborn 1915:309 and 310). It was a 15-hand high horse (Ewart 1911:364), which is good height even for a tall horse. The shorter limbs of the European horse are consistent with the Allen's rule and the stout body of the European ones follows the Bergmann's Rule of zoology. The Swat horse's anatomy did not exhibit any impact of the Allen's and the Burgmann's rules during its phylogenic evolution. Thus it was a characteristically southern horse evolved in a relatively warmer climate.

Turkmenistan and Bactria, although termed as south Central Asia, did not have horse before the Bronze Age (BMAC phase). The first generalized horse with rider was recovered from a seal recovered from a looted grave in Afghanistan (Sarianidi 1986; Anthony 2010:415, Fig 16.3, middle). It is exactly like the Marwari horse of India, implying that the domestic Indian horses had reached Afghanistan and Bactria by 2000 BC, the end of the Bronze Age. Unfortunately the authors like Anthony have often mentioned it as Turkmenistani (BMAC) horse. On the other hand the equid depictions from Turkmenistan (Gonur, Malyan, Godin III etc) are of *Equus hemionus*, and not of the true horse (Anthony 1989). The first evidence of riding in West Asia (Ur, Sumer) is later (1900 BC), that too not of true horse but of a *hemionus* equid (Owen 1991; Anthony 2010:415). Thus Afghanistan horse is the oldest depiction of horse with a rider anywhere in the world. The Swat horse too was similar to this Afghanistan horse.

The southern Caspian banks in Iran and the areas of Turkmenistan adjoining the Iranaian boarders (e.g. Anau IA) had the wild caballus horse from 4000 BC (Duerst 1908; Moore 2003:154) when mid-Holocene optimum changed the climate from desert to grassland (savannah). These were most probably the remaining stock of the wild *Sivalensis* of the Early Holocene northwest India, who were forced to move out as India became less hospitable and Iran more hospitable to their survival about 5000 BC climate change.

Azzaroli (1985) noted that the bones were "slenderer than those of Pleistocene wild horses of the same size and also than those of the Mongolian wild horse, Equus Przewalskii." The horse was an adult of seven years with a height of 13 hands (132 cms; *ibid*), clearly shorter than the average height of horse. However, this is the usual height for the native Himalayan horses of India like the Bhutia and the Spiti horses (Hendricks 1995:76; Pundir 2004:75), and Swat too being within the Himalayan region, must have had horse similar to these. Hence its importation from Central Asia is no more than a pure imagination based on poor knowledge of horse breeds.

The Etruscan horses from Populonia and Castro (Italy) from the first millennium BCE resembled the Swat horse and did not resemble the Bronze or Iron Age horse from other parts of Italy or the rest of Europe as well as the Pleistocene horse from the same area (Azzaroli 1985:146). Hence the light "oriental breed" which Azzaroli mentioned is a distinct entity, and must have derived from the residual Indian stock from the *sivalensis* horse.

Louise Firouz studied the DNA of the famous Oriental breeds of horse like the Arab, Barb, Akhal Teke, Caspian etc and found that they all are located south-south from East Iran to North Africa, and genetically constitute a family tree. The fossils recovered from Iran dating back to 4000 BC had made it clear to Sander Bokonyi that the Iranian horse type Turkoman had contributed to the improvement in the quality of the horse breeds since about 4000 BC (cited in Firouz:1 pdf). These horses had evolved in Turkmenistan and Iran over the last 6000 year as the DNA analysis (Dendrogram by Dr E. Gus Cothram, University of Kentukey, cited Firouz) as well as the fossils recovered revealed (*ibid*).

This horse stock is the same horse which came and settled in Iran about 4000 BC, after the arrival of the mid-Holocene Optimum had converted the arid country into pleasant grassland. And this is the time when the Indus Valley wild horses died wholesale due to conversion of the region into a dense forest. Some wild horses survived in the Thar (Rajasthan) and the Himalayan highlands and others in Iran. But the local horses which stayed in the Indus valley were all domestic, because the wild horses had all died in the region.

The domesticated horses of the Bronze and Iron Ages in Europe had "slender limbs but of weak constitution, with thin shafts in their long bones but relatively massive joints" as a result of irrational breeding. "This is not the case in the horse from Katelai T.40" (*ibid*). Clearly this rules out any fraternity of the light Swat horse with the European horse. The Katelai graves, many of which contained horse figurines, had the oldest date of 1520 ± 150 BCE (1877 calBCE[12] ± 197, Azzaroli:1975). The horse skeleton itself has been dated 1200 BCE (1500 calBCE, Azzaroli 1985:94). Yet there were horse figurines at Swat dating back to c. 1900 calBC in tombs numbered Katelai T242 and Loebnr T19, indicates presence of the horse in Swat since at least 1900 BC (Azzaroli 1975).

This rules out the arrival of the horse and the Aryans from Arkaim which was at least two centuries later than the horse figurines found from Pirak and Katelai in India. In fact when these figurines of horse were being made in Pirak and Katelai, the BMAC had no horse nearly the same time in the south Central Asia, and the Andronovo culture of the steppe too did not exist that much early.

---

12 Calibrated with the help of 'quickcal 2007' software available at the calpal web site.

Figure 1. Terracotta winged horse of Etruscan period, kept at Museo archaeologico nazionale tarquiniense. Tall limbs, head bent down, slender face, broad forehead, high-set tail, long neck, slender belly are the features common to Indian, Iranian, Etruscan and sivalensis horses. Source: http://commons.wikimedia.org/wiki/File:Etruscan_Horses_Tarquinia.jpg. Accessed 15 June 2014.

Clearly the light domestic horse had been domesticated from the sivalensis in India before the latter became extinct sometime after 8000 BCE. But did it become extinct in the true sense? Or, it did survive as the domestic ones, and became extinct only from the wild existence? Climatic factors are identifiable which must have restricted the distribution of the horse population to the high mountains of the Himalayas and the Thar during the mid-Holocene period up to the Harappa period. The modern Marwari horse of India, considered indigenous and closely resembling another indigenous breed the Kathiawari horse of the arid regions of Gujarat, owes its origin to

Marwar which belongs to the Thar region. Probably the large scale capture for domestication and also ruthless slaughter for the "horse-sacrifice" and the funeral rites, ultimately led to the extinction of this horse from the wild.

There is evidence to suggest that the domesticated Sivalensis type migrated to South China, Southeast Asia, Central Asia, the steppe (with the Scythian nomads too, *vide supra*) and also to Italy through Iran and West Asia following domestication. The Etruscan horse must have been brought by the Etruscans arriving to Italy from West Asia and here it had in all probability arrived with some Indo-Aryan arrival to West Asia like the Mittani. There is evidence from cattle DNA that the Etruscans arrived into Europe from West Asia (Pellecchia).

That the Swat horse and chariot had not arrived to India from West Asia is made explicit by Azzaroli (1985), who found that the Indian chariots were different from the West Asian ones. The petroglyphs at Swat depict chariots that are same in style as that of Central Asia and the steppe. This, given the earlier presence of chariot in Harappa (*infra*), implies an Indian migration of chariot to Central Asia with technology and culture. The sixth century BC horse burials at Padova (Padua, north Italy) too resemble the Swat burial in style (Azzaroli 1985:137).

Chapter 13

Anatolian Origin Claim

When the DNA studies of the peoples of the regions involved proved wrong any such migratory event about 1500 BC, the proponents of the Aryan Invasion Theory added to it that the migrations were decimal numerically, yet the victorious Aryans had the might which was able to convert the languages of the people subjugated—the so called "elite dominance" model. This happened in India, Iran, Europe and Anatolia (ancient Turkey) they claimed. Such possibility made the role of the DNA studies of migrations redundant for the purpose of the studies of the Indo-European linguistic migration, because the language could travel without the DNA or in other words without the humans. However one basic criterion in the theory of "elite dominance" was that the victorious elites must be equipped with the farming techniques and the subjugated onces must be hunter-gatherers (Renfrew 1990; Bellwood 2002). Ironically, the same authors do not apply this premise to case of the AIT wherein the subjugated Indus-Valley people were the farmers and the invaders were barbaric nomads in the Aryan Invasion Theory.

With the sole motive of proving this theory (AIT) correct the entire histories of these peoples were designed so as to make them consistent with the Aryan Invasion Theory. In this effort, archaeological findings were concocted or distorted, often the findings of horse and camel from India in the pre-history were denied. Anyone in the West who went against this theory was marginalized in his or her academic career. Peers rejected the publications of academic papers by such scholars who went against the Aryan Invasion Theory. Such scholars were often humiliated and even abused.

However it soon became clear that the Aryans were not pastoral-nomads, but were pastoral-farmers (Comrie 2002; Puhvel 1964; Bloch 1936). Some DNA studies have found farming and Indo-European cultural migration taking place together with the identifiable DNA lineages' migrations (King and Underhill 2002). It was claimed by many that the spread of the Indo-European languages into Europe occurred with the archaeological evidence of concomitant migration of farming-culture, the source for both being Anatolia (Renfrew 1990; Bellwood 2002; Gray and Atkinson 2003).

West Asia particularly Anatolia being the source of culture and Indo-European language to southern Europe undermined the position of the steppe as the claimed homeland. The situation brought about a split in the school and now one camp of AIT supporters claimed Anatolia to be the Aryan Homeland and the other camp claimed the Ukrainian steppe to be so. The Anatolia supporters included Renfrew (1990), Gray and Atkinsosn (2002), Bellwood (2002, 2005, 2008) etc who claimed that the Indo-European languages originated in Anatolia with farming about 7000 BC from where the langage and farming spread to Europe in the west, and Iran and India in the east. They rejected the steppe's claim with formidable evidence.

Initially some archaeologists like proposed that the wave of Indo-European and farming had reached India from Anatolia. However soon it became clear that the South Asian Neolithic complex including the Ganga Valley Neolithic, the Vindhyan Neolithic and the Mehrgarh Neolithic were at least as old as Anatolia. The domesticated cattle (Zebu) and cereals (barley, wheat and rice) too were unique and distinct in their genetic constitution indicating local domestication.

The latest effort by the group supporting Anatolia as the home of the Indo-Europeans was to publish a paper (Bouckaert *et al* 2012) in which statistical treatment of the philological data was done in such a manipulated way so as to prove that the Anatolian Hittite language was the oldest of the Indo-European languages and Anatolia was the homeland of all the Aryans. The results of the statistical examinations depend on the data fed into the process. In this case many wrong data inputs were made so as to achieve the single desired results.

Bouckaert's study was designed such that the meanings (words) which were listed for the various languages for the comparative study did not include any farming related words like horse, cow, bull, goat, lamb, sheep, pig, chariot, wheel, mouse, cook, grind, mill and similar Neolithic associated meanings, which were in fact most relevant to the study of the farming related Indo-European migrations (which the article claims to have studied).

The study was biased too, because it considered only two options or possibilities for the homeland—Anatolia and the steppe (p.959), and no third or fourth country were placed into the contest. The result is marred by the use of the wrong data for the Indian languages. The Swadesh Lists for Hindi, Nepali etc used in this study have included many loan words from Persian, which were borrowed over the last 800 years of Persian influence in India. Only original words should have been included in the study. One such example is "janwar" (Persian) for "animal" in Nepali which should have been "*pashu*" (see IELEX list).

Other such wrong data fed in the compilation are: for "sea" Vedic *samudras* and not *mīra*; for "sky" Vedic *daus* and not *nabha*. The Vedic word (*paśu*, from PIE *pek*, cattle; Pokorny:797) for the meaning "animal" has been given a low rating (single star), while more obscure words from the many European languages have been given high ratings (up to three stars). Often, words have been chosen from the Vedic in such a way that these would be scored "not cognate" in the computerized analysis. One simple example of such manipulation is the meaning "warm": for Vedic Sanskrit they have listed *uṣṇa*, instead of the

Vedic word *gharma-* (cognate to PIE *$*g^{hw}$*er-*) reducing one mark to the Vedic.[13] This completely erodes the credibility of the study. Even after committing such errors, the Vedic stands older (2,900 BCE) than the European languages in the study.

The discrepancies have been reflected in the results too. For example Dunn, Gray *etc* (2011) had found, applying the same kind of computer analysis that the Indo-Iranian is the youngest of all branches of the IE family (Dunn *et al* 2011:80, Fig.1). However, Bouckaert *et al* (2012) found that the Indo-Iranian is older than the European branches, and only Armenian, Tocharian, Lycian, Luvian and Hittite are older than the Indo-Iranian (p.959, Fig.2). This clearly indicates the problems with the materials, methods and designs of the studies.

There are more serious objections to Anatolia being the Aryan homeland. One such objection comes from linguistics and archaeology. Cognate word for *akwa* (horse), an animal considered so crucial to the Indo-European theme is absent from the vocabulary of the Anatolian Hittite language (Kazanas 2009). In fact horse is very late in the Anatolian archaeology. The Anatolian Hittite vocabulary is deficient in the basic Indo-European words for cow, goat, sheep, pig (see later in this book) and also the core IE kinship terminology (Kazanas 2009). Thus Anatolia's claims must be considered closed.

It is relevant to mention here that the prime Neolithic equipment the 'plough' was an Indian word, originally from the Austro-Asiatic family of languages. From there it entered the Indo-European family and then spread to other countries. The philological material is as follows:

---

13 **Other such manipulations in compilation are: for "sea" Vedic *samudras* and not *mīra*; for "sky" Vedic *daus* and not *nabha*; see the list at http://ielex.mpi.nl/wordlist/all/. This data location has been provided in the supplementary attached to the article: http://www.sciencemag.org/content/suppl/2012/08/22/337.6097.957.DC1/Bouckaert.SM.pdf**

> Sanskrit *lāṅgala* (plough, *RV* 4.57.4), Bihari *teṅārī* (axe), Bangali *tengari* (axe); Persian *langar* (anchor, equipoise, counterpoise, weight, gravity, dignity); English 'plough', O.E. *plog, ploh* (to plow), Scandenevian *plogr* (to plow), Old Frisian *ploch-* (to plow), Middle Dutch *ploech* (to plow), Proto-Germanic **plogo*; Lithuanian *plugas*; Pliny noted that Latin *plovus* (to plow) was a loan word from Rhaetian.

Semantic analysis of cognates reveals that root is "*ank, ang*" which has the meaning "bent solid object". From this has come anchor (E.) from *anker* (German). However the German word is a borrowing from Latin *ancora* < from *ankyra* (Gk. anchor, hook). The word is present in the Dravidian and Austro-Asiatic as well as some Semitic languages too:

> Austro-Asiatic: Munda **na-kel, nan-kel* (Zide & Zide 1973: 5), Santali *nahel*, Khasi *lynkor* [*lənkor*] < **lēnkol*, Khmer *aṅkal* (Witzel 1999).
>
> Dravidian: Tamil *nancil, nancil*, Kannada *nẽgal*, Gadba *nangal* (DED 2907), Brahui *langar* (plough).
>
> Austronesian forms: Malay *tengala*, Cham *langal, langar*, Batak *tingala*, Bugi *rakala*,Makassar *naṅkala*.
>
> Sino-Tibetan : Kanauri *hāloṅ*.
>
> Afro-Asiatic **nigal* (to reap, reaping sickle), Sumer *nig-gala*$_x$*l* or *nig-gal* (sickle).

This lexical material helps us conclude that the word originated in India in the context of emerging Neolithic technology and got quickly adopted by the three language families evolving in Central India India that time the Dravidian, Austro-Asiatic and the Indo-European. It was with the spread of the farming technology with the out of India first wave of migration about 8000 BC that the word dispersed in the Indo-European speaking regions (Primary Dispersal). However, later during the Bronze Age the word was adopted by the Austronesian, Sino-Tibetan and Afro-Asiatic languages too, as exemplified above.

Chapter 14

The Homeland Debate and the Horse

The Aryan Invasion Theory (AIT) claimed that the cognate words for horse and wheel are found in all the branches of the Indo-European language family, therefore the Aryan homeland must have had horse and cart before their dispersal out of the homeland.

The theory thought that the horse was domesticated before 1600 BC in the steppe or Central Asia from the wild Przewalskii horse that lived there. The theory added--with the horse and the chariot the Aryans arrived at Iran and from there to India after 1500 BC. In this theory, the horse had been the main source of power or superiority, which made the Aryans victorious in India, Iran and also in Europe.

The Dereivka Horse of 4200 BC

In 1991, David Anthony reported in the *Antiquity* a horse-and-dog burial from Dereivka (Ukraine) from a layer dated 4200-3700 BCE. This became widely accepted as the earliest domesticated horse, bringing the location of the Aryan home in the Ukrainian steppe at about 4,200 BCE. However, Levine (cited in Anthony 2009:214-215) in her detailed study of the horse-bones from the same layer of Dereivka and from another steppe site Botai (3700-3000 BCE, Kazakhstan) inferred that none of the horses found at these two places had actually been ever domesticated (cited *ibid*:205). Hausler (cited *ibid*:214-215) and many other specialists of ancient horse bones too never accepted the 4200 BCE date for the domestic horse in the steppe.

In fact at the time 4200 BCE the region was not a steppe but a dense forest because of the climate amelioration caused by the mid-Holocene optimum (Zhao 2008, 2009; Miehe 2007:163; 156 Table 1). Such ecosystems harbour carnivores like tiger, which can hunt very efficiently in the dense forests, and are not good for the survival of the horse whose survival in the wild depends on the fast escape-speed. The 4200 BC was a wet time for the region. In such ecosystem, hunter-gatherer and primitive farming with cattle and goat pastoralism could have been possible, not the horse nomadism. Any horse seen there must be considered a capture from the distant grasslands. Hence the claim for the presence of the horse there at that time must be seen with suspicion.

Then the skull bone of the horse was directly radiocarbon dated and found to be from 3000 BCE, which Anthony (1997) interpreted as contamination in the museum. However it was soon obvious that this radiocarbon report was wrong as the bone tested did not actually belong to the horse.

Thereafter another radiocarbon dating of the horse skull was done, giving the date 800-200 BCE (Scythian era). The conclusion emerged that the horse-burial had been dug deeper into the lower layers of the soil. David Anthony, author of the Dereivka story was left with no other choice, but to retract the claim, which he quickly did (Anthony:2000; 2009:215). He wrote, "New radiocarbon dates from Oxford and Kiev indicate that the Dereivka `cult stallion' should be withdrawn from discussions of Eneolithic horse-keeping. The Dereivka horse died between about 700 and 200 BC." (Anthony in *Antiquity* 2000).

This episode bulldozed the steppe-horse theory completely. Yet the Dereivka hosre has been kept alive by many Eurocentic authors in the field. The belief in 4200 BC steppe horse is perpetuated by the unscrupulous writings of prominent authorities like Trautmann (2005) who control and regulate the academic world. Trautmann republished in 2005 (and 2007:251-253) extracts from David Anthonyís oldest article claiming the 4200 BC domestic horse of Dereivka (Ukraine). Trautmann did this and the Oxford University Press published it in spite of the fact that David Anthony had retracted from this older claim (of year 1991) in year 2000 (*Antiquity*). The history writing has been brought down to the level of racist conspiracy.

In views of most of the specialist in animal archaeology the wild Indian type of *Equus caballus* or the *sivalensis* horse became extinct from India after the early Holocene (Priyadarshi 2012, 2013; Bokonyi 2005:238). Apart from *Equus sivalensis* bones of which have been recovered from the Himalayas, the ones recovered from Central India have been named as the *Equus namadicus*. G.R. Sharma (1980) noted horse bones from the end of the early Holocene dated 6570-4530 BC. The same bones were re-examined by D.K. Chakrabarti who gave a date earlier than about 5000 BC (1999).

Other findings of horse bones from Harappa culture, generally ignored by mainstream authors, too need to be recorded here. Allchin and Joshi found "lumbar vertebrae of horse" at Malvan, a Harappan site at Shaurastra (1995: 95). Dhavalikar reported horse bones unearthed at Kuntasi, periods I and II which date back to 2300-2000 BC. (1995: 116-117). Thomas and Joglekar (1995) found 9 bones of true horse (0.13% of the total faunal remains) and 9 bones of the onager at Shikarpur from mature Harappan levels, ie c. 2300 (cited by U. Singh:158).

There is evidence of entry of the *sivalensis* horse into Tajikistan during Late Pleistocene (Forsten and Sharapov 2000:309). During the Last Glacial Maximum (18,000 BCE-14,000 BCE) and the Late Glacial (11,000-9,500 BCE) there was a wholesale extinction of horse from Eurasia, except from the warmer southern regions like India and Iberian Peninsula (Achilli 2011:4 of pdf version). Thus any wild horse living in Tajikistan during the early or mid-Holocene must have entered this province of Central Asia from south only after the end of the peak of glacial period.

Bones of wild *Equus namadicus* and *Equus sivalensis* (specimen names for *Equus caballus*), have been found from 18,000 BCE Inamgaon, 75,000-50,000 BCE Narmada basin and the Siwalik Hills (Badam 1985:413; Falconer and Cautley 1849; Sonakia and Biswas 1998). Although the wild horse became rare following conversion of the Indian steppes into dense forests after 6000 BCE, it never went completely extinct from India as it survived as the domesticated one. There is evidence from the anatomy of the surviving native horses of the Southeast Asia and from the SEA fossil horses that the domesticated Indian *sivalensis* horse had been transported to the SEA region during the Neolithic period itself (*vide infra*).

In fact the absence of any animal should not be taken very seriously by the archaeologists. For example, we know that the "Dog and cat bones were rare" in the Indus Valley Civilization (Goyal 2013). It would be utterly foolish to suggest on this account that the dogs and cats were not among the common domestic pets in the Harappan Civilization. The cats and dogs certainly lived in the Indus Valley Civilization can be said by understanding the basic survival requirements of the three man, dog and cat. Paucity of bones should never mean that the cat and the domestic dog, and for that matter any animal pig, camel, crow or parrot, were not there in that civilization. And this general rule must apply to the horse too.

In spite of the denials by many mainstream historians, many horse bones older than 1500 BCE have been attested from Indian archaeology. Upinder Singh noted horse bones in many cities of Harappa, "Horse remains have been reported at Harappa, Lothal, Surkotada, Kuntasi, and Kalibangan, and at superficial level at Mohenjodaro." (U.Singh 208:157). Fentress mentions presence of horse bones at Mohenjo-Daro but not at Harappa (364:Table 2). This is because of the nearness of Mohenjo-Daro from Thar grasslands in which the the horse might have survived in the wild during the mid-Holocene optimum.

G.R. Sharma noted the domestic horse bones from 6500 BCE and 4500 BCE, Bolan and Son valleys and even older specimens from many sites in Central India (G.R. Sharma 1980a:22, 220, 224; 1980b 110 ff.). Bryant lists reports of archaeological remains of horse being found from Harappa, and cites Sewell and Guha (1931), Bholanath (1963), Wheeler (1953:92), Mackey (1938) and Piggott (1952:126, 130), in his book (2001:170-171).

R.S. Sharma reports domesticated horse from Mahagara Neolithic complex dated 5000 BCE and Bagor in Rajasthan dated 4500 BCE (R.S. Sharma:16, 17). However he most ingenuinely argues that it is "an isolated species of horse distinct from the one inhabiting the areas in the USSR, Iran, Afghanistan etc and associated with the Aryans" (R.S. Sharma:17). Prof R.S. Sharma obviously does not know that there is only one species of real horse for the whole of the world in the Holocene; and the other species Przewalskii which never lived in India, cannot not be considered a true horse after we came to know the DNA and chromosomal study of the Przewalskii.

R.S. Sharma's statement is full of confusion and contradictions. It suggests that the horse which lived in Iran and Afghanistan at about 4,500 BC was associated with the Aryans. It also suggests that the domestic horse had two species, one which lived in India and the other which lived in Afghanistan, Iran and USSR. No biologist has ever noted this.

From the Harappa Civilization many domesticated horse bones have been found by this time (Bokonyi 2005; Lal 2005; Gupta 2005:186-191). Wild true horse (*E. namadicus*) bones were found from 18,000 BCE strata of Bolan and Son valleys (G.R. Sharma 1980b:110 ff.; Kazanas 1999:33-34). Only archaeologist who did not accept the presence of horse in India before 1500 BC was Meadow (1998a:18; 1998b). But his sole opinion cannot be trusted in view of his ethnocentric trend of writing.

Meadow's Eurocentric pretentions are not secret. He has seen Harappa as the "eastern margin" of the great Middle Eastern Civilization, and not the western margin of India which had Ganga Valley Neolithic too (Meadow 1984, 1993). Moreover, he himself emphasized that it is extremely difficult to distinguish the bones of *E. caballus*, *E. asinus* and *E. hemionus* (Meadow 1986, cited by Rissmann:19). Hence this lone voice of Meadow against the Indian horse should be discounted and should be kept away from any genuine enquiry of the the presence of horse in prehistoric India. It may be noted here that *Equus caballus* along with the *hemionus* and other species was noted by Meadow at Aq Kupruk of Afghanistan dating back from 6,000 to 14,000 BCE (Meadow 1989:25-26, Table 2). During this period the northwest Indian steppe extended from Afghanistan to Punjab, and there is no reason why this horse should not have lived in the northwest Indian steppe in the same period. Clearly Meadows heart is not clean.

From Mohenjo-Daro John Marshall recorded a horse-jaw, which was in no way different from the modern caballus horse samples: "In size the fragment of jaw corresponds exactly to that of a skull of a modern horse in the collection of the Zoological Survey of India" (Marshall, John 1931:653). Marshall gives the detailed measurements of the mandible with comparisons from Anau horse and the museum specimen of the *Equus caballus* (654). He by this means concludes that "it is probable that the Anau horse, the Mohenjo-daro horse, and the example of *Equus caballus* of the Zoological Survey of India, are all of the type of the Indian 'country bred', a small breed of horse, the Anau horse being slightly smaller than the others" (Marshall 1931:654). We can say, this small "Indian country bred" horse of Marshall is the *Sivalensis* horse.

At Shikarpur (Mature Harappa period, Gujarat) at least 0.13 percent of all bones belonged to horse (Upinder Singh:158; Thomas and Joglekar 1995). V.N. Misra (2001:515) noted horse bones from Kayatha from the Harappa period: "The presence of horse bones in the layers of the Kayatha and succeeding Chalcolithic cultures as also a terracotta figurine of a mare at Kayatha is interesting because it takes back the antiquity of this animal to the late third millennium B.C."

Lal mentions, "The latest evidence regarding the association of horse with the Harappan Civilization comes from the excavations carried by J.-F. Jarrige and his colleagues from the well known site of Nausharo" (2005:71). Beside these, plenty of horse figurines, sketches and engravings have been found from the Harappa Civilization.

Kennedy mentions that Dupree in 1966 found horse bones from *Darra-I-Kur* in Northeast Afghanistan dating back to 1580 ± 130 BC (radiocarbon date), which on calibration gives the age 1882 BC, and the calculated collagen date was 1945 BC. Hence 1900 BC to 2000 BC is the approximate age of these horse bones (Kennedy 2000:253).

Dupree in 1972 found the skeletal remains of the caballus horse which he identified as the *Equus Przewalskii* from a Neolithic complex lying along with domestic goat, cattle, onegar and rodents from northeast Afghanistan, Darra-I-Kur (Kennedy:279). Dupree named it the *Goat-Cult Neolithic*. The presence of cattle, domestic goat and horse in the same complex is indicative of domestication. Although Dupree identified it so, most probably this caballus horse was certainly not the Przewalskii because the latter was never domesticated and South Asia was out of its natural range.

Forsten and Sharapov noted that the *namadicus* horse was larger, and comparatively younger in archaeological findings than the *sivalensis* (2000:310). It is generally said that the *sivalensis* became extinct from India after 8,000 BCE. However, no cause or evidence was ever given. Ghosh correctly pointed out that "The rarity of horse is surprising. For on one hand it existed in India in the end of Pleistocene and on the other the grasslands afforded a good pasture" (1990:211). No one ever bothered to answer this riddle.

The most well accepted presence of the domestic horse in India comes from Pirak (periods IB, II and IIIB). The uncalibrated radiocarbon date of Pirak IB is 1460 ±140 BCE (Kuz'mina and Mallory:434), which on calibration gives the calendar date 1794 calBCE (say 1800 BCE).[14] At 1800 BCE, there was no horse or its related furniture in the BMAC (Witzel 2003:7 of 12, pdf).

Lamberg-Karlovsky (2002:73) noted "in Bactrian Margiana communities there is scant evidence for steppe ceramics and a complete absence of horses and their equipment or their depiction". The date of Pirak 1800 BCE is older than the Indo-Aryan culture of Arkaim by 200 years. Thus we can say that the Pirak horse was not brought from the steppe through the Bactria-Margiana region by the Aryans.

However, one seal with horse-rider from BMAC has been reported by Sarianidi (1986, cited by Anthony 2009:504, n17). The horse on the seal characteristically belongs to the Marwari breed of India, and is identical with the Etruscan horse. The seal also depicts on its round surface a humped bull, which is undisputedly Indian (S. Chen 2009). Clearly the seal was made by someone of Indian origin, or might have been imported from India.

Many people had doubted the claimed date 4200 BCE for the onset of riding in the steppe before Anthony was forced to withdraw his claim. Even after the withdrawal the theory is often kept alive by a few authors. Such view has been opposed by many scholars. Renfrew (2000:44; quoted by Drews 2004) wrote, "The mounted warrior nomad horseman does not make his appearance until the end of the second millennium". Kuz'mina (2000:122) wrote "warrior-horsemen appear in the steppe not in the fourth millennium BC but at the end of the second millennium BC" (quoted by Drews 2004:132). Rassamakin (1999), and Benecke and Driesch (2003) too express similar opinion (both cited by Koryakova and Epimakhov 2007). We find no reason to distrust the views of Renfrew, Kuzmina or Drews on this matter. Thus the late Harappan (Pirak) horsemen of 1800 BCE are the oldest unequivocal evidence of riding the horseback in the world.

---

[14] Calibration done with the 'quickcal 2007' software.

It will not be out of context to cite a few examples of the light chariot recovered from Harappa Culture. In spite of denials of older two-wheel chariots by the western historians, the excavation report (1920-21 and 1933-34) of Harappa clearly mentions a roofed copper chariot model recovered from Harappa (Vats 1940:452) and should be dated at least 2500 BCE. Many chariot toys, particularly the bird-chariots too were found from that date. This finding fits well with an older date of the *Rig-Veda* which quite often mentions the chariots. Later another copper chariot from 2300 BCE layer was found from Daimabad in Maharashtra (Sali 1986:477-479). Mackay found proper chariot models and toys from Chanhudaro (Mackay 1943: 160, 164). There were many samples of bird-chariot and at least one ram-chariot was found (*ibid*:160). Chariot appears in any other civilization only after 2000 BCE (Egypt, Mesopotamia, Sintashta etc). He noted, "...the people of Harappa culture were well acquainted with the Sumerians, it is not surprising that both two-wheeled and four-wheeled vehicles were were in use in both countries" (*ibid*:164). India could have been the source of the chariot for Sumeria, because Mackey notes that the Indian chariots recovered were of more primitive type than the Sumerian ones (*ibid*).

Mackey described one metal chariot in detail which he thought was a war-chariot. He wrote, "But the shield-like front of the chariot shown in Pl LVIII 9,13—obviously intended to protect the driver—do certainly suggest something in the nature of a vehicle used in warfare" (1943:164). He describes two bronze chariots there. One of them he notes, resembled exactly like a modern Indian *ekka*: "The other metal vehicle found (Pl LVIII, 2) is of quite different pattern; in some respects it resembles the *ekka* of modern India" (*ibid*:164). Again he notes, "From these little model catrs we can visulalize the actual vehicles that took people to and fro between the cities and the various ferries across the river, and most likely in the evenings carried people to pleasure resorts outside their cities; in fact, which served all the purposes of "tonga" or the "*ekka*" of the modern day" (*ibid*: 165). The *ekka* of modern India is a single-horse driven two-wheeled light chariot still surviving in rural modern India. Mackay also described the metal chariot found from Harappa by M.S. Vatsa (*ibid*).

In fact the Harappa Civilization people used horse and chariot for rapid communication. Such a huge civilization with distant trade related, monetary and diplomatic relations could not have been successful on the bullock-carts. It certainly had fast vehicles. Regarding the chariot wheels, Marshall noted that the models of the ones found from Mohenjo-Daro almost exactly resembled the Sumerian ones (Marshall:554). In fact it is surprising that the entire excavation reports have been dumped and fictional stories have been concocted to create an impression that the Harappa people did not have fast chariots.

Equus sivalensis: the Horse of India

Before the late twentieth century many European horse-specialists viewed the modern Indian native horse as the lineal descendant of the *sivalensis* horse. British archaeologist Lydekkar posted in India wrote in 1887 in the *Records of the Geological Survey of India*, "There is also a species of horse (*Equus namadicus*) which seems to be a survivor from the Siwaliks, and is allied to the existing species of the genus." (1887:53) When Sir John Marshall examined the Mohenjo-Daro specimen of the horse bone, he reached the conclusion that the Mohenjo-Daro horse was of the same breed as the Indian small country horse of today (1931:654).

Crooke (1906) inferred that the *sivalensis* was not only the ancestor of the modern Indian horse, but also that of the Arab and the British thoroughbred horse: "It is almost certain that the Indian horse is a descendant of the fossil horse of the Siwaliks, in which the skull pit is larger. A similar pit was found in the skulls of 'Eclipse', 'Bend Or' and 'Stockwell' and hence it has been concluded that the Arab stock from which our thoroughbreds are derived was originally imported in ancient times from India." (Crooke: 1906:253).

Crooke's study found that that the original Western European breed of horse was different from the many prestigious breeds of modern Europe, and also from the Arab (and the English throroughbred *i.e.* the British bred Arab) as well as the Kathiawar breed of India. He noted, "Mr Lydekker has recently discovered in the skull of the modern Indian horse a vestige of the pre-orbital depression or pit which must, as in living deer, at one time have sheltered a tear-gland. He regards the Arab and the English thoroughbred as distinct from the *Equus caballus* of Western Europe, of which the original tint seems to have been dun with black marking on the legs, and sparse development of hair on mane and tail, like the Kathiawar breed. The Arab variety, with a bright bay colour, white star on forehead, and not in frequently a black bar round the fetlock, is quite different." (Crooke 1906:253)

However what Crooke noted was forgotten later. He also mentioned the belief of the horse specialists that the Indian Kathiawar breed of horse is a "very primitive" and "distinct" type which possibly emerged from the Indian mares and Libyan or some other stallion long back (*ibid*). Ewart wrote, "*Equus sivalensis* is the oldest true horse known, it has more highly specialised teeth than the Oreston and Newstead ponies" (1911: 366; also see 1909:393). It was possibly domesticated at 8000 BCE in India.

The first domestication of horse in India at the Neolithic period at the early Holocene was earlier accepted by everyone in the field. Rissman (1989:15) noted, "The region defined by the boarders of modern India contains a number of domesticable wild animal species, as well as long record of human habitation. These factors have led some scholars to distinguish India as a hearth of domestication, where in various points in time, local taming and/or breeding of cattle, buffalo, elephant, horse, camel, sheep, goat, pig, dog and foul took place."

Ridgeway noted: "Mr Lyddeker holds that because *E. sivalensis* of the Indian Pliocene is usually characterized by large first premolar teeth in the upper jaw, and as large functional premolars are found in some Javanese and Sulu ponies,.. lineal and somewhat modified descendants of *E. sivalensis* still survive." "Prof Huxley in 1870 indicated the existence of a rudimentary pre-orbital pit in the skull of *Equus sivalensis*, an Indian fossil species, and Dr Forsyth Major in 1880 pointed out the existence of a similar feature in *Equus stenonis*,... and he also showed its existence in the *Quagga*"...

..."Mr Lydekker has recently directed attention to the occurrence of what he considers 'a vestige of the *Hipparion* face-pit in the skull of an Indian domesticated horse in the collection of the British museum'... 'from the occurrence of the feature in question in these skulls, both of which probably belonged to horses of eastern origin and its entire absence in the skull of prehistoric European horse', Mr Lydekker has suggested that the blood-horse unlike the cold-blooded-horse of Western Europe, may possibly have been the descendant of *Equus sivalensis*." ... "Mr Lydekker thus holds that the thoroughbred horse as well as the ponies of Java and Sulu is lineal descendants of *E. sivalensis*..." (Ridgeway 1905:142-143)

These descriptions imply domestication of *sivalensis* horse in India before 8000 BCE (10,000 BP). The DNA studies too indicate that the horse was domesticated soon after the end of the glaciations, i.e. about 8000-6000 BCE, and not about 4000 or 2000 BCE. If this premise is accepted, then many of the Rock Paintings of Bhimbetka depicting horse with riders may be from the early Holocene or the Mesolithic period, the date generally reserved for the Rock Paintings of Bhimbetka which do not depict horse. Iberia and India were the places where horse could have survived well during the glacial, and their immediate post-Pleistocene presence has not been denied by anyone. Moreover, all the Bhimbetka depictions of horse are hunting scenarios, and they do not contain evidence of Neolithic culture. Of the other places only Crimea and Romania stand some chance for having saved some horses during the Late Glacial peak. Some authors (like Bokonyi 2005:238) say that the Indian wild horse (sivalensis) suddenly became extinct at about 8,000 BCE after having survived the most difficult glacial period. This is partly because of their large scale capture, domestication and the ritualistic killings.

Osborn (1915:310) noted "A possible contributory to the desert breed of the Pleistocene and of the modern domesticated horses is the animal of the *E. sivalensis* type of the Upper Pliocene in the Siwaliks of India. This animal is tall, with long, fairly slender limbs, long neck, well elevated tail, long face, which is strongly deflected on the cranium with a slightly convex profile and broad brow, and teeth with a narrow protocone."

Ewart (1909:392-3) noted, "Of the possible ancestors of the domestic breeds, the following may be mentioned:-- *Equus sivalensis, E. stenonis, E. gracilis* (Owen's *Asinus fossilis*), *E. namadicus, E. fossilis* and *E. robustus*"... "It used to be said that *E. sivalensis* could not be regarded as an ancestor of domestic horses because of the shortness of the anterior pillar of the cheek teeth. I find, however, that in some modern horses, the anterior pillars are decidedly shorter than in *E. sivalensis*, and that in some of the short-pillared domestic horses the face is nearly as strongly deflected on the cranium as in *E. sivalensis*. There is hence no longer any reason for assuming that this ancient Indian species had no share in the making of domestic breeds. But in the absence of a large and representative collection of skulls of domestic horses, it is impossible to say which modern breeds are most indebted to the large-headed, long- limbed race, which in Pliocene times frequented the area to the east of the Jhelum River, now occupied by the Siwalik Hills. Mr. Lydekker thinks E. sivalensis or some closely allied race " may have been the ancestral stock from which Barbs, Arabs and Thoroughbreds are derived.""

The view can be further supported by the finding that the *Rig-Vedic* horse, the extant native Indian horse, the *Sivalensis* horse, the Arab and the Southeast Asian native horse Sulu (considered evolved from *Sivalensis*) all exhibit 17 pairs of ribs. (*Rig-Vedic* horse, *RV* 1.162.18; modern native Indian horse, Manansala 2006:447; Arab horse, Murray 2010:14; Sulu horse of Indonesia, Bankoff 2004:19) while the rest of the horses of the world exhibit 18 pairs of ribs or more (Hawkins 1866:14).

"*Equus sivalensis* of India was a tall, broad-browed horse characterized by a long tapering deflected face and an inter-orbital prominence, a long neck, high withers and a high-set-on tail." (United States Bureau Report: 174). The Report suggested that like the Arab and the Indian horses, which descended from the *sivalensis*, the latter too may have been a fleet race characterized by an indomitable disposition: "light as well as heavy horses characterized by long pointed ears and a prominence between the eyes, by a long deflected face, high withers (shoulder ridge), and a high-set-on tail include horses of the Siwalik type as their ancestor" (*ibid*:174).

Certain breeds of modern British racehorses have descended from Newstead horse which was a connecting link between the modern British horse breeds and the Indian *sivalensis* (Ewart 1911:370). The British breed "thoroughbred" too has descended from *sivalensis* (*ibid*:369). The Barb breed of North African coast and also the so called Arab breed of horse are descendants of *Equus sivalensis* (*ibid*:369).

Lydekker, another specialist of equine breeds too opined that the horses of Arabia, North African coast and the Thoroughbred breed have descended from the Indian *Equus sivalensis* (quoted in *ibid*:369; also Lydekker:19-21). Lydekker, and also Ray Lankester, found that the "blood-horse" too was of Indian origin (Ridgeway 1905:469-470).

US Bureau on Animal Industry Report noted that "Throughbreds built on the lines of Stockwell and Persimmons are probably more intimately related to *Equus sivalensis* than to Prof Ridgeway's 'fine bay horse' (*Equus caballus libycus*) of North Africa." (page 174).

Manansala (p. 396) notes, "In other words, Lydekker now realizes that all the modern breeds are not characterized by long-pillared molars, and says that there is a probability that Barbs, Arabs and Thoroughbreds are descended from *Equus sivalensis*". He further adds, "However, rather fully *sivalensis* types have been described from Neolithic strata (8000-4000 BCE) at Lemery, Batangas in the Philippines together with dog remains." (*ibid*).

The horse of Philippines retains many features of the Sulu horse of Malaya like the 17 pair of ribs instead of the usual 18 (Animal Industry 1911:479, cited in Bankoff 2004:19), which is the characteristic feature of the *sivalensis* horse. Paterno noted, "This contention is based on some isolated preservation of *E. sivalensis* traits. However, rather fully-sivalensis types have been described from Neolithic strata (8000-4000 BCE) at Lemery, Batangas in the Philippines together with dog remains." (Paterno 1981, cited in Manansala 2006:396). Alba (1994) too notes that the *E. sivalensis* features are still found in the horses of the so-called "Sulu Horse" and its relatives in Borneo, Sumatra and Malacca.

Establishing the origin of the Arab breed of horse from the *Sivalensis*, J.A. Thompson (1922:1109) wrote "One of these, which flourished during Pliocene times, was a slender-limbed species, standing about 15 hands high, and having a broad forehead and tapering face, and certain peculiarities of the molar teeth. This type is represented by the Siwalik horse (*Equus sivalensis*). The Arab may be a descendant of this stock."

He also noted that the ancestor of the other type of horse, the heavy draught or daft type horse was domesticated from the Tarpan which was surviving in Europe at the time when he wrote the book (*ibid*). He suggested that the Przewalskii too could have been the ancestor of the heavy daft type horse. However for the light racehorses, he considered only the *Sivalensis*. He was a meticulous observer and his viws cannot be just dust-binned.

We know from the latest scientific techniques that the Przewalskii branched off the lineage of horse about 200,000 years back, and it was not the stock from which the horse has been domesticated. We also cannot sustain the deception that that the steppe horse could have been light horse. The steppe wild horse of 2000 BC or earlier resembled the Tarpan or the Kazakh breed of modern horse, was heavy and was principally used for meat, milk and draught even after domestication which took place much later. It was not used, and in fact could not have been used, for riding (on the back) or racing in the chariot. For the racing purposes, it were the southern horses, whether from South China, or India or Iran, it had to reach the steppe and Central Asia with the late Bronze Age contacts.

The Arab horse does not only resemble the Indian horse externally, but it has only 17 pairs of ribs, just like the *Rig-Vedic* Indian horse (*vide supra*). The Barb horse (North Africa), which seems to be a kin of the Arab horse, too has only 17 pairs of ribs, while the horses in general have 18 (and sometimes 19) pairs of ribs (Higgins 2012:21).

The Philippines Agricultural Review noted, "Some palaeontologists believe that the Indian species (*E. sivalensis* and *nomadicus*) became extinct and the *E. stenonis* gave rise through *E. robustus* to the modern breeds. But the presence in the Java, Sulu, and Borneo horses of the above-mentioned vestiges of the preorbital depression and the large premolars make it appear that some modified descendants of *E. sivalensis* survived" (Mackie 1911:477). Ridgeway too made a nearly identical statement (1905:10-11).

Montemayor too noted, "Evidence tend to show that in all probability the latter is an offshoot of one of the Indian horses (*Equus sivalensis*) since physical characteristics such as pre-orbital depression, large development of the first premolars of the upper jaw and the presence of but 17 pairs of ribs inherent to the prehistoric Indian horse occasionally appear in the anatomy of the Sulu horse (1954: 307)".

Horse depicted as Unicorn in Indus Valley Seals

The claim that the Indus Valley Civilization did not have horse has been proved to be wrong, as we noted enough archaeological remains of the horse from that culture. However one objection finding has not been explained why there was no horse seal found from that civilization. Kazanas noted that the frequency of the horse bones do not increase in the north Indian archaeology even after 1500

BC, the claimed date of arrival of the horse to India (Kazanas 2013). Hence particular neclect of the horse in depiction on the seals by the Harappans needs careful consideration.

One thing is clear that the horse had become an essential element in the burial practices of the well off. Hence there might have been an associated taboo against depiction of this animal on anything. However, we can guess, such taboo would not apply to depiction of the sacred horse of the horse sacrifice.

In the *Rig-Veda* the *Aśvinī kumaras* as well as the horse meant for the sacrifice had horns, of course bridle in nature. It was usually golden in colour (*RV* 1.162.9, 1.162.11; *TS* 4.6.7.4). Therefore a large number of the unicorn seals depict no other animal but the horn-bridled horse. Moreover the sacrificial bowl put below their heads signify that they were probably the sacrificial horses.

M.S. Vats, the archaeologist who wrote of the Harappa Excavation Report thought that the incense-burner depicted in the Harappa seals is intimately associated with the 'cult of unicorn' (p. 322). In fact the unicorn has always been shown with the incense-burner, which is placed in below the head of the creature. Vats expressed a possibility "—but nothing more than a possibility—that the so called unicorn may, after all, be no other than the Indian ox so posed that one horn is completely hidden behind the other." (Vats:321). Ever since this unicorn has been considered/mentioned as a unicorn-bull. [Vats, M.S., 1940, *Excavations at Harappa*, Vol. 1, Manager of Publications to the Govt of India, Delhi]

However such a view is not correct because of the following reasons. The Indus bull has a large fold of skin or platysma hanging down its neck, which is absent from all the unicorns in the Harappan seals. The typical bovine-hump too is absent from all the unicorns. An Indus Valley bull (zebu) must have had a characteristic hump. The head of the unicorn is elongated while that of the bulls depicted on the other seals is more rounded. The "overlap" of horns, one covering the other in the profile views is a wrong and misleading argument. Because none of the bulls' depicted in the Harappan seals have horns which cover each other in such a way that only one can be seen. All the bulls have been depicted with two, clear from each other, horns. Then why should this particular way of depicting 'two horns as one' be applied only to the unicorns?

In fact many of the Harappan unicorns are composit animals in the Harappan seals, some having the torso of the bull, others having multiple heads of different animals. Natawar Jha and B.K. Jha have identified some of the unicorn seals as that of the *eka-shringi Varaha* of the Pauranic literature. The *Varaha* has an alternative meaning 'bull'. In their learned view, the Harappa unicorn was a chimera which had the head and neck of a horse, and the torso and tail of a bull. Natwar Jha cited the example of the *Haya-grīva* of the *Puranas*, which too was in fact not dissimilar from the unicorn and had the 'neck' and head of the horse. *Mahabharata* mentions the *ekashringi* (literally, 'unicorn') at quite a large number of places (*e.g. MB* 12.330.027, 12.330.027). *Mahabharata* also mentions a composit animal (*trikakuta*) having three heads which is a manifestation of the divine (*MB* 12.330.028). The three headed beast has been depicted in some of the Harappan seals.

Even during the *Rig-Veda* stage of the evolution of the Hindu theology, some divinities were assigned horn possibly as costume. This trend is visible in the Harappa iconography too where the *paśupati* has been depicted having a horn. Most of the hornless animals have been depicted in the seals as having horns. Not only in Harappa but in Iran, China and Central Asia too horses were depicted having horns. Most of the Central Asian horses recovered from the Scythian Kurgans (graves) were decorated with artificial horns, sometimes made of wood, and other times of gold. The wooden horns were shaped like that of wild ram (ibex), or sometimes like the antlers of deer. They were often covered with gold foil (Azzaroli 1985:76; Rudenko 1970).

However, we can assume that not only the horses, but women too adorned themselves with horns. This we can say on the basis of the word *shringara* or *śṛñgāra*, which is derived from *śṛñga* (horn, antler) and which has the applied meaning as the adornments and make up used by women.

We know of the *Ṛṣya-śṛñga ṛṣi* who was contemporary to the King Dasharatha. He is known to have one single antler of deer. *Ṛṣya* and *ṛśya* mean deer (and also antelope; Monier-Williams Dictionary). *Mahabharata* mentions many kings and fighters who were *ārṣya-śṛñgī* ('one who has antlers of deer'; *ārṣya* is an adjective of *ṛṣya*; *MB* 06.086.045a, 06.086.064a, 06.096.021e etc). King Duryodhana too has been named with the epithet *ārṣya-śṛñgī* (MB 06.096.021e), indicating that he too wore the deer-antlers. Another verse describes the Goddess who is adorned with the copper axe (weapon), is dressed in leather, and has the ibex-ram's horns (on her head): *lohacarmavatī cāpi sāgnih sahuḍaśṛṅgikā* (*Mahabharata* 03.016.008c).

It was usual in the Harappa culture to add horns to any animals' head. For example, Kenoyer reports an elephant with horns found in one of the clay-tag impressions of the Kalibangan seals: "At the site of Kalibangan, a clay tag was found impressed by a seal that has an elephant with the horns of a bull" (Kenoyer, J.M. 1998:88). Adding horn to elephant was done in this case to add divine status to the elephant, which possibly was the *airavata* in this case.

Horse in the Vedic India and its philology

The horse was slaughtered and cooked for food during the *Rig-Vedic* age (*RV* 1.162.6, 12, 13). There is clear mention of the wild horses (*RV* 8.17.15; Griffith) in the *Rig-Veda*. Hence we can date the *Rig-Veda* to the early Holocene when the wild horse lived in northwest India. It is known that the Indian wild horse (*sivalensis*) became extinct from the wild existence soon after early Holocene. Our study dates the *Rig-Veda* to the early Holocene by other parameters too. Horse can survive in the open thin forests intermingled with the grasslands, but cannot in the dense closed forests, where it would be predated and devoured by the carnivores owing to impedance in the escape velocity caused by the obstructing trees. The *Rig-Vedic* time was a semi-arid period in the early Holocene having lots of grassland, semi-deserts and open forests wherein horse could live happily.

The *Rig-Veda* mentions horses sent to the people as gift by the God Indra (*RV* 6.44.12; 6.47.22; 6.53.10). The gift means herds of wild horses, which would be captured by the people of the *Rig-Veda*. Horses have been described in herd of hundreds, and at one place sixty thousand, which might have been large wild herds (*RV* 8.46.22; 8.1.9; 1.103.5; 1.184.3; 4.16.11; 5.36.6).

This is consistent with our finding that the *Rig-Veda* belongs to the early Holocene. The *Yajur-Veda* belongs to the mid-Holocene Optimum, whichwas a time of dense afforestation for the northwest India. Hence the mention of the horse in the *Yajur-Veda* should be considered exclusive to the domestic horse, because the forest ecosystem surrounding the region must have extincted all the wild horses. In fact the *Yajur-Veda* does not mention any wild or feral horse.

The word for desert or grassland was *araṇya* in the *Rig-Veda*, in which the horses ran and lived (*RV* 1.163.11). This meaning has survived in the place-name "*Runn* (short form of *araṇya*) of Kutch" where a species of wild ass '*ghur*' is still found. The dwelling huts and pits were often surrounded by the grasslands in the *Rig-Vedic* times. In the expression *amā cainaṃ araṇye* (at home or in the grassland; *RV* 6.24.10), the the word *araṇya* means the grasslands located just 'outside' the homes. However it is likely that the same landscape got filled with forests, and then the meaning of the word *araṇya* got changed to 'forest' during the mid-Holocene Optimum.

Harappa and Mohenjo-Daro, being surrounded by the dense forests, must have lacked the wild horses. Most of the domesticated horses must have been slaughtered in the horse-sacrifices and the horse-burials by the time of the Mature Harappa. That is why there is a paucity of horse in Harappa archaeology and only a few horse bones have been found from the Harappan archaeology like Mohenjo-daro (Marshall 1931:653-4), Surkotada (Bokonyi) and Shikarpur (U. Singh). Its association with the burial rites attached stigma of bad omen to this animal. Hence it was not depicted over the Harappan seals, except in a modified horned form (unicorn) in association with the sacrificial bowl. If at all some wild horses had survived in India during the mid-Holocene Optimum, they must have done so in the Himalayan mountains. However, they too must have got captured and domesticated by the mature Harappan times. Thus we find today many native domestic horse breeds of Himalayan origins namely Manipuri, Bhutia, Zanskari etc, which are light bodied typical *Sivalensis* horses.

The Indian wild ass *Equus hemionus* (*gardabha*) has been mentioned in the *Rig-Veda*, *Yajur-Veda* and *Atharva-Veda*. The Sanskrit word *gardabha* is Indo-European in origin and its reconstructed PIE form is **gordebhos* (Mallory and Adams 1997:33,35). In Tocharian B cognate is *kercapo*, indicating that the original meaning was 'onager' or *hemionus* and not the donkey or *E. asinus* which came to these regions very late (*ibid*). The name was borrowed into the Nuzi (Akkadian) language: *šintarpu* (donkey, Black 2000:375; *k>s* change). This name was thrust on to the donkey when this animal reached India from Africa, precisely because the two look very similar to each other. There is archaeological evidence of the presence of the onager in the domestic form in Mesopotamia about 2000 BC.

The words English 'ass', Hittite *anše*, Latin *asinus*, Mycedonian *o-no*, Greek *onos*, Slovanian *osol* etc are not Indo-European but are borrowings from Mesopotamian vocabulary for onager like Sumerian *anšu*, Hebrew *athon* (Mallory and Adams 1997:34). It means that on reaching Turkey and Europe, the Indo-Europeans had lost their original word for onager, and later they borrowed the words which today mean 'donkey' in the European languages only during the late Bronze Age from the Semitic languages of West Asia.

Other words used for this animal or its other sub-species in the several Indo-European languages are: Sanskrit *khara* (donkey), Gujarati *ghur*, *khur* (wild ass), Gypsi *ḳăr, kari, xari* (donkey), Kashmiri *khar,* Marathi *khar,* Sindhi *kharu* (donkey, ass), Bashgali (Indo-Aryan of Pakistan) *kurē* (onager, donkey; Konow 2001:149), Kohistani i.e. Dardic-Indo-Aryan *xar* (donkey; Zoller 2005:131; CDIAL 3818); Tocharian B *khare* (onegar, ?donkey; Adams 1999:244); Persian *gur, goor* (donkey), Kurdish *ker* (donkey). Thus the cognates with meaning 'donkey' or 'onager' have been preserved in Indo-Aryan, Iranian and Tocharian branches, and in Latin with change of meaning to "running'.

It is certainly the Indo-European name of the ass. These words prototype of which is *khara* were lost from the Indo-European tongues of Europe when the Indo-Europeans arrived into Europe except Latin *currere* ('to run'). This linguistic finding means that the *hemions* were a part of the original Indo-European fauna and these animals were not present in Europe when the Indo-Europeans arrived there for the first time. These wild asses are characteristically Asian animals, and the philological evidence suggests that the Indo-European originated in Asia, where the *Equus hemionus* too lived.

Philology of horse:

Most of the European branches of the Indo-European languages are poor in cognate words of *ek(w)a.* This seriously erodes their claims for being the first domesticators of the horse. These languages show loss of the word or the meaning or both. Often they have retained only a very remote semantic connection with horse. Thus, in the Germanic branch, apart from the Old English *eoh* 'horse', the Gothic *aihwa-* occurs only as the compound word *aihwatundi* 'the herb bramble, prickly bush'[15] and the Old Saxon *ehu-* is found only as a compound word in *ehu-scalc* 'stable-keeper' (Lehmann:15).

---

15 It has been claimed that 'bramble' is a herb which was fed to horse in the past, hence named ***aihwatundi***. However, ***aihwa*** as an independent word meaning 'horse' itself does not exist in Gothic.

The Gaul *epo-* 'horse' also does not occur independently, but as the first part of the compound word *eporedorix* 'horse-(of)-the chariot-(of)-the king' and in the name of the goddess *Epona*. Greek *hippos* is another puzzle, but Mycenaean *iqe-/iqo-* and dialectical *ikko-* are clearly enough related to PIE **aqva* (Kazanas, personal communication).

The Baltic languages have: Old Prussian *ašva, ešva* 'mare', *aswinan* 'army, mare's milk', Old Lithuanian *ašvíenis* 'stallion' and Lithuanian family-name *Ašvine* and *Ašva*. However, in the languages of the steppe—the so called home of the horse—no cognate of the word *akwa* (horse) exists. The Old Church Slavic *ehu-* may in fact be a borrowing from the Germanic (OS *ehu-*), and in reality no cognate of *ek(w)a* exists in the Slavic. This is a severe blow to the steppe's claim of the homeland status.

Lehmann remarks that "phonological difficulties may point to borrowing introduced when the horse became known to the Indo-Europeans through an unidentified steppe people." (*ibid*). Moreover "p" in these words may have come from the Iranian *aspa* (< Indian *aśva*), and the loss of "s" may have occurred rather than the claimed k>p mutation in the formation of the words like *hippo-*, *epo-* etc. Probably in *hippo-*, the Iranian "s" has changed to "h": *asva* > *aspa* >**ahpa* > *hippo*. Thus the mutation is v >>> p. Similarly, Latin *Equus* may be derived from the Persian *aqva, ākẖẉur* (horse); but the ś/q correspondence is common enough.

However in the cases of the Indian and the Iranian languages, we do not find any phonological difficulty happening. We can also say that the domestic horse was lost from the lives and therefore vocabulary of the Indo-Europeans on arriving at Anatolia (Hittite) and the steppe (Slavic) because the domestic horse was not there.

This is obvious from the discussion that the original inhabitants of the steppe had some other language in place when the Indo-European arrived there. Hence, after settling in the steppe, the proto-Slavic branch borrowed the word for the horse (*konj*) from the substratum or the pre-IE language of the region. That is why the Slavic word for horse *konj* is not found in any other branch of Indo-European (Kazanas 2009:36, 117), except a stray -*konj* in a compound word meaning footwear in Albanian.

However, Pokorny preferred to claim *konj* to be of PIE origin. He reconstructed the PIE **kab-n-io-* and listed as its cognates the following: Ukrainian *kin'*, Old Church Slavonic *kon"ъ*, Russian *kon"*, Czech *kůň*, *koně*, Slovak *kôň*, *koňa*, Polish *koń*, Serbo-Croatian *kòńj*, Slovene *kònj*, all meaning 'horse' (Pokorny:301-302). But the presence of this word only in Slavic does not warrant IE origins!

Pokorny claimed that the Italic words for horse like the Italian *cavallo* and Spanish *caballo* too are from the PIE PIE **kab-n-io-* and are cognates of the Slavic *konj*. However, this is unique and suggested only for the occasion! *Cavallo, caballo* and the Irish *capall* (all meaning horse) may be related to the Sanskrit word *kapila* (brown-red animal; ant, horse, ape), and needs a re-examination. In a nutshell we can say that the Slavic languages do not show evidence of early contact with the domestic horse, and the PIE root-word **aqva* is completely absent from the Slavic languages. This indicates late acquaintance with the domestic horse after having remained away from the homeland for a few millennia.

The cognate word for PIE **aqva* or **ek(w)a-* (horse) is not found in any of the languages of the ancient Anatolia either *e.g.* the Hittite (Kazanas 2009:174). Most importantly, West Asia did not have horse until 2000 BCE, although there were domestic donkeys in Levant at about 4,000 BCE and domestic onegar at Ur at about 3,000-2,600 BCE (Sherrat 1983, quoted in Barker 1985:33; Renfrew 1990:201).

The PIE root-word for horse *eḱ u̯o-s* (Pokorny:301-302) has been derived from another PIE root *ak^{w}ā-*, *ək^{w}ā* or *ēk^w-* ('water, river, sea', Pokorny:23). Starostin (p. 824) thinks that the horses were sacrificed to the sea-god (for navigational safely), hence they got named after "water". This may be true for the early Indus people. However, sacrifices evolved in civilizations much later than the languages, and the words for animals like horse must have been coined much earlier than any sacrificial rituals came into practice.

The derivation *ek̂ u̯o-s* (horse) from *akʷā* (water) cannot be explained unless we take into account the *Rig-Vedic* descriptions of origin of the horse from the ocean. *Rig-Veda* 1.163 (*Hymns for the Horse*) says:

> 1.163.1: What time, first springing into life, thou neighedst, proceeding from the sea or upper waters, Limbs of the deer hadst thou, and eagle pinions. O Steed, thy birth is nigh and must be lauded.
>
> 1.163.4: Three bonds, they say, thou hast in heaven that bind thee, three in the waters, three within the ocean. To me thou seernest Varuna, O Courser, there where they say is thy sublimest birth-place.

The abode of Varuna, the God of waters, is in the Arabian Sea. The foregoing is a picturesque description of retreating horses from the submerging coasts of the Gulf of Cambay in the Arabian Sea following the sea-level rise after the LGM. Just after the Last Glacial Maximum, about 16,000 years back, the sea-level started rising, forcing the coastal fauna, which included the wild horse, into mainland. The process continued up to the early Holocene. It may be noted that the horse does not want to live in dense forests (Linlater), and it must have lived in the coasts in large numbers in India. Possibly this would have given impression to the people at that time that the horses were coming out of the sea.

The Domestication of Horse

It has been proved from the scientific (DNA) studies that the steppe-horse or the Przewalskii is not the ancestor of the domestic horse, and is only very remotely related to the domestic horse. The other blow to Aryan-Horse-Steppe theory came from archaeology. The

Mohenjo-Daro excavations recorded that the horse was present in the mature Harappa (Marshall 1931:653-4). From Chanhudaro, Harappa, Surkotada and Kayatha too horse bones were found from the third millennium BC layer, predating the antiquity of the 2000 BC the date of the oldest steppe horse.

The popularity of the steppe theory owes itself to the Kurgan Hypothesis of Gimbutas (1956) which was supported later by Mallory (1989) who noted and emphasized the combined findings of horse and the Aryan cultural features in the steppe. Since then, 'the steppe origin of the Indo-Europeans' has become the mainstream hypothesis of the Indo-European origin. In this hypothesis the Indo-Iranian language had split from the rest of the Indo-European in the steppe itself, lived there in the form of Andronovo etc cultures, and then migrated south to reach the northern Iran and thence to India.

Was the wild steppe horse ever domesticated? Archaeology and DNA

Sir William Ridgeway had noted on anatomical grounds that the Przewalskii was not the ancestor of the caballus horses (1905:425). Further than this the US Bureau of Animal Husbandry noted in its Report (1910:165) that the modern horse had come from many sources: "But notwithstanding the absence of well preserved skulls it has been possible by making use of the new methods to obtain a considerable amount of evidence that **the domestic horses had a multiple origin, that they include amongst their ancestors not only varieties allied to the wild horse which still survives in Mongolia, and varieties adapted for a forest life, but also varieties specialized for ranging over boundless deserts and plateaus, and for living amongst foothills and upland valleys.**" (emphasis added). The contribution of the horse genes from many regions in the domestication of horse has been proved, yet any contribution from the steppe-horse has not been supported by these DNA studies of the caballus and the Przewalskii horses (Jansen 2002; Bowling 2003; Wade 2009; Cai 2009:481; Achilli 2011).

The official position in science is that the steppe horse *Equus przewalskii* has different chromosome number, and that has not been found in any domestic horse and hence it is an entirely different species (Oakenfull 2000; Clark 2006) from which the modern caballus horse could not have descended.

Confirming the non-domesticablility of the Przewalskii horse, Jansen *et al* (2002:10910) noted, "Modern breeding of the wild Przewalski's horse initially encountered problems such as pacing, excessive aggression, impotence, and infanticide, leading the Przewalski's horse to the brink of extinction. The Przewalski's horse is not ancestral to domestic horses, but if their wild ancestors were similarly intractable, it is unlikely that the technique was mastered many times independently during prehistory. The ease of domestic horse breeding today may be the genetic consequence of selections of particularly amenable beasts some thousands of years ago."

It can be proposed that the true horse might have lived along with the Przewalskii in the steppe. But that imagination is not allowed. The non-Przewalskii horse could not have lived along with the Przewalskii in the steppe because of the Gause's Law of Competitive Exclusion, which states: "No two species can equally and successfully occupy the same niche in the same habitat at the same time." With time one species completely eliminates the other by competition. Hence all the horse bones recovered from the steppe must be considered those of the wild Przewalski. This view is consistent with Levine's findings too; and the bones with evidence of domestication must be considered imported from outside into the steppe-region.

None of the archaeological claims made so far for the presence of the domestic horse in the steppe have been uncontestable. Outram (2009) found evidence of mare's milk on pottery at Botai. It does not necessarily mean evidence of domestication. It was easy to capture a Przewalskii full-term pregnant mare, keep her captive through delivery, then use her milk for some time before slaughter. For the domestication status of any animal there should be complete package of evidence, not just a stray finding.

The Botai horse examined by Outram was indeed an import from outside, as Outram noted: "Metrical analysis of horse metacarpals shows that Botai horses resemble Bronze Age domestic horses rather than Palaeolithic wild horses from the same region." Other studies too have shown that metrically, the Bronze Age and later domestic horses of Eurasia resembled the European and Indian fossil horses (*stenonis, sivalensis etc*), but not with the steppe horse.

The ancient DNA study of the domestic horse remains from the Scythian Period found within the steppe proved that they all had been imported from outside regions like Anatolia, China etc (Keyser-Tracqui 2005). None of the thirteen such DNAs matched the DNA of today's horse breeds from Central Asian, steppe and other neighbouring region such as Yakut, Mongolian, Akhal Teke (Turkmenistan) horses, or the Pleistocene horse from northeast Asia, which are generally conjectured as the close relatives of the ancient steppe horse.

These Scythian Era DNAs did not form a single cluster. If they had been locally domesticated within in the steppe or its vicinity, then they should have formed a single cluster. The study revealed that the DNAs had come from six different clades of Vila. "No clear geographical affiliation of the specimens studied was thus determined", they noted.

These DNA findings are consistent with the archaeological finding from the Scythian era that the domestic horse of the south Ural region (Siberia; *e.g.* Rostovka, Preobrazhenka, Samus' IV etc) came from Central Asia at about 1300 BCE (Kuz'mina and Mallory 2007:200). In our study, we surmise that these horses had reached Central Asia from further south like Iran and India, and not from north to south. It is consistent with Warmuth's DNA study which found that the no horse migration from north to south took place in Eurasia (2012b:7).

DNA-matching of the ancient Scythian Era domestic horses of the steppe with the DNAs of the modern Chinese breeds revealed two matches with the Chinese Guanzhong and Tuva horses located in the northeast and northwest of China respectively. On the other hand, in a similar study of horse DNA from ancient horse remains found from China showed 75% of Chinese horses (from 2000 BCE and later) had same DNA as those found from earlier periods, implying their local domestication from the pre-existing wild Chinese horse (Cai 2009:481). The remaining 25% DNAs of post-2000 BCE were new arrivals from outside, but not from the steppe. The conclusion is that the 75% of the late Bronze Age horses of China had been domesticated locally from the wild Chinese horses, and they had contributed to the steppe domestic horse population too; however, none of the Late Bronze Age domestic horses of the steppe had any local ancestry from the wild steppe horse.

Similar DNA study of ancient horse remains from Iberian Peninsula (Spain) revealed many of the modern Spanish lineages had been present throughout the early Neolithic, Copper Age, Bronze Age and Iron Age, indicating a local domestication within the Iberian Peninsula itself from the local wild horse population (Warmuth 2011). Cieslak found that the domestic horse's DNA lineages B, H1 and J originated from within the Iberian Peninsula and were domesticated probably during the Copper/Bronze Age. However, some East/Southeast Asian lineages (namely A, D2, X4a) were too present in Iberia at the Bronze Age indicating an early arrival of some domestic horses from outside from the south-east Eurasia possibly through North Africa and India (Cieslak 2010:3). In our view, horse migration from Southeast Asia to the Iberian Peninsula necessarily involved passing through South Asia under a state of domestication.

Cieslak found that all the regions of Eurasia had local Pleistocene horse DNAs preserved in continuity into the modern primitive breeds of the regions. The steppe region, however, was the only exception in this respect which showed no such continuity of lineages in Cieslak's study.

His has been supported from the DNA study of the second millennium BCE remains of horse from the steppe (*supra*).

Warmuth (2011:4 pdf, Fig 1B) noted that apart from Iberia, the other likely site of the first domestication of horse was the region of Iran south of the Caspian Sea (the Caspian breed). The study was not extended to the further east and had not included India and China. However the study noted (p. 4, Fig 1C) that desert conditions prevailed in the south Caspian region of Iran before 4,000 BCE. Horse cannot survive in the desert. That means the Caspian horse was domesticated in north Iran only after it had reached there from somewhere else in the wild form when the desert-like condition of the region improved after 4000 BC. One source of such arrival into Iran, in our view, could have been South Asia.

Study of the autosomal genes by Warmuth (2012b:7pdf) demonstrated that there was a general migration of the true horse from east to west before domestication. However, horses of Lithuania and Kazakhstan showed evidence of recent arrival from the East, implying import after domestication. This fact about Kazakhstan militates against Central Asia having been a place of domestication of horse.

The study (2012b:7) ruled out any migration of horse from north to south: "There was no significant correlation between genetic diversity and latitude, despite written accounts documenting a continued flux of horses from the steppe lands in the north into both India and much of China (Gommans 1994)" (Warmuth 2012b:7pdf). This finding rules out the common conjecture that the horse arrived into Iran and India from north.

DNA study of living Greek horses revealed that many of them (Crete, Pindos and Pinias breeds) had arrived there from the Middle East route, and not from Ukraine/East Europe route (Bömcke 2010:7/9pdf). This too goes against the domestication of the horse in the steppe, and is consistent with the arrival of the horse from Iran and India to Middle East and from there to Southeast Europe.

Hence the steppe region of today was not the source of the horse populations for Central Asia, China, India, Iran, Greece and Spain--we can say from the above studies. The study by Warmuth (2012b:5,Table 1) also showed that Ukraine, Kalmykia (Russia) and Kyzilorda (Kazakhstan) of the steppe had no private or unique alleles, while other regions like Jammu (India), Yunnan (Southwest China adjoining northeast India) and Naryn (Kyrgyzstan not far from the northern reaches of India) had many unique alleles each indicating local evolution in these areas.[16] Thus Kyrgyzstan, located immediately to the north of Pamir, was the only place north of the Indo-Iranian plains where we find any evidence of *in-situ* horse domestication. No place to the further north, including Ukraine, Kazakhstan, Mongolia and Siberia has any DNA evidence of local domestication of horse.

This reflects that Ukraine and the other steppe regions possibly had received all their domestic horse DNAs from outside, while Jammu, Kyrgyzstan and Yunnan—the regions adjoining the Himalayas where *sivalensis*, the Indian wild horse once prevailed--had local domestication of horse. Considering facts from every angle it becomes obvious that the steppe origin of horse domestication cannot be sustained any more, and it was an academic hoax.

The Multiple Primary Domestication events of Horse:

Necessarily associating the horse domestication with the Aryans was the most unfortunate event of historiography. The DNA studies revealed that horse had not been domesticated only at one or a few places, but at seventy seven places throughout Eurasia, and can be grouped into seventeen DNA types (Jansen, 2002; Vila, 2001; Lippold 2011a; Cieslak 2010). Lippold (2011b) noted that the DNA remains of the wild horse from ancient Siberia, Alaska and Yukon proved that

16 Number of private alleles: Whole of Europe 3; Whole of Kazakhstan 2; Kyrgyzstan 5; Xinjiang 5; India (only Jammu district) 4; Altai 2; Mongolia 2; Yunnan (Southeast Asia, politically part of Republic of China) 3.

they all belonged to the Przewalskii, and it is enough to prove that the caballus horse had not lived there in the wild then. Lippold also found that all the ancient remains of horse with features of domestication (dated 800 BCE) belong to the non-Przewalskii type of DNA, clearly indicating the arrival of the domestic horse from outside the range of the Przewalskii horse.

All the regions of Eurasia other than Mongolia, Siberia and the steppe at the Bronze Age had domestic horses which had been locally captured (Kavar 2008). Clearly Siberia, Mongolia (and North America and steppe) were the regions where ancient domestic horses had been imported from outside, and not locally domesticated.

Lindgren (2004) and Lau (2009) found (DNA study) that although wild mares had been recruited from all over Eurasia, yet on the male side there were only one or just a few stallions. It was also confirmed that none of the male progenitors was the steppe or Central Asian Przewalskii stallion (Lindgren:336). In our opinion this progenitor stallion could have been from the *sivalensis* stock (*vide infra*).

DNA studies found that some northwest European domestic ponies namely the Fjord, Icelandic and Shetland ponies have a single cluster of DNA, which originated very early just after the Late Glacial period (about 10,000 BCE; Jansen:10908). Achilli (2011) found one lineage of European horse (haplogroup L) was domesticated in Europe from where it seems to have spread to Middle East and Asia.

Study of DNA recovered from the Neolithic and Bronze Age horse bones showed that many of the extant European lineages had already been there at those times, and some even during the late Pleistocene (Achilli 2011:3-4 pdf; Cieslak 2010:3; Lira 2012). In fact at least one lineage of modern domestic horse Lusitani Group C had been domesticated quite early, possibly during the Neolithic period itself (Lira 2009). The haplogroup D lineage, which is the most prominent lineage of Iberia, arrived here only during the Bronze Age. Another study found that at least one breed of horse had been domesticated in Spain much before

Indo-European linguistic arrival to the area (Achilli *et al* 2011:4 pdf). Solis (2005) showed many horse breeds of the Iberian Peninsula are autochthonous and have been domesticated locally in Europe itself (Solis: 677). The study by Royo noted common DNA motifs in Iberian and Barb (North African) horses, which is consistent with our view that the late Bronze Age arrivals of the domestic horse to Iberia took place through North Africa. These studies rule out the association of the European horse with the Indo-European culture.

A recent study by Devi (2013) revealed that the 59 Indian horse samples studied carried 35 haplotypes, which gives one of the highest index of genetic diversity in the word. Such figure is consistent with the oldest horse domestication event having taken place in India. A total of seven major mtDNA haplogroups (A–G) was identified in the Indian horse breeds that indicated the abundance of mtDNA diversity. The haplogroup D constituted 33% of Indian horse breeds. The Manipuri breed of horse comes from the eastern end of India and it has remained segregated from the other horse breeds of India and outside. It is presumed to be the local descendant of the Wild Asiatic Horse. However, it was noted that the Manipuri horse showed closest affinity with the various Indian horse breeds as well as the Thoroughbred horse, and not with the Chinese or Central Asian breeds (*ibid*).

Horse statue (three feet tall) dating 7000 BCE was found recently from Asir (Arabia Felix, near Abha, southwest Arabia; Science News, BBC News, Reuters etc). Arabia was not inhabitable by horse during the last glacial owing to cold desert like conditions. Any early Holocene presence of the horse must have been from India, where the *sivalensis* horse had survived the Last Glacial maximum. There is plenty of evidence of Indian migration to the East Arabian coast (human DNA, Underhill 2009:2 and 3; shrew, mice, Duplantier) during late Pleistocene and early Holocene. Evidence from the other regions indicates that the Indian *sivalensis* was domesticated as early as 8,000 BCE. Hence it could have been taken to the Arabian coastal region by the early Holocene migrants.

Climate change and the arrival of the Domestic Horse in Central Asia:

The archaeology of the steppe has confused the archaeologists because the steppe sites contain ancient horse bones which had been hunted for meat, or captured live then sacrificed ritually, and these belonged to the Przewalskii horse which was never domesticated. It is difficult, if not impossible, to make distinction between the Przewalskii and the true-horse bone. There is no evidence to support that any non-Przewalskii horse lived in the steppe about 2000 BCE or earlier.

In spite of the several horse hoaxes raised about the steppe, the recent archaeological studies serious challenge the long held view that steppe was the home of the true horse. The archaeological study done at Begash (Kazakhistan) confirmed in a recent study: "While pastoral herding of sheep and goats is evident from the Early Bronze Age, the horse appears only in small numbers before the end of the first millennium BC" (Frachetti and Benecke 2009: Abstract).

The paper adds the "horse use seems to commence gradually and is not highly associated with early and middle Bronze Age pastoralists." (*ibid*:1025). The authors find, the "**percentages of horse remains at Begash remain below 6 per cent until approximately AD 50 (Phase 3b)**", and "The domestic horse is documented at Begash by the start of the second millennium BC, but its impact on pastoralism is not clear." In our view, such stray domestic horses as ones documented from second millennium Begash, were Bronze Age imports from the further south *i.e.* Iran and northwest India. Challenging the whole hypothesis, Frachetti and Benecke note: "Thus the data from Begash draw into question the general view that Eurasian pastoralism diffused eastward as a result of mounted horsemen in the Bronze Age".

A study at Tentek-sor (northern Caspian, Kazakhstan) revealed that horse bones do not increase between 4000 BCE and 2000 BCE (Koryakova), and the samples did not contain any domestic sheep or cattle, even wild aurochs was only 5% (Frachetti 2012:7; Koryakova

2007). However, after 2000 BCE, we get a very large number of domestic cattle (60 to 90%) in the steppe and Central Asia, indicating the arrival of pastoralism into this region only after 2000 BC (Koryakova:88, 65, 146-147). This indicates that probably all the horse bones from earlier than 2000 BC dates are of the wild horses. Koryakova (p.54) noted "but horse bones are extremely rare in the Kurgans", and "a larger group of specialists share the idea that classical steppe nomadism appeared in the first millennium BCE" (*ibid*:55). This is consistent with the palaeo-climatic studies of Asia too. Earlier than this period there were forests in Central Asia and South Siberia although breaking and fast changing into steppe and desert after 3000 BC. Yet patches of forest would support hunter-gatherer and farming economy. However, it is the total conversion into grassland and desert ecosystem which forces man to adopt the nomad existence. Thus nomadism was not the product of the mood or temperament of the particular nationality, but a geographic-ecological compulsion. It was a niche for man.

The fossil pollen studies from Central Asia, South Siberia, Northern and Western China and other steppe zones have shown that the steppes converted into forests in the early Holocene (8000-6000 BC). Jiang (2006) found that the inner Mongolian steppe changed into birch-pine (*Betula/Pinus*) forest at 10,500 BC-7,200 BC period, and evolved into woodland with these trees dominating at 7,200-4,700 BC period, but reverted back to the steppe after 4,700 BC.

Conversion back to the steppe and desert ecosystems took place at different times in different areas. Many areas remained forest as late as 2000 BC. At Yolin Am steppe (Southern Mongolia), it was found that it was a forest between c. 3600 BC and 2000 BC, and *Betula* (birch) and *Salix* (willow) trees dominated (Miehe 2007:156, Table 1). In general, however, after 3000 BC, more and more of Central Asia converted into steppe and desert (Zhao 2009; Zhao 2008: cited in F. Chen Editorial 2009:1). There was an abrupt change to arid climate at 2500 BC in many regions of China (Zhao 2009: Abstract; Chen, W. 2009). Miehe *et al* noted in their study of the succession of ecologies in the Gobi desert, that birch and willow pollens and charcoal were present in the soil layers up to 3000 BC (calibrated radiocarbon date), however birch became extinct from that site after that time (Miehe 2007:163; 156 Table 1).

Dense forest and desert are the places where horses die. In the dense forest, that harbours tiger, panther etc, horse can be easily predated because it cannot run fast enough in there to escape from the carnivores. Hence in all likelihood, hardly any horse may have lived before 4000 BC in the regions which we know today as the Eurasian steppe.

On the other hand, northwest India became a semi-arid region in about 33,000 BC and continued to be so until the end of the Glacial period (Petraglia 2009). Semi-arid ecosystems consist of deserts and grasslands like savannah, steppe, sahel etc, but no dense forests. The *sivalensis* horse must have found the northwest Indian grasslands as the ideal habitat. This situation lasted up to 6,000 BC, after which the region became moist leading to the growth of dense forests in Northwest India, which was not a friendly ecosystem for the horse. But then, the former Thar Desert evolved into grasslands (Deotare 2004a:Abstract), which stayed so until 2200 BC. Thus horses could have lived conveniently in the Thar between 6,000 BC and 2200 BC.

On the basis of the recent archaeological and palaeo-environmental studies, we are in a position to say that the horse domestication could have been possible in Central Asia and the north Caspian steppe only after 2000 BC. The Bronze Age economy of this region remained mainly cattle and goat dominated and the classical horse based nomadism appeared only in the first millennium BCE after the aridity of the region increased enough to eliminate the possibility of farming-pastoralism.

Section III

Forest Trees of northwest India

Chapter 15

The Golden Willow an extinct ancient Indian tree: References in the Vedic texts

So far many authors have assumed that the climates of India and Europe have remained throughout the Holocene the same as they are today, and that the same plants have always grown in the two regions throughout the Holocene. This thinking has produced a wrong history of India so far and is not correct.

Willow (*Salix* sp; Sanskrit *vetasa*)

Identification:

Although willow does not grow in the Indian plains today, many botanists have identified it in the descriptions contained in the Sanskrit literature. Nambiar and Raveendran (2008:71, Table 1, Sr 139) identified the willow tree (*Salix tetraspermia*) from the description given in the *Amarakosa* of Amarasimha, a Sanskrit text of *circa* fourth century AD.

We find in the Vedas, description of the willow tree at several places. It was known then by the Vedic/ Sanskrit word *vetasa*, the Sanskrit cognate of 'willow'. As per the Vedic accounts the tree had riparian habitat. Its variant with the golden colour was considered particularly important. This means the particular species was the golden willow or *Salix alba*. The Vedas also mention the medicinal properties of the plant. The plant was used mainly to treat fever and pain. In modern terminology it was analgesic and antipyretic, with anti-inflammatory properties. Such description confirms that the Vedic plant *vetasa* is nothing other than the willow tree (*Salix*) which contains in it the salicylic acid which is a well-known fever-lowering and pain-relieving drug.

The crude willow-extract called salicin contains both quinine and salicylic acid (Brittain 1846:152). Quinine is a strong anti-malarial medicine and the both must have acted in unison in bringing about the cure of the febrile illnesses particularly these caused by malaria, which must have been very common during the wetter times of the northwest Indian plains. Salicin is also found in the *Populus* tree which too like the willow belongs to the same plant family *Salicaceae* and was found in the Indus region before 4000 BC (Jarrige).

From Mehrgarh sites of the Indus plain, willow (*Salix*) pollen have been found in abundance since the very beginning of the Holocene, and up to the fourth millennium BC (Jarrige). Absence of the willow pollen beyond that time means that the tree became either extremely rare or extinct from the Indus Valley soon after the early Harappa period. However the willow species continued to grow in the Himalayan altitudes like Nepal, Kashmir and higher reaches of Pakistan and Afghanistan. With the loss of the tree in the plains, the later Indo-Aryan cognates of the word *vetasa* such as *bent* etc were often applied to mean the *Calamus rotang*, which too is a flexible woody tree. However many of the north Indian languages have retained the meaning 'willow'.

Willow, although generally a temperate region plant, has many species which grow only in the South Asia (*e.g. Salix tetraspermia*)[17]. Willows characteristically require wetlands, particularly the alluvial or riparian ones-- however very humid climate is not needed and 20 to 45 centimeters of annual rainfall is enough. The alluvial and riverine features being absent from the steppes, the willows are not found in the steppe. However, some willow trees grow in the mountains located within the steppes where the annual rainfall is from 20 to 45 centimetres (Zhao:246, Table 2; Miehe:151).

Paleoclimate records of effective moisture (precipitation minus evaporation, or P- E) show a dry (low effective moisture) period in mid-latitude arid/semi-arid central Asia during the early Holocene (11,000-8,000 years ago) relative to the middle and late Holocene, in contrast to evidence for greater-than-present precipitation at the same time in the south and east Asian monsoonal areas (Liya 2012).

However Central Asia had plenty of willow (*Salix*) forest at the early Holocene. Cermac *et al* noted "All evidence collected about the three *Betula-Salix* forest islands of the Govi Altay supports the hypothesis that today's isolated forests are the last remnants of a former forest belt spanning the entire Govi Altay. Charcoal findings and floristic evidence link the present-day forest islands to periods past." (p. 269). The early Holocene steppes converted into forests for some millennia, when the willow tree grew there. Willow (*Salix*) pollen was found from Gobi desert-steppe soils dating 3000 BC (Miehe:156, Table 1) but not after that.

From our knowledge of the past climates we can say that the willow was not found in the steppe at late Bronze Age, say 1500 BC, the alleged time of Indo-European migration into India. This fact frustrates the possibility of the steppe being the homeland of the Indo-European speakers, because it has been settled (from philology) that the willow

---

17 http://www.efloras.org/florataxon.aspx?flora_id=5&taxon_id=200005744 accessed 28 May 2013.

tree was certainly found in the Indo-European homeland (Witzel, *vide infra*). If the Homeland was in the steppe, then the date of migration of the Indo-Aryan to India cannot be after 4000 BC, if we trust the palynological data of willow from the steppe. However in that case then the whole of the Indus Civilization will have to be accepted as the Vedic Civilization. This fact too thus frustrates the ethnocentric designs of the Eurocentric authors.

Golden willow (*Salix alba*), a plant mentioned in the Vedic literature (*hiraṇyamaya vetasa*) and found till today in the northern reaches of South Asia, requires a soil of the type "deep, moist loams", usually located along stream beds and wetlands and cannot tolerate prolonged drought.[18] The loam retains moisture and is a mixture of sand, silt and clay, which is the characteristic soil type of the wetter regions of the Indus-Sarasvati valley civilisation, not a feature of the steppe or the Central Asia. Willow grows along the rivers and ponds. The dry climate of the steppe and of the Gobi Desert was thoroughly hostile to the growth of the willow tree. The knowledge of the original IE speakers about willow rules out the steppe from being the homeland of the Indo-Europeans at 1500 BC, and implies that the homeland was in a wetter region and there too they lived at an older colder time (*vide infra*).

The ecological habitat needed for the golden willow matches well with that described for the Vedic *vetasa* tree. For example the *Taittiriya Samhita* (*Yajur-Veda*) mentions that the *vetasa* plant grew in the wetlands: *apsujo vetasah* (*TS* 5.3.12.2). *Atharva-Veda* (10.7.41) mentions that the golden *vetasa* grows amid floods. Again the *Atharva-Veda* (18.3.5) mentions that the rivers love *vetasa* (*upadyāmupa vetasamsvattaro nadīnām*). It is possible that the Vedic river *Vitastā* (Kashmiri *Vyeth*, Hindi Jhelum) too was named after this plant. On the other hand the word used to mean the 'reed' in the *Atahrva Veda* is *naḍa* or *nāḍa* (*Atahrva-Veda* 12.2.50 etc),

18 Goden Willow http://www.ag.ndsu.edu/trees/handbook/th-3-139.pdf, accessed 30 May 2013.

which is an Indo-European word and is the cognate word of PIE *nedo* ('reed'; Pokorny:759).

This date corroborates well with the palynological evidence for the presence of the willow tree (*Salix*) which is the recovery of the abundant fossil pollen from the soils of that region dating back to 7,000-5000 BC (Costantini 2008:171-2). In 1997, an extensive palynological examination of Mehrgarh and Nausharo of the Indus Valley region was conducted by Lorenzo Costantini and Alessandro Lentini (2000, cited by Jarrige 2008). Jarrige citing that work, notes, "The results of the pollen analysis show that, from the beginning of the Mehrgarh occupation till the 4th millennium BC, 'the region was probably dominated by a semilacustrine or humid environment with a riparian vegetation, characterized by *Populus*, *Salix*, *Fraxinus*, *Ulmus* and *Vitis*, associated in a typical hydrophytic complex, arranged in dense gallery forests'." (Jarrige 2008:151).

In a similar study conducted in Jammu, willow (*Salix*) pollens were found from the soil layer dating back to 7500-5700 BC (Trivedi and Chauhan 2009:406-8). They were found in continuity in the layer of 2000 BC to 150 BC (*ibid*:407). The work noted its continued presence in the region from then till date (*ibid*:403, 407, 410).

Other cold climate forest trees which existed until the fourth millennium in the Indus Valley region included *Populus* (poplar), *Fraxinus* (Ash Tree), *Ulmus* (elm), *Vitis* (grape), *Abies, Picea, Tsuga, Pinus, Juniperus, Quercus, Tilia* and *Corylus*. Hydrophytic plants included *Cyperaceae, Phragmites, Typha, Alisma, Myriophyllum,* and *Nymphea* (Jarrige 2008:139; Costantini 2008:172). Along with these Peregrine mentions the presence of *Cedrus* (cedar) and *Betula* (birch) between 5500-2600 BC in the northwest Indus Valley (2002:118).

Costantini noted the evidence for the ancient presence of the oak-forests in the region. There was the evidence for the presence of *Tamarix, Palmae, Smilax* and *Fumaria* in the Mehrgarh periods I and II (*ibid*). Out of these, ones that are found today in the Himalayas, although not in the Indus plains, include *Populus* (poplar), *Salix* (willow), *Abies* (fir), *Juniperus*, *Corylus* (Himalayan hazel) etc.

We have noted that the Old Indo-Aryan cognate word for 'willow' is *vetasa* (Pokorny:1120-22). However there has been an element of confusion among the European Indologists and philologists about the Indian willow tree, none of whom had any study of either the present or the past flora of India. Griffith who translated the Vedas and Pokorny, the author of Indo-European dictionary thought that the Vedic *vetasa* was one of the 'grass-reeds' which are in the family Gramineae or Poaceae. However the grass-reeds are not known by the name *bent* (or by any other cognate of *vetasa*, *vēta*, *vētra*) in any Indian language. All the cognates of Sanskrit *vēta* surviving till date mean 'willow' (CDIAL 12097). Cognates of Sanskrit *vētra* and *vētasa* mean either the willow or the cane (*Calamus rotang*) in the modern Indo-Aryan languages (CDIAL 12101 & 12099). Thus the use of word 'grass-reed' as the translation of *vētasa* etc by Griffith and other translators of the Vedas is unreasonable.

Similarly Monier-Williams, author of the Sanskrit dictionary, thought that *vetasa* or *vetra* was the Asian furniture-reed *Calamus rotang* (rattan palm, cane-reed), which is a climber found in Sri Lanka, South India, Assam, Southeast Asia and West Asia, and which belongs to an entirely different family *Arecales*. Witzel opted for this view.

The *Ayurvedic Pharmacopoeia of India* lists *vetasa* as *Salix* (p. 169) and *vetra* as *Calamus*. Khare too holds the same view (Khare 2007:110-111). *Calamus rotang* is not found in north/ northwest India (*ibid.*:110). Loon prefers to use the untranslated words *vetasa* and *vetra* in his English edition of the *Charaka Samhita* (Loon:427, 428, 500 etc) and does not use *Calamus* for either of them, which in his view is *vaca* in Sanskrit (*ibid*:428).

The confusion was created and spread by the misleading writings of Eurocentric authors like Witzel who falsely claimed that willow is not found in India, nor was it found there when the Aryans arrived. The

Aryans thrust the name *vetasa* on to the 'reeds', after finding no willow tree in northwest India. None of these claims can be substantiated by archaeo-botanical studies. It is interesting to see what Witzel wrote (Witzel 2005:373):

> "Some of them [names of the plants] therefore exhibit a slight change in meaning; a few others possibly are applications of old, temperate zone names to newly encountered plants, such as 'willow'> 'reed, cane'. Again, this change in meaning indicates the path of the migration, from the temperate zone *into* India" (box bracket added).

He again wrote (2009 Fulltext:5 n32),

> "In addition to the birch, the IE word for ... 'willow' [may be found] in *vetasa* > '*Calamus rotang*' (*EWA* II 578), if so, then both with change of meaning in the Indian climatic context" (box bracket added).

Today, at least 40 species of willow (*Salix*) are native to northwest India (Pakistan), Nepal, Kashmir and many other high altitude regions of north India zone, in over and above the species of willow present in Afghanistan.[19] Many species such as *Salix tetraspermia* are found exclusively in India. In the pre-history too, willow, particularly the "golden willow" (*i.e. Salix alba* and *S. babylonica*; Taylor:124, cited by Roth:289) was native specifically to the northwest India. It is

[19] http://www.efloras.org/browse.aspx?flora_id=110&name_str=salix&btnSearch=Search
http://www.efloras.org/florataxon.aspx?flora_id=110&taxon_id=129059
http://www.efloras.org/browse.aspx?flora_id=5&name_str=salix&btnSearch=Search
http://www.efloras.org/florataxon.aspx?flora_id=5&taxon_id=129059
All accessed 28 May 2013

noteworthy that the *Salix babylonica* is found in Jammu till date (Trivedi and Chauhan:403). However, we do not get evidence of the willow in the Indus plains anytime after 4000 BC (Costantiny 2008) or the latest 3000 BC (Jarrige 2008). Hence the dates of composition of the *Rig-Veda* and the *Taittiriya Samhita* (*Yajur-veda*) cannot be later than this time.

The Vedic Description of *Vetasa*

The *Taittiriya Samhita* (5.4.4.2-3) mentions the use of *vetasa* in the context of pain. It is understandable. Because the willow (*Salix*) contains salicylic acid, a remedy for fever and pain used in modern medicine too (Jeffreys 2008). This property of willow was known to the ancient Greek, Egyptian and Indian people. However its rediscovery goes to the credit of Edmund Stone (1763 AD). No such pain relieving property has ever been attributed to the grass-reed or the cane-reed. This fact confirms that the Vedic *vetasa* was nothing else but willow.

Max Muller (1897/2004:308) gives details of the charms associated with making of a medicinal drink from the *vetasa*, which was used to treat a thirsty person with high fever (as described in the *Atharva-Veda*). The drink was made in a cup made of *vetasa* (willow), and was stirred by the branches of *vetasa*. This must have caused the salicylic acid in willow to be dissolved in water, leading to the relief in the symptoms of fever and thirst on drinking the syrup. Max Muller also mentions some other Vedic texts (*viz. TS* 5.6.1.2-4; *Kaushik* 40.1-6; *AV* 3.13) wherein the same process has been described (Muller:308).

All the Vedic accounts of the *vetasa* plant match the description of the willow tree and not that of the cane-reed or the grass reed. The *Rig-Veda* (*RV* 4.58.5) mentions *vetasa* (willow) as the 'golden willow' (*hiraṇyāyo vetaso*). The 'golden willow' or *Salix alba* is found in northwest India even today, and its twigs are exactly like gold in colour.[20]

---

20 Golden Willow in Pakistan: http://www.efloras.org/florataxon.aspx?flora_id=5&taxon_id=200005744

The Vedic *vetasa* could not have been any reed, whether the *Calamus rotang* or the 'grass-reed'. The 'golden reed' (as in the translation by Griffith; *Phragmites australis aurea*) is a grass-reed native to North America and Australia. The grass-reed species that is found in South Asia *Phragmites karka* (Khagra reed) is not golden in colour and is different from the 'golden reed' of America. It does not in any way fit with the description of *vetasa* as described in the Vedic texts. Hence the identification of the golden *vetasa* as the "golden reed" as done by Griffith is wrong.

The habitat of the *vetasa* plant, as we get from the Vedic mantras, is amidst waters. *Rig-Veda* (4.58.5) mentions that the *hiranyayao vetaso* (golden willow) lives along the brook. *Taittiriya Samhita* (5.4.4.2) too says the same thing (*apām va etad puṣpam yad vetasas).*[21] The *Atharva Veda* writes that the *vetasa* plant stays within the waters (10.7.41; 18.3.5). These descriptions of the *vetasa* are consistent with the description of the morphology and the habitat of the 'golden willow', and not that of a reed. They also point out a wet climate in the region where the *Rig-Veda* was composed.

Yajurveda too describes the willow (*vetasa*) at many places. The *Kṛṣṇ-Yajurveda* (or the *Taittiriya Samhita*, 5.4.4.3) mentions the branches of *vetasa* (willow). We know that the grass-reeds do not branch, and it is the willow which has numerous branches. The *Taittiriya Samhita* mentions an eagle sitting in the branches of the 'golden willow' (*hiraṇyayo vetaso, TS* 4.2.9.6). The eagle would prefer to sit in the camouflage of the dense branches of trees like the willow, not in the grass-reed. Hence the meaning of *vetasa* in these contexts is 'willow' not the grass-reed. We have discussed elsewhere the diffance in the treatment of the willow by the different Vedas—while the *Rig-Veda* describes it as something extant, the *Atharva-Veda* describes it a something distant and difficult to be known.

---

21 ***vetas*** (willow) is the flower of the waters. Here the context is that of the golden willow.

Philology of willow: Latin *salix*, English 'willow' and Sanskrit *vetasa*

Witzel relied on the biased Eurocentric philology of *vetasa* given by others, and did not check whether any modern Indo-Aryan language has a cognate word of *vetasa* meaning 'willow'. He as well as Monier-Williams gave the meaning 'cane-reed' for Sanskrit *vetasa*, which was wrong because the later Indo-Aryan derivatives of *vetasa* like *bet*, *bed* etc certainly mean 'willow' in languages like Prakrit, Nepali, Kashmiri and Dardic etc. Michael Witzel is also silent about the origin or etymology of the unique Latin word *salix* (willow). We shall now examine the etymology of *salix* below.

Etymology of Salix, sallow

Lat. *salix* (willow) is a loanword from Germanic (Valpi 1828:415). The cognates are found only in the Celtic and Germanic branches, and that cannot warrant its inclusion as an Indo-European word. Cognates are: M. Irish *sail*, *sa(i)lech*, Welsh *helyg-en*, O. Brit. name *Salico-dūnon*, Gaul. name *Salicilla*; O.H.G. *sal(a)ha*, M.H.G. *salhe*, Ger. *Salweide*; O.E. *sealh*, O.Ice. *selja* (willow, from **salhjōn*). It has been suggested that the source of all these cognates is the Saxon root **sal* meaning 'black' (Valpi:415), and at PIE level **sal* meaning 'salt', 'grey', 'saliva' etc (Pokorny:879). These roots have no specific semantic feature which could be associated with the willow tree, and clearly the etymology suggested is wrong. The sound resemblance between the Saxon *sal*, PIE *sal* and the tree *salix* is only superficial, and gives no idea of the real etymology of the word *salix*.

If we think laterally, we find that, in all probability, the cognate words of *salix* represent an older linguistic substratum of Europe. The Altaic words like Tungus-Manchu **ǯalikta* and Uralic like Finnish *salava*, *jalava* and Hungarian *szilfa* meaning 'elm' are enough evidence to suggest this fact (see Starostin Database).

willow-*vetasa*

The other word which needs etymological discussion is Sanskrit '*vetasa*'. Its other names in Sanskrit are *vidula*[22], *vēta-*, *vētasá* and *vētra*. Its cognates mean willow in Indo-Aryan, Iranian, Germanic, Baltic and Greek branches. However in the Slavic languages of the steppe the cognates of 'willow' do not mean 'willow' but 'branch' and 'twig'. This indicates the absence of the willow in the steppe which is likely because of the very dry climate of the steppe. Hence the Indo-Aryan homeland could not have been the steppe of 1500 BC.

Lith. Inf. *vūti, vytìs* (acc. *vỹtį*; willow rod), ablaut. *žil-vìtis* (grey willow), Ltv. *vīte* (branch, tendril), *vîtuõls* (willow), O.Pruss. *witwan* (willow), *apewitwo* (willow of the river-banks); Old Church Slavonic *větvь* (twig, branch), O.C.S. *viti, vitь* (a loan word from Lith. *vytìs*), Russ. *vítvina* (twig, branch, rod), Sloven. *vitika* (ring); Avestan *vaēiti* (willow, willow-stick); Gk. ἰτέα (*itea*); O.Ice. *vīðir*, O.E. *wīðig*; M.L.G. *wīde*, O.H.G. *wīda* all meaning 'willow' (Pokorny: 1120-1122).

If the Indo-European had originated within Europe in the Ukrainian steppe, how did the cognates of 'willow' like Slavic *vítvina* (twig) and Latin *vitis* (grape-vine) etc lose the real meaning 'willow'? Latin *vitis* does not mean 'willow' but *vine*. Contrasting this, Sanskrit *vēta-*, *vētasá*, *vētra* etc all are cognates to this group of words, and their derivatives mean 'willow' in northern Indo-Aryan languages even today.

Clearly the meaning 'willow' was lost from the southern branch of the IE during transit from India to Southeast Europe through the Iranian route (the southern route of migration; J2b), because there was no willow in Iran during the Holocene. Although willow, which is a riverine tree, may have occurred in northern Iran near the Caspian coasts (Akhani 2010:239), Turkey (Wick 2003:670) and in Syria (Hussein 2006:336), yet it was absent from the arid Iran in general. Even in East

22 *Sushruta Samhita, Uttara-tantra* XLVII.18-19.

Turkey Wick mentions the occurrence of willow (*Salix*) only during 10,750 to 9,630 BC which is before the early Holocene.

Thus the word *vetasa* (willow) lost its real meaning, and acquired the meaning 'grape-vine' which too is very flexible, at the time when the language was passing through Iran in the early Holocene. The grape-vine (*Vitis*) was distributed all the way along India to Turkey through Iran, although willow was not there. Hence the Latin word *vitis* means the grape vine and not the 'willow'.

Vitis has been in the Southwest Asia since the earliest known history (Beck 2005:183). Djamali noted presence of *vitis* pollens in Northwest Iran at about 1500 BC (2009:1372), and its quantity indicated that it was wild. In the northern Zargos mountains of Iran, archaeological evidence of wine making (from the *vitis* plants) has been found dating 5500-5000 BC (Bouby 2013:2). Similar economic exploitation of grapes took place in northern Greece (at Dikil Tash) about 4500-4000 BC (*ibid*), indicating migration of the art of wine making from Iran to North Greece.

It is generally thought by the European scholars that the *soma* of the *Rig-Veda* was not grape, but ephedra. The reason stated is the general belief assuming the absence of grape from ancient India at 1500 BC. However Costantini demonstrated from his fossil pollen studies that the grape (*Vitis*) was found in the northwest India at 7000-5000 BC, the deepest layers of the excavation by him (2008:172). The presence of *vitis* in the region continued certainly up to 4000 BC (*ibid*:173), and possibly up to 3000 BC (Jarrige). But the less known fact is that India has been home of some unique varieties of the wild grapes such as *Ampelocissus indica*, *A. filipes*, *A. barbata* etc which have always been in India at some place or the other through the ages.

Thus we see that during the early Holocene, the grape was available from India to Europe in both of the routes, the northern and the southern. Although the etymology of the Sanskrit word *soma* (grapevine, grape) has not been examined by anyone so far, it is likely that the word *soma* may have survived in the following words of the Balto-Slavic languages: Proto-Balto-Slavic **kama-* (clump); Serb. *kȍm* (grape-vine), Serb. *kȍmina* (pressed grape refuge), Russ. *kom* (clump), Russ. *komúlja* (clump), Proto-Slav **kamli̯a-*; Ltv. *kams* (clump), Lith. *kẽmuras* (grape); Ltv. *kamuolis* (ball), *cę̄mu(o)rs* (grape).

The latest estimate of the date of composing the *Rig-Veda* goes back to before 4000 BC by other authors (Kazanas 2009) and before 5500 BC or 6000 BC by us. From archaeology we know that grape (*Vitis*) was present in India at that time since the early Holocene. In the north Indian masses, traditionally the meaning of the word *soma-rasa* (the juice of *soma*) is understood as wine and spirits. Thus even after the disappearance of grapes from the Indian plains, the folk memory retained its association with wine, which was probably once made in India from the grapes.

Vitis contains in it the chemical resveratrol, which has properties of providing vitality and mental and physical energy. It strengthens the neurones, slows down aging, and prevents disease and fights cancer and death (Jang 2003; Anekonda 2006; Athar 2007; Barger 2008). The properties described of the *soma* in the *Rig-Veda* resemble that of *Vitis*, not ephedra. The latter is in fact very toxic and bad for the health, and is a poison taking away the senses and often life too (Hellar and Beniwits 2000). Some workers report that *Vitis* leaves are useful in the treatment of tuberculosis (Vardhan 2006:914), which is consistent with the medicinal properties of *soma* described in the Vedas.

On the other hand the meaning 'willow' was conserved in the northern route of Indo-European migration which took place through Central Asia and the steppe. The Gobi desert of Central Asia had converted into wet forest during early Holocene and it had willow (*Salix*) trees lasting up to 3000 BC (Miehe 2007:163; 156 Table 1). Kaiser (2009:1550, Table 3) studied the fossil pollens from Tibet and found *Salix* (willow) pollen present at Rutok from 11,000-9,900 BC and 9,300-4,800 BC; same from Nienang 8,000-1500 BC. Another fossil pollen study done in the south-west Siberia (Tuva Republic) showed dense presence of willow

(*Salix*) at Akkol at 8500-7000 BC in continuity, then interrupted low intensity presence up to the onset of the Common Era 2000 years back (Blyakharchuk 2007:527Fig 5); at Grusha at 9,000-7,000 BC and 6,000-5,000 BC (*ibid*:526 Fig 4). Another study from Ulugan (South Siberian steppe) showed similar presence of Salix dated 6,000-5,500 BC (Blyakharchuk 2004:267 Table 2). At Alashan, fossil pollen of *Salix* was in the abundance from 9,000-6,200 BC, however its later presence became very intermittent and thin (Herzschuh:12 Fig 4). Similar study from peat mire in northern Kazakhstan revealed the presence of willow at 8,500-6,200 BC (Kremenetski and Velichko: Abstract).

The periods 8,000-7,000 BC and 6,000-5,000 BC exhibit the densest presence of *Salix* from almost all the places in Central Asia and western steppe. Thus the Indo-Europeans were crossing Central Asia during the early Holocene about 8000-7000 BC or 6000-5000 BC, otherwise the IE word for 'willow' should have been lost from the Indo-European vocabulary, or would have changed the meaning. This fixes the date of migration of the Indo-European speakers through Central Asia region at any or both of the time-hiatuses *viz.* 8,000-7,000 BC and 6,000-5,000 BC.

At these two periods, the region was like a forest dominated by willow, birch and pine in patches over the region. This is the reason why the names of the willow and the pine trees (or their cognates) in many languages of Europe have often taken the general meaning of 'tree', although Pokorny assigns different roots to these words *e.g.*

> O.Ice. *viðr, viðar* (wood, forest, tree), O.E. *widu, wudu*, O.H.G. *witu, wito* (wood) from PIE *u̯idhu-* (tree, Pokorny:1177); *c.f.* Sanskrit *veta, vetra* (willow) and Sanskrit *viṭapa* (tree).
>
> O.Ir. *fid, fedo* (tree, wood, forest), Welsh *gwŷdd*, O.Corn. *guiden, gwez*, Welsh *syb-wydd* (pine). (*c.f.* Sanskrit *pitu-* 'pine').

There are many cognate words in the Indo-Aryan branch which mean 'willow' or are semantically related to willow. Sanskrit *vīḍu, vīḷu* (strong) seems to be related with Proto-Indo-Aryan *vēḍu* (bamboo, willow) and the latter's derivative Kashmiri *vīr, vīrü* (white willow; CDIAL 12091). Other cognate words with the meaning 'willow' are (Turner):

> Proto-Indo-Aryan *vēta* (willow, CDIAL 12097), Pashai-Dardic *vei, wēu* (willow), Dardic *bīk* (willow), Shina-Dard *bĕu, bĕvĕ* (willow); Proto-Indo-Aryan *veta-daṇḍa* (willow-stem, CDIAL 12098); From Sanskrit *vetasa* (CDIAL 12099), Prakrit *vēdasa, vēasa* (willow), Ashkun-Kaffiri *wiẽs* (willow), Kashmiri *bisa* (willow), Lahnda *bīs*, Nepali *baĩs* (willow), Dameli-Kafiri-Dardic *bigyē* (willow), Proto-Indo-Aryan **vēḍu--, vētrá--. *vētuka*—(willow).

Other Indo-Aryan cognates meaning 'willow' and listed by other authors include: Assamese *bheha* (*Salix*), Punjabi *bed* (willow, *Salix species*, Singh:110); Nepali *beu* (Turner 1931 Nepali:456), *bais, biu* (*ibid*:458). Persian cognates meaning 'willow' are: *bada, bīd, bed, bīdī, bīde* (Steingass:165, 217-8).

The examination of the cognate words meaning 'willow' from the modern and the extinct Indo-Aryan languages reveals that the real meaning of the Old Indian or Vedic *vetasa* was 'willow', not the reed or cane. We note above that the Prakrit, Northwest Indo-Aryan (Dardic), Kashmiri, Lahnda, Nepali and Assamese cognates of 'willow' mean 'willow' only and nothing else. Hence the Eurocentric stand taken by some scholars, that the meaning 'willow' was lost from the cognate words after the Aryan arrival into India cannot be supported.

We may then conclude that the willow (*Salix sp*) was native to the Indus-Sarasvati region up to the fourth millennium BC (*vide supra*). Golden willow (*Salix alba*), described well in the Vedic texts, grew along the rivers in the moist soil. As described in the *Yajur* and the *Atharva* Vedas, it was used for the medicinal purposes of treatment of pain and fever because of the salicylic acid content of it. However it became extinct from the Indus-Sarasvati plains following the fourth millennium BC, when the region became drier. It fixes the dates for composing the three Vedas cited (*Rig*, *Yajur* and *Atharva*) to before 3,000 BCE.

Chapter 16

Kustha, Kutsa and *Nard* (*nalada*) plants

There was a change in climate, environment and flora with time during the Holocene. This resulted in the application of the older names of the extinct plants and animals to the newer plants and trees found in the region. Bloomfield's statement that the Vedic mantras and words acquired new meanins as the climate and ecology changed can be best illustrated by this example.

The *Atharva Vedic* medicinal and aroma-bearing plant *kuṣṭha* has been mentioned as the curative medicine for fever (*takmāna*, possibly malaria; *AV* 5.4.1). It has also been called *amṛtasya puṣpam* or 'the flower of immortality' signifying its medicinal properties (*AV* 5.4.4). Many authors have identified it as the *Costus speciosus* (*Cheilocostus speciousus*; crape ginger)--a rhizome-bearing plant resembling ginger (MacDonald and Keith: 175; Monier-Williams). However this identification is wrong on many accounts. *Costus* is a tropical plant which grows in the warm and humid climates which have plenty of rains *e.g.* Indonesia and Fiji. This plant does not grow in the cold dry high altitudes of the Himalayas where the *Atharva-Veda* mentions the *kuṣṭha* plant to have been growing then (*AV* 5.4.1-2). Clearly the *Atharva-Vedic* description of the *kuṣṭha* plant growing in 'the third heaven' and in the high peaks of the Himalayas (MacDonald and Keith:175) does not match the tropical *Costus* plant. The *Atharva-Veda* also mentions that the *kuṣṭha* plant did not grow in the Northwest Indian plains, but grew on the snowy mountains, from where it was brought down and sold in the market (*AV* 5.4.1-2):--

> "Thou who wast born on mountains, thou most mighty of all plants that grow. Thou Banisher of Fever, come, *kuṣṭha*! make Fever pass away. (*AV* 5.4.1)

Brought from the Snowy Mountain, born on the high hill where eagles breed, Men seek to buy thee when they hear: for Fever's Banisher". (*AV* 5.4.2; Griffith's Translation)

The Veda also mentions that the plant *kuṣṭha* spread from the Himalayas into the region to the north of the Himalayas (Tibet) and from there to the further East (China). The people of the latter country (*i.e.* the Chinese) dealt in this medicinal plant (*AV* 5.4.8). The Indians of the *Atharva-Vedic* times brought this medicinal plant by the sea-route too coming across the Southeast Asian seas (*AV* 5.4.3-4). This whole is a vivid description of the *Artemisia* plant which grows today in western Himalayas, Tibet, Korea, China and Japan and has been used in the Chinese medicine to cure the febrile illnesses like malaria. Its derivative artemisinin is one of the most powerful anti-malarials known today (Miller and Su 2011). Mannan (2010) showed that its Pakistani/Indian Himalayan species *Artemisia indica* contains the medicinal substance artimisinin.

The *Atharva-Veda* also mentions the role of the plant (*kuṣṭha*) in curing the tuberculosis (*yakṣma*) and leprosy (*AV* 5.4.9; McDonald and Keith:175). Recent experiments have proved that the artimisinin has anti-mycobacterial property too, although demonstrated in *vitro* only so far (Ntutela 2009). That means it could be effective against tuberculosis and leprosy, both of which are caused by the mycobacteria. This finding too is consistent with our identification of the *Atharva-Vedic kuṣṭha* as the *Artemisia* plant.

Another plant, the *Rig-Vedic kutsa*, too has been identified by most of the authors as the *Costus* (MWD). This identification too like that of the *kuṣṭha* is wrong. The Veda mentions the plant (*kutsa*) metaphorically as a seer. Troubled by the bad elements, the seer was finally rescued by the Rain-God *Indra* (*RV* 1.106.6). It is possible that the *Atharva-Vedic kuṣṭha* and the *Rig-Vedic kutsa* were the two names given to the same plant at the different periods of time. This we can say because we know that many of the plants and trees found at the time of the *Atharva-Veda* (1500-1300 BC) in the higher altitudes of the Himalayas were found in the northwest Indian plains much earlier, during the *Rig-Vedic* times (6000-8000 BC). There is a trend in the *Rig-Veda* to personify the plants and trees. The *Kutsa* has been mentioned in association with the *aśvinī kumaras*, the divine physicians, pointing to the likelihood of its being a medicinal plant (*RV* 1.112.9). Such description matches the artemisia plant, which was widely distributed in north India during the early Holocene (Vishnu-Mittre:550,551; Trivedi and Chauhan 2009; Tewari 2008:350, 352, 355). Pollens of of Artemisia have been recovered from the early Holocene Didwana in Rajasthan (Madella and Fuller 2006:1287). However, it is quite possible that the two—*kutsa* and *kuṣṭha* are distinct and unrelated plants.

This view however would contrast with that generated from the comparative philology. The philology strongly demonstrates that the *kuṣṭha* was *Saussurea* plant which is closely related to another such plant nard (*Nardostachys*, Sanskrit *nalada*). These two are fragarence-bearing (incense) plants and they do not posses medicinal properties against malaria and tuberculosis which have been claimed for the *kuṣṭha* in the *Atharva-Veda*.

The *Saussurea lappa* growing at the heights of 2500-3500 meters above the sea level in the Himalayas today has been extensively used in the *Ayurvedic* medicine. Its names are: *kuutth* (folk name, Hindi), costus (folk name, Indian English), *kuṣṭha* (*Ayurvedic* texts), *qust* (Yunani or Greek-Arab medicine), and *kostum* and *kottam* (Tamil), which all are obvious cognates of the *Atharva-Vedic* word *kuṣṭha* (see Khare:586; Madhuri 2011:Abstract; Waly 2009). Waly too found in his study that the *qust* (Arabic for *kuṣṭha*) was not the *Costus*, but the *Saussurea lappa* plant. Thus we can say that the *kuṣṭha* was the anti-malarial Himalayan and East Asian plant at the time of the *Atharva-Veda*, yet because of some reasons the name got applied to the *Saussurea* plant quite early in history.

Adding to the confusion, the word *costum*, a cognate of the Sanskrit *kuṣṭha* has been applied to a third plant 'nard plant' in the Latin language (Valpi:104). Like the *Saussurea* (*kuṣṭha*; see above), nard too is a medicinal plant as well as incense plant belonging to the same botanical class *Asterids*, yet the two are different and are not the same plant. The word 'nard' is a cognate of Sanskrit *nalada* which means *Nardostachys jatamansi.*

The *Atharva Veda* mentions the plant *nalada* along with the *kuṣṭha* to be used by the husbands as ointment for massaging the wives for sexual activation (*AV* 6.102.3: *āñjanasya mayughasya kuṣṭhasya naladasya ca*). *Nalada* has been identified by many scholars as the fragrant plant *Nardostachys jatamansi i.e.* the spikenard or 'nard' (Khare:433; MacDonald and Keith:175). That means the *nalada* and the *kuṣṭha* are two different plants, not 'one'. Nard has been used for making incense powder in many cultures. Its other names are Latin *nardus*, Greek *nardos*, Arabic *nard* (Valpi:279) and Portuguese *nardo indiano.* The word is present in Tamil and Malayalam as *naṛu* (fragrant; Yule/ Hobson-Jobson:642).

Nardostachys jatamansi grows in the colder Himalayan territories of India and Nepal. It is a medicinal plant used for the treatment of epilepsy and the psychiatric and menstrual disorders. It is possible that the close taxonomic relationship of the two exotic fragrant plants--*Nardostachys jatamansi* and *Saussurea lappa*—may have created the confusion of names, and that is the reason for the Latin word *costum*, which sounds to be the cognate of *kuṣṭha*, being applied to the 'nard' or the 'spikenard' (Valpi:104).

However, the identification of *nalada* (with the nard) is too not free from confusion. The Sanskrit *nalada* has often been identified with some other aroma-bearing trees also. Khare (2007:701) notes the application of the Sanskrit word *nalada* for the *Vetiveria zizaniodes* (Hindi *khas*, Arabic *cusus*) in the *Ayurveda*. This tropical plant too bears a very strong perfume. The Hindi and Arabic names (*khas*, *cuscus*) of the plant hint that this plant too was confused not only with the *nalada* but also with the *kuṣṭha* in the past. Another tropical plant which has often been confused for *kuṣṭha* is *Costus species* (discussed above). However the two, the *khas* and the costus which grow in the hot tropical climates, not in the Himalayas were certainly not the *Atharva Vedic* Himalayan cold adapted *kuṣṭha* or *nalada*.

Thus the conclusion which finally emerges can be summarized like this: The transfer of name *kuṣṭha* from *Artemisia* to the incense plant *Saussurea* took place because originally it was the *Artemisia* plant which was used as incense plant and burnt in the sacrificial fires. But when it became extinct from the plains, it was brought from the Himalayas for the medicinal purposes up to the *Atharva-Veda* period. However still later its traditional use was lost from India and the plant too was lost from the popular memory lending the name to the other incense plants like *Saussurea*.

This we can say with certainty because the practice of burning the *Artemisia* as incense has survived in those regions of the Himalayan districts where the plant grows even today. The practice survives in the Kullu and Lahoul district of the Himachal Pradesh (Kibber, Jahalman and Beeling tribes), Uttaranchal (Kumaon people), the Indus-Valley of Laddakh region and mountainous regions of Nepal (Pennacchio 2010:46-49; Sood 2001; B. Singh 1996; G.S. Singh 2000; Manandhar 2002; Shah and Joshi 1971; Bhattacharya 1991; Pohle 1990).

Kutsa, although translated as 'name of a *ṛṣi*' may well have been the name of a plant during the *Rig-Vedic* period. Monier-Williams, citing 'lexicographer', mentions that *kutsa* was another Sanskrit name of the *Costus* plant, apart from being the names of many individuals. If that is true then *kutsa* is just an older name of the *kuṣṭha* plant. *Kutsa* was tormented by the demon of the drought *śuṣṇa*, and was saved by the efforts of *Indra* who brought the relief (rain) to the region (*RV* 4.16.10-12). Possibly the *Rig-Vedic* individuals often adopted for themselves the names of plants and trees, as is done in many cultures even today. Word meaning lotus etc are used as human proper names in India today. Thus this plant *kutsa* may be just the name of a plant of the *Rig-Vedic* times adopted by a saint of that age.

Although the glaciers were melting and the rivers were full, the climate was cold-dry at the beginning of the Holocene in Northwest India-Pakistan (Mayewski 2004:249), because the melting glaciers absorbed lots of heat (Latent Heat of melting). And the air in Northwest India was dry, because cold air cannot hold much water-vapour. This stage has been depicted in the *Rig-Veda* as the *śuṣṇa* (the demon of drought, Monier-Williams:1085) and should correspond to the 7000-6000 BC period of RCC (Rapid Climate Change) leading to the region becoming drier (Mayewski 2004:249 Fig5). This cooling also overlaps 'the 8.2K Cooling Event', which took place about 6,250 BC.

Chapter 17

Birch (*Betula species*)

Birch was present in the forests surrounding the oldest home of the Indo-European speaking people. This we can say because its cognate words are present in many (it is wrong to say 'all') of the branches of the Indo-European speech and the tree is known by the derivatives of the same oldest name in most parts of Europe and India (Pokorny:139-140). This is in spite of the geographical discontinuity of the modern natural ranges of the birch.

However, the cognate words of 'birch' are not found in the languages of South Europe and Iran. Thus the cognates are **not found in Italic, Greek, Celtic, Albanian, Hittite, Iranian and Tocharian** branches—seven branches out of the eleven, and are present only in Indo-Aryan, Slavic, Baltic and Germanic branches, indicating a clear geographical pattern overlying the colder northern route of migration. However Ossetic, a northern Iranian language, lying on the northern fringe of the southern route of migration, has retained the cognate. Its many cognates like the Latin *fraxinus* (ash tree), Albanian-Gheg *frashen* (ash tree) do not mean 'birch'. The Indo-European cognates retaining the meaning 'birch' are:

> Sanskrit *bhūja*; English 'birch', Old English *beorc*, *birce*, Old High German *birihha*; Lithuanian *béržas,* Latvian

> *bę̃rzs*, Old Prussian *berse*; Russian *berëza*, Serbian-Croatian *brȅza*; Ossetic (North Iranian) *boerz*--all meaning 'birch' (Pokorny:139-140).

The languages of South Europe and Celtic do not have the cognates for Sanskrit *bhūrja*, but have the name of this tree from some other source, like the Latin *betula* from the Proto-Celtic **betwā* (Gaul *betu*, Middle Irish *beithe* box-tree; Welsh *bedwen* birch). The ancient Greek had no word for birch. Thus cognates with intact meaning are found only in the four branches of Indo-European family *viz.* Indo-Aryan, Germanic, Slavic and Baltic--the languages located in the northern part of Europe and the Indo-Aryan. That means, even without much knowledge of the prehistoric climate, the northern languages did not reach their present locations by the way of the southern European territories where the cognates of birch do not exist. The etymology of 'birch' thus rules out the Anatolian origin of IE.

As we move south from North Europe, we find the loss of the meaning 'birch' from the cognates although the cognates themselves have been retained with altered meanings in some languages. Thus the meaning 'birch' gets lost from the Bulgarian *brěz* (white spotted), Slovakian *bręza* (white spotted cow or goat) and Albanian *brez* (stripe) because of the paleo-climatic factors (discussed below). We have just mentioned the Latin *fraxinus* (ash tree) where the original meaning has been lost (Pokorny:139-140). Persian *burj* (fortified tower), Avestan *bərəz-* (high; high mountain) can too be cognates where substitution of meaning has occurred. These indicate the absence of birch during Holocene from the Iranian plains in general. However birch is found in the mountains of north Iranian, and that is why the northern Iranian language Ossetic has retained the meaning.

That the tree is known today by the cognates of the same name in the IE languages of India and North Europe prompted Witzel to make the conjectural and false claim that the birch tree is found today all the way from India to Europe (Witzel 2001:51 fn 113). This claim is wrong. Although birch grows in the northern part of the Siberia region, in

Mongolia and in the Ukrainian forest highlands, it does not grow in the steppe, and there is great discontinuity between the Himalayan birch forests and the European birch forests (Hytteborn:74 Fig 2.22a & b; Crystal:296).

The philological presence in many European and Indian languages (with meaning conserved) could have been possible only if the tree had been present throughout the course of migration at the time when the migration took place. Each successive generation of the migrating humans needed to come across the birch tree if the name of this tree had to be retained as the same by the migrating population. This fact provides us with a unique method of knowing, and excellent insight into, the history of the Indo-European migration.

Birch (Sanskrit *bhurja*) is found in many of the Himalayan districts of India, where regular snowfall occurs (Elvin and Liu: 65). Birch derives its water-supply from the snow-melts, and is a cold-resistant tree. The cold periods with widespread snowfall in north India were the Last Glacial Maximum, Older Dryas (12,000 BC), Younger Dryas (10,800-9,500 BC) and the 8.2 Kilo-year event (6,200 BC; Starkel 1999; Hijma and Cohen). The tree was widespread in north India during these times. A study of the fossil pollens in the Jammu region showed that the birch (*Betula*) was present there from 7,500 BC until the medieval period (Trivedi and Chauhan 2009).

During the glacial peaks, India had acted like a refugium for many trees of Asia including birch and oak. Although Central Asia was not covered under ice-sheets during the last glacial period, yet no tree grew there during the Last Glacial Maximum and the Late Glacial. In Europe too trees did not grow during the glacial peaks except in the few refugia in the Iberian, Balkan and Italian Peninsulae, which were located to the south of the tree-line. Thus these three peninsulae and India were the prime reservoirs of tree-stocks which would expand into the rest of Europe, and Central Asia respectively as soon as the glacial peaks receded.

Immediately after the late glacial peak, when ice melted, the Central Asian level of humidity started increasing. Between 7000 BC and 5000 BC the lake levels went up in Pamir, Kazakhstan and Tibet (Starkel:117). At this time birch being the cold-resistant taxon, expanded quickly over most of Asia and Europe except in the Iranian plateau, as the birch-willow (*Betula-Salix*) forests about 10,700-8600 BC (Zhao 2009:248) and the birch-pine forests (*Betula-Pinus*; Jiang 2006). Its arrival, expansion and maximum in Finland correspond to dates—9,500 BC, 7,000 BC and 6,500 BC respectively (Elina 2010:154, Fig 78). In contrast to birch, oak was slow to expand in Europe and the beech was even slower than the two. So if Indo-European speakers arrived at Finland about 6,000 BC, or 7,000 BC, they would be getting the birch but not oak or beech (Bolte 2007), and such conditions are reflected by the presence of the cognate words for birch but not for beech or oak in the northern Baltic language. The IE word for the birch would be conserved but not for the other two in the Baltic branch of IE.

And therefore in the Baltic branch of IE languages, we get cognate words of birch with the meaning intact, but not that of 'oak' or 'beech'. Thus selective loss of the name of one tree and the selective retention of the name of the other in the vocabulary of the Baltic languages is an important indicator of the date of migration of the Indo-European speakers.

The oak reached North Europe by 3,600 BC. But before making any conclusion we have to take into account the presence or absence of the trees on the way too. We know from the fossil pollen studies of Central Asia that the oak was restricted only to the mid-Holocene in that region. Thus a migration during the early Holocene through Central Asia would lose the word for oak if it took place during the early Holocene when oak was not there. By this method, we can exactly date the arrival of Indo-European at any place in Europe.

There is absence of the cognate words having the preserved meaning oak for *quercus* in the North European languages. On the basis of this evidence, we can say that the oak which was present in the southern Europe, was not found either on the way (in Central Asia) or in North Europe or both, when the IE migration to North Europe took place. The cognate words of *quercus*, if at all present in the North European languages have meanings quite different from the oak (Pokorny:822-823).

It was only birch which was present all the way round from India to North Europe (on the northern route) when the migration took place, because we find its cognates with meaning preserved in India and North Europe, but not in South Europe. These philological conclusions are further supported and clarified by the palynological studies.

The fossil pollen studies of Central Asia and the Eurasian steppe have shown that the steppes converted into forests in the early Holocene (8000-6000 BC). Jiang (2006) found that the inner Mongolian steppe changed into birch-pine (*Betula/Pinus*) forest at 10,500 BC-7,200 BC period, and evolved into woodland with these trees dominating at 7,200-4,700 BC period, but reverted back to steppe after 4,700 BC. In general birch was present in most of the forests at 10,000-8,000 BC period in the areas where we get steppe toady. It continued to exist in most of those regions up to about 5000 BC.

Thus birch constituted an important part of the forest flora during 8000 BC to 6000 BC period throughout the entire distance intervening between India and the European steppe, the time when the R1a1a migration from north-west India to the north Black Sea region was taking place (Underhill 2009).

Thereafter the distribution of the birch became patchy. The birch lasted in Central Asia and South Siberia up to 3,000 BC in patchy distribution. Thereafter the steppe and the desert ecosystems prevailed in the entire region and birch trees became extinct from the entire zone (Zhao 2009). Miehe *et al* noted in their study of succession of ecologies in the Gobi desert that the birch and willow pollens and charcoal were present in the soil layers up to 3000 BC (calibrated radiocarbon date), however birch became extinct from that site after that time (Miehe

2007:163; 156 Table 1). This paleoclimatic description explains why cognates of 'birch' are not found in the Tocharian language. Clearly the word must have been present in the beginning, but was lost after about 3000 BC or so from Tocharian which was a Central Asian IE language when the birch became extinct there.

We get pollen evidence of the birch tree in patches from the Central Asian core region up to 3000 BC. However birch trees were present in continuity throughout the IE migration route starting from India to Europe through Central Asia only before 6,000 BC. Thus the only time when the birch was present in the continuity was 8,000-6,000 BC. This time-window of 8000 BC to 6000 BC for IE linguistic migration from India to north Europe through Central Asia and steppe correlates well with the well studied R1a1a (male DNA) human migration from northwest India going through Central Asia to East Europe and our date of the *Rig-Veda* (Underhill 2009).

Hence we can say that the R1a1a migration was 'the Indo-European migration' too. Otherwise the word 'birch' would not have survived till today, and would have been found either in the Indo-Iranian or in the European IE languages, but not in both, depending on the place of the origin of the mother of the IE languages.

The absence of the cognates for 'birch' from Greek and Latin can too be understood from the pollen studies. The birch was not a regular feature in the southern Indo-European route *i.e.* the Iranian route, although it was present in the early Holocene South Europe. In Southern Europe (East France) it disappears after 5,000 BC (data from Seille Valley; Riddiford:17). Tonkov (2005) found the evidence of birch forest growth between 7600-6800 BC in the Balkans. Then birch it disappeared from the Balkans. Indo-European along with the Neolithic reached the Balkans and then France only after the respective dates for the disappearance of the birch. Such dates have been been estimated from genetics and archaeology (Ammerman and Kavalli-Sforza 1984; Semino 2004; King and Underhill 2002; Underhill 2002).

Birch is found in some isolated regions of Turkey today (Ozturk 2013). The tree is not present today in the distance extending from India to Turkey except in Iran at the high altitudes of the mountains in the northern colder regions. In the Iranian plains, birch pollens are conspicuous by their absence during the Holocene. Even if a few isolated localities might host the birch in the northern Iranian mountains, the tree was not generally present in the route from India to West Asia, which was mainly coastal southern Iran. The absence of birch in Iran was primarily because of aridity, and secondarily because of the absence of annual snow fall during most of the Holocene in the southern plains of Iran. Thus the word 'birch' or its cognate was lost from the southern IE during transit through Iran. And this is the reason why the cognate word for 'birch' is absent from the Hittite (Anatolian), Albanian and ancient Greek languages too.

For this reason, we do not find the cognate words of birch in Greek, Italic and Celtic languages: Proto-Celt **betwā-*; Latin *betula*, Portugese *bétula*, Italian *betulla*, Spanish *abedul*, French *bouleau*; Greek *simyda*, *rabdizo* all meaning 'birch' but none being its cognate. Another Greek word *berga* (birch) is actually not a cognate of Sanskrit *bhūrja* or English 'birch', but that of **berg-* meaning 'strong, powerful and large' (Pokorny:140-141). Thus no cognate word of 'birch' exists in Latin, Greek or in any Southern European language. This is consistent with the absence of birch en route if the migration to South Europe took place by the southern route through Iran. We can say that the South European languages have retained the words for birch in the extinct substrate language of South Europe.

Chapter 18

Oak (*Quercus*)

No common name for oak in
the European languages

David Crystal wrote about the oak: "On the other hand, there is little evidence of a common word for 'oak', which is also a European tree, and if this word was not known to the Indo-Europeans, the view is supported that their migration must have begun in Asia after all" (Crystal:296).

We cannot disagree with this statement which is a very onjective observation. There is no cognate relationship between the names of oak in different branches of IE in Europe. The names are not the same even within the same branch (*e.g.* Italic). This can be seen from the following examples which all mean 'oak' in the different European languages:

> Latin *quercus, glans, robur, sūber, aesculeus, ilex* (holm-oak), *ilignum*; French *chêne*; Romanian *stejar*; Portugese *carvalho*; Spanish *roble*; Albanian *lis, drushk, artikuj*; Proto-Celtic **dari(k)-*, Irish *dair, darach*; German *eichen,*

eiche; Greek *phegos, phagos, drys, balanidia*, Old Greek *balano-s*; Croatian *hrasto*; Lithuanian *azuolas, azoulinis.*

Linguists have in general circumvented the issue as to why the oak does not have a common name in the languages of Europe. They do not like to answer the question as to how it happened. It could not have happened without any underlying cause.

Examining the claimed PIE root **park^{w}u-s*

On the other hand some authors have disproportionately highlighted the Indo-European status of the Latin word *quercus* meaning 'oak' and have reconstructed its ancestral root-word as PIE **perk^{w}u-* ('oak'; Pokorni:822-823; Witzel 2009 Fulltext:5 fn32). The Sanskrit *parkaṭī* (*Ficus infectoria*; a type of fig-tree) has been claimed as its derivative (*ibid*). It has also been claimed that the original meaning of the **perk^{w}u-/ parkaṭī* was oak, and the name was applied to the *ficus* when the arriving Indo-Europeans did not find the oak tree in India (Pokorny; Witzel; Lehmann:105 F12).

Valpi however gives a different etymology of *quercus* from *ker-kaleos* meaning 'rough bark' (Valpi: 388), and it is possible that *quercus*, cork and cortex etc are from a root entirely unrelated to the oak-tree. Ironically the word *quercus* is exclusive to Latin and its absence from French, Spanish and Portugese even within the Italic branch cannot be explained. Its meaning has changed in the Italic-trent cognate *porca* to pine (Pokorny:822-23). Valpi's hypothesis seems to be likely in view of the presence of many cognates of the *quercus* in Indo-Aryan which are certainly not related to the PIE **perk^{w}u-* or the Sanskrit *parkaṭī* (*vide infra*).

On critical examination of the etymology of **park^{w}u-s*, it seems possible that this root-word is arbitrary, false and chimera created from fusion of two words--Sanskrit *parkatī* and Latin *quercus*. Thus the Italic *porca* (pine) could be just a cognate of Sanskrit *parkaṭī* with meaning altered to 'pine' on arrival to South Europe.

Out of the many cognates claimed to have been derived from the PIE _*park_^{w}_u-s_ only the claimedly Latin cognate (*quercus*) means 'oak', and no other cognate from any other language means 'oak'. Thus the trees claimed to have been named after the PIE _*perk_^{w}_u-s_ in the languages other than Latin have always meant some tree other than the oak.

Often such claimed cognates mean entirely different objects like 'mountain', 'thunder' and 'cloud'. Presence of the meaning 'oak' in just a single language cannot justify the assigning of the meaning 'oak' to this root. Hence attributing the meaning 'oak' to PIE _*park_^{w}_u-s_ is misplaced judgement. We can see how wildly the meanings of cognates vary:

> Latin *quercus* (oak); Italian *porca* (pine); Old English *furh* (pine), Old Icelandic *fura* (pine), OHG *for(a)ha* (pine); OHG *fereh-eih* oak; OHG *Fergunna* (birch forest), MHG name *Virgunt* (birch forest); Irish *ceirt* (*quiert*, apple tree); Welsh *perth* (bush, hedge); Hittite *peruna* (cliff); Lith. *perkunas* (thunder), O. Pruss. *percunis* (thunder), Gothic *faírguni* (mountain range), etc (Lehmann:105 no. F12; Pokorny:822-23). Friedrich (1952:167-8) thinks that the Hittite *peruna* (cliff) is not from PIE _*park_^{w}_u-s_, but is a cognate of Sanskrit *parvata* (mountain, hill).

Indian cognates of Latin *quercus* (oak)

In fact the Indo-European words which can truly qualify to be the cognates of *quercus*, a word etymologically not related to the Sanskrit *parkaṭī* in our view, should be searched for in the Indo-Aryan and Iranian branches. The likely candidates that emerge are: Pašai-Dardic *kaṛék* (oak; CDIAL 3228), Hindi *karhār* and *kharhar* (a kind of oak; CDIAL 2802), Pashto *kharawa'h* (oak; Raverty) and Sanskrit *karkaṭa* (literally:

hard, an ancient Indian tree not identified so far). The meaning and the phonology match so well with the Latin *quercus* that there should not be no doubt about them all being mutually cognates.

Related to this group of words may be the Hindi *kakar-singhi*, *kākṛā-singi*, *kakra* and *kakring* which mean the Indian *Pistacia integerrima* (CDIAL 2818). Literally *kakar-singhi* (same as Sanskrit *karkaṭa-śṛñgī*) would mean "having hard-thing at the end". Although the words mean today *Pistacia*, they might have earlier included the meaning the 'oak' which too has a nut at the top of the twigs. Pistachio and oak grew together as the most dominant trees of the forests in northwest India and Iran during the early Holocene. This we name today as the *Pistacia-Quercus* or the Pistachio-oak forest. Sanskrit *karkaṭa*, Hindi *karkar* etc etymologically mean 'hard'. Possibly the nuts or the trees *Pistacia* and *Quercus* were known by such words like *karkarī* to imply hardness (*AV* 20.132.8).

However, after the extinction of the oak from the South Asian plains, the words *karkar* etc that otherwise might have meant 'oak', got applied to the nuts of *Pistacia*. Sanskrit *karkaṭa-śṛñgī* (lit. 'one which grows on the top of *karkaṭa*') means 'gallnut' (CDIAL 2818) and *karkaṭa* means 'various plants' (CDIAL 2817). Gallnuts are intimately associated with the oak trees on which they generally grow. This is the reason why the Latin *galla* (gall) means an oak-apple. Persian *karkarūhan* (a drink made from oak-apple; Seingass) may be a cognate word of the foregoing. Thus all these may be semantically traced to the oak.

The Sanskrit word *karkaśa* (bitter, rancid) resembles the *quercus*. However, it means the *Cassia* tree and not the oak. Gypsy word *kerko* (bitter, rancid; CDIAL 2641) too can have semantic association with *quercus* (oak) nuts which are bitter to taste.

The Sanskrit tree-name *karka* (or *karkaṭa*), which has been mentioned by Monier-Williams as names of an ancient Indian tree, citing Sanskrit lexicographers too could be related to the foregoing words. Turner mentions other cognates like Sanskrit *karahāṭa* (*Vangueria spinosa*;

Monier-Williams), Prakrit *karahāḍa* and Gujarati *karāṛ* (a particular tree; CDIAL 2802). These must be examined seriously rather than applying the the usual knee jerk reflex to label them as convergent evolutions.

After this much of review, we are in a position to say that *quercus* is not etymologically related to Sanskrit *parkaṭī*, and has its origin from the hardness of the nuts of the oak tree. Its cognates mean oak, pistachio and often other hard things in the modern Indo-Aryan languages, and in the early Holocene it may have meant the oak tree or nut.

Examining the Sanskrit word *parkaṭī*

Unlike the European languages, the Indian words related to *parkaṭī* have a more or less particular meaning—some species of the '*ficus* tree' *e.g.* Sanskrit *parkaṭī* and Hindi *pakar* (*Ficus infectoria*; MWD; CDIAL 9022). Members of this *genus* have arial roots. The word *parkaṭī* has migrated to Southeast Asia also, retaining the meaning some species of '*ficus*', its 'aerial roots' or any 'root' in the Austronesian languages:

> Kalimantan Island Languages *pakat* (root); Merina Language (of Madagascar) *fahani* (from **paka*, aerial root); Bismark Archaepelago *paka* (*Ficus nodosa*, Tolai and Pala languages); Fiji *mbaka* (*Ficus oblique*, Mbau language); Vanuatu (several languages) *mbak*, *paka*, *nu-mbak*, *na-pak*, *na-ban*, *pan* all meaning *Ficus prolixa* (Mahdi:203). Apart from these other cognates of *pakur* or *parkaṭī* in Austronesia are *uakat*, *oakat*, **uakaR*, *akar*, *okor*, etc (Mahdi: 204-6).

Thus we find that the cognates of the Sanskrit *parkaṭī* in the Austronesian languages mean some form of the *ficus* tree or the 'aerial root' or simply the 'root'. Probably the spread of this word took place during the exploration of the Indian Ocean by the Indians during the Bronze Age (*q.v.*). The above discussion indicates that *parkaṭī* was originally an Indian word meaning the *Ficus infectoria* during the Bronze Age, although out of India it acquired some related meanings.

Thus the out of India distribution of the cognates of *parkaṭī* is the product of the Indian migration to island Southeast Asia during the Bronze Age about 2,200 BC while on the way to Australia as proved by the recent studies by Pugach (2013), Karafet (2005:94) etc. The Indians arrived there in large numbers (10-15% of the local population) and influenced the local language by introducing the names of plants etc. There is evidence of similar Indian migration to the Middle East, Arabia, East Africa and possibly even Madagascar at the Bronze Age (third millennium BC).

Many authors (like Valpi:153) hold that *ficus* is a loan from the Semitic (Hebrew *fag* and Phoenician *pagh* "half ripe 'fig'). It is more likely that the Indo-Aryan derivatives from *parkaṭī* like *paka* and *pakar* entered the Semitic languages during the Bronze Age Indian contact with West Asia. Thus the evolution of the cognates took place like this: Indo-Aryan *parkaṭī, paka, pakur* > Phoenician *pagh,* Hebrew *fag* > Latin *ficus.* The masse of evidence rules out the European or even steppe origin of the word *parkaṭī* (or **perk^{w}u-s* of Pokorny) etc, and fixes its origin in India where it has been used to name the the *Ficus infectoria* tree since the Bronze Age migrating to the Southeast Asia with time.

However it is very much likely that *parkaṭī*, but not the reconstructed chimera**perk^{w}u-s*, was another name of the oak tree in India during early Holocene. However the word did not recorded in the *Rig-Veda*. It was because of the general resemblance of general features of the oak trees with the *Ficus infectoria* trees, that the Indians named the latter as *parkaī* when the oak became extinct from the Indian plains. When the oak became extinct from northwest India, the word *parkaṭī* got applied not only to the *Ficus infectoria* but also to the betel-nut (see MWD). The nuts of this tree (*Areca*, betel nut) very much resemble the acorn nuts of the oak. In fact not only the word *parkaī* but almost every other name of the oak got applied to the betel-nut (*vide infra*).

Etymology of Latin *suber*, another name of oak

Not only '*quercus*' (oak) but many other European names of oak too have survived in India, usually with the altered meanings. The folk name of *Quercus incana* or *Q. leucotrichophora* (Himalayan oak) is *shilā supāri* (literally, Himalayan *supāri*) in the Kashmiri language (Khare: 531) and sounds to be cognate of the Latin word *suber* (oak). Hence this needs further examination.

For the modern Indo-Aryan *supārī*, Turner reconstructs the Old Indo-Aryan word **suppāra* which means the *Areca* (or betel-) nut that is shaped like an oak-acorn and also looks like the glans penis of the human males. In the north Indian plains, where people do not know the oak tree, the words *supārā* and *supārī* mean the "glans penis" (see **suppāri*, CDIAL 13482). Turner does not provide its Sanskrit cognate.

However considering the Indo-Aryan status of the reconstructed word **suppāra* (of Turner), it may be assumed that the word was present in the Vedic Sanskrit too, compelling us to look for its Sanskrit cognate. The nearest matches to Hindi *supārā* are the Sanskrit *suparṇā*, *suparṇī* and *suparṇikā*. The Sanskrit (Vedic) word *suparṇā* occurs as the name of a tree in the *Yajur-Veda* (*TS* 2.1.4.2). In the *Rig-Veda* the word *suparṇā* does mean a tree, yet the word has been often used as the name of a bird too. It is possible that the *suparṇā* or *suparṇī* was the name of the oak tree at the *Rig-* and *Yajur-Veda's* times and has been retained as the Kashmiri *shilā-supāri* (mountain-oak).

Griffith translates the frequently used *Rig-Vedic* word *suparṇā* as the 'bird with beautiful feathers' (Griffith). At some places this meaning as the bird with beautiful feathers is appropriate. However this meaning stands out as inappropriate at several places where the oak tree seems to be the more plausible and the only meaning.

For example the *Rig-Veda* (9.86.1) mentions the *suparṇā* in the context of fast maturing/purification (*pavamāma*) of the wine which had been made from *soma*. Here the phrases used are "*suparṇā madhumanta*" (*suparṇā* which contains wine) and "*indavah madintama asah pari-koṣam āsate*" (the most intoxicating drops are these; filled up fully, in the jar are they). In this mantra, the meaning of *suparṇā* is clearly the 'oak-wood', and the wine has been kept in a container (or jar) made from this wood. This meaning makes better sense. Even today wine is matured in oak barrels (George 2003a; George 2003b: 6). On the other hand, the meaning provided by Griffith ('a bird') makes the mantra meaningless, obscure and absurd for the context, and therefore is not tenable.

When the oak became extinct from the north Indian plains and the tropical trees of moister climates arrived in the Indus-Sarasvati region about 3000 BC, the words which meant the 'oak' earlier (*suparṇā* etc) got applied to the betel nut, glans penis etc, which looked exactly like the oak-nut (acorn). And it is from there that we get the Hindi and other north Indian words *suppārā* etc for these things (betel-nut, glans-penis). The applicatin of same words for oak and the glans penis is not unique to India. The Greek *balanidia* and Old Greek *balano-s* too mean the glans penis and oak both.

The word *suparṇā* or *suparṇī* has survived in Europe as the Latin *suber* (oak; cork-oak). From Turner we learn that the Sanskrit *suparṇikā* (? *suparṇī* tree, *TS* 6.1.6.1) was a type of oak with good leaves edible to the cattle and this meaning has survived in the Pashai-Dard word *suplaĩ* (a particular type of oak which has good leaves; CDIAL 13477). The Persian *ẓubbār* is an Iranian tree "resembling oak" (Steingass:799), and it can too be cognate of *suparṇā* as it sounds like the Indo-Aryan *suppārā* (betel-nut, glans penis). Whatever philological material survies today after a gap of eight thousand years is a miracle, and should not be considered inadequate evidence.

Thus we are in a position to say that at least two European names of oak *viz quercus* and *suber* have cognates in Old Indian with meaning intact, and also that these words have no other cognates in any European language with intact meaning. Thus oak grew in India and South Europe, but not in the steppe at early Holocene.

Etymology of Greek word *phagos*

Valpi notes that Latin *fagus* (beech) is from *phagos* (Greek, oak), which is from *phegos* (Gk. esculent oak; Valpi:146; also Powell:372). Pokorny reconstructs the PIE root as **bhāgó-s* (Pokorny:107-8). He presents a list of cognate words out of which only the Germanic words mean the 'beech': German *Buche*, OHG *buohha*, O. Icelandic *bōk*, O. English *bōc, bēce.*

However the meanings of this PIE root (**bhāgó-s*) include the names of almost every forest tree of Europe in the various European languages, and the names are not specific to the beech:

> Greek *phagos* (oak); Latin *fagus* (beech); Slav. **buza-*, **bъzъ-* (elder tree *sambucus*), Russ. *buz*, Slovac *bεz*, Russ. dial. *boz*, Kurd. *būz* (a kind of elm).

Greek being earlier than Latin, archaeologically, palynologically and by DNA studies, should have retained the original meaning which as our study indicates was oak. There are many Indian cognates of these words, not mentioned by Pokorny, which generally mean the 'oak', but sometimes other trees also. The etymology of these words was suggested as *vṛkṣa* by Turner. (see in CDIAL 12067; also see Turner CEDNL:451 and CDIAL 11209, 12067, Witzel 2001:51n). However this etymology is not convincing and they should be considered the cognates of the German *Buche* etc:

> Nepali *buk*, *buka* (oak), Hindi *bā̃j* (oak),; Dardic (dialects) *wṓzu* (oak), *bōñǰ*, *bonz* (oak), Shina-Dardic *bŭċh* (chenar-tree, *Planus species*), Ḍumaki *bīk*, Dameki *bigyē̃´s* (willow), Tirahi *brīč*, Maiya *biċh* (pine tree), Shina *bŭċh*, *bŭç* (plane or *Platanus* tree), Kohistani *bīċh* (*Pinus excels*); West Pahari (Kochi) *bīkh* (tree).

Only three words in the Sanskrit language very closely resemble Greek *phagos* or PIE *bhāgó*, and they are--*bhāga, pūga* and *bhoja*. The word *pūga* means 'the betel-nut'. It is possible that the older Indian oak had a name *pūga* which was applied to the betel-nut once the oak became extinct (because of the oak-nut's resemblance with the betel-nut). Thus this gives one possibility that the Greek *phago-s* is a relic of the ancient Indian name of oak '*pūga*' surviving in India as the name of the betel-nut and in Greek as the name of 'oak'.

The words *bhoja* and *bhāga* could be candidates, however their usage in the Vedas is associated with the meanings 'joy, pleasure, food' etc, none of which has any strong semantic correlation with oak. However Nostratic protagonist Blapek's comparative study suggested that the Latin *fagus* and Greek *phagos* name is connected with the act of 'eating' and that the ultimate source of *phagos* (and also of Latin *fagus*) is an ancient word with the meaning "tree with edible fruits". "However, Blapek (2000/1) shows new evidence for an ultimate Nostratic origin ("tree with edible fruits") from Semitic, Egyptian, Berber, Chadic, Dravidian, and Altaic." (Witzel:394 n 176).

Bhoja has been name of some regions (*Bhoj-pur*; *Bhoja-kshetra*), rulers of the region (*Bhoja-rāja*) and possibly a tree too in India. Laity thinks that the word *bhoja* tree and *bhoja-patra* (leaf of *bhoja*) mean the 'birch' tree and its bark respectively (Khare: 91-92). For the Sanskrit word *bhoja*, however, the meaning birch or any tree has not been recorded by the Monier-Williams Dictionary. It is true that the Sanskrit word *bhūrja* would have evolved in the Praktit as *bhujja*, which may be loosely spoken as *bhoj* in Hindi, Oriya etc (CDIAL 9570). Yet there is a Sanskrit word *bhoja* too, which was used to name a Central Indian region. But the word *bhoja* has no evidence of having been the name of any tree in the Sanskrit language.

The palaeo-climatic evidence generated by scientific studies of the past say much on this. Costantini's study of the fossil pollen in Mehrgarh region did not reveal evidence of birch (*Betula*) between 6,900 BC and 5,000 BC (2008:171-3). At the Bolan River site no birch pollen was found between 6000 BC and 4000 BC, while those of poplar, willow, ash, elm and *vitis* were found (Costantini in FAO Document; Jarrige 2008:139).

And that is why the word *bhūrja* (birch) is missing from the *Rig* and the other *Vedas*. Possibly the Sanskrit name of the tree was retained by the masses from early Holocene up to later times, and it came into the written or recorded language only after its bark was brought into use for writing, sometime at the Bronze. Before that the role of birch was that of fire-wood, hence the name *bhūrja* from the Sanskrit root *bhṛjj-* (to fry, to burn).

Since the IE names of oak could not have travelled by the northern route through Central Asia (ecological reasons; *vide infra*), only the southeast European names of oak *viz. phagos* (Greek), Latin *quercus* and *suber* stand any chance of being the cognates of the original name of the oak tree.

Correlation of with the migration studies

We know from archaeobotany that the oak was present only in the southern countries of Europe during the early Holocene. That time its distribution was south-south. Recent migration studies have revealed that Indo-European speakers arrived in Greece and the Balkans before penetrating further in Europe as the J2 DNA (Y-Chromosomal) related migration (Priyadarshi 2011; King and Underhill).

Thus the ancestors of the Greeks were possibly the first IE speaking people arriving in the southern Europe, and had entered Europe by the Anatolia route. They must have encountered 'oak' on arrival into southeast Europe, and should have applied certain name/names to this tree. The names given by the earliest IE speakers who ever lived in Greece must therefore be the most original and truest of all the names given to the oak tree in all the European languages. The J2b (M12) arrived at Greece about 4,700 BC (King 2008:209-10 Table2; Battaglia:Table 1&2). The male chromosomal lineage J2b2 (M-241) originated in north India about 11,800 BC (Sengupta 2006:216), reached Turkey and Sicily about 8000 BC (Battaglia 2009:826 Table 2).

Hence it is chronologically wrong to think that the Indo-Europeans had first colonized the Italian Penninsula or the Proto-Italic linguistic regions and then from there spread to Greece to give birth to the Proto-Greek language. It is wrong to think that the Latin *fagus* is the predecessor of the Greek *phagos*. It is factually wrong to say that Greece was a beech-less country, and the Indo-Europeans applied the Latin name of the beech-tree (*fagus*) on to the oak-tree when they did not get any beech in Greece. This hypothesis assumes that there was no oak in the Italain Penninsula, and no beech in the Balkans; and the name of the Italian beech (*fagus*) was transposed to the Greek oak tree. We can very well see that every assumption/statement in this hypothesis is wrong.

We may for sometime imagine Witzel's claims that the Indo-Aryans came to India from the steppe about 1500 BC are true. We may also assume to be true his next premise that on not finding the oak there in India, the Aryans thrust the name of oak (PIE *perk*^{w}*u-s*) on to the Indian fig tree.

However we note that any such concessions to Witzel's proposal cannot be granted. There are non-manageable problems in his scheme. The steppe region never had any oak since its conversion into steppe about 2000 BC. Hence there was no probability at all that the people coming out from the steppe to India at 1500 BC could have had any word meaning 'oak'. This forces us to reject both--the received etymology of the Latin *quercus* from PIE **perk*^{w}*u-s* and the claimed derivation of Sanskrit *parkaṭī* from 'oak'.

If one claims that the Indo-Europeans originated in Central Europe and therefore they had known oak as *perk*^{w}*u* or *parkaṭī* from Central Europe at 1500 BC. But if the IA speakers had come from Central Europe walking down through the steppe even in that case the meaning of the word *perk*^{w}*u* (*parkaṭī*) would have been lost from the mass vocabulary, once the tree was out of sight for several generations. Hence we can reject all these claims as wrong.

The palaeo-ecological influences on the naming of oak, beech and pine in early to mid Holocene Europe

Let us discuss first the word *dāru* (also *taru*, Sanskrit for 'tree') meaning 'oak' in some European languages. Application of the generic word *dāru* (Sanskrit tree) for naming 'oak' in the several languages of Southern Europe like Celtic **dair*, Gaul *Dervus* (place name meaning "oak forest"), Welsh *derwen*, Old Irish *daro*; Albanian *drushk*; Macedonian *darullos*, Old Greek *drus* and Greek *drys* indicates that oak was probably the most common tree in the southern regions of Europe (south of the Alps) at the time of Indo-European arrival in the Balkans and the subsequent south-south spread from there. At the same time no application of the cognates for the purpose of naming 'oak' in the north European languages makes it clear that oak was perhaps not there in North Europe then or en route to Europe at that time.

Precisely because of the analogous reasons, the word *dāru* in various cognatic versions was applied to name the pine tree and pine-wood in the North European languages. Pine was the commonest tree at about 6000 BC north Europe (Giesecke 2012:9). Thus as the result of the effect of climate of North Europe of about 6000 BC over the north European language, we get: Old Norse *tyrvi, tyri* (pinewood), *tyrr* (pine), M.H.G. *zirwe, zirbel* (pine cone); Lithuanian *dervà* (chip of pinewood), etc. Later the pine wood was distilled to produce tar since the Bronze Age in North Europe, particularly Scandenevia. In fact making tar from pine, and storing this tar were the main utilities of the ceramic pottery recovered from the Bronze Age Scandenevia (Isaksson:137, 138). The practice of making tar from pine continued there till recent days (Isassson:139). It is after the pine's Nordic name, that the wood distillate (tar) has received its names in many North European languages: Lith. *dervà*, Latvian *dar̃ va*, Old Norse *terva*, Old English *teoru, tierwe*, German *Teer* all meaning the black material known in English as 'tar'.

At early Holocene oak was principally a south-south tree, distributed in South Europe, Southwest Asia, Iran and South Asia. It was the most common tree in the route from India to Europe through Iran and Turkey at the time when the migration was taking place in the early Holocene (as pistachio-oak forest). Hence the word *dāru* became synonymous with oak by the time the Indo-Europeans reached Southeast Europe. Palynological study of Greece demonstrates that the tree was there for the whole length of the Holocene (Digerfeldt 2007:363 Fig 3). However oak disappeared from nearly the rest of South Europe at about mid-Holocene because of too mush of rain. Hence its original PIE name cannot be expected to have penetrated and survived anywhere to east of the Balkans at that time.

In South Spain, oak flourished from the early Holocene to about 3,400 BC (Fernández 2007). However in the study conducted by Issar, oak disappeared from the Iberian Peninsula about 5000 BC (p. 41). Oak forests declined in Romania about 6600 BC (Elina 2010: 135). Soil charcoal studies at Palmi, South Italy, showed presence of oak forest only during the Neolithic and post-Bronze Age horizons, and absence of the tree from the Chalcolithic and Bronze Age periods (Allevato 2011:74; Pelle 2013). Finsinger found that the *Quercus ilex* (evergreen oak) abundance was low at Lago dell'Accesa (Central Italy) between 5700 and 4000 calBC (2010:1244). The Lake Accesa (Lago dell'Accesa) which is located in Tuscany province of Italy, a persistent decline of *Quercus ilex* taking place around 5700 calBC was reported by other scientists too (Peyron 2013:1237).

Summarizing these archaeobotanical reports, we can conclude that the evergreen oak, a summer-drought adapted forest, disappeared about 5700 BC from Italy perhaps due to the increased rainfall occurring during the moist mid-Holocene Optimum. It is during this period of absence of oak from Italy that the name of the oak (*phagos*) got applied to the beech in Italic branch of IE, resulting in the Italic name of beech as *fagus*. It was further modification from this word that the other names of beech (like *boc*, 'beech' etc) developed in the Germanic and other languages of Europe as and when the beech reached their respective territories from Italy carrying its name *fagus* in several modifications.

Thus the reality is just reverse of what Wizel had claimed. He had claimed that Greece was a beech-less country, and therefore the name of the 'beech' was applied on the oak tree (Witzel 2001:51 fn120). The truth as revealed from archaeobotany is just the reverse--when the Indo-Europeans arrive, it was Italy which was oak-less and the name of oak was thrust on the beech in the Italic language.

Similar study from the Lake Zaribar site in Iran showed that the upland vegetation in the western Iran changed to a pistachio-oak savanna when the low temperatures and the severe aridity ameliorated at the early Holocene (Steven 2001). Since the early Holocene (8,000 BC) up to at least 5000 BC, the oak (*Quercus sp.*) was found in the Kachi plain of the Indus Valley (Costantini:172-3).

In the case of India, Costantini studied the soil column pertaining to the period 7000 cal BC-5000 cal BC along the Bolan River of Baluchistan and found pollens of oak there. Although oak pollen can be transferred in the river flow to long distances, yet Costantini thinks that the oak stands "might grow in the interior plains and hills as well as in the mountainous slopes", because that type of climate and soil which existed there then was the natural habitat of oak. Costantini's study noted a rapid warming event at 5600 BC (2008:174). Many similar studies from Turkey, Iran and India evidence the simultaneous presence of the oak tree in these three countries at about 8000-7000 BC, making it possible to retain the cognates if the migration had taken place in that time window.

We can expect a declined in oak stands following the end of the dry period and arrival of the wet period. However Central India became drier during the mid-Holocene Optimum because monsoon had shifted from east to west of India. This made Central India a better place for the growth of *Qurcus ilex*, which likes to grow where summer rainfall is less. In Jammu region oak was in abundance since the beginning of the Holocene up to 2000 BC, after which it declined owing to aridity (Trivedi and Chauhan 2009), and it declined in Nepal about 2000 years back (Yasuda 1988; Yonebayashi 1997/online 2003). Pollen studies conducted for Nepal showed that the oak forests prevailed in west Nepal until 2000 years back (Yasuda 1988).

We can understand the causes for the limited presence of IE words for oak in the modern Indian languages, because the tree is not generally found in the north Indian plains where most of the Indo-Aryan languages are spoken. The near complete absence of the cognate words from the Iranian languages too requires explanation from climatology. Today Iran and Turkey have scattered oak forests (Marvie Mohdjer:1983; Akhani 2010). Oak has been in this route in patches, interruptedly, throughout the Holocene. It was present in Syria for the whole length of Holocene (Hussein:336 Table 1). Oak was present in Iran at the onset of the Holocene in the grass dominated savannah which had interspersed oak and pistachio trees (Schmidt 2011:4).

Djamali studied the Almalou Lake (West Iran) since 1700 BC till date, and found presence of oak pollen for the whole length of the 3700 years period (2009:1368). Similar study done by Kehl for the Zagros Mountain showed that the ecosystem turned into a pistachio-oak savannah about 12,000 BC (2009:10). Following 8,000 BC to 3,500 BC, there was the progressive invasion by oak (*Quercus aegilops*) and pistachio forest (El-Moslimany). Since about 4000 BC the oak forests have invaded into in the catchment of the Lake Zaribar and Lake Mirabad (Kehl:10).

Thus if the human migration took place by the southern route any time between 8000 BC and 5000 BC, the oak would be the commonest tree, although in a savannah background, and would be found throughout the way, leading to the application of *dāru* etc the general word for 'tree' to the oak tree as noted above. However those who migrated into northeast Europe by the northern route would get pine forests in North Europe at 8000 BC to 6000 BC period instead of the oak forest.

In the Iranian language the cognate words of oak are not present. This is because there were periods of severe droughts when oak vanished from most of Iran for long periods. Oak declined at Zaribar lake site from 4,500 BC and reached a pronounced depression there about 2500

BC and continued to be low for 900 years up to 1600 BC. The latter was also a time of peak of aridity, and is often called the 4.2 K event (Schmidt 2011:5). In the relatively drier areas of Iran, which constitutes most of Iran, oak became extinct when the pronounced periods of climatic aridity arrived. Between 1000 BC and 100 AD again it was dry, and oak disappeared from nearly whole of Iran (*ibid.*). The interrupted existence of oak in Iran is probably the reason why the cognate words have been lost from the Iranian languages.

Other fossil pollen studies of oak

Oak needs humid climate to survive, and hence is not found in Central Asia, particularly the steppe and the Gobi region. But the region was not always so dry. Oak grew in the western steppe and Central Asia for a few millennia during the "Mid-Holocene Optimum". However Central Asia became dry again subsequently and converted into steppe-desert at about 2000 BC. Since then no oak has grown there. The philology of oak can be clarified further by examination of the unique geological history of the oak tree in Asia and Europe.

Witzel's claim that beech was the original meaning of *fagus/phagos* does not stand the examination of the fossil pollen studies of Europe for the Holocene (as discussed above). Beech was not found anywhere out of the Balkans, Italy and South France till late, and the cognate words of its Latin name *fagus* (beech, *boc* etc) in the Germanic languages are the results of borrowing by the latter from the former (*vide supra*).

The Italic word *fagus* reached Germany with the beech tree from Italy and France about 1000-2000 BC. Thus the seemingly widespread presence of the cognate words for *fagus* (beech) is spurious and is the result of the late migration of the tree from Italy, and of borrowing of its Latin name into other European regions (and languages). Not only the Indo-European languages of Europe but also the Finno-Ugric ones borrowed the word *fagus* when beech arrived into their countries, examples being Hungarian (*bükkfa*) and Finnish (*pyokki*) both meaning 'beech'. Therefore, not beech but 'oak' could have been the original meaning of the IE root-word **bhago-s* which has been preserved as the Greek *phagos* (oak) till today.

In Europe and Asia no tree grew beyond the tree line during the LGM and also during the late glacial peak. Hence oak tree survived in the southern refugia like Italy and Greece. On the other hand, India being comparatively humid even during the glacial period, particularly on the eastern side, must have been a refugium for oak at the glacial climatic extremes. From that stock, oak was surviving in the Kachi plain (of the Indus Valley) in continuity since the Glacial up to the Neolithic Phase I (period 7000 BC-5000 BC; Costantini:172), and has survived till today in the Himalayas. Clearly if the northern route Indian migration took place at about 8000 BC to 6000 BC only then the names of both the oak and the birch tree (*q.v.*) would survive in the emigrant population. But even in that condition, oak was required to be present in North Europe at the time of the IE arrival for preservation of any name of oak in North Europe.

In Europe, during the end-phase of the Glacial Period, oak expanded out from the Italian refugium (Petit 2002; Fineschi 2002), and reached the south of the Alps very quickly, by 11,000 BC (Finsinger 2006:615, Table 1). However it did not cross the Alps for many millennia. It appeared in Southwest France and Spain during early Holocene (Finsinger:623). It crossed to the north of Alps (Switzerland) at about 9000 BC (Finsinger:622).

It reaches the northern part of the Central Europe only after 8700 BC (Bolte:417). At that very time it reached northwest Romania and became established there by 6600 BC (Feurdean:125, 135, 138). Its arrival and maximum growth in the Finland corresponds to the dates 5,800 BC and 3,600 BC respectively, although it never expanded too much in this region (Elina 2010: 154, Fig 78). Thus in North Europe, it became an important tree only about 3600 BC. It shows decline in Romania between 6600 and 2800 BC (*ibid*:135). Roughly the same time, it disappeared from the Iberian Peninsula about 5000 BC and again reappeared about 2,500 BC (Issar:41). Thus history of oak in Europe is not the simultaneous presence in all the places. In Russia, any date has not been provided so far, but the date of arrival must be still later than the two.

If Indo-European languages arrived in the North-East Europe about 8,000 BC, or even at 6,000 BC, there would be no oak tree there. However if they came through Central Asia after 5000 BC, only then their each generation would be able to see oak on the way. In fact in Central Asia, oak will not be visible in the western side. In the Eastern Central Asia, like Mongolia, any oak would be visible only after 5000 BC (Holocene Optimum). Thus the absence of a common name for oak in the European languages implies that the migration took place when the birch was there in Central Asia but **oak was not.** This fixes the time before 5000 BC.

Oak displays poor tolerance of extreme of aridity. It generally tolerates mild cold if humidity is present, but cannot tolerate extreme cold like minus twenty ^{0}C. It is essentially a tree of the humid Mediterranean region, although may be found in the colder regions if they are humid. However the *Quercus ilex* can tolerate the summer draught well, and is killed by too much of rain. Thus the oak has not grown in the northernmost regions of Europe and the Western steppe. The steppe areas to the north and east of the Black Sea were always dry steppes except for a few moist millennia in the middle of Holocene. That is why oak could not grow there. It could not survive in the steppe and desert climates of the alleged Aryan home, and any suggestion that there was a word for the oak in the steppe is wrong. Its past distribution in space and time in Europe has been very unpredictable and the linguists need to exercise restraint in formulating hypothesis without knowing the archaeobotany of the oak tree.

The steppes became a bit humid during the mid-Holocene time (see above). It is only then that some oak was found in the Eastern Central Asia and Southeast Siberia regions (like Mongolia). In Mongolia, when the climate changed to steppe-forest type, even then, only scanty oak trees appeared and that too for a very short time (5000-3000 BC; Zhao 2009:249). The western steppe, being much drier than Mongolia, had much less chances of getting any oak tree, although some oak at the humid period 5000-3000 BC could have grown.

Thus at 8000 BC to 6000 BC, most of the way from India to north Black Sea region was not humid enough for the survival of the oak tree, and thus was devoid of this tree, although birch and willow were there. The oak pollens recovered from the Central Asia core region before about 3000 BC were brought there by rain washouts from the further southward regions fed by the Indian Ocean monsoon which were humid (Miehe:163). However such washed out oak pollens too disappeared when the southern monsoon became much weaker after 2300 BC (*ibid*). This happened almost the same time when oak diminished in Jammu and disappeared from Indus Valley (Costantini's date).

This finding trashes the claim of the Indo-Europeanists (Pokorny, Starostin, Witzel etc) that the original word *perk*^{w}*u-s* meant 'oak' in the homeland--then the migration to India took place at 1500 BC--on arrival into India, they did not find the oak tree--then thrust this name (Sanskrit *parkaṭī*) on to the fig (*Ficus*) trees which were available in India in the plenty then.

This story also clearly implies that up to the Indian boarders, there were the oak trees in Central Asia and that the oak trees were found absent only on arrival into the Indian territory. And the next implication of the claim is that the general Indo-European names of 'oak' in Europe are cognates of *quercus* (PIE **perk*^{w}*u-s,* oak; Pokorny:822-823).

But this all is untrue. Pollen studies have made it clear that about 1500 BC **no oak tree existed in the claimed steppe homeland and no oak tree existed in Central Asia *en route*.** More than this, the cognates of *quercus* in no European language other than Latin mean oak (see Pokorny's list). If 'oak' was the original meaning, the meaning should have survived in at least one more branch of IE language in Europe.

Quercus is the lone European cognate with this meaning, although there are many likely cognates of *quercus* in Indian with the retained meaning 'oak' (*q.v.*).

Thus the last but not the least conclusion we can make is that the Sanskrit *parkaṭī* only sounds like *quercus*, but the two are not cognates. In fact many different words from many different and unrelated roots having wildly separate meanings have been clubbed together as the cognates of *quercus*. If *quercus* is a cognate word of *burgundy* (as claimed by Pokorny) then why not of the Indian '*bargad*' tree (*Ficus bengalensis*) too, which has at least the berries of the burgundy colour. Thus the entire etymology is concocted and wrong, suffers from Eurocenticism, false stories and wrong history and palaeo-climatic claims; and we need to reconstruct the etymology of *quercus* and *phagos* afresh after trashing much of the earlier conclusions.

This discussion makes it abundantly clear that oak was not present in Central Asian route from India to the steppe at the time migration took place, i.e. the period 8000 to 6000 BC. This is the time of R1a1a migration. At this time birch was however present there. Hence we get the Indo-European cognates of 'birch' but not that of 'oak' in the European languages. That is how the PIE names of the oak tree was nearly lost from Europe.

Chapter 19

Beech (*Fagus sylvestica*)

Philologists have been able to reconstruct a PIE root **bhāǵo-s* (Pokorny:107-108) which has been identified as the beech tree (Latin *fagus*). The available philological material clearly shows that the reconstructed PIE **bhāǵo-* was the name of a tree present in the homeland before the Indo-European languages dispersed. However its identification with beech is wrong, unfortunate and claimed on the basis of non-existing archaeological claims. Such claims are clearly wrong on the archaeobotanical grounds. Witzel claimed "The word for 'beech' etc. is not found, also not by local adaptation for other trees, in Iranian (Blapek 2001: 84 sq.) or in South Asian languages." (Witzel 2005:394, n176).

However the archaeobotanical fact is that the beech did not grow beyond some restricted locations namely Southeast France, Italy and the Balkans until very late times (fossil pollen and ecological evidence, *vide infra*), and it was certainly not a tree present in the homeland whether in India or in the steppe. Witzel's claim that beech grew in the steppe during the Atlanticum period is a first class example of concoction by fertile brains, and has not been supported by archaeobotanical studies (see Witzel 2001:51 n120; 61 n 146).

Beech is a tree of sub-tropical to temperate climate, and requires warm and humid climate for survival. Other than Europe, it is found in Turkey, Caspian region, north Iran (*Fagus orientalis*; Kandemir and Kaya; Ahmadi 2011; Erkan 2011), China, Japan (*Fagus japonica*), North America and New Zealand (*Nothofagus* sp.). Today it is not found in East Europe, Siberia, Central Asia and India. It survived the Last Glacial Maximum by taking refuge in the Balkans and the South France refugia. It started expanding out of these regions very late and that too quite slowly.

It reached its modern frontiers in the North Europe only a thousand years back (Bolte 2007:417; Giesecke 2007). Until now, no evidence of beech from India has been indicated. In spite of Witzel's daring claim that the beech was present in the steppe during the Atlanticum period (5,500 to 3,000 BC; see Witzel 2001:51 n120; 61 n146) beech did not grow in the steppe and Central Asia during the entire Holocene. It was also not found in most of Europe at the claimed date 4000 BC for the Indo-European linguistic origin. Thus if we identify the **bhā́ǵo-s* with Latin *fagus* (beech) and claim that the beech has an original IE name then we will have to place the homeland somewhere in France, Italy or the Balkans!!

Romania was one of the first places where beech reached first from the Balkan and Fanco-Italian region. Feurdean (2001) wrote "In the North-west Romania (Steregoiu site), at 2,800 BC *Fagus* became established and rapidly expanded in the local forest. The regular presence of *Fagus* pollen grains start around 6,000 BC, but it was first at c. 2,800 BC, that *Fagus* suddenly became widespread in the local forest. Around 2,000 BC, *Fagus* became the dominant tree in the canopy. *Fagus* has held this dominance until the present day. The presence of *Fagus* is recorded earlier in other regions of country. For instance, it started to appear around 3,000 years ago in the north-eastern and south-western Carpathians Mountains (Farcas, 1999)."

Beech is not found to the east of the beech-line, a line joining a point in Poland to another in Romania (Bolte 2007:414, 415 Fig.1; Thieme

1954:16, cited in Witzel 2001:51,61). Beech is not found in the steppe, the claimed homeland, which is much to the east of the beech line. This is a clear case of concoction. Since the beginning of the Holocene up to 3000 BC, beech was nowhere found in Central Asia, the steppe or Europe except South France and the Balkans (Magri 2008).

Beech seeds cannot tolerate dry climate at all, and this rules out any possibility of the growth of beech in the steppe. Fossil pollen studies from Gobi, Central Asia, Mongolia and North China have not shown any evidence of beech in the steppe and desert regions even when they had converted into forests during the Mid-Holocene Optimum (Miehe 2007; Zhao 2009). Clearly beech is neither found in the steppe, nor was it ever found there at any time during the Holocene.

Figure 2. The beech line passing through Poland and Romania, East of which beech tree is not found. A more detailed figure has been presented by Bolte: 415 Fig 1.

The archaeological evidence (fossil pollen) shows that beech (*Fagus sylvatica*) was restricted to only three *refugia* located in South France, South Italy and the south Balkans (Greece and Macedonia etc) during glacial peaks (Bolte). From the French refugium site it started expanding very slowly and remained confined within the boundaries of France up to 3000 BC (Tonkov; Feurdean). At Marsal (South France, at the neck of Iberian Peninsula) beech occurs between 9,500 BC and 3,500 BC. At Solennes (north-east France) beech occurs between 7000 BC and 3000 BC (Riddiford:14-15, Fig 4a). Earliest beech on the Spanish side of the Pyrenees appears about 3000 BC and at Salada Pequena about 1000 BC (Davis 1994:186; Montserrat 1992; Tonkov).

Although its expansion started about 8000 BC, yet beech was very slow to move, taking 7000 years to reach Germany (Bolte:417). It reached north Spain by 3000 BC (Davis 1994:186), and reached northern Balkans by 2000 BC (Tonkov). It arrived into Romania by 2,700 BC, but established itself in the Romanian forests only by 1300 BC (Feurdean 2001:135-36). From its glacial home in South France, *Fagus* reached Salonnes in the North-East France by 1000 BC (Riddiford 2012, Fig. 4b). It reached northern Germany by 1000 BC and the northern Poland by 1500 BC (Bolte:417). Clearly, the Indo-Europeans reaching Germany from the steppe side did not come across any beech tree either en route, or on arrival in Germany. Hence the cognate words of beech have been carried from the South Europe (South France) location as and when the beech inched towards Germany.

Radiocarbon study of *Fagus* charcoal recovered from Hechtensee (near Mariazell) indicated that in Austria, the first maximum of *Fagus* took place *circa* 3063 calBC (Vogel 1963:198). Schwarz noted its presence in the eastern Alps at late Bronze Age (2013:84). These are the earliest dates. If IE speakers reached these places any time before these respective dates they would not find the beech there.

It has also been proved archaeologically that the steppe never had beech over the last 12,000 years; and the beech forests nearest to the steppe were in the mountains of Ukraine adjoining Romania only for the last 4000 years (*i.e.* after about 2000 BC). Thus the claim that beech was present in the steppe can be proved bogus on the basis of sound material evidence.

It is an example how the Eurocentric authors have taken recourse to deception and concoction to write whatever they wanted to prove, and the thing was accepted as fact by others. Even Elst in his contradiction to the Witzel's 'beech argument' does not suspect that Witzel had lied about archaeobotany of beech in the steppe.[23] The great difficulty for history was that the hard evidence was circumvented by lies, and even the opponents could never suspect that it was all lie.

Witzel tells another untruth in the same article that the beech tree is not found in Greece, and adds that the Latin word for beech tree *fagus* was adopted in the Greek language to mean 'oak'. Reason for this was, Witzel claimed, that Greece is a beech-less country (2001:51, 61; 2005:394). This is again a huge deception. Forest survey reports from Greece indicate that beech is found there in plenty, and the Balkan Mountains are one of the three densest homes of beech in Europe (Bergmeier and Dimopoulos 2001; Brunet 2010:77). Archaeology too proves that the Balkan Peninsula, in which Greece is located, is one of the oldest homes of beech in Europe and beech has always been in the Balkance since the glacial age (Bergmeier and Dimopoulos:110; Magri; Tonkov; Feurdean).

Thus the beech tree has been found in ancient Greece (and Italy and South France) since at least 12,000 years back, and has been present only recently at other places. The IE speakers entering Europe by the southern (Iranian) route first settled in the Balkans. But the Indo-European immigrants had never before seen this tree. Hence they adopted the substrate language word which has survived today in Greek as *oxya* and in French as *hêtre* both meaning 'beech'. Thereafter the Greek speaking people should never have had the identification problem for 'beech'. However other European people faced difficulty in

23 Koenraad Elst, http://voi.org/books/ait/ch33.htm

identifying and naming the beech tree, and they erroneously named it *fagus*, 'beech' etc when the tree first reached them.

Why does *fagus* mean 'beech' in Latin?

We have evidence of oak in northwest India from 8000 BC to 3000 BC. Hence the human migration through Iran and Turkey must retain the original IE word for oak when it reaches Greece. It is the Greek word *phagos* (oak) which has retained the oldest (and perhaps the original) meaning of the cognates of the word *fagus* among all the European languages. This we can because beech tree was present in Greece when the IE speakers arrived at the Balkans Peninsula by the southern route (J2b migration, Priyadarshi 2012:336-338). King found the date of arrival of J2b at Macedonia about 5000 BC (2008:210 table 2), when oak was there. However its descendant J2b2 reached Central Italy about 3000 BC and to South France still later, when oak was not there. Hence we can say that the Latin *fagus* is a borrowing into Latin (Gk *phagos,* oak > L. *fagus*) with associated change of meaning from 'oak' to 'beech'.

This is possible because we know that 'oak' had disappeared from the Italic speaking southwest Europe between 5,000 BC and 2,500 BC, the probable time when the IE speakers may have reached the Italic territory from the Greek speaking territory. Thus the application of the word *fagus* originally meaning the 'oak-tree' to another tree beech on arrival to South France (where beech was present then) is quite logical. This new meaning has been retained in the Latin language as well as in the Germanic branch. Hence we can date the arrival of Indo-European into the South-West Europe (particularly South France) to a date between 5000 and 2,500 BC, the time when oak was absent from the region but beech was present in South France.

Hence we can conclude that the knowledge of the tree (beech) is not possible at 4000 BC, or even 1500 BC, in the steppe region. Thus even if this is accepted that beech was the PIE *bhāǵo-s*, this philological evidence goes against steppe being the Indo-European homeland.

If the PIE *bhāģo-s* meant the 'beech' then only South France or the Balkan Peninsula could have been the IE home. The fact from archeo-geography about absence of beech in North Europe, Germany, Russia, Ukraine, Asian steppe and Central Asia at about 4000 BC rules out these countries from being the place of origin of the Indo-European languages at 4,000 BC.

Philologically too, the European languages lack a common word for beech. Only some of the Germanic languages have in common the cognate words meaning 'beech' e.g. English 'beech', German *Buche*, Icelandic *beyki* etc. Otherwise, there is complete irregularity in the naming of this tree. Some examples are: Greek *oxya*; Spanish *haya*, French *hetre*, Portugese *faia*, Romanian *fag*; Albanian *ah*; Irish *feá*, *fáibhile*, Welsh *ffewydden* (all meaning 'beech'). Out of these, only Portugese (*faia*) and Romanian (*fag*) resemble the Latin *fagus*.

On the other hand, the listed cognates of PIE *bhago-s* mean different trees in different languages of Europe for example: German *Buche* (beech), Greek *phago-s* (oak), Russian *buz* (elder tree), Icelandic *beykir* (cooper) etc. People have considered Celtic (Gaul) *bāgos* too to be cognate of Latin *fagus* or 'beech'. However this is in all likelihood, a loan word from Greek or Latin because the other Celtic languages do not share this word for beech: Irish *feá*, *fáibhile* (beech), Welsh *ffewydden* (beech) are not from Proto-Celtic *bagos*.

Words for 'beech' in the non-IE languages Hungarian (*bükkfa*) and Finnish (*pyokki*) are closer to the Germanic words for beech, and could have been a loan from Italic when the tree reached these territories. Thus after the name *fagus* was snatched by beech from oak, beech-tree propagated slowly north carrying this name attached into Germanic, Hungarian, Finnish and Gaul languages. In other languages, the tree 'beech' was named independently on encounter.

Chapter 20

Juniper, the Gymnosperm plant of the Indus Valley region before 3000 BC

Indian Juniper: Identification

Juniper is a conifer tree within the same order as pine (order *Pinales*) belonging to the larger class gymnosperm or the 'flower-less' trees. It is a cold loving tree of moderately drier environment, and does not grow in very dry regions like the steppe and the Gobi cold-desert. Juniper is not found in the Indian plains today. It, however, grows in the remote heights of the Himalayas (1800 meters to 3000 meters) in Tibet, Pamir, Ladakh, Northwest Pakistan, Afghanistan, Nepal and Bhutan, and has been named *Juniperus wallichiana* or *indica* (Hook and Thomson 1874:537, cited in R.P. Adams 2014:201).

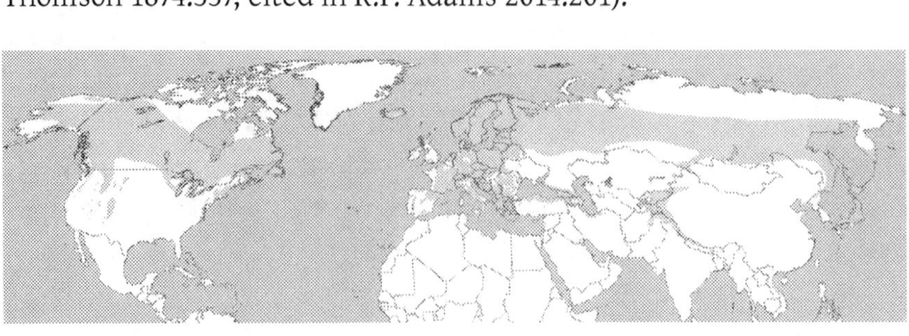

Figure 3. Modern distribution of juniper. Source: http://en.wikipedia.org/wiki/Juniperus_communis#mediaviewer/File:Juniperus_communis_range_map.png; accessed 15 June 2014.

Its wood has been traditionally burnt in the sacrificial fires in both the Vedic and the Buddhist traditions of India, Nepal and Tibet (Pennacchio:108) and wood as well as resin and leaves have been used for making incense sticks and powder. Mesopotamian inscriptions mention the burning of juniper rasin and wood in fire as incense to please the gods (Black 2006:267; *Asir-namursaga to Inana for Iddin-dagan*, hymn 195-202). Sanskrit *dhupa* (Hindi *dhūwan*; Bajjika *humād*) is the common name of all types of incense in India and it includes the juniper wood which is commercially available in Nepal and the central and eastern zones of north India. However the name of the tree from which the *dhupa*-wood comes is not known to the masses that are the end-users, perhaps because it does not grow in non-Himalayan regions of India anymore.

The *dhūpa* available in South India and also in most of the shops in Delhi are different from the juniper. In Iran and Pakistan, the incense is made from the juniper, and the incense tree is known as *sanobar.* However Khare identifies *sanobar* as *Pinus longifolia* Roxb. (Khare: 488). The incense contains aromatic oils, some of which belong to the terpenes family. We are aware that juniper and *Pinus* are important sources of terpene and other aromatic oils. (Breitmaier: 54; Bower MS. JRAS 1942, 32, cited in CDIAL 4837).

However the so called 'Indian pine' *deva-dāru* or *deodar* (*Cedrus deodara*) is not a pine at all, it is a cedar tree and it has much less aromatic property. The name of the tree, from which terpene could be made has been given as *cīḍā* in the Bower Manuscript, a Buddhist medicinal text of Central Asia. This is the name of a perfume too (MWD). Although the word *cīḍā* sounds like *cedar,* it is most probably the name of the juniper or pine. Because the modern Indian cognates e.g. *cīḍ, cīr, cilli* etc. mean juniper and pine in different Indo-Aryan languages but do not mean the cedar (CDIAL 4837). That means the cedar tree has acquired its name from some other tree--either the pine or the juniper—which existed in India before the cedar had arrived into this country.

The meaning of Sanskrit word *cīḍa* (and its derivatives) as juniper has been retained only in the dialects of the Dardic Indo-Aryan language (CDIAL 4837; Phal. *čili* juniper, Sh. *čĩlī* juniper) of Northwest Pakistan. In the other languages of India like Kashmiri, Hindi and Nepali the same name (*cīḍa etc*) has been applied to pine (*ibid*). The Bihari *cailā* (fire-wood), *silli* (log of wood) and Persian *chīda* (dwarf-pine, Steingass:405) too are its cognates.

Cedar tree itself arrived in India quite late. Stratigraphic study in a Jammu lake reports that the cedar (*Cedrus*) pollen is "met with for the first time with extremely low frequency" in the 2050 BC--150 BC layer (Trivedi and Chauhan 2009:407). A careful philological examination of the available lexical and archaeological material reveals that the cedar has acquired the name *deodara* only lately after the extinction of the juniper (and pine) tree from most of India.

This conclusion results from the examination of the following lexical material: Greek δᾳδουργός (*dadoryos*, pine-wood-cutter); Persian (Steingass) *dev-dār* (juniper), *dubūdār* (juniper), *devārū* or *deva-dārū* (pine), *dev-dāl* (white poplar tree), *dev-k̲h̲ār* (juniper, pine, bramble), *dev-āward* (pine); Indo-Aryan *Devadāru* (cedar or *Cedrus*, Turner, CDIAL 6531; also see Khare:133); Tamil-Siddha medicine *simai-devadaru* (*Pinus longifolia*; Khare: 488).

Thus the *devadāru* was most probably juniper, but it might have sometimes included *Pinus* too. This inference is evidence based. Juniper (and also pine) are used for their aromatic properties for religious rituals offered to god, hence the name *deva-dāru* (god's wood) should be applied to either or both of them. But any tree which does not have profound aromatic property could not have acquired this name. Secondly, it is the medicinal property of the wood too which contributes to the acquisition of the grandiose title "God's wood". It is only the juniper which has spectacular medicinal property like anti-tuberculosis effect. Pinus too has important medicinal properties. *Cedrus* has minor anti-inflammatory, anti-fungal and other medicinal properties (Khare:133).

Archaeological evidence of presence of juniper in India's past

Cedrus arrived into India quite late from North Iran and it was found for the first time in small numbers in Jammu at about 2000 BC (Trivedi and Chauhan:407). Trivedi (2012:1458) found trace of *Cedrus* pollen (0.5%) from Madhya Pradesh 3500-2000 calBC layer. These were probably drifted pollens from Himalayan regions (*ibid*:1457). Hence *Cedrus* was not known to the *Rig-Vedic* Indians. However the later *Yajur-Vedic* Indians may have known it.

Pollen studies of the archaeological remains from the north Indus Valley region have revealed that it was not the cedar but the juniper and pine trees which were present since the beginning of the Mehrgarh culture up to 4,000 BC (Costantini 2008:172-73). However a small last remaining forest of juniper with thousands of years old trees is still surviving in the Zirat Valley of the Kanchi plain in Pakistan (Costantini 2008:172). "The juniper forest at Ziarat is a relict of past vegetations, which probably covered a more extensive area" (Costantini:172). McIntosh too metions modern presence of juniper in the adjoining Quetta Valley (McIntosh: 12).

On this basis we can say that juniper may have grown at the outskirts of the northwest Indus Valley region during the later Harappa Civilization too. There is evidence from the Harappan artefacts for the presence of juniper in the mature Harappa Civilization (*vide infra*). It is possible that even the much later Indians particularly the practitioners of medicine like Sushruta had the knowledge of juniper, and his reference to the *deva-dāru* should be construed to be that for juniper (or may be pine) but not for the cedar.

The confusion in the names

Thus the *devadāra* tree must have originally meant the juniper, or the juniper and pine both before 4000 BC. This we can say because the medicinal properties classically attributed to the *devadāra* tree in the medicinal texts of ancient India are absent from the cedar and actually they belong to juniper.

For example, Sushruta mentions the use of the bark of *deva-daru* for the treatment of *yakṣmā* (tuberculosis), a disease caused by *Mycobacterum tuberculosis* (*Sushruta-Samhita*, *Uttaratantra*, XLI.27). No anti-tuberculosis property has so far been demonstrated for the cedar trees or even the pine tree. On the other hand, Carpenter (2010) demonstrated the anti-tuberculosis effects of juniper in a recent scientific study, which is consistent with the account by Sushruta. Thus the anti-tuberculosis medicine *devadāru*, mentioned by the *Sushruta-Samhita* was actually 'juniper' and not the *Cedrus deo-dara.*

Many authors have mentioned that juniper has anti-bacterial, anti-fungal and anti-viral properties apart from the tonic effect (Boon and Smith:186-87; Purkayastha 2012). In the Western complementary medicine, juniper has been used widely. It gives relief from abdominal pain of intestinal, kidney and bladder diseases, and treats backache, menstrual pain and oligomenorrhoea of the women (Crellin 1994:171; Culpeper 1816(original 1653AD):339,349). Juniper has expectorant, anti-viral, diuretic and anti-diabetic properties (Boon and Smith 2004:187).

The Seven Divine Mothers (*sapta-mātrikā*) depicted in a Harappan seal are wearing juniper branches attached to their heads as adornment (Mohenjo-daro DK 6847, Islamabad Museum; Aruz 2003:403, stamp seal no 294). The identification of the twigs in the seal with Himalayan pencil cedar, which is in fact not a cedar but a juniper (*Juniperus macropodis*), was made by Sir John Marshall, who wrote, "The seven figures in a line at the bottom ... female officiants or ministrants of the goddess... The plumes on their heads might be feathers; but it is probable that they are small branches, such as in Kafiristan are still worn on the head by officiannts at the worship of ... the Himalayan pencil cedar, when branches are also burn in honour of the tree spirit" (Marshall 1931 vol 1: 65, quoted in Possehl 2007:439).

In general the *Rig-Veda* addresses the seven rivers of northwest India as the "seven mothers" (*RV* 1.34.8, 8.85.1, 9.86.36, 9.102.4, 10.17.10 etc). Probably there were juniper forests along the banks of these rivers. Hence the seven mothers on the seal have been depicted wearing adornments of juniper branches. The seal also hints about the possible medicinal role of the juniper tree. Another goddess in a Harappan terracotta figurine (National Museum, Karachi HP 1603; also Aruz: 291, no 278b) wears berries, which look like the juniper-berries, as the head and waist adornment. This latter lady may be the goddess of life and health.

The juniper was an important tree of Harappa (Meluhha) from where it was brought to Mesopotamia by the merchants on boats, as mentions an Early Bronze Age inscription from Syria (*A hymn to Shamash*, cited by Aruz: 237; 465). The inscription mentions the "smoke of the God" which clearly means the incense. The commodities imported by the Mesopotamians from this distant land included lapis lazuli, silver, cedar wood, box-wood, cypress, emblems, vegetable oil, honey, juniper etc. The inscription also adds that the sun-god living on the other shore of the sea had a bull as his vehicle. It is important to recognize here that the oldest meaning of the Vedic *śiva* was 'sun-god'.

Black gives the translation of an ancient Sumerian text describing the home-country of a traveller to Sumer. The description of the home of the traveller sounds more or less to be that of the Indus Valley India: the country had rain from heaven, water for agriculture, harvest of fine barley, well irrigated pine trees and adorned junipers. The country also had palm tree, chariot made of juniper wood, fine cloth, boxwood etc (Black 2006:191-2). The boxwood mentioned here was possibly the cedar (*Cedrus deodara*) which makes excellent packing boxes even today, and which had arrived in India by the time the Sumerian Civilizarion had developed in Mesopotamia.

The Confusion in the names of juniper, pine and cedar

Although, the *pinus* and *juniperus* have become extinct from India in general their name/names must have survived till later times applied to other Indian trees growing in the lowere altitudes of the Himalayas or even in South India till today. Today, we have a large number of trees in India that are known by the common name *'deva-dāru'* or its variants. Some examples of such trees, possessing the name *devadaru* are *Polyalthia longifolia* (Khare:505), *Vepris bilocularis* (Khare:698), *Erythroxylum monogynum* (*ibid*: 246) etc.

One such tree is the Himalayan cedar (*Cedrus deodara*), wrongly translated as the *dev-dār* or the 'Indian pine'. Its wood is resistant from insect-pest like termite and moth and has been used for making storage rooms and boxes for dress, food materials etc in the mountainous regions and in Europe. In fact it is even till date used as box-material for packing the fruits grown over the Himalayan hills. The box-wood mentioned in the Mesopotamian text (Black 2006: 191) was probably this same cedar or the *dev-dār* wood.

It is interesting to know that the 'store-room' in the *Yajur-Veda* was called *kṛdara* (*Taittiriya Samhita* 5.1.11.1), which is not much removed from the word "*cedar*" and *kedāra*. It is likely that the cedar tree had arrived into India during the period of the *Yajur-Veda*, and was present in India during the Bronze Age, and had acquired the Sanskrit name *kṛdara* by that time. However the older meaning of the word *kṛdara* might have been the 'juniper' before juniper had become extinct.

Another seemingly related word *'kedāra'* means the name of a Himalayan region (*Kedar-nath*) which was mentioned in the *Mahabharata* too (*MB* 4.427, 3.6042). Its later meaning 'a field under water' is perhaps a late application of the word. Thus we can visualize that there was a Himalayan region where this tree *kedara* grew, and that this tree could have been the 'cedar' or *Cedrus*, because the time of the *Mahabharata* could be 3500-3000 BC. However some cognate of the word *kedāra* may have existed in India even before 3500 BC, the time of arrival of the cedar in India and then it must have been the name of either juniper or pine or both.

Pokorny gives the meaning 'fume' for the reconstruct PIE root **ked-* (Pokorny:537). Pokorny gives the following words relevant to our study: Sanskrit *kadru* (brown); Old Church Slavonic *kadilo* (incense), *kaditi* (to burn incense); Russian *čad* (haze, fog), Russian *kedr* (cedar), Serbian *čad* (soot), *čaditi* (to become sooty); Greek *kedros* (juniper, later *Pinus cedros*); Latin '*cedar*' and *Cedros* (pine); German *zeder* (cedar), *kiefer* (pine), Lith. *kadagỹs* (juniper), O.Pruss. *kadegis* (juniper).

It clearly proves that the meaning was originally the incense-wood which give red-brown fume on burning. The chips of juniper uded as the incense-wood too are 'red-brown' coloured. Hence the meaning 'red-brown' became the meaning of the root. Anything particularly fruits which were red-brown or tawny in colour derived their names from this root. The Sanskrit word *kadru*, which literally means 'red-brown', often means the 'bottle-gourd' or 'melon' in the *Rig-Veda*. However, either this or its related word must have meant the 'juniper' in some remote pre-history of Indian northwest.

We can examine the different meanings and usage of the word *kadru* in the literature. A word which has occurred in the *Rig-Veda* at several places is *tri-kadruka* 'three beakers' (*RV* 1.32.3; 2.11.17; 2.15.1; 2.22.1; 8.13.18; 8.92.21; 10.14.16). Beakers (*kamaṇḍalu*) were made in India from dried bottle-gourds until recently. The word "three-beakers" used regularly and consistently indicates the fact that the beaker was made up of three chambers. The bottle-gourd is a tricarpellary fruit, and has three chambers on drying. Macdonell and Keith think that the word *kadru* (*RV* 8.45.26) was some type of vessel meant for keeping drinks (Macdonnel and Keith vol 1:134).

This *tri-kadru* is probably the modern north Indian gourd *kaddu* (*Lagenaria siceraria*; Hindi, Bengali, Nepali), which is green in colour when unripe but becomes tawny or red-brown. In Punjabi language, the name *kaddu* is applied to pumpkin, which is similar, but of American origin. However, the unripe fruits or even melons too must have been often named *kadru* as is hinted in the expression: "*apibat kadruvaḥ*" (drank the *kadru*-juice, RV 8.45.26). The juice of the bottle-gourd although drunk by many naturopathy fans in India, it is distasteful. Most probably it is the 'melon' which is the meaning here.

There is mention of a tree named *kadru* too in the *Taittiriya Samhita* (2.1.4.2), where the tree has been depicted as a lady having dialogue with another lady-tree *suparṇā*. Most probably the *kadru* tree is the juniper tree in this context (Greek *kedros* juniper), which provided the incense and has red-brown wood. The *suparṇā* is the oak tree (Latin *sūber* oak). Oak is particularly known for its good leaves, sutable as food for the cattle. This identification was not made earlier because most of the Indologists like Monier-Williams and Griffith did not know that the juniper or oak ever grew in India.

Thus we get a large number of possibly related words: Sanskrit *kedara* (an unidentified tree MWD), *kedāra* (a region in the Himalayas, *Mahabharata*), *kadru* (tawny-red colour *Taittirīya Samhitā* 2.1.4.2; a particular tree *TS* 6.1.6.1-2), *tri-kadru* (three-chambered beaker or bottle-gourd, *RV*); *kadru* a fruit of which some drink was made; *kṛdara* (store-room *TS* 5.1.11.1, ?sacrificial fire-wood).

The meaning of *kṛdara* as store-room given by Griffith (tr of Black *Yajur-Veda*) may not be correct, and it might mean the juniper incense-wood alternatively. The mantra is as follows: *samiddho añjan kṛdaram matīnām ghṛtam agne madhumat pinvamānaḥ*. A proper rearrangement of words would result in the following: *samiddho añjan kṛdaram/ ghṛtam agne/ matīnām madhumat pinvamānaḥ*. This arrangemet gives the meaning 'incense-wood' which was juniper. However if the meaning 'store-room' is accepted, cedar would be the more appropriate meaning of *kṛdara*.

There is the confusion of names between pine and juniper in Europe too, where both the trees are regularly encountered by the people.

Thus Greek *kedros* (juniper) and Latin *cedar* (pine) are in fact the same word applied to two different trees in the two languages of Europe.

Sanskrit word *pṛthu-dāru* and *pūtudrū* meaning the *Pinus* tree in Vedic times too has been confused and variously applied to pine, cedar and juniper in Europe: Albanian *bredh* (pine; Lehmann: 66); Greek *brathu* (juniper, Lehmann:66), Greek *pitys* (pine); Latin *pinus* (pine). Another example of such confusion is the set of cognates: Armenian *ełevni, ełevin* (cedar), Lithuanian Lith. *ẽglius* (juniper) and Russ. *jáłovec* (juniper; Pokorny:302-304).

The word 'cedar' too has been widely applied to name the cedar, pine and juniper trees in the various regions of Europe and the European speaking Americans: the Prickly Cedar (*oxykedrus*, ὀξύκεδρος), Mountain cedar, Sharp Cedar, Bermuda Cedar and Eastern Red Cedar are the types of junipers. The Atlas Cedar and Cyprus Cedar are the pine trees. Marshall noted identified the Himalayan Pencil Cedar in Mohenjo-Daro seal which is in fact a *juniper* (Marshall 1931 vol1:63, cited by Sastri 1957:17). The incense-cedar *Calocedrus* too is a tree of the juniper family (*Cupressaceae*), not of the pine family (*Pinaceae*).

Hence there is no reason to believe that the ancient Indians did not have this confusion of applying the same name to the three gymnosperm trees pine, cedar and juniper. Following the extinction of the juniper and pine, the names the two got applied to the cedar and other trees which were their survivors.

A *Rig-Vedic* hymn picturized in Harappan seal

We can note that the *Rig-Vedic* hymn (*RV* 10.97) has been graphically represented in a Mohenjo-Daro seal (Seal no. Mohenjo-daro DK 6847; Islamabad Museum, NMP 50.295). This seal was originally described by Mackay (1938: pl. XCIV, 430; pl. XCIX, 686a; cited by Aruz 2003: 403, topic no 294), however its depiction in the *Rig-Veda* text was not noticed by him nor anyone else so far.

The moribund infirm man with frail limbs lying to the left of the shaman (or, priest) is the patient, or his dummy. The shaman/priest is passionately pleading to the Goddess who lives in the *pipal* (?*aśvattha*; *Ficus religiosa*) tree to procure her favour in the form of the cure of the person who is his client. A ram (or he-goat) has been brought for sacrifice to be offered to the goddess. The underlying principle behind this is 'life for life'. Ram's life is being offered to the Goddess in lieu of the parient's life. In the seal there are seven ladies—the *sapta-mātrikā's*--standing on the one side. The *Rig-Veda* mentions : *RV* (10.97.4-5): "Mothers, to you the Goddesses... The *aśvattha* is your home,", *RV* (10.97.22): "With Soma as their Sovran Lord the Plants hold colloquy and say: O King, we save from death the man whose cure a Brahman undertakes."

These Seven Divine Mothers (*sapta-mātrikā*) have been depicted wearing juniper twigs as adornments or ornaments (Marshall vol 1:65). Thus the seven mothers, which were originally the seven great rivers of the *Rig-Veda*, have been deified here as the medicinal goddesses. However the Supreme Goddess in this seal resides in the *aśvattha* tree which is consistent with the *Rig-Vedic* description: *RV* (10.97.4-5): "The *aśvattha* is your home". the *Yajur-Veda* also repeats the same assertoion: "In the *aśvattha* is your seat," (*TS* 4.2.6.2; also repeated in *SB* 8.8.3.1).

The other medicinal mother-trees have been further explained in the same hymn of the *Rig-Veda* as the trees with flowers and without them, and trees with fruits and without them (*RV* 10.97.3, 15). Of note here is the Akkadian name of juniper that is *supalu(m)* which might be from Sanskrit *suphala* (one with good fruits) and has been considered a medicine (Jeremy Black:328). The *Rig-Vedic* hymn mentions the *apuṣpī* (non-flowering) plant which mixed with some other plants had been used to treat the person who has fever and pain (*RV* 10.97.15). It further clarifies that the other mother goddesses join in chorus in support of the shaman's request for favour in the following words: RV 10.97.22: "With Soma as their Sovran Lord the Plants hold colloquy and say: O King, we save from death the man whose cure a Brahman undertakes."

The *Rig-Vedic* medicinal tree *apuṣpī* (literally 'gymnosperm') must have been the juniper. It does not have flower and it contains anti-bacterials, steroids, cardiac glycosides and anti-tuberculosis substances of high medicinal value. The other non-flowering (*apuṣpī*) tree (*i.e. Pinus*) from the *Rig-Vedic* times did not have enough medicinal properties however it had anti-inflammatory properties helpful in painful conditions. It also has some cough-suppressant properties (*Ayurvedic* Pharmacopeia of India, Govt of India:28).

The *Rig-Veda* (*RV* 10.97.15) mentions the *apuṣpā* (without flower, gymnosperm) tree in the context of treatment of a seriously ill patient with *yakṣma* (*RV* 10.97.11-13). We know from the description of *yakṣma* (*yakṣmā*) in later medical texts that this was nothing other than the consumptive disease of the lungs, caused by *Mycobacterium tuberculosis* (*Sushruta-Samhita*, *Uttaratantra*, XLI.2 & 4-6).

Thus the high esteem for its medicinal properties showed for the *apuṣpā* tree in the *Rig-Veda* makes the reference to the gymnosperm plants predominantly to the juniper. Therefore we conclude that *apuṣpā* of the *Rig-Veda* was juniper, and its common name was *kṛdara/ kadru* (later *kedara* although the word *kedara* itself has missed mention in the *Rig-Veda*). It is also likely that owing to the medicinal properties, juniper was considered divine. No doubt the tree was revered in the Vedas as 'mother' (*RV* 10.97.2). It is also possible that the Akkadian word *kullaru* (kullar-juniper, a type of juniper) is from Sanskrit *kadru* (see Jeremy Black).

Hence it is very likely that in the early Harappa culture (before 3000 BC) when the juniper was available in the Indus Valley region, the goddess of health was depicted decorated with the juniper berries in terracotta art. However, later the epithet goddess of life and health seems to have been transferred to the 'pine', and after its extinction, the name went to the cedar, during mature and later Harappa times. This we can say on the basis of the fact that in many Harappan seals a female deity is sitting on the branch of a tree, which can be identified as pine.

Chapter 21

Pine (*Pinus*) and Ash (*Fraxinus*)

The pine (*Pinus*), Himalayan pine or cedar (*Cedrus deodara*) and fir (*Abies*) are gymnosperm conifer trees in the *Pinales* family having naked seeds and no flower. The leaves are acicular and sharply pointed (like needles). Their branches are nearly horizontal (Bhatnagar and Moitra 1996:210; Farjon 2010:256). Fir is closer to the cedar tree. These three and the juniper are quite similar in many ways and their names have often been confused in the different languages and locations.

Pinus was present in the northwest Indian plains from about 7,000 BC to 4,000 BC (Costantini 2008:171-2). In Jammu it was present from 7500 BC till present (Trivedi and Chauhan 2009:405-7), although the pollen counts are very low after 100 BC. In Europe's northern regions, there was a peak of pine pollens between 6600 BC and 5800 BC (Starkel 1999:111). In the east of the Central Asia region the pine was present in Southwest China (near Tibet) before 8,000 BC, however it declined there soon after that time (Zhao 2009:248). The temperate steppe (of Inner Mongolia) changed into birch-pine forest at early Holocene changing back to the steppe climate by 4700 BC (*ibid*:248-9). From these date it can be guessed that the presence of the pine is possible during the early Holocene at the Western steppe. It is true that too much rain kills pine yet it needs minimum 300-350 mm of rainfall every year to survive (Cermak 2005: 254) which was not available there at 1500 BC in the steppe, the generally claimed place of Indo-European origin.

The pollen studies showed that the vegetation around Dadiwan (China) was of a desert-steppe type in the early Holocene. However it changed into *Pinus* dominated steppe between 6,500 BC and 4,400 BC period (Zhao 2009:249), and then again returned to the desert-steppe condition after that. A study from Kazakhstan revealed the invasion by pine on the *Betula-Salix* and other forests between 4,500 and 4,000 BC in different parts of the region, increasing progressively with passing time (Kremenetski and Velichko 2007).

Diaojiao Lake site had pine trees between 5,000 BC and 3000 BC (Zhao 2009:249). At present pine is not found in the steppe (see distribution map below). At Yolin Am (Central Asia), pine pollens occurred in the mid-Holocene before 2300 BC, and decreased following this time (Miehe 2007). However they noted that the pine pollens found there had in fact come from south, washed out by the rains during the strong summer Indian Ocean monsoons (Miehe 2007:163). The presence of pine forest is not uniform in the region, we see from the data. The absence of pine-forest is notable in Kazakhstan before 4500 BC. Hence if the migration had taken place before 4,500 BC, the name of 'pine' would be lost from the vocabulary by the time people reached north Europe from India. Instead the general word for 'tree' *dāru* would be applied to the pine tree when these people encounter pine again on reaching North Europe.

On the other hand pine trees were present in Anatolia as fir-pine forst 7000-1500 BC (Bottema cited by Roberts 2011:149, table 1). The study of Lake Van (East Anatolia) fossil pollens indicated the enhanced presence of pine at 8,100 BC to 6250 BC period (Wick 2003:671 Table 1). They also noted earlier evidence of cedar (*Cedrus*) to the north of the lake between 9,500 BC to 8,500 BC period (*ibid*:670).

In such a study done from Syria, the pine was present in the early part of Holocene in abundance, but decreases in the later part (Hussein

2006:337). In Western and Southern Iran early Holocene had dry and cold climatic conditions (Kehl 2009:1,8), yet the actual precipitation in Southern Iran was more then than it gets today (*ibid*:10). These conditions were conducive to the growth of pine. In the Zagros, more humid conditions would arrive only after 5000 BC (*ibid*:11), which would lead to establishment of oak, beech and other trees replacing the pine.

In the Caucasus region, pine was abundant in the late Pleistocene early Holocene (Conner 2006:26, 27, 29). The mid-Holocene is warmer and more humid leading to growth of beech and oak. Obviously this period was not favourable to pine. However when the pine again increased at the late Holocene, we can infer decreasing humidity of the region (*ibid*:26).

Thus we find that it was only during the early Holocene (roughly 8,000-6000 BC) when pine species were regularly present in Iran, Syria and Turkey. In Greece pine is found at 4300 BC in abundance (Digerfeldt 2007:364). Thus a migration starting from India about 8,000 to 6,000 BC and reaching the Balkans by 4000 BC would come across the pine trees throughout the way and get it there in Greece too. Thus it would be able to conserve the name of 'pine'.

The cognates words--*pitu*, *pūtu* and *pṛthu* (Sanskrit, 'pine tree'), Latin *pinus*, Greek *pytis* and Albanian *pishë*—are unique to the southern route and have not been identified so far in the languages of northern Europe. However, the Old Prussian *peuse* (pine), Lith *pušìs* (pine); O.H.G. *fiuhta, fiuhtia* (fir); Old Irish *fid*, gen. *fedo* (tree) etc could be possible cognates (see PIE *peuĝ*, Pokorny:828). In the northern route the cognates of *dāru* were used to name the pine, because it was the most frequent tree in that route.

This relationship of the Sanskrit word *pitu* with Greek *pytis* etc claimed by earlier authors was rejected by Mayerhofer (1956-80, II:293), however, Friedrich (1970:31-38) reaffirmed this relationship (see Lehmann:120, for these references; also Valpi:343, CDIAL 8236, and Harper). We too find the cognate relationship with Sanskrit *pitu* convincing, especially in view of the near cosmopolitan presence of the pine tree in Eurasia during the Early Holocene, the putative time of these migrations.

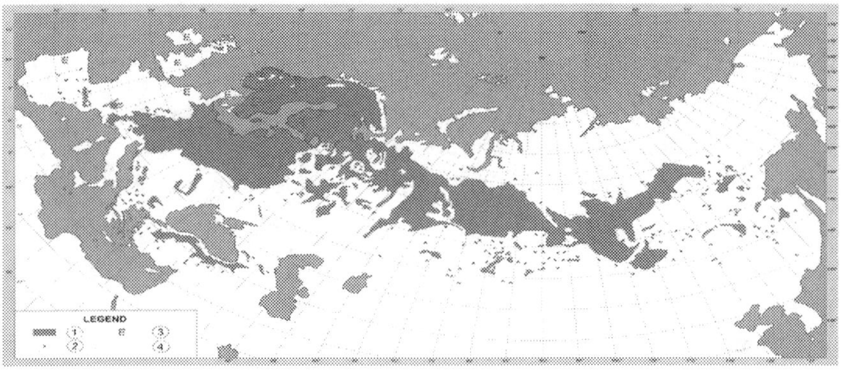

Figure 4: Map depicting the distribution of the pine trees as grey and dark regions. Source: http://upload.wikimedia.org/wikipedia/commons/5/5e/Pinus_sylvestris_range-01.png. Accessed 15 June 2014.

Modern distribution of *Pinus*

Although a reference to this tree can be construed in the *Rig-Veda* (10.97) where flowerless trees have been mentioned, yet it is more likely from the context that this *Rig-Vedic* reference pertains to the non-flowering medicinal tree the juniper. There are trees depicted in the Harappan seals which look like the pine. A goddess has often been shown sitting over one of its branches and often she appears to be one with the tree.

In the Mohenjo-Daro seal (M-478A) which depicts a pine tree, the leaves are sharp and acute. There is a tiger, which looks a bit frustrated. The tiger is probably the symbol of threat (disease/death). Clearly the female deity is the goddess of life/healing. Many seals with identical depiction have been found from the Harappan Civilization.

Thus the concept of the mother goddess (of health, medicine and life) described in the *Rig-Veda* (10.97) continues into the Harappa

Civilization. In fact the contemporary folk Hinduism has attributed the disease curing powers to the 'mother deity' or the *mātā* till very recent times, and even today by the rural folks. This belief may be traced back to the *Rig-Veda* passing through the Harappa culture.

The *Rig-Veda* (10.97.5) mentions the "*parṇa* tree" as the name of a particular tree, and states that this tree is the mansion of the mother-goddess of health and life. We do not know what this tree is, but it the description makes it clear that it was a medicinal plant. It could have been fern (German *farn*), we can say because of philological resemblance. Ferns are important medicinal herbs used in ancient Indian medicine (Mannan 2008). Fern plant was found in India (single study done in Jammu) from 7500 BC until medieval times (Trivedi and Chauhan 2009). Alternatively it could be the pine. Or, this could have bben the same as the *farn*-herb (*Asparagus*), which has medicinal properties against many diseases (Pokorny:816-17; Khare: 68). The issue needs further examination.

Fraxinus or Ash Tree

The ash-tree (Latin *Frāxinus*; Romanian *frasin*; Greek *fraxo*; Albanian *frashër*) which is the first class firewood and burns with bright light with little smoke, has been considered present at the PIE stage by the name **bherəĝ-* or **bhrēĝ-* (Pokorny:139-140), which is philologically the nearest for the *Rig-Vedic* word *bhṛgu*, which was a group of men specializing in lighting, burning and preservation of fire (*RV* 1.58.6; 6.15.2). Possibly the ash-tree too was called *bhṛgu* in the beginning. Today this tree *fraxinus* is not found in India, but was there in the Indus Valley region (Mehrgarh) in the oldest aceramic period between 7,000 and 5,000 calBC period (Costantini 2008: 171-2). *Fraxinus* tree is found in Iran (Hossein Akhani 2010) and Turkey (Ozturk 2013:193) even today. It has been there since mid-Holocene (Hussein 2006:336). It has increased in Northwest Iran since 1600 BC (Djamali 2009).

The Vedic fire-specialists the *bhṛgu*-s must have been named after this tree (PIE **bhrēĝ-*) which is one of the best woods for burning. The word *bhṛgu* has been used in context of 'car' (*ratha*) building too (*RV* 4.16.20), indicating that the same specialists could also make carts from this wood. It is known that the bodies of cars (but not the wheels) were built from this wood in Europe because of the flexibility of the wood (Hammond:87; Porcher:494).

Obviously, when the tree became extinct in India, following warming and drying of the region, the meaning of the word as the particular tree was lost; and the word *bhṛgu* came to be remembered only for the specialists who specialized in maintaining the fire, or lighting it, and worked with this wood. The English word 'bright' is the cognate of *bhṛgu*. Hence we need to fix the date of the *Rig-Veda* before 4000 BC, after which this tree has become extinct from northwest India.

Chapter 22

Aspen and poplar in Indian archaeology and Vedic texts

The fossil pollen studies done in India reveal that the *Populus species* were common trees in India during early and mid Holocene, and fossil pollens have been recovered from Mehrgarh dating up to 4000 BC (Jarrige; Costantini) and the Harappa Civilization up to 2600 BC (Peregrine and Ember vol 8 2003:118). At Kot Daji (near Harappa) poplar charcoal was found in all the layers of the Harrappan period (Fuller and Madella 2001:365), and that would mean up to 1900 BC. However given the general extinction of the tree from the region in the early fourth millennium BC, it can be understood that these later poplar trees must have been cultivated.

They do not occur in the Indian plains any more. However trees of this genus (*Populus*) grow even today at 3,800 meters above sea level near Bhoj-basa village in the proximity of the Gangotri glacier in the Himalayas (Ranhotra and Bhattacharya 2011: 24). It is not possible to identify the exact species of the *Populus* from the Mehrgarh pollens because both the trees namely aspen (*Populus tremula*) and poplar (*Populus alba*) have similar pollens (Costantini in his personal correspondence to me). So far no attept to identify these trees in the Vedic texts has been made. This matter therefore requires enquiry and investigation.

Bloomfield noted regarding the Vedas that as the climate, and thereby flora, changed with the passing time the names of the older plants and trees got applied to the newer ones (Bloomfield 1897: Introduction). There has been enormous climate change almost every two thousand years, and to expect that the same flora and fauna have existed over the ages is doing injustice with history. Hence we must accept that most likely the Vedic names of the *Populus alba* and *P. tremula* were thrust on to some other Indian trees during the Bronze Age about the mid-Holocene when these trees became extinct and many other trees like *Ficus religiosa* etc arrived into the region.

Identification

Poplar and aspen belong to the same genus *Populus*, however the aspen is known scientifically as the *P. tremula* and poplar the *P. alba, nigra* etc. Leaves of aspen and some of the poplars resemble the *Ficus religiosa* leaves not only in shape but also in their ever-trembling nature. Even then, poplar is warmth tolerant and aspen is cold adapted.

Poplar spent the Late Glacial period in the Italian and Romanian refugia, while the aspen was distributed to the north and spent the glacial period in the refugia located about the snow caps. Subsequently the two expanded during the Holocene, meeting and hybridizing in Central Europe. However the frquency of the tree was very low because not much fossil pollen of any *Populus* species has been found from the Holocene Europe (Giesecke 2012; Bjune 2004; Gaillard 2010; Elina 2010; Fussi 2010). However it has been claimed by the palynologists that the pollens of the *Pupulus* species are perishable. But this latter argument should be taken with caution (read suspicion) because quite often large quantities of *Populus* pollens have been recovered from the archaeological soil samples. The current distribution of the aspen is in the colder extreme north Europe, whereas that of poplar is in the warmer South and Central regions of Europe.

Philological Material for poplar:

English 'poplar', 'popal'; Greek *pelea* (elm); Latin *populus*, *populnus*, *populinus* (poplar; Valpi:353), Italian *pioppo*, Romanian *plop*; German *pappel* (poplar); OCS *topoli* (poplar); Sanskrit *pippala* (*Ficus religiosa*), Hindi *pipal* (*Ficus religiosa*). The German word is a borrowing from the Italic. However these words have not been recognised as IE words by Pokorny. Pokorny and other German Indo-Europeanists had the ethnocentric habit of not accepting any word as Indo-European unless its cognate occured in the Germanic languages.

However the list of cognates presented above makes it clear that the Indo-Europeans entered South Europe not from the north but from the south-east direction. It is also possible that these words ('popler' etc) arrived later in Europe only after the first wave of Indo-Europeans had arrived and settled there long back. The absence of the poplar tree from North Europe is reflected in the absence of cognate words of 'poplar' from the languages of that region. The linguistic distribution of the cognates of 'poplar' also indicates that this word travelled by the southern coastal route to Europe.

The Indo-Europeans were not native of Europe. That is why there is no fixed nomenclature for this tree in Europian IE languages. As for example, the Cornish (Celtic) word *bedewen* means 'poplar' (*c.f.* Pushto *badar* 'poplar'), however its cognates the Breton word *bezuen* and Gall word *betulla* do not mean 'poplar' but mean the 'birch'. (Pokorny:480). Similarly the Albanian *verrë* (poplar) is a cognate of Breton *gwern* (alder; Pokorny: 1169). The Macedonian **elisā* (poplar) is a cognate of Latin *alnus* (alder). Greek *kabaki* (poplar) is another mystery.

This inconsistency in naming is enough evidence to bring home that although the tree was in Europe since the early Holocene no doubt, yet poplar may not have been present throughout the route from India to South Europe going through Iran. Poplar is a stream-bank tree and Iran did not have enough of the streams all along to have had the poplar throughout Iran. Thus the Indo-European name for the tree (?

pippala) was lost during the first wave of migration associated with the Neolothic. The names possibly reached there during the Bronze Age.

Poplar became extinct from India when the end of the mid-Holocene Optimum was approaching. Since the early Bronze Age it must have been cultivated in India, Iran and Turkey. Djamali studies the fossil pollens from 1700 BC Iran and found the evidence of its cultivation there (Djamali 2009: 1370, Fig. 5). Older periods have not been studied so far. Hoever there is literary evidence for the cultivation of poplar (*pippala*) in the *Yajur-Veda.*

It is possible that the people of the *Rig-Veda* made distinction between the poplar (*pippala*) and aspen (*aśvattha*), although later both the words were used synonymously to name the *Ficus religiosa* tree. Clearly the Vedic word *pippala* is not too far removed from *Populus* etc. Hence we may conclude that during *Rig-Vedic* India, *Populus* was called *pippala.* But the *Ficus religiosa* was not there in the northwest India during the *Rig-Vedic* times which was a dry period and it invaded the region only during the mid-Holocene Optimum which was the period of the *Yajur-Veda.*

There was a small window of time when both the poplar and the *Ficus religiosa* may have existed in the region. The poplar must have become extinct before 3000 BC or even 4000 BC, yet its presence up to 1900 BC Harappa (Fuller and Madella 2002:365) indicates its cultivation. The poplar tree was cultivated and irrigated has been mentioned explicitly in the *Yajur-Veda* (*TS* 4.1.2.4) and the *Atharva-Veda* (*AV* 3.17.5). The poplar has been addressed regularly as "the medicinal plant good-*pippala* (*oṣadhi su-pippala*)" in the *yajur-Veda* (*TS* 1.2.2.3; 1.3.6.1; 4.1.2.4; 5.1.5.10; 6.1.3.7; 6.3.4.2 etc), and possibly because of her medicinal value the tree was widely cultivated.

However, after the *Populus* became extinct completely even from the cultivated stock, the name was retained only by *Ficus religiosa* in India. The *Rig-Veda* mentions the name *pippala* only once: *supippala oṣadhiḥ* (good *pippala*, the medicinal tree; *RV* 7.101.5). The hymn prays to the rain-god to give rains which may protect the "medicinal good-*pippala*" trees. However, by the time of the *Yajur-Veda* the artificial irrigation too was used (*TS* 4.1.2.4; *AV* 3.17.5). This "good-*pippala*" mentioned in the *Rig-Veda* is in all likelihood the salicylic acid containing tree *Populus*. It is the *Populus* tree which is riparian in habitat and needs rain or irrigation for survival--that is the reason for the *Rig-Vedic* prayer. *Populus* not only contained salicylic acid but also contained quinine, the anti-malarial medicine (Zavaleta:153; Anonymous in Magazine of Science 1848:152).

The poplar leaves and bark are the favourite food of horse and they act as tonic to these (Stewart 1869:131). The Non-Steroidal-Anti-Inflammatory drug present in the bark of this tree removes the muscle cramps of humans too, and it may be one of the reasons for the popularity of this tree among the horses just as the anti-inflammatory drugs are popular among the athletes. Withering (1776:614) and later Buxton (1849:126-7) too wrote that horses like to eat the poplar leaves, while cows do not.

Hence the wild and feral horses must have thronged the poplar forests in good numbers. We also know that the poplar has riverine habitat and it tends to grow naturally along the banks of the rivers. Hence there must have been poplar forests along the northwest Indian rivers, particularly the Sarasvati and Indus. And being the natual addictant to the wild horse, the wild horses must have thronged these forests in large numbers (*RV* 7.95.2-3). It is because of the horses roaming over the banks of the rivers, that the Sarasvati has been called *vājinī-vatī* (rich in mares) in the *Rig-Veda* (*RV* 1.3.10). DNA studies have proved that the mares were captured from the wild while the stallions were not after the first stallion had been domesticated. (Lindgren 2004; Lau 2009). Hence the epthet "rich in mares" to Sarasvati is significant. These were the wild mares which were of the economic importance to the early Holocene Indians, not the wild horses.

This understanding helps us explain the *Rig-Vedic* mantra (*RV* 10.097.7) which says that the medinal herbs were "rich in steed", and were given to an ill person with the intent of curing him. This is a clear reference to poplar which was loved and thronged by the horses and which had spectacular medicinal properties too.

The *Rig-Vedic Aśvins* (or, the *Aśvinī Kumāra-s*) are two gods which are of the shape of horses (*RV* 1.118-119). They are the first medical physicians too. Indeed poplar was a medicinal plant for the Vedic horses as well as the humans. It is possible that the primitive Indians of early Holocene thought that god of the horses lived in the poplar tree. That was why the horses thronged the tree, they would think. However later when they knew the medicinal value of the tree, they attributed properties of physicians to these divine horse-beings who lived inside the poplar trees.

It is possible that the tree was believed to be the home to the *Aśvinī Kumāra*-s. In one of the Harappan seals, the *aśvattha* tree has been depicted as harbouring two horses within its stem, and the neck and head of the horses are projecting out. Both the horses are having 'horns' (Harappan Seal M-296 A). The *Rig-Veda* mentions the *Aśvins* as horse-shaped gods having horns (*RV* 1.118.10; 1.163.9). Hence this Harappan seal should be considered an icon of the *Aśvinī Kumāra*-s living in a poplar tree (or its Harappan replacement *pippala* tree) and curing the infirm people.

Philology of Aspen:

English 'aspen' and 'asp', Old Eng. *aespe*, German *espe*, Old High German *aspa*, Middle Dutch *espe*, Norse *ösp*, Old Norse *ǫsp*; Latvian *apse*, Old Prussian *abse*, Lithuanian *apušě*; Russian *osína*, Polish *osa, osina* all meaning 'aspen' (Pokorny:55). Also of interest is Persian *aspe-dār* (aspen; literally horse-tree) and *aqwāq* (white poplar), where *dār* means 'tree' and *aspa* and *aqva* mean 'horse'. The common syllable here is '*asp*' which is there in the IE word for horse also—Iranian *asp*, Sanskrit *aśva*.

Clearly *aśvattha*, the name of a *Rig-Vedic* tree, is a cognate of these words at the very face value. This word (*aśvattha*) is no more used by most of the Indian masses yet has been extensively used in Sanskrit literature and has been understood by the readers as the *Ficus religiosa*. However its cognates are used today only in the modern Assamese, Bengali and Sindhi languages where they mean not the *Ficus religiosa*, but the *Ficus tsiela* tree (CDIAL 922 and 1470).

In case of the philology of aspen, we get a story different from the poplar. Aspen has a precise meaning in all the North European languages and there is no multiplicity of names for this tree or overlap of its name with other trees. This also indicates that the tree was present throughout the way when the Indo-European migration took place. Hence the name was not forgotton. The northern route to Europe went from northwest India along the Oxus River and thereafter along the north Caspian. The ecology was riparian and cold at 7000-6000 BC and the aspen was present on the way along the river. The cognates of the "aspen" are also cognates of Sanskrit '*aśva*' and Iranian *aspa* indicating some sort of etymological connection with horse. This possibility cannot be ingonored in view of the fact that the association with horse has been philologically claimed by many Indologists with regard to the Indian tree *aśvattha*.

The Horse Connection of *aśvattha* and aspen

It has been claimed on the basis of philology that the word *aśvattha* means the 'horse-stand' (*aśva-stha*= horse-stay; MacDonald and Keith:43; Dikshit 1938:40; also MWD). Today although the word *aśvattha* is no more used in any Indian vernacular language, yet the *aśvattha* tree is identified as the *Ficus religiosa* or the *pipal* tree by the scholars.

It is a common knowledge that the *Ficus religiosa* tree is not at all the most fancied place for keeping the horses under, although there is no prohibition. Then why this name? Why did the ancient Indo-Europeans keep their horse below the *aśvattha* tree? Was the *aśvattha* the same as today's *pipal* (*Ficus religiosa*) or was it something else? We have noted in this book that during the early Vedic period, the *Ficus* trees were not there in northwest India. Hence no question of keeping the horse below this tree could have ever emerged.

However, the aspen tree, which was present in the cold early Holocene Indian stream-banks, has been one of the most favoured trees for tying the horse to the stem or for keeping a horse under it, because of the horse's dislike for the bark and leaves of this tree. Withering (1776:614), Souter (1805:543) and Buxton (1849:126-7) mention that there is a special type of *Populus* (*tremula* species) known as 'aspen' which horses refuse to eat. Horses often have a habit of bitting if they get bored. In this process they can severely damage the trunk of any tree. Therefore it becomes necessary to keep them tied to some tree whose bark or leaves they do not like to chew. Aspen meets this requirement and horses do not bit its bark.

In the English fiction, the horsemen have been often dipected tying their horses to the aspen tree (*e.g.* Lo-Johansson 1991: 217; Harman 2010:31; Dyer 2013). Hence one should not be surperized if the ancient Indians too tied their horses to the aspen trees when these trees grew in India. Moreover the *Taittiriya Brahmana* (3.8.12.2) clearly mentions that the horse for the horse-sacrifice should be kept in a pen (stall) made of the *aśvattha* wood in the last two months before the sacrifice (cited Eggeling Part 5, 1900:*xxx* fn3; 364, fn 2).

Thus it is very much likely that the Vedic *aśvattha* was nothing other than the aspen tree (*Pupulus tremula* or 'trembling poplar'). In that case, the early Vedic people would have liked to keep their horses under this tree, because the horses disliked aspen and never bit its bark. This might have made aspen trees in India the favourite place to keep the horses tied with its stem. It is remarkable to note that about 8000 BC all the combination was present in northwest India: the cold climate, grassland ecosystem with plenty of horses, river full of glacial waters with aspen trees along the banks.

However, the *Ficus religiodsa* too had acquired the name *aśvattha* some time during the period of the *Yajur-Veda* itself, because the *aśvattha* tree has been listed along with the three other trees of the *Ficus* genus in a mantra (*TS* 3.4.8.3). The *Shatapatha Brahmana*, a 3000 BC text (astronomical date; Kak; Achar), often mentions the *araṇī* made of the *aśvattha* tree which had grown as epiphyte over the *sāmī* (*Prosopis*) tree. It is the *Ficus religiosa* which commonly grows over the *Prosopis* tree. Thus the *Ficus religiosa* had arrived in the Indus-Sarasvati region and acquired the name *aśvattha* by the time of the *Yajur-Veda* and the *Shatapatha Brahmana*. However for some centuries the the aspen and *Ficus religiosa* both must have coexisted in the region before aspen finally became extinct.

Study by Thiebault (1988) revealed that at 3000 BC, there was no *Ficus religiosa* tree at Lal Shah and Mehrgarh. However at Nausharo, three out of 4035 samples of charcoal had trace resemblance with *Ficus* wood, although there was no element of certainty to call it *Ficus*. Seventeen samples at the same place and six at Lal Shah and seven samples at Mehrgarh belonged to the *Populus sp*. Thus it was the transition point when the *Populus sp* was becoming extinct (see Constantini), and the *Ficus* had just entered the region in the negligible numbers.

During the Vedic age fire was produced by churning one piece of wood (upper rotating piece called *araṇī*) over the other made (base). The texts repaeatedly mention that the upper piece was made of *aśvattha* wood and the lower of the *sāmī* (*SB* 11.5.1.15).

It is the aspen (and also poplar) which makes excellent fire-wood and catches fire easily even if not fully dry. It "gives intense heat with nearly no smoke, lasts well, does not blacken utensils" (Tawrell 2006: 430). *Ficus religiosa* or *pipal* is in fact a fire-retardant, and is not good as firewood. However, the smaller baby *aśvattha* grown as epiphyte plants over the *Proposis* tree burns well and was used for kindling the holy fire for the Vedic rituals (*SB* 2.1.4.5). However this text mentions the word *su-pippala* only once and the usage mentioned is entirely different (*SB*

3.7.1.12). In fact many authors have also cofused the *pippala* with the *pippali* which is a bitter medicinal berry used to suppress cough.

Having said this there is another important point to consider. The *Shatapatha Brahmana* makes it clear that there was utter confusion in identifying the *aśvattha*, and the people were in general wrongly naming the *kārṣmarya* wood as *aśvattha* (*Shatapatha Brahmana* 4.3.3.6), which the author of the *Shatapatha Brahmana* did not approve of. What was this *kārṣmarya* wood we do not know. However from the name of the tree itself it becomes obvious that about 3000 BC it was grown in Kashmir and brought to the Indus-Sarasvati region from there. The *Gmelina species* suggested as the meaning of the *kārṣmarya* by the MWD and also Khare (p. 290) is not convincing because this tree (*Gmelina*) grows even in the Andaman and Nicobar Islands, and has no particular affinity with cold climate or with Kashmir. Although the *Gmelina* tree resembles the aspen tree and has antibiotic substances in it (Sudhakar 2006) which should have been highly valued as medicine those days, we cannot accept the view of Monier-Williams without more evidence.

But one thing is amply clear that we name the *Ficus religiosa* as *aśvattha* today, but this was not the case always in the past, and once upon a time different trees were called *aśvattha* in northwest India, and about 3000 BC there was utter confusion in identifying the *aśvattha* tree.

Some other mentions of *pippala* and *aśvattha* in the Vedic texts

In the *Rig-Veda*'s tenth *mandala* we find the medicinal trees being addressed as the 'mothers', and a medical professional (shaman) is pleading emotively to obtain the cure of his client (*RV* 10.97). This has been discussed in this book in the context of juniper. The shaman also says that the mother's (Goddess's) abode is inside the *aśvattha* tree (10.97.4-5; also quoted in *TS* 4.2.6.2 and *SB* 8.8.3.1).

However this *Rig-Vedic aśvattha* was certainly not the *Ficus religiosa* that has no spectracular medicinal property. It must have been the aspen (or poplar), which has leaves resembling the holy fig tree's, both in shape and in tremulousness, but has very high medicinal value even in some critical medical emergencies. This is because of the salicylic acid content in it which is extremely beneficial in Coronary Artery Disease, fever, arthritis and gout. It can avert or even revert the heart attacks and strokes and save the lives. Aspirin or acetyl salicylic acid is a derivative of salicylic acid the active component of the aspen and poplar trees. Hence the identification of the *Rig-Vedic aśvattha* as aspen is quite convincing.

In one mantra (*TS* 5.1.5.10) the *su-pippala* tree has been claimed to be rich in flowers and fruits. Another mantra (*TS* 6.1.3.7) mentions the handsome fruits of the *su-pippala* tree. This feature also matches the poplar. The *Populus* has impressive catkins and beautiful flowers, while we are not aware of any flower of the *Ficus religiosa* known outside the botanists' circles. Hence the *su-pippala* is certainly the *Populus* tree. It is however possible that the word *pippala* without the prefix "*su-*" was used as the generic term for all those trees which had the tremulous, shaking leaves and when the *Ficus religiosa* arrived in the region, the name was applied to it too. *Ficus religiosa* and poplar both the trees are famous for their ever-shaking leaves (James: 24).

This shaking as an essential semantic aspect of *pippala* can be suggested from the Indo-European etymology too, as the words for 'butterfly' in some of the Indo-European languages would suggest: Hindi *titlī* (butterfly), West Pahari *phímpəṛi* (butterfly, CDIAL 8201 *Addenda*), Nepali *titili* (butterfly, Turner Nepali CEDNL), Sindhi *popaṭa* (butterfly); Latin *pāpiliō*, French *papillon* (butterfly); Slovenian *prepelíca* (butterfly); also Greek *pallo* (tremble). Other likely cognates are Albanian *palun* (fluttering); Latin *palpito* (shake), *palpebrae* (eyelids), Sanskrit *pallava* (leaf) etc (see Pokorny:798-801).

Certainly the *Ficus religiosa* too might have been known as *pippala* particularly in the third millennium BC because of its ever-trembling leaves. However the Indo-European words meaning the female 'nipple' are often the cognate words of *pippala*, and the berry of the *pippala* exactly resembles the nipple of a mature woman. This is an example of semantic shift of the meaning of the root with changing environment. The cognate words covering this semantic aspect, *i.e.* 'nipple' or 'berry' of *pippala* (*Ficus religiosa*) are: Sanskrit *pippalaka* (nipple); English 'nipple'; Latin *papilla* (nipple); Lith. *pãpas* (nipple); Middle English and Swedish *pappe* (nipple; see Pokorny: 91). This is clearly the result of a secondary semantic shift, and later transmission of the words carrying this meaning (nipple, berry) during the Bronze Age.

The *Ficus* wasp (Sanskrit *pipīlikā*)

There is another semantic derivative of the word *pippala*. The ant was originally known as the *vamra* (*RV* 1.51.9), *vamraka* (*RV* 10.99.12) and *valmī* during the PIE stage and the *Rig-Vedic* times. Their cognate, Latin *formica*, means 'ant' (Pokorny:749). Although not noted by anyone so far, the Latin *vermis* (insect) may be a cognate of these, rather than of the Sanskrit *kṛmi*. Old Icelandic *ormer*, Old High Germanic *wurm* which meant 'insect' and 'snake' (Lehmann:397) may too be cognate words of the Vedic *vamra* etc apart from the Goethic *miera* and Middle Dutch *mure* meaning ant (Lehmann:253).

However, by the time of the *Atharva-Veda* the words *pipilī*, *pipīla*, *pipīlikā* etc (*AV* 7.56.7) meaning 'ant' appear, obviously derived from the Sanskrit word "*pippala*" which is name of the the *Ficus religiosa* tree at the time of the *Atharva-Veda*. These Sanskrit words meaning 'ant' did not occur in the *Rig*- and the *Yajur*- Vedas. That means the *Ficus religiosa* either had not existed or had not acquired the name *pippala* by the time of these Vedas. We know from zoology, in the berry of the *Ficus* trees live thousands of tiny symbiotic wasps which look almost exactly like the tiniest ants.

In our study, the *Atharva-Veda* has been dated 1500-1300 BC. By this time the *Ficus religiosa* tree had established itself in the region and the poplar had been extinct. The absence of the words *pipīla* etc for 'ant' from the *Rig-Veda* indicates the absence of the *Ficus religiosa* tree from the *Rig-Vedic* age of northwest India. The *Ficus* trees arrived in the region about 3000 BC. The oldest charcoal sample of *Ficus* has been found from about 3000 BC. In the *Yajur-Veda* there is evidence of the *Ficus religiosa* tree being named *aśvattha*, but not yet *pippala*. This we can infer from the list of some trees where the name *aśvattha* has been listed with other *Ficus* trees (*TS* 3.4.8.4). But, nowhere in the *Yajur-Veda* would the context suggest that the name *pippala* has been used to mean the *Ficus religiosa*. Over and above this, the word *pipīla* (tiny 'fig-wasp', ant) has nowhere been used in this text to name the ants, a usage which occurs for the first time in the *Atharva-Veda* (Macdonell and Keith vol 2:531; *AV* 7.56.7).

That means the *Ficus religiosa* had not acquired the name *pippala* by the time of the *Yajur-Veda*, although it had acquired the name *aśvattha*. Why this? Aspen being a cold-adapted tree must have become extinct from the region much before the poplar, possibly by the sixth millennium BC. Aspen could not have been cultivated once the climate became hot enough for its extinction, because it is a cold adapted tree. Hence the name *aśvattha* became (trade-mark) free! And, therafter the name was acquisitioned by the *Ficus religiosa* tree.

Moreover there is evidence that the poplar, but not aspen, was cultivated in the region even after extinction from the wild existence, and the word *su-pippala* was applied to name the poplar tree in the *Yajur-Veda*. Poplar can grow in hot regions provided enough irrigation is provided. However the climate became drier more and more when even artificial irrigation became impossible by 1900 BC. Then the poplar tree became completely extinct even from the cultivated existence. Hence following the Indus Valley Civilization, the name *pippala* too became available (or free) to be applied to the *Ficus religiosa* tree. This is possibly the reason why this Sanskrit name of the tiny 'fig-wasp' *pipīla* does not occur before the *Atharva Veda*. Hence the *Atarva-Veda* is later than 1900 BC on this account alone. We find in our study that it pertains to 1500-1300 BC.

The *pippala* (*Ficus religiosa*) tree was not there during the early Holocene at all and appeared in the NW India only during the later part of the mid-Holocene Optimum. This we can say from the fact that the native range of the tree is only thropical Africa (Chad) and India, and the tree requires a good rainfall of between 500 and 5000 mm and a warm temperature of between 16 and 35 degree Celsius (Orwa 2009). Thus it could not have grown in the NW India during the dry and cold *Rig-Vedic* period, and any mention of the *pippala* in the *Rig-Veda* pertains to the poplar species (*e.g. RV* 7.101.5). This becomes more probable in view of the fact that the Veda mentions that the *pippala* is a medicinal tree protected by gods, which is true for the *populus* but not for the *Ficus religiosa*. The latter is good spiritually but unlike the *Populus* this is not of much medicinal value.

We get mention of the *aśvattha* tree twice in the *Rig-Veda*. One is the prayer to the mother goddess of medicine, which resides within the *aśvattha* tree (*RV* 10.97.5)[24]. The hymn adds the name of another tree *parṇa* as the mansion of the medicine-goddess. *Parṇa* is cognate word of 'fern', which could have been the medicinal fern asparagus or some other fern tree.

By the time of the Indus Valley Civilization, the aspen might however have grown in the Jammu and Kashmir which is much colder, particularly in the regions like Swat. This makes us wonder whether the *kārṣmarya* tree of 3000 BC *Shatapatha Brahmana* was aspen!

Thus we can say that the famous doctrin of Witzel was based on the lack of the knowledge of the historical ecology of the region. He had said, "Finally, it must be considered that, generally, the IE plants and animals are those of the temperate climate and include the otter, beaver... ... birch, willow, elm, ash, oak, (by and large, also the beech129); juniper, poplar, apple, maple, alder, hazel, nut, linden,

---

24 RV 10.097.05 ***aśvatthe vo niṣādanam parṇe vo vasatiṣkṛtā***,
Griffith's translation: "The ***aśvattha*** tree is your home; your mansion is the ***Parna*** tree."

hornbeam, and cherry (Mallory 1989: 114-116). Some of them are found in South Asia, ... But most of them are not found in India and their designations have either been adapted ... or they have simply not been used any longer." (2001:54).

Chapter 23

The Indian names of the Ficus Trees

We have already examined the *Ficus* trees in the context of other trees. We shall only discuss some philological aspects hare.

Parkati

The cognate words of *parkati* listed by Pokorny (1959) and other authors are:

> Pokorny: 822-823-- PIE **perkṷu-* (?) "oak-tree"; Sanskrit *parkaṭī* (sacred fig tree); Latin *quercus* (oak tree); Italian –trent *porca* (pine tree); Celt name *Hercynia* (forest-cliff, mountain range from *perkuniā*; see GED by Lehmann:104-5), Welsh *perth* (bush); OHG *Fergunnea* (mountain chains with mines or pine), MHG *firgunt* (forest-mountain), Goth. *faírguni* (mountain range), O.E. *firgen (forest-hill)*; O.H.G. *forha* (pine tree; from this English "forest"), German *Forst* (pine), O.E. *furh* (pine), O.Ice. *fura* (pine), *fȳri* (forest of "Scots pine tree"), O.H.G. **forh-is* (Scots pine forest). Some other cognates meaning "mountain" are OHG *Virgunnia, Virgundia* etc. (Lehmann:104 F11).

The list makes it amply clear that the words in European languages for Sanskrit *parkatī* generally mean "pine" or "pine forest" (Germanic and Italian), or "mountain covered with forest" (Celtic and Germanic), or "bush" (Celtic), and not the "oak". This is contrary to what the mainstream historians have been telling us so far. The Latin *quercus* meaning "oak tree" could be an exception, or it might have an altogether different etymology (*vide supra*). Other than this, nowhere else in any language, the words cognate to *parkaṭī* mean "oak". The fact as noted by Crystal is that oak, a tree found all over Europe, has no common word in the various Indo-European languages.

Ficus (and fig), a loan into Latin from Hebrew (Valpi:153) may have come from India into Arabic, and most likely is derived from Sanskrit *parkatī*: Arabic *fijj* (unripe fig), Hebrew *pag* (fig), Syrian (*paga*) fig etc. Witzel (2009 fulltext :5, fn 32) too thinks that *ficus* has derived from PIE **perku̯u-*. The word may have entered Hebrew language from India in the Bronze Age when lot of Indian migration to Arabia took place across Arabian coast and sea. Such migrations have been proved by recent DNA studies. Also remarkable is to note that not only in India but also in Southeast Asia and Polynesia, cognate words of *parkaṭī* mean the various species of *ficus* (fig) trees (*vide supra*). Hence an Indian origin of the word *parkaṭī* having a meaning *ficus* trees is the only plausible explanation.

There are cognate words of *parkaṭī* which mean "thunder-god", "thunder" or "thunder-storm" in many European languages as well as in Sanskrit.

> Pokorny: 822-23—Sanskrit *Parjánya-* (thunderstorm God); Albanian *Perëndi* (a goddess); O.H.G. *ferah* (life); Russ. *Perunъ* (thunder-god), Russ. *perún* (thunderbolt, lightning); Old Prussian *Perkūns* (the god of thunder), O. Lith. *perkúnas* (thunder-god), Lith. *perkúnas* (thunder), *perkúnija* (thunder-storm), Ltv. *pḕ rkuôns* (thunder, god of thunder); borrowed into Finnish as *Perkele*, and into Mordvinic *Pur'gine-paz* (the god of rainstorms and

thunder); Thracian *Perkon/Perkos* with same meaning. Some other cognates suggested by other authors are: Armenian *harkanem* (felling trees, slaying); Old Irish *orcaid* (slay); Hittite *harganu-* (destroy); Albanian *perëndim* (West, sunset), *perëndoj* (to set--about sun).

Thus a large number of cognates from the root **perku̯u-* in the Indo-European languages have the meanings associated with "thunder" or "rain", indicating origin of the word in a country where the rains were torrential and often associated with the thunder-storms—a monsoon region. The words having meanings "thunder" or "rain-god" have survived only in the Indian, Baltic and Slavic vocabularies.

The meanings "rock" or "mountain" have been preserved in the cognate words in Indian, Germanic and Hittite languages. The meaning "fullness" or "abundance" has been preserved only in the Indian and Celtic branches for PIE **prek-* to fill (*vide infra*). The only possible semantic link of "rock" or "mountain" with this set of words can be the mountain-like shape of the *Ficus infectoria* tree or the *parkaṭī*. The Arabic *barq* (lightening) and *baraqat* (Arabic→Persian as per Steingass:177; plenty, affluence) in fact appear to be loan words into Arabic carrying only two semantic aspects.

Pokorny noted the Old Indian word *pr̥ṇákti* (*pr̥ñcati*, *piparkti*), the participle form *pr̥kta-* and *pracura-* had all meaning "full" or "abundance" (PIE **perk-*[1]; Pokorny:820). He noted that the cognate words retaining the meaning have survived only in the Indic and Irish (Middle Irish *ercaim* "full"). The semantic element "fullness" in the PIE root-word **perk-* has been fully preserved in the Vedic word *parjanya* (Pokorny:822-823; cloud, rain-god), and is evidence that the PIE root **perku̯u-* is a derivative of another root **perk-*[1]. The word *parjanya* derives from Sanskrit root *pr̥j-* which means "to fill".

The same semantic element (*i.e.* "fullness") is discernible in the word *parkaṭi*. These trees provided shelter from rain and sun, fire-wood, fodder and bark and fibres for covering bodies. Even the berries could be eaten. The *Rig-Veda* says:

> "Sing forth and laud *Parjanya*, son of Heaven, who sends the gift of rain. May he provide our pasturage. *Parjanya* is the God who forms in kine, in mares, in plants of earth, and womankind, the germ of life. Offer and pour into his mouth oblation rich in savoury juice. May he for ever give us food." (*Rig-Veda* 7.102).

All these attributes of the Vedic *parjanya* fit well to that of the *ficus* tree. In India today, fig trees are considered divine along with the gods. Indian women even today pour milk or water into the roots of the sacred fig tree, and offer fabric-threads as symbolic dress (possibly an old practice of return-gift, staying as folk-custom till today, for the fibres received from the tree in the forgotten remote past).

Some words left out by Pokorny from PIE **perku̯u-* but listed with PIE **bheregh-* (high, mountain; Pokorny:140-141) merit inclusion here, because they can be connected with *parkaṭī* (and Hindi *bargat* etc) semantically and phonetically.

> Pokorny: 140-141-- PIE **bheregh-* (high, mountain); German *burgund* "a particular deep-red colour", "high-rising" (E. "burgundy"; *c.f.* OHG *Virgundia* "high mountain"; also, *c.f.* Hindi *bargat Ficus bengalensis*), Old English *burg*, *burh*, German *Burg* "hill-fort", O.H.G. woman's name *Purgunt* "highness"; Persian *burz* "high"; Tocharian A and B *pärk* rise, Toch A *pärkant* (c.f. *burgund*) rising, Toch A *pärkär* tall (c.f. Hindi *pākar* name of a large tree); Hittite *pár-ku-uš* (*parkus*) "high"; Albanian (**parkus*) *pragu* "threshold, elevation before the door"; Lat. *for(c)tis* (dial. *horctus*) "strong, robust.

Quite surprisingly, the colour of the ripe berries of the *Ficus bengalensis* and *F. religiosa* is burgundy, while none of the mountains associated with the Burgund region have this particular colour. Here the word *burgundy* (colour) can be seen to have carried with itself the meaning of the colour of ripe fruit of the *bargad* (*Ficus bengalensis*) in the folk memory of the migrating Indo-Europeans. And the "large size" reflected in the mountains of Burgundy was another feature lasting in the folk memory of the migrants. Hence we need to examine the Hindi word *bargad* or *bargat* (Platts:148; Fallon:250). For *bargat* or *bargad*, no etymology has been suggested so far. However, Fallen writes that it is an Eastern Hindi word. Among other words, phonologically and semantically similar, *parquet* "wooden flooring", Dutch and English *park* originally meaning "the wooden fencing of fold for sheep" etc point to a relationship of the tree or wood with this group of words meaning "high" or "hill". However much deeper and extensive dissection is required before anything can be said with any degree of certainty about all these words.

In Indo-Aryan, the derivatives of PIE **perku̯u-* are Sanskrit *parkaṭī*, Hindi *pākar, pākhur*, Oriya *pākura* "*Ficus infectoria*"; Eastern Hindi *bargat* (or *bargad*) "*Ficus bengalensis*". Turner (CDIAL 505) disagrees with the stray view that these words have derived from *plākṣa* and are not Indo-European but from an Austro-Asiatic source. Witzel however tempts to associate *plākṣa* with these (2009 Fulltext: 32 fn 5).

The *plākṣa* tree

Another word in Sanskrit for *Ficus* is *plākṣa* which appears to be a cognate of Latin *plexus* and Enflish "flax". All the ficus species have special fibrous aerial roots, which provided fibre for textile and for the fishing-nets to the pre-historic people. In fact different textiles are still woven of the *ficus* aerial root fibres by many New Guinea tribes (Mackenzie: 68-70, 83, 209, 87 plates 51, 52). The fibre produced by beating the bark of the ficus trees was considered sacred in India and Indonesia (Kearsley 2010:200, 201). Such textile was in use in Congo (Africa) when the British traveller Andrew Battel visited Congo (old name Zaire) in the sixteenth century AD. He noted the use of the cloth made from the fibres of the *Isande* tree (*Ficus lutata*, wild fig) (cited by W. Gillon 1984, and Gillon in turn cited by Kearsley 2010:199).

Moreover there is evidence that weaving activities were not restricted to the relatively later times, and archaeological evidence of weaving goes back to 30,000 years before present (Kvavadze). DNA studies of the cloth-lice too shows that some sort of cloth was worn by the ancient humans, at least about 40,000 years back (Kittler) or even 80,000 years back (Toups). Those cloths may have been made of the fibres derived from any of the the *Ficus* trees which grow in India and Africa. The sedcendants of the same lice have survived as the cloth lice till today.

Other features of *ficus* trees are stilts or board-like projections from stems, wood, trembling leaves (particularly in *Ficus religiosa*) and the berries. Although the meaning "*ficus* tree" has been lost from the European branches of the IE languages, yet the features of the tree (semantic features of *plākṣa*) have been preserved in many of the words in the European branches of the Indo-European family.

We can list some of the important words here. The philological material is being present not for the sake of arriving at any conclusion or hypothesis but just to present some material which had been ignored and was out of purview so far.

> Sanskrit *plākṣa* (*Ficus religiosa, infectoria* etc); Latin *plexus* (net of fibres); English "flax" (linen); English "ply" (to weave); Greek *plektos* (twisted), from Gk. **plek-* (to weave, to strip fibres) etc. The cognate words of *plākṣa* have preserved the meanings "fibre", "weaving" etc.

In spite of availability of huge philological material, the Sanskrit word *plakṣa* (*Ficus religiosa* and *F. infectoria*; MWD) and *plākṣa* (*Ficus infectoria, bengalensis*, and the fig-trees *F. racemosa* or *glomerata* and *F. carica*) have not been considered Indo-European, and have often been dubbed loan into the Indo-Aryan from some unknown source. This has been done not on the basis of any philological evidence, but only because the ficus trees do not grow in the Eurasian steppe and Germany. Thus it is a clear-cut example of Eurocentric manipulation of linguistics.

Although, not recording the word *plākṣa*, Pokorny has inadvertently assembled three sets of words for three PIE roots, all of which are only the different forms of the root for the Sanskrit word *plākṣa*:

1. *plā-k-*[1] "wide and flat",
2. *plāk-*[2] "to hit, to tremble" and
3. *plek̂* - "to weave".

All of the three converge semantically and phonetically to the Sanskrit words *plakṣa* and *plākṣa*.

Many words in Pokorny's material for the *plā-k-*[1] mean "wood", "peaceful" etc, which we can relate with the *Ficus* trees without difficulty.

> *plā-k-*[1] "wide and flat" (Pokorny: 831-832)-- Gk. πλάξ (*plaks*, surface, plain, area, piece of wood, board), πλακόεις (*plakoeis*, wood); Lat. *placeō, -ēre* (pleasent, compliant), *placidus* (flat, even, smooth, peaceful); O.Ice. *flaki, fleki* (wooden shed), *flecken* (board, plank, balk); German *Flũhe*, Swiss *Fluh, Flũh* (all meaning cliff, rock-wood), O.Ice. *flǣr* pl. from **flahiz* (wooden board); Toch. AB *plāk-* "to agree, to please"; Lith. *plãkanas* (flat), *plõkas* (stone floor) etc.

However, some words in Pokorny's the list (*plā-k-*[1]) resemble the shape of the *Ficus* leaves which are ovoid, flat and smooth. The "turnip" in the list for *plāk-*[1] is not flat, yet its shape exactly resembles leaf of *Ficus religiosa*.

> Mod. Ice. *flōki*, O.E. *flōc* (fluke-worm), Eng. flook-footed (flat-footed), O.H.G. *flah-*, Dutch *flak, flach* (smooth), O.S. *flaka* (sole of foot), Nor. *flak* n. (disc, slice, window-pane, a flat flowing ice or floe), Lith. *plãkė* (the lead,

> brake), *pleksne˜* (large beet, turnip), *plei-k-* in *pleikiù, pleĩkti* (to broaden); Ltv. *plāce* (scapula), Ltv. *plece* (a flat-fish; anything handmade).

Other words in the *plāk-*[1] list of Pokorny have semantic association with dressing:

> M.H.G. *vlīen* and *vlīgen* (layers of coat), *fūgen* (sort, order, to dress up, adorn), Lith. *plaikstūti* (the outer garment about chest and shoulder, to ventilate); Latin *plagula* (piece of toga garment, sheet of paper), *plagella* (rag).

The second PIE root mentioned by Pokorny is *plāk-*[2] "to hit, to flicker" (Pokorny: 832-833). The *pippala* (*Ficus religiosa*) leaves are famous for trembling. We are aware that the *Ficus religiosa* (and also the *Ficus bengalensis*) have been associated with divinity and sacred practices in India. Hence some spiritual and cultic features have been retained in many European words listed by Pokorny for *plāk-*[2]:

> Old Saxon *flōcan* (to bewitch); O.H.G. *fluohhon ds., fluoh* (curse, oath); O.Ice. *flōki* (felt hat).

Many words from this list have preserved the meanings "impact, gust of wind, to flap wings, to flutter, to flicker" etc. *Ficus religiosa* leaves flutter too much on the tree, and fly away too a lot if detached from the tree. Such features are displayed by many of the words listed by Pokorny under the head *plāk-*[2]:

> O.E. *flōcan* (to applaud, clapping), German *Flūgeln* (to flap wings), Old Icelandic *flaga* (sudden attack), M.L.G. & M.H.G. *vlage* (shove, attack, storm)", Eng. *flaw* "gust of wind, jump, crack", O.Ice. *flǫgra* "flutter", O.H.G. *flagarōn* "to fly or to flog", O.Icelandic *flǫkra* (*flakurōn*) "to wander about", M.H.G. *vlackern*, Dutch *vlakkeren* "flicker", O.E. *flacor* "to fly", *flicorian* "flicker", O.Ice. *flǫkta* (**flakutōn*) "flutter", O.Ice. *flakka* "flutter, to

> wander", older Dutch *vlacken* "twitch", M.L.G. *vlunke* "wing", O.Ice. *flengja* "thrash", Eng. *fling* "throw", Lat. *lancea*, Spanish *Lanze* (Celt. word).

The above words have retained some religious and spiritual connotation, along with that of "fluttering"—the features associated with *Ficus religiosa*. The *Ficus religiosa* has been associated with shamanic ideas too. Hence we find a strong semantic association of all these words with *plakṣa*.

> PIE **plek̂* - (to weave); Greek πλέκω *pleko* (lichen, braid), πλεκτός *plektos* (rope, net), πλέκος *plekos* (netting, wickerwork); πλοκή *ploke* (netting, tendtil, branch, shoot), πλόκος *plakos* (braid); Lat. *plicō* (braid), Lat. *plectō* (flax, wattle, braid); Alb. *plaf* (woollen cover), *plëhurë* (bad quality canvas, fabric); O.H.G. *flehtan*, O.E. *fleohtan* (in addition *flustrian* ds.), O.Ice. *flētta* (flax, wattle, braid), O.Ice. *flētta* f. (*lichen*), O.E. *fleohta* m. (hurdle), Goth. *flahta* (hair lock), O.H.G. *flahs*, O.E. *fleax* n. (*Flachs*), Dutch *vlijen* (flax, wattle, braid), O.C.S. *pletǫ*, *plesti* (flax, wattle, braid), O.C.S. *plotъ* (fence); (Pokorny:834-835).

If this word (*plākṣa*) is of Indo-European origin, its Germanic form would be "flax", "*flacks*" or "*flachs*", and the Latin form would be "*plexus*".

Originally, the *plakṣa* tree may have been named so because its leaves are always fluttering. PIE **plak*- (to hit, Pokorny:832-833); Greek *plazo* (πλάζω, to hit, thrash); Latin *plāga* (to blow, knock), *plectō* (punish); O.E. *flōcan* (to applaud, clap), *flicorian* (flicker), *flacor* (flying); Old Icelandic *flǫgra*, *flǫkra*, *flakka* and *flǫkta* (flutter), *flaga* (attack); Sanskrit *pala* (a moment, time taken to complete a blink of eye); Persian *palak* (eyelid, to blink the eyelid; Steingass:225; c.f. Eng. *flaw* 'gust of wind').

Plexiform roots called the prop-roots, grow down in air from the branches of the *plakṣa* or *plākṣa* tree. The semantic sense of "whip" has been carried into the words: PIE **bhlag-* (Pokorny:154); Lat. *flagrum* and *flagellum* (whip, scourge) etc. Words plak, plaque, plank and German *Plakat* (placard, poster) too seem to be related. Another likely cognate "flax" is the name of a plant which is a cultivated shrub gives fibres. Flax fibres were used to make linen.

Chapter 24

Some Typical Indian Plants

Mulberry (*Morus*)

In spite of the claims to the fairness, the European Indo-Europeanists never philologically examined the names of any of the typically Indian trees and herbs for assessment whether these belonged to the Indo-European vocabulary. Often many distortions of facts and wrong assumptions were used as evidence to support the claims which were not correct. The case of the mulberry tree well exemplifies this.

Mulberry is a sub-Himalayan forest tree, which grows mainly in India but also in East China, Japan and the Americas (Suttie). It has spread to Europe as a cultivated tree owing to human activity. In Europe, the oldest pollen of the *Morus* tree has been found from Belgium dating the Late Bronze Age otherwise the botanical samples of the *Morus* tree are only known as Roman introductions in nearby regions such as France, Germany and the British Isles (Vanessa 2005).

Girdini (2013) reported finding of the mulberry remains from the historical period of Rome. Carroll (2012) noted the presence of *Morus* pollens from 400-800 BC in the islands of Malta. Anderson *et al* noted the presence of the mulberry pollens only during the last 100 years in Spain in their study of the pollens from a period spanning about

11,500 years of Spain (2011:1622). Hence it is safe to conclude that the mulberry tree was not found in North Europe and the Western steppe until quite late. It is as late as the first millennium BC that the tree reached Southeast Europe and was cultivated in significant numbers. However the Bronze Age migrations from India to Europe had probably carried some mulberry trees from India to North Europe (Belgium) by the Late Bronze Age (Vanessa 2005).

Several species of *Morus indica* are found in India. With the growth of the silk trade the tree has spread to Central Asia, Near East and Europe (Sanchez 2000). It was never grown, or even known, in the steppe. However we note that there are at least two PIE reconstructions possible for the mulberry tree, indicating that the Indo-European home was located at a place where mulberry grew, and thus it was not the steppe nor even Europe but most likely in India. One reconstructed word is **moro* (Pokorny:749 &), and the other **brahma* (of this author, or * *bherem* of Pokorny:142).

Mulberry 1: PIE *moro-* (mulberry[25], Pokorny:749); Sanskrit *madhura-vṛkṣa* (mulberry-tree; Pokorny does not list this Sanskrit word, however, the word has been recorded by Turner in CDIAL 14733); Arm. *mor, mori, moreni* (blackberry); Gk. *moron* (μόρον, mulberry, blackberry); Welsh *merwydden* (mulberry); Lat. *mōrum* (mulberry, blackberry; Valpi:271), *mōrus* (mulberry, Valpi:271); Spanish *morera* (mulberry), French *murier* (mulberry); O.H.G. *mūr-, mōrbere*, M.H.G. *mūlber* (mulberry); Lith. *mõras* (mulberry). Cognates of **moro* are absent from the IE language of the steppe i.e. Ukrainian, where the mulberry is called *shovkoveetsya*. This indicates that the steppe was not the source of the PIE word for the mulberry.

A wild mulberry tree *Artocarpus lacucha* (within the mulberry family Moraceae) has identical fruits and leaves to the mulberry, and has been named *madar* in Assamese and Bengali languages (CDIAL 9849;

25 Pokorny thinks "blackberry" which cannot be supported on the basis of available philological material

madhura>madāra). These words must have migrated with the tree itself when the human contact brought the mulberry tree to Europe during the Bronze Age. Hence there is no identification problem or confusion with the names of other plants and trees. However this contact was not the Indo-European migration which had already taken place many millennia ago in our study.

Mulberry 2: Sanskrit *brahma-niṣṭha, brahma-bīja, brahma-bhāga, brahma-sthana, brahmaṇya, brāhmaṇya* (all meaning 'mulberry', *q.v.* MWD). The common part is *brahma*. The mulberry does not grow in the wild in North Europe. Yet, the cognate words of its name have travelled into the Nordic territory and are well represented in the Germanic languages as words which mean the "blackberry". The migration of this set of cognates must have taken place with the original Indo-European migration. The mulberry did not grow in Europe then, hence the name got applied to blackberry which has similar fruits. These words are:

> Proto-Germanic **brāmil*, English "broom", O.E. *brōm* (broom brush), M.L.G. *brām* (blackberry bush), O.H.G. *brāmo, brāma* (blackberry bush), *brāmberi* (PIE **bherem*, Pokorny:142). Other cognates are: Ger. *Brombeere*, O.E. *brēmel*, Eng. *bramble* all meaning the "blackberry".

The Gothic word *bagms* (tree) as in *baíra-bagms* (mulberry tree, Lehmann: 55 note B5) may too be a cognate of the Sanskrit word *brahma*. Central Indian archaic language Nihali which is not related to the IE, has the word *baru* (mulberry; Witzel Fulltext:21) which may be an early borrowing of the Indo-European *brahma*. These cognates probably migrated along with the first post-glacial migration from India to Europe taking place at the early Holocene as R1a1a migration.

It may be noted that although the bramble or the blackberry is a bush, and mulberry is a huge tree, yet the fruits of both look alike, and in the absence of mulberry, the words were rightly applied to the blackberry in North Europe. Just as the cognates of *morus*, the cognates of *brahma-* etc too are absent from the modern steppe's IE languages like Ukrainian, where the bramble is called *ozheena.*

Kikkar (*Acacia*)

The *kikkar, kīkara, kikkir* (Hindi, Punjabi, Bihari etc) is the Indian name of the *Acacia arabica* tree, which grows in the drier climates. It has not been found in the extant Sanskrit literature. However, Turner reconstructed the Proto-Indo-Aryan for this tree-name as **kikkara* (CDIAL 3151). Pokorny has not included any Indo-Aryan cognates in his list for PIE **k̂ik̂er-* pea, although linguistically it is same as the Indian *kīkara* (see Pokorny: 598). Its other form, again not included by Pokorny, is the Iranian Pushto *kī-kar* (*Acacia*; Raverty: 828). The cognates are present in Germanic and Italic where they mean the chick-pea (Mallory and Adams 1997:106). Acacia and chick-pea both are leguminous plants belonging to the same family and their pods have lot of similarity.

In the *Rig-Veda* a word *kīkaṭa* occurs (*RV* 3.53.14). No one has been able to give its actual meaning, and it has been guessed that probably it was the name of a province in Magadha (Bihar). However the *Rig-Vedic* says, "*kiṃ te kṛṇvantī kīkaṭeṣu gāvo*". This literally means: "what those cows are doing among the *kīkaṭa*-(shrubs)" (bracket added).

The mantra further adds that they (cows) are not able to give any milk. This clearly means that the comment is at the poor nutritional condition of the cows which were trying to graze in a land which was devoid of grasses but full of thorny (*acacia*) bushes. Such climatic conditions existed in the northwest India about 8000-6000 BC. The person in the mantra wanted to take those cows away to his own homeplace which seems to have had good water supply (from the Sarasvati River). Moreover, it is difficult to assume that someone at the time of the *Rig-Veda* would have travelled down to Bihar in east India just to bring some poorly cows. The context suggests the Thar region and the meaning of the word *kīkaṭa* seems more appropriately to be the thorny bushy forest of *Acacia*. However, just like the other meanings provided by the other authors (like MWD) this one too is a pure guess.

PIE *k̂ik̂er-* pea (Pokorny: 598); Arm. *siseṙn* (chickpea); Gk. Maced. *kikerroi*, Gk. *krios* (chickpea) <**kikrios*; Lat. *cicer* (chickpea); Lith. *keke* (grape), Ltv. *k"ekars* (shine), Ltv. *k"eḱis* (umbels like cumin, coriander; grape), Lithuanian and Ltv. *cekulis* (flamingo plant, tassel, jute, tussock grass), *cecers* (frizzy hair); Cz. *čečeřiti* (to make shaggy or frizzy); Alb. (**k"ekar*) *kokër* "grain, bean".

The *kikkar* fruits are legumes and its seeds resemble the chickpeas, hence Armenian *siseṙn* and Latin *cicer* etc. Its inflorescence is umbel hence Ltv. *k"eḱis* (umbel). Its flowers look like tassel or spike of tussock grass, hence Latvian *cekulis* (tussock grass). Clearly the most original meaning seems to be the name of a leguminous plant, which obviously is Indian *kikkar*.

Calotropis and *Madar* plants

Madar or *Calotropis* is an Indian plant. Therefore the words meaning the *madar* plant cannot be expected to exist in the European languages. However they can be traced there too with altered meanings. It is a plant growing in relatively arid climates, and could have existed in the *Rig-Vedic* times too which was a dry period for the Indus-Sarasvati region. In spite of so many odds (distance and time of migration etc) the word *madar* has survived in the European languages applied to some other meanings. We can say that the PIE **modhro-* or **madhro-* (Pokorny:747; blue colour; a fiber plant) is the same word as the name of the Indian *madar*, which has purple and blue flowers and the pigment was used in the dying industry in the past and the fibre was used for making cushion etc.

Pokorny omitted from his list the Sanskrit plant names *mandāra* (*Calotropis indica*) and *madāra* (thorn-apple, *Datura*), both of which have purple/ blue flowers and provide fibre for making cushions (*Calotropis*) and ropes (thorn-apple). The thorn-apple has lost this name in the modern Indian languages, and the *Calotropis indica* is generally known by the names *madār* (Hindi, Assamese), *mādār* (Bengali) and *madara* (Sindhi). These names are also used to name a smalled variety of *Calotropis* whose botanical name is *Asclepias gigantean* (CDIAL 9849).

All of these three Indian plants *viz. Calotropis, Asclepias* and *Datura* give intoxicating or poisonous products, have medicinal usage and have flowers light purple or blue in colour. They have extractable blue-dye. The bast fibre of the thorn-apple resembles the flax fibres. The white silky fibres of *Calotropis* and *Asclepias* are used for filling the cushions and missio. Thus both the semantic aspects (blue colour & fibre) suggested by Pokorny are fulfilled by these Indian plants, particularly the *Calotropis*. The names of the plants too resemble the PIE **modhro-*. Hence not including the two Sanskrit words in this list is an act of mission.

The tree *Erythrina variegate* (Indian Coral Tree) too is named *madar* and *mandar* in some Indian languages like Bengali, Assamese, Pali, Prakrit and Sanskrit (CDIAL 9849). But this Indian tree produces a red dye and not the blue dye. But this is not a serious matter. Many Germanic cognate words of the PIE **madhro-* listed by Pokorny too mean the plant *Rubia*, which produces red dyes. The cognates of PIE **madhro-* are absent from most of the branches of Indo-European being present only in the Indo-Aryan, Slavic and Germanic branches.

Some of the European cognates to this root are: Old Icelandic *maðra* (*Galium verum*, the Lady's bedstraw, with yellow flowers, fibres used in cushions), modern Icelandic *Kross-maðra* (*Galium boreale*, Northern Bedstraw has purple-white flowers), Old High German *matara* (dyer's red). Then there are words like English 'madder', 'Mader' (name), O.E. *mædere, mæddre*, M.L.G. *mēde*, O.Fris. *mīde*; Slav.**modr□* (e.g. Cz. *modrū*) which mean *Rubia tinctorum* and *R. cordifolia* (dyer's madder), whose roots produce red dye. However the fruits (tiny berries) are purple.

The "madder plant" of South Europe too belongs to the tropical and sub-tropical climates and not to the temperate. The word Madder has also meant the professions carpentry and textile-trading which used the dyes in their professions. In a nut shell none of the trees or plants associated with this group of cognate words is found in the temperate regions except the Icelandic *Kross-maðra* (*Galium boreale*). This finding too rules out the steppe from being the homeland of the Indo-Europeans.

It is clear that this group of plants was associated with the dying industry both blue as well as red dyes extracted from various plants. Possibly dying, textile and cushion production were controlled by the same group of artisans during the Bronze Age, and Indus Valley was the hub of these. Hence these words might represent the trade related migrations out from the Indus Valley, and are consistent with Indo-Aryan location within the Indus Valley during the Bronze Age. There is skeletal and DNA evidence to support that people from Indus were going and settling out and also *vice-versa* during the Bronze Age (third millennium BCE). (Kenoyer 2013).

Possibly it is because of the contact related technology transfer that the word has travelled to the Indonesian language too where the flowers of the plant *Colotropis* are called *widuri* (from *madāra*). The Tibetan name "*man da ra ba*" (*Erythrina* tree) might be the result of the Bronze Age trade related contact, or the later transfer of the Sanskrit word *mandāra* in association with Buddhism.

Intoxicants and Opium

Opium plant certainly grew in the IE homeland. The Sanskrit word *mohana*, means "depriving of consciousness, bewildering, confusing, perplexing, leading astray, illusion and delusion" (MWD). Its past participle form *mugdha* (Sanskrit) means "hypnotised". This is the most appropriate description of the effects of opium.

The MWD does not give the meaning 'opium' but gives another meaning the 'thorn-apple', which too is an intoxicating fruit (*Datura fastuosa*). However 'opium' is the more appropriate meaning of the Sanskrit word *mohana*. Persian *mahānul* (opium; Steingass) seems to be a cognate of the Sanskrit *mohana*. Hindi *māhur* (poison, very bitter in taste) may be related to *mohana*, although Turner (CDIAL 10035) thinks this word has derived from Sanskrit *madhura* (sweet, honey, wine). Monier-Williams is wrong because honey is not poisonous in any lay non-philosophical state of language which was the PIE and PIA.

Thus we can say that PIE **mā̆ k(en)-* (poppy, Pokorny:698) is represented in Sanskrit by the word *mohana*. The cognate words of **mā̆ k(en)-* provided by Pokorny are:

PIE **mā̆ k(en)-* (poppy, Pokorny:698); Gk. μήκων (*mekon*); German *Mohn*, O.H.G. & O.S. *māho*, M.H.G. *māhen*, *mān* and O.H.G. *măgo*, M.H.G. *mage*; N.Ger. *mån*, Dutch *maan-kop,* O.S. *val-mughi*, *-moghi*; M.Lat. *mahonus*; Lith. *magônė*, O.Pruss. *moke*; Church Slavic (etc.) *makъ*, Russian *mak*, all meaning "opium".

Thus we find that the Sanskrit cognate is more generic in nature, because of the availability of a large number of intoxicating herbs in India. Whereas the cognates are restricted to the opium and poppy in Europe, where people knew the opium, because it is king of all intoxicants, yet the other Indian intoxicants were not known to the Europeans in General.

Another Sanskrit word *ahi-phena* (opium) has widespread cognates in the Indo-European family. Such words have not been recorded by Pokorny. Sanskrit *āphīna*, *āphūka*, *aphena* and *ahi-phena* all mean 'opium', the last one literally the "snake-venom". Other cognates are: Greek *opos* (vegetable juice) > *opion* > Latin *opium* [Harper]; Persian *afyūn*, *apyūn*, *abyūn*, *hapyūn* (opium). Opium never grew in the steppe or North Europe.

Lotus

There are at least two Sanskrit words with the meaning 'lotus' which have cognates in many European languages, although lotus was not found in Europe. Meanings have naturally changed to the plants growing in Europe. On this basis we can say that lotus was present in the Indo-European homeland. When the IE speakers went out of India, they applied these names to mean other flowers and plants, all of which have co-incidentally purple or blue flowers.

> PIE **ereg^w(h)o-* (pea, Pokorny: 335); Sk. *aravinda*; Gk. ὄροβος (*orobos*), ἐρέβινθος (*erevindos*, chickpea); O.H.G. *araweiz, arwiz*, Ger. *Erbse* (in proper name only, 'pea'); M.Ir. *orbaind* (grains) from **arbainn* and older *arbanna* (Starostin:902).

> PIE **kemero-*, **komero-* (Pokorny:558); O.H.G. *hemera*, Proto-Germanic **hamirō* (hellebore flower), Ger. dial. *hemern* ds. (hellbore), RCS (Russian Church Slavonic) *čemerъ* (poison, originally 'hellbore'), Russ. *čemeríca* f. (hellebore); Lith. *kemerai* (*Eupatorium cannabinum*); Greek κάμαρος (*kamaros, Delphinium*), Greek κάμμαρον (*kammaron, Aconitum* flower); Indian *Chamarikā* (*camarikā*) from *kamal-ikā*.

Lily: The European flower "lily" is perhaps a cognate word of Sanskrit *nalina* meaning "lotus".

Jambula (rose apple)> > apple

The Sanskrit word *jāmbūla* stands for two different species of *Eugenia* or *Syzygium*, one of which resembles apple and is called "rose-apple" while the other is smaller dark purple fruit generally called the Indian plum or *jāmun*.

The word *jāmbūla* shows a regular change spatially until it becomes "apple": *jāmbūla* (South Asia) > *jáblonь* (Russ.), *jáblan* (Sloven.) > **āboln-* (Aus idg.)> *avallo, Aballō* (Gaul) > *apfel* (Germany), apple (see Pokorny:1-2 and also Turner CDIAL 5131, p. 283). The word *jāmbūla* also migrated to the southeast Asia from India. In the Thai language the word *jāmbūla* has survived as *chompoo* (rose apple). The Sanskrit word *jāmbūla* also gave birth to the Albanian word *kumbull* ("plum, round fruit").

Another European set of words for apple *malum* (Latin) and *mollë* (Alb.) have been derived from the Luvian word **šamlu* (Pokorny:1-2; Pokorny and Starostin:248). The Luvian word **šamlu* is easy to derive from Sanskrit *jāmbūla*. French *melon* (from *melo-peponem*) too is derived from Luvian **šamlu*.

Flax (*Linum*)

Flax (*Linum*, linseed) originated in India (Vavilov 1992; Vaisey-Genser and Morris 2003; Sfetcu 2014). Vaise-Genser and Morris explain that it was the rich data collected by Vavilov (1992) that it could become clear that the flax was domesticated in India (2003:3). However it reached Europe with the Neolithic through West Asia (Mallory and Adams 1997:8, 206). The Indians cultivated the linseed primarily for oil (Fuller 2008:6), while the West Asian and the Europeans for the fibre. It has been revealed by DNA examination that the oil-yeilding varieties occupy the root of the family tree indicating the original domestication, and the fibre yielding varieties were pnly later developed from it (Allaby 2005). Its cultivation needs lot of water (>750 mm) and its first domestication in India is very much plausible.

Its proto-European reconstructed form is **līnom* (Mallory and Adams 1997), and it is well represented in nearly all the European branches of IE language family, *viz.* Celtic, Italic, Greek, Germanic, Baltic and Slavic (*ibid*:206). However the flax plant reached the steppe (located north of the Black Sea) quite late in history (*ibid*:433). This fact rules out the steppe from being the homeland.

Flax flowers are deep blue and the plant is a commercial source of blue dye in some parts of the world (Sfetchu). It is perhaps because of this that the flax was named in Sanskrit *sunīla* (MWD; *su*, good; *nīla* blue). From the Old Indian word *nīla* (blue) has been derived the Latin word *linum*, just as from the Old India *nalina* (lotus) has derived the word 'lilly'. Its chrred seeds have been found from Pakistan's Miri Qalat dating to about 4000 BC (Tengberg 1999).

Chapter 25

Farming related flora

Karpāsa (cotton tree)

Cotton is of Indian origin. Philology shows that it was either present at the IE homeland at the early Holocene, or the cognates travelled later during the Bronze Age trade related contact.

The lexical material available is: Sanskrit *karpāsa* (cotton), Hindi *kapas* (cotton); Latin *carbasus* (cotton), Spanish *ceiba* (silk-cotton); Greek *karpasus* (cotton); Persian *kirbasa, karābīs, karābīsī, karbas* (cotton, linen, muslin), *kirbasi* (cloth). PIE *kerəp* and *krep* (cloth, Pokorny:581 and 620) should be considered here.

The word has migrated widely to many countries, probably during the Bronze Age: Nubian (North Sudan) *koshmaag*; Sumerian *kapazum*; Old Khmer *krəpa:s*, Proto-Viet-Muong **k-pa:lh*, Proto-Katuic, Proto-Banharic and Proto-Pearic **kə-pa:jh*; Javanese *kapok* (Silk-cotton) etc.

At the time of out of India migration, cotton was not cultivated. However it must have been gathered from the wild trees. Yet the ancestor of the word *karpāsa* was not semantically exclusive to cotton, but was also used to mean any plant fruition (like Gk. καρπός, *karpos* "fruit"), and particularly those ripening in the autumn. Hence Germanic words: O.H.G. *herbist*, O.E. *hærfest* (autumn) and English "harvest". The emigrant Indo-Europeans were farmers--at least early farmers. They had cutting tools made of stone and bone before metal was available. The Sanskrit word *kṛpāṇa* (knife, sword) and Latvian *cir̃pe* (sickle) are cognates to these words. (Pokorny:938-947).

Sesame

Charred sesame seeds have been found from ancient remains at Harappa (Indus Valley) from a layer dating back to 3500 BCE or 5500 years before present (Bedigian and Harlan 2005: Abstract). Bedigian and Harlan noted that outside India, archaeological findings supporting sesame cultivation are from much later dates.

The oldest findings outside India are from: *Uratul* in Armenia 600 BCE, *Hajar bin Umeid* in South Arabia 450 BCE and Egypt and China 3rd century BCE (*ibid*), all dating much later than the Indus finds. New evidence suggests that the "Mesopotamian oil plant *śe-giś-i* was sesame" and "that the crop and one name for its oil *ellu* were introduced from India" (*ibid*). The Akkadian *ellu/ūlu* 'sesame oil' and Sumerian *ili* 'sesame' are clearly derived from the South Dravidian words *el, ellu* meaning '*Sesamum indicum*' (*ibid.*, also Southworth:203-4 and Witzel 1999:28 pdf). Witzel also noted that the Indo-Aryan *tila* and the Dravidian *ellu* are related words. Greek *elaia* and Latin *oliva* meant "olive", and the Greek words *elaion* and Latin *oleum* meant "olive oil" from which Germanic "oil" (E.), *olie* (Du. oil) etc have derived. The Proto-Italic form was **elaiuom*. These all are related to the Indian word *ellu*.

Clearly the archaeological, linguistic and ancillary evidence all point to the Indian origin of the cultivation of sesame and the word *ellu* (oil) and their subsequent transmission to other parts of the world. However, the transmission of the word into other Indo-European languages must have occurred earlier when the Indo-Europeans started migrating out of India to be differentiated into various linguistic branches.

The Proto-Indo-Europeans knew 'oil' and oilseed *tila* (Sanskrit, sesame). Although the Sanskrit word *tila* has been thought by Burrow (1947:142, 1948:380) to have been a loan word from the Dravidian into Sanskrit, Turner (CDIAL 5827) and Witzel (Fulltext:15, 2.4.7) seem to agree more with Kuiper (1955:157), who thought these words to be of Munda (Austro-Asiatic) origin. Thus there is a widespread confusion about linguistic origin of the words for "oil", however all agreeing that the word was a loan one into the Indo-European. Such an early borrowing at the very pre-split level of PIE could not have taken place unless PIE was evolving in India itself, along with Munda and Dravidian languages evolving in the vicinity.

Sanskrit and other Indo-Aryan languages, word *tila* (CDIAL 5827) means *Sesamum indicum* plant or its seed. However, it also means the black mark (mole) on skin (CDIAL 5828), which resembles the black seeds of sesame plant. In Dravidian *ellu* means the sesame seed, oil and even "bone" (DED 854, 839). The semantic association between sesame and bone might have been through association with "fat". Early humans procured fat by heating animal bones.

The Indo-Aryan word *tila* too has migrated with the early migrations, although losing the meaning "sesame" yet retaining the semantic association with the colour "black". Such philological relationship although not examined thus far, probably does exists between Sanskrit *tila* and Greek τιλίαι (*tiliai*, black popler); Greek *stear* (fat, oil) > English "tallow" solid fat (*c.f.* Sanskrit *tela* oil); Proto-Gmc. **dilja*, O.E. *dile*, O.S. *dilli*, O.H.G. *tilli*, *dilli* a strongly smelling plant umbel which have small seeds resembling the size and shape of sesame; Alb. *dyllë* wax (see Pokorny: 234).

Although the Germanic words English "tallow", Norwegian *talg* etc have retained the meaning "fat", their cognates from warmer parts of Europe have retained the semantic aspect "liquidity" of the sesame oil. Thus we have: Armenian *teł* (rain), *tełam* (to rain); M. Irish *delt* (dew) etc. (Pokorny:196 has failed to note this relationship).

Sugar and Sugarcane

The word sugar is present in almost all of the languages of the Indo-European family. Sanskrit *śarkarā*, Hindi *sakkar*; Irish *siúcra*; Eng "sugar", German *zucker*, Dutch *suiker*, Swedish *socker*, Danish *sakker*; Lithuanian *cukrinis*, Latvian *cukurs*; Russian *sakhar*, Slovak *sukor*, Serbian *shye-chyerni*, Bulgarian *zakharyen*; Latin *saccharum*, Italian *zucchero*, Portugese *açúcar*, French *sucre*, Spanish *azucar*; Greek *zakhare*; Albanian *sheqer*; Tocharian B *śakkār* (Adams 1999:620) all meaning 'sugar'; Persian *sakr* (wine, a fine variety of date, sugar, see Steingass:688), Pashto *sukr* wine (Raverty:609). It has been borrowes in many languages like Estonian *suhkur* and Arabic *sukar*.

Clearly the word is present in all the branches of Indo-European, and with adequate diverse forms. Hence it cannot be a loan from Indian to other European languages through Arabic, and should be called an Indo-European word. Yet all sorts of somersaults were made to avoid this very obvious conclusion. Przyluski claimed that the word was of Mon-Khmer origin (quoted by Turner, see CDIAL 12338). Others claimed that it was borrowed by Persian from India, then from Persian to Arabic, then from Arabic to Latin, then from Latin to German and Russian etc (see Harper). We cannot be sure whether these cognates made their ways during the primary migration or later during the Bronze Age migration when India had a monopoly over production of sugar.

Sugarcane was present in India since the very beginning, before the Indo-European migrations came out from India. The cognates have been retained in many European languages often with altered meanings but retaining one semantic aspect or the other. With the passage of time the word *kāṇḍa* (Sanskrti, cane, reed) and *khāṇḍa* (raw-sugar) lost their meanings in the European languages as these were not available inEurope.

Sanskrit words *kāṇḍa* (sugar-cane, reed, segmented-stem of a plant), *kaṇḍa* (joint); English "cane" (reed); Old French *cane* (reed, cane, spear),

Latin *canna* (reed); Gk. *kanna* (tube, reed, c.f. Hindi *ganna* 'sugar-cane'); loanwords into Assyrian *qanu* (tube, reed), Hebrew *qaneh* and Arabic *qanah* (reed). The Sumerian *gin* (reed) also seems to be a loan from Indo-European. Other cognate words which should be included here are candy/ candid (English), and Persian *qand* (cane sugar). Tamil *kantu* (candy), *kattu* (to harden) and Arabic *qandi* (sweet) are possibly loanwords from Sanskrit.

Indo-European Fauna:

Chapter 26

Aquatic and Semi-aquatic animals

Pearl (a produce of oyster)

Philology: Sanskrit *manjari* (also *mandara, madrura*) pearl; English (female) names *Marjorie, Margery, Marjory*, O.E. *meregrot* (loans from Old French); Old French *Margaret*; Gk. *margarites* (all mean pearl, Harper). Persian *marjān* (pearl; Steingass: 1210). There are words in the modern Indo-Aryan with the meaning 'coral, pearl and precious stone' which can be cited as cognates: Gypsi *minrikló* (ornament), *mərənkló, miriklo* (pearl, coral), *miliklo, merikle* (agate), *mérikli* (bead) *etc* (see CDIAL 9731). Sanskrit *mañjú-, mañjulá-* (beautiful; women's names) and *mañgala* (good omen) may be related to this set of words.

Pearl is made by the oysters living in salt-water under hot climates. The mollusk *Pinctada vulgaris* cannot survive below 6° Celsius. Philological comparisons show that the word for pearl was present in the Proto-Indo-European language before dispersal. This implies that the IE home was located near warmer seas in a southern location. It rules out the "Steppe-Region" as the Indo-European homeland. Apart from this set of words, there are other Indo-Aryan words too (like the Pali *sippikā* and Sanskrit *patolaka*) which mean oyster and which can be traced to the other branches of the IE family (*vide infra*).

Oyster

By the presence of "pearl", availability of oysters in the urheimat is proved. Words meaning "oyster" in the Indo-Aryan branch are *sippikā, sippi, sīpa, sīp* (oyster; CDIAL 13417). Similar to these are Italian *sepia*, Latin and Greek *sepia* (cuttlefish) which has the skeleton looking exactly like one of a oyster.

Pali *sippikā* is the Sanskrit *śilpikā* (a piece of handicraft or artefact), oldest of which were made of bones and mollusk-shells. The word had an early penetration into the Dravidian too (*cippi*, Burrow DED 2089), indicating origin of the word in India and not in South Europe. However, in South Europe, the cuttlefish bone was found to be similar to the oyster-shell. Hence, most plausibly, the word *sepia* was thrust on to the cuttlefish bones.

The patella (limpet) too has the external looks of the oysters. Similarity between the Sanskrit word *patolaka* (oyster) and English *patella* (a mollusk resembling oyster shell and found in the sea-waters off the Western Europe) is not coincidental but indicates common origin of the names.

Conch

Conch is a mollusk found in the warmer latitudes in the oceans. The word "conch" is of definite Indo-European origin. However, it has been largely lost from the northern European languages—Balto-Slavic and Germanic.[26] The fact that the early Indo-Europeans had "conch" in their homeland's vocabulary rules out the steppe region as the possible home of the Indo-Europeans.

Cognates are: English "conch" (loanword from Latin); Sanskrit *śaṅkha*; Latin *concha* and *cochlea* (snail); Greek *konkhe*; PIE **konkho* (Pokorny:

[26] In German language, cognate of the word "conch" has become extinct, and it is translated as ***Meeres-schnecke*** (sea-snake, sea-snail).

614). Other cognate words are Latin *congius* (measure of capacity) and Latvian *sence* (oyster). The Hindi (IA) word *ghoṅghā* (snail) is a cognate of "conch" and a vestige of the centum past of the Indo-Aryan languages.

We have a large number of words surviving in Sanskrit from the PIE root *konkh-* e.g. *kaṅkata* (hair-comb, *AV* 14.2.68; *kaṅgha* in Hindi). That the conchs were used as the hair-combs is clear from the fact that the Venus Comb Shell which looks like a fantastic hair-comb is in fact a natural conch-shell or mollusk skeleton.

The *Rig-Veda* (1.191.1) mentions a poisonous mollusc by the name *kaṅkata* which lived in the midst of the aquatic weeds and injected the venom by means of needles, often killing the victim. The description best resembles the various tropical snail species within the genus *Conus* which generally inhabit the Indian and the Pacific Oceans. They have poison-injecting radulae which are like the venom-fangs and look like needles (Haddad Junior).

The mention of this Indian Ocean poisonous mollusc in *Rig-Veda* is very significant. It is generally found in the coastal Indian Ocean. It is possible that the Sanskrit word *saṅkaṭa* ('danger') evolved semantically out of the word *kaṅkata* ('poisonous snail'). The words *śaṅka* and *śaṅkā* meaning 'fear' are the other Sanskrit cognates of 'conch', and indicate the fear of this poisonous mollusk *Conus* within the minds of the early hunter-gatherers.

The Harappan people used the conch-shell of the *Conus* species as jewellery (Kenoyer 2000). Related to the word *kaṅkata* are the Sanskrit words *kaṅkaṇī*, *kaṅkaṇa* (ornament, bangle) and *kaṅkaṭa* (Sk. armor). Other words related to the 'conch' are *śaṅku* (cone) and the Bangla *śākhā* (bangle, made of the conchshells). It entered Tamil too *e.g. sanku* (conch; Tamil).

Conch and other mollusk shells are widely used in Africa, India, Southeast Asia and Polynesia often as jewellery and/or currency.

Cognates of the word 'conch' have been borrowed by many non-IE languages too, probably as the result of the Bronze Age trade with India. Examples are *Keong* (Indonesian) and *Kuanaka* (Hawaiian) both meaning the conch-shell. It is remarkable to note that just by the change of one sound from '*k*' to '*c*' (*kañcana*) the meaning of the word changes to 'wealth' or 'gold'. It may be assumed what is gold today for man, was conch shell to the man in the remote prehistory.

The Indo-European status of the word "conch" rules out the steppe from being the Indo-European home. Another set of Indo-European cognates represented by the word 'comb' too actually meant the conch-shell: Sanskrit *kambu*, *kambuka* (shell, conch); English 'comb', '-kempt', Proto-Germanic **kamb-* (comb) etc. Earlier the comb was made of bones and shells (c.f. Venus comb shell). The discussion amply demonstrates that the conch was a very pervasive element of the ancient past of India and the Indo-Aryan language and its cognates have survived in the European branches of the IE too.

Crab

Crab is again an aquatic animal of the warmer climates, inhabiting the tropical and semi-tropical regions of the world. On the basis of philology we can say that the crab was certainly present in the homeland of the Proto-Indo-European speakers. The words are: Sanskrit *karkaṭa*, *karka*, Hindi *kenkarā*; Persian *kark*; Greek *karkinos* all meaning the 'crab'.

Pokorny reconstructs the PIE root for Sanskrit *karkaṭa* etc as **kar-3*, reduplicated to *karkar-* (Pokorny: 531-532). Reduplication of the PIE stem suggests Indian origin of the word because reduplication of stem is a feature of the southern languages (Indian, Southeast Asian, African), and not of the European languages (Rubino 2013).

In the Persian language *kark* means "crab", however, it has acquired additional meanings *viz.* domestic fowl and partridge, both edible animals in the Persian speaking region. It is interesting to note that the Tocharian B word *kran.ko* too means a fowl. Thus going just beyond the region of India, wherever crab was not found, the word *karka* (crab) was applied to many small edible animals.

The Indo-European migration to the Balkans took place via the Iranian coast (J2b migration). The cognate words *kark* etc with the meaning 'crab' were retained in the languages along this route, because the crab was found along this route. Hence the word *kark-* retained its meaning "crab" in the coastal Iran, and Greece.

However in the non-coastal, northern arid regions of Iran where "crab" was not found, the word acquires other meanings like fowl and partridge. This is true for Tocharian B too. In the same way, in northern and East Europe, where crabs were not found, this word acquired the meaning the spiders, however here the ssemantic relationship was not of edibility but of the shape of the creature. With time the cognates acquired the meaning 'weaving' etc and even the meaning 'spider' was lost from many languages.

Thus we have: M.H.G. Ger. dial. *kanker* (spider), Finnish (loan from dem Gmc.) *kangas* (web, webbing, strong cloth or fabric, net-like weave), Swe. dial. *kang* (droopy slender branch), *kāng* (esp. from horses: agile, lively, excited, aroused; actually "spinning violently"), *kynge* (bundle), O.N. *kǫngull* (bundle of berries), (see Starostin:1018; Pokorny:380). Germanic word "crab" is not related to the word *kark-*.

Tortoise and Turtles

These are cold-blooded reptiles which live in or near water. They are not found in the cold regions or very dry regions of world. These animals are not found in Europe except Greece and adjoining areas. They are found in the most parts of Asia including Central Asia. The phrase Russian Tortoise is a misnomer, because this is found in the Central Asian countries, not in Russia. Linguistic evidence favouring the presence of the tortoise in the Indo-European homeland indicates that the homeland was not in Russia or Ukraine where the tortoise did not live.

kamaṭha: Sanskrit word for tortoise is *kamaṭha* (which also means 'porcupine', MWD; also see CDIAL 2760). Clearly the meaning 'tortoise' was lost once people migrated out of India, and the word was applied to another aquatic edible animal, the lobster. The Indo-European status has been accepted for this word (PIE $*k_{e}mer$- the animal with armour, crab, turtle, Pokorny: 558;).

Its cognates are Greek *kammaros* (lobster) > Latin *cammarus* (lobster); O. Norse *humarr* (lobster) and German family name *Hummer* (lobster). Also compare with Indo-Aryan *kammal*, *kambalin*, *kambu* (conch-shell) and *kamra* (CDIAL 2771-2773, 2775). Cognates present only in Indian, Greek, Italic and Germanic.

Turtle: Other name of the tortoise is the Sanskrit *dadru* (also *duḍi*, *druḍi*, *duli*, *ḍuli*, *dulī*, *dauleya* and *druṇi*). Its cognates are French *tortue*, Middle Latin *tortuca*, Latin *turtur*; Old English *tortuse*, English "turtle" and "tortoise". Before the Neolithic revolution, man must have used tortoise shells as bowls etc. Hence the Sanskrit word *druṇi* (and related words *droṇi*, *droṇa* etc) also means wooden bowls, or pots in general.

Frog and Toad

Toad (E.): The amphibian "toad" is inhabitant of warmer climates and lays eggs in the warmer waters. Cognate words are: English "toad", O.E. *tadige*, *tadie* (toad); Sanskrit *taduri*, *dardarika*, *dardura*, *dādura* (frog, toad). The word has been lost from the other branches of IE.

Frog (E.) again is amphibian which resembles the toad almost exactly. It has the same habitat as the toads, but it needs more rain waters.

Cognates are: Pokorny (845-846; root PIE **preu-* to jump); Sanskrit *plava, plavaka* (frog, see CDIAL 8772); Romanian **breuska, broască* (tortoise, frog); Alb. **breustka* (toad, frog), Proto-Alb. **breuska* (tortoise); Greek *batraxos* (frog); Old Icelandic *frauki*, Old English *frogga* (frog), Middle English *frude, froud* from O.N. *fraudr* (c.f. Sanskrit *plava + udra*); Greek *frune, frunos* (toad); Persian *farg͟hūr* (frog; Steingass:920).

Otter:

Many linguists (e.g. Witzel) think that "otter" is a European animal, and that it is not found in India. In fact otter is very much an Indian animal and some species of otters are found exclusively in India and Southeast Asia (**Indian Smooth-coated** Otter, *Lutrogale perspicillata* and **Oriental Small-clawed** Otter, *Aonyx cinerea*). It is Europe where the name of the otter has often lost its real meaning and acquired different meanings (like *hydra*).

The word (Sk. *udra*; Hindi *ud*) is well represented in the modern Indo-Aryan languages (see CDIAL 2056). Pokorny (p. 78-81) lists Sanskrit (*udra*), Avestan (*udra*), Greek (*udros*, "water-snake"), Latin (*lutra*), O.H.G. *ottar* and Lith. (*ūdra*). Other cognates are Old English *oter* and Old Icelandic *otr* (Lehmann).

The cognates are from Indian, Iranian, Greek, Latin, Germanic, Baltic and Celtic. Out of these only the Indian, Iranian, Baltic and English languages have preserved the meaning "otter". The cognates have lost the meaning 'otter' from South and Central Europe. Even the German word 'otter' originally means snake and adder, and the meaning 'otter' is a recent adoption.

Had "otter" been originally a European word, its cognates should have been in use in most of the the European languages, particularly those in the north. However, the European cognates of "otter" (from

Sanskrit *udra*) often mean animals other than otter in most of the linguistic provinces of Europe *e.g.* O.H.G. *ottar* (water-snake), Greek *udros* (*hydra*, water-snake), Old Irish *odar* "brown". In Old Irish, the word "*odar*" was snatched away from the poor animal "otter", and this animal was granted an entirely different name, *coin fodorne, i.e.* water dog (Pokorny:78-81; Starostin:229-230). This shows that Europeans had not had this word "otter" from the very beginning--otherwise the confusion in use of this word would not have previled so widely.

Thus we can conclude that when the IE speakers arrived into Europe, they applied different words to mean the animal "otter", and also they applied the word "otter" to different animals or things in different regions of Europe.

Beaver (*Castor*)

Witzel's claim (2001:53,54,55) that "beaver" was not native of India during the Vedic age had been proved wrong by archaeological findings coming from India, much before Witzel actually wrote his article!

Lot of beaver bones with evidence of hunting have been found from the archaeological remains in India e.g. Kashmir Valley Neolithic sites Burzahom and Gufkral (3100 cal BC & 1800 cal BC; V.N. Misra 2001:507-8; U. Singh 2008:114; IAR 1962). However, later beaver became extinct from India, primarily due to the development of the thick human settlements along the river banks, resulting in the loss of habitat for the beavers and secondarily because of weakening monsoon and increasing temperature of the climate. They were hunted ruthlessly for the musk, meat and fur too.

Mentions of beaver in the *Yajur-Veda*, and later Vedic texts only prove that they are very old texts, composed when beaver had not been extinct from northwest India. Following extinction of the beaver, the same term *babhru* came to be applied to the mongoose in India and to mice in north Iran (*bibar* Persian mouse, Steingass:154). However Persian *babr* and Kurdish *bebir* mean 'tiger'. In the Black *Yajur-Veda* the animals mongoose (*nakula*) and the veaver (*babhru*) have been mentioned in the same verse as different animals (*q.v.*). Hence the Neninger's claim oft cited by Witzel, that the mongoose was the meaning of Vedic *babhru*, is just a wrong guess.

In fact it is Europe where the word "beaver" (Pokorny 1959: 136) arrived later. This we can say because we find the clear confusion in the meaning of the word and in the naming of the animal in Europe. Thus the new-comer Indo-Europeans to Europe applied this word to mean several other things too, like "fibre", "brush" etc. In the north European languages its cognates often mean anything brown, including even "bear". In Latin there has been a semantic change and the *fiber/ fibra* means "soft" or "extremity of anything" (Valpi:152-3).

Purely on linguistic grounds too, the PIE word for "beaver" **bhebhru* does not stand to be of northern origin. In **bhebhru*, we find a reduplication of stem "*bh*". Such reduplication is not a feature of the northern languages at all. On the other hand it is an important areal feature of the southern languages (Austro-Asiatic, Austronesian, Dravidian, Indo-Aryan and African) languages (Rubino, Feature 27-27A).

Herodotus (fifth century BC) too uses the word *kastor* to mean 'beaver' (Powell 1938: 184). It is derived from the Indian word *kastūri* which is the name of a particular aphrodisiac perfume and also name of the perfume-carrying Himalayan deer 'musk-deer'. The perfume has been considered aphrodisiac in action. There was a hunt for this poor animal's testicles. Hence has derived the word 'castration'. The oil-seed 'castor' (*Ricinus communis*) too resembles testicles in shape, hence acquired the name (Pokorny: 516-517; also see Harper).

Crocodile

Crocodile and alligator live in the tropical rivers and swamps. In the past their leather was used for making bag etc. They are not found in Europe in general. Hence the meaning "crocodile" was lost from the European cognates derived from the Old Indian word *makara*, yet vestiges of the word have survived in European languages retaining some semantic aspect of the crocodile *viz* bag or article made of leather, swamp, to weep, slender and long.

Material: PIE **mak-* (leather pouch, Pokorny:698); Welsh *megin* (bellows); OHG *Magen*, O.E. *maga*, E. *maw*, O. Ice. *magi* (stomach); Latvian *maks*, *mekelis* (bag, purse), Lith. *mãkas, mẽkeris* (purse); Lith. *makšnà* (sheath); O.Ir. *mēn* from **makno-* or **mekno-* (mouth, bay).

PIE *mă̄k*-1 (damp, swamp, Pokorny:698); Proto-Armenian **mākri-* (swamp, marsh); Alb. *make* (skin of water-cat); Slav **mākati* (to weep). It may be noted that in folk thinking, weeping is usually associated with crocodiles.

māk̂ -, mək̂ - (long and slender; Pokorny:699); Av. *mas-* large; Greek *macros* large.

Fishes

Carp (*Cyprinus sophore* fish)

The wild form of this tropical small fish is found in the fresh waters of South Asia, China and Southeast Asia. However it is also found in Europe up to the Denube River, Caspian Sea and Central Asia. Its cognates are present in most of the languages of Europe, and the carp fishes lived in the Indo-European homeland can be made ot from this.

Sanskrit *śaphara* (masculine), *śapharī* (f.), PIE *k̂ op(h)elo-s or k̂ ap(h)elo-s*, Lithuanian *šãpalas*, Latin *Cyprinus*, Greek *kuprinos*, German *Karpfen* (found only as family names), English "carp" (Pokorny:614).

Small Fish Minnow/ Min

Sanskrit *mīna* (fish), English "minnow", O.E. *myne*, OHG *muniwa*, *munuwa*, German *munne* (fish); Greek *maine, mainis* (a small sea-fish); Latin *maena* (a small sea-fish); Russ *menЪ* (eel caterpillar); PIE $*m_{e}ni$ (fish; Pokorny:731).

However, Purpola, Witzel and many others quite wrongly think that Sanskrit *mina* (fish) is a loanword from Dravidian (*min*, fish). Other similar words related to the meanings 'food' and 'small' are North German *minn*, *mine* (small, little), *menu*, *minus*, "miniature" etc, which may or may not have some relationship with the word *mina* (see Pokorny: 728-729, PIE **men-* small), and the subject needs further exploration.

Salmon fish and the Lachs Theory

The Lachs Theory: Mehendale (2005:58-59), Witzel (2003; 2001:53) etc refer to Thieme's Lach's Theory with great enthusiasm. Mahendale summarizes the theory as follows: "Old HG *lachs*, Anglo-Saxon *leax*, Old Norse *lax* etc. point out to a common origin of IE **laks-/*lakso-* for salmon fish. This kind of fish is to be found only in the rivers which flow into the northern oceans (the North Sea and the Baltic Sea) and their tributaries. There is no salmon in Greece and Italy. Hence we have no correspondence of IE **laks-/*lakso-* in Greek and Latin and also in south Slavic. The Celts had their own word which was later borrowed as *salmo* in Latin."

However, the argument is self contradictory, flawed and based on manipulated and wrong data. The Tocharian word *laksi* does not mean "salmon", but means "fish". This clearly proves that the PIE root **laks-* could have survived even in the non-salmon regions of Europe--Greece and Italy. Hence it should have survived not only in the Greek, Latin and the Celtic speeches but also in the in the Indian languages retaining the meaning 'fish' or 'large fish'. However, this has not happened raising serious doubt over the validity of the hypothesis.

The first and the most likely possibility is that the Nordic languages and Tocharian received this word from some source other than the PIE language that was the substrate language of the northern, Central and Western Eurasian regions before the IE arrival there. Our further exploration proves this suspicion as fact (*vide infra*).

Mahendale proceeds to complete the hypothesis in the following manner: "That the word in Tocharian does not mean 'salmon' is understandable, since there are no salmon in Central Asia. The Tocharian branch has thus preserved the old IE word but given it a more general meaning 'fish'."

However Thieme, Mahendale etc do not reply to the question as to why the same did not happen in South Europe and South Asia. The theory further assumes, from the first principles, that the word corresponding to German '*lachs*' in Sanskrit should be *lakṣa* (one hundred thousand) and *lākṣā* (the red resin "lac").

The hypothesis argues that salmons are always found in large numbers, hence "Sanskrit has preserved IE word **lakso-* in the form *lakṣa-,* not in the meaning salmon but in the meaning 'one hundred thousand'." For *lākṣā* (a red resin found in India), the Theory argues that the flesh of the salmon is red and the lac resin is also red. Thus the Indian lac which is a red resin made by insects living on a particular tree had been thrust the name *lākṣā* when the Indo-European speakers arrived into India. But the theory does not say why this happened selectively in India and why any analogous thing did not happen in Iran, Anatolia or Southern Europe retaining any of the three semantic aspects of *lakso* namely the "very large number", "red colour" or "large fish".

Defects in the Lachs Theory:

The foremost defect in the theory was a large set of assumption without any evidence to support them. Thus the assumption that the early Indo-European word **lakso* meant only the 'salmon' and no other fish, and that it could not have meant any other fish are both wrong. The action which followed these assumptions was taking no note of the cognate words of **lakso* in the Vedic which could have meant 'fish' (*vide infra*). These semantic presumptions and the assumed semantic evolutions have been challenged by many on the basis of irrationality (Zimmer 2003).

The cognates of **lakso-* (salmon, fish) are found in only four branches of the IE family (out of the twelve) namely Baltic, Slavic, Germanic and Tocharian, all located on the northern limb of the Indo-European spread (R1a1a route).

Material: Proto-Germanic **lakhs*; MHG *lahs*; German *lachs*, Yiddish *lahs*, Icelandic *lax*, Danish *laks* (all meaning salmon), Old English **lax* (fish); Russian *losos*, Czec *losos*, Polish *losos*; Lithuanian *lašiša*, Old Prussian *lasasâ* (salmon).

However, many Germanic languages do not have any cognate word for **lakso-* at all-- neither for the meaning salmon, nor for any fish. Thus instead of any cognate of **lakso*, Dutch has *zalm* and Frisian *salm* (salmon). Italic and Celtic languages also have *salmo-*. Thus *salmo* is more popular in the European languages and has a greater chance of having been of IE origin rather than **lakso-*.

> Pokorny (*lak̂-*, *lagh-* 653) and other phylologists should have discarded the meaning "salmon" for PIE **lak-* and **laĝh-*. The only appropriate meaning of this word in the Indo-European, which should have been retained in the PIE root-list, is "to be spotted". This meaning has two semantic connotations: to have spots (on the surface), and to be noticed/ located), both of which are

> the meanings of the root in Sanskrit. This meaning covers all the derived meanings of the root like the 'salmon' as well as the 'lac-resin' and the 'large number'.

This we can say because this word *lachs* (salmon) is found only in the few languages of the Germanic and Balto-Slavic groups. Outside the two, it is found only in Tocharian B *laks* (fish; Central Asia, extinct) and Ossetic *läsäg* (salmon; a south Central Asian Iranian dialect) with the meaning 'fish'. In Ossetic, the word probably represents a loan-word from Central Asian substrate language (Altaic, *vide infra*), because the word (with meaning "fish" or "salmon" is completely absent from the other languages of the Iranian branch of IE.

In the Indo-Iranian as a whole, the words sounding similar in configuration are : Iranian, **raxša* (dark colored), N. Pers. *raxš* '(red-white), Vedic (Old Indian) *lākṣā* (red resin lacquer or lac). None of the phonologically possible cognate words mean "fish" at all. However the word is present in most of the Central Asian Turkic languages with the meaning "fish".

The ultimate source of the word "lachs" meaning "big fish":

The word lakso/lachs is entirely absent from European IE languages except Germanic and Balto-Slavic region, but is present in all the Uralic languages of Europe, and the Altaic languages of Asia, reaching even up to North America (*vide infra*).

By genetic and skeletal studies it has become clear by now that the Uralic (Finno-Ugric) languages are in their present location since the days before Indo-European languages came there (Niskanen; Villems 1998, 2002). "Therefore, the genetic ancestors of the Baltic-Finns have lived in the Baltic region more likely for 10,000 years rather than for 3000 years..." (Niskanen:122).[27] However the genetic ancestors for

---

27 Kalevi Wiik argued that the Finno-Ugric-speaking people lived during the Mesolithic period as far west as the westernmost regions of the

the rest of the Europeans including Germany have been not the pre-Neolithic European people and they have arrived in Europe after 5,500 BC (Haak 2010, 2005; Bramanti 2009).

It also became clear by genetic studies that the north Europeans in general arrived into Europe from Central Asia. "This admixture indicates that North Eurasia was colonized through Central Asia/ South Siberia by human groups already carrying both West and East Eurasian lineages". (Pimenoff 2008:39) Thus it follows that the Central Asians and the north Europe's pre-Indo-European population spoke languages of same stock which was probably the Proto-Uralic-Altaic language.

A search in the dictionaries of Uralic-Altaic languages clarifies that this word (*lachs* 'fish') is not of Indo-European origin, and is in fact 'Uralic-Altaic' in origin, being present in all the languages of the Uralic and Altaic families, reaching up to Japan and Dene-Yeniseian of North America. In these languages it means either of the two "salmon" or "a large fish".

Uralic Languages: Finnish *lohi*, Hungarian *lazac*, Sami *luossa*, Estonian *lõhe, lõhi* (all 'salmon').

Dene-Yeniseian (North Amerindian): Navajo *Loo* (fish), Dena"ina *lika* (fish), Tlingit *l'ook*, x̲*áat* (salmon); (Source—Swadesh List for Dené-Yeniseian languages at Wictionary).

North European Plain (quoted by Niskanen:122). The continuity theory practically replaced the migration theory in 1980 at the "roots" symposium held in Tvärminne, Finland. According to the continuity theory, the Uralic-speakers arrived long back in the Baltic region most likely when when the earliest post-Glacial inhabitants of the region arrived about 11,000 years ago (Nuñez 1987, Julku 1995, Wiik 1995, Salo 1996, all quoted by Niskanen:122). DNA study by Villems et al (1998, 2002) too supported the continuity theory for the Baltic.

Altaic: Proto-Altaic **lak`a*, a kind of big fish; **Proto-Mongolian** *\*laka*, Mongolian *laqa*, Khalkha *lax*; **Proto-Tungus-Manchu** *\*laka*, Evenki *laka*, Negidal *laxana*, Manchu *laqačan nisiχa, laqča nimaχa*, Ulcha *laqa*, Orok *lāqqa* herring, Nanai *lāqa*, Oroch *laka*, Udighe *la`sā* all meaning "a particular big fish". **Japanese** **nakatai, ru:* salmon.

Mongolian form is also present in the Turkic having the meaning "sheat-fish" or "catfish", although a suffix *balig* or *baliq* meaning "fish" is added: Turkmenistanian *laGGa balɨq*, Uzbek *laqqa baliq*, Azeri (Azerbaijani) *naqqa-balig* (Doerfer G.; also Tsintsius). Uzbek *losos* (salmon).

This survey makes it eminently obvious that the Germanic-Balto-Slavic word *laks* is actually of Uralic-Altaic extraction of the European substrate. Uralic-Altaic was the linguistic substratum before Indo-European advance (of R1a1a migration) into the north Caspian area, the Russian-Ukrainian steppe and north Black Sea region.

The source of Indo-European **lak-* and the Sanskrit word *lākṣā* etc:

The lac resin was used for industrial purposes in the Indus Valley Civilization (Kenoyer 1992: 504). The tree on which the lac resin was formed by the lac-insects has been mentioned in the *Athatva-Veda* by the name *lākṣā* (*AV* 5.5.7). *Lākṣā* was known to the people of the *Atharva Veda*, which fits into our chronological scheme of dating this Veda after to the Harappa period.

Because the Lachs-Theory is one of the core arguments of AIT, it must be discussed and dissected out threadbare. Therefore it is desirable to examine the Sanskrit word *lākṣā* and its etymology, whether it could be related with Germanic *laks* (salmon) even remotely. If there could be a link at all, in that case the Indo-European and the Uralic-Altaic etymology of the words like *lak'a* etc should be considered a case of convergent evolution.

Monier-Williams Sanskrit Dictionary gives meanings of *lākṣa* as: a 'mark, sign or token'. In fact even the token-money used in gambling has been named *lakṣā* in the *Rig-Veda* where a winning gambler collects the tokens (*lakṣā*) of the defeated players (*RV* 2.12.4). A related Sanskrit word *lakṣmī* too means 'mark', 'tocken' etc, and during the recent times 'wealth'. It is possible that during the proto-historic trading period (Indus Civilization), traded goods were marked with signs (Indus seals) using the lac resin. Thus the word *lakṣmī* acquired additional meaning "wealth", and the maker/sealing resin was thrust with the name *lākṣā*. A related word in Sanskrit is *lāñchana*, which means 'stigma, burn mark of punishment' etc. Another related word *lakṣya* means 'target, goal'. The whole set of the Sanskrit words have been derived from the root *lakṣa*- meaning "to see".

One more word of the same stock is *lakṣaṇa* which means signs (and symptoms). Its derivative is *lakṣmaṇa* that means "having marks or signs or charecteristics". In the *Taittiriya Samhita* (7.1.6.3), the word has been used with this very meaning (MWD). The phrase is "*rohiṇī lakṣmaṇā*". *Rohiṇī* means 'red' (feminine). Literally the phrase means 'one with the red sign' and it is the epithet of a sacrificial being (?fish) which has come out of water and is meant for sacrifice/slaughter to please the water-god Indra.

Although the translators like Keith have conjectured that the meaning is a 'red coloured cow with good signs or omens' this meaning is wrong on several accounts. Firstly, fish is the more appropriate being/animal for sacrifice to the water-god Indra, not the cow. Secondly the hymn mentions that it had come out of water, which applies to the fish and not to the cow. Thirdly, the red-sign is checked by the Indians in case of the fishes, which have red gills if fresh and dirty dark-grey gills if they are rotten, and the 'red sign' or 'red-carecteristic' has no meaning for the cow. The phrase is meaningless if taken to mean a red cow with good charecteristics as has been assumed by Kieth. The phrase does not tell "charecteristics" of what?

Clearly *rohiṇī lakṣmaṇā* means the fresh *Labeo rohita* fish, with demonstrable red-gill sign of freshness. Out of the full phrase *rohiṇī lakṣmaṇā* only the first part has survived in the modern Indo-Aryan languages as the *rohu, rehu, rohi* etc (CDIAL 10866) meaning the fish *Labeo* particularly the species *boga* and *rohita*. The out of India people to the North Europe have retained the latter part of the phrase (*i.e. lakṣmaṇā*) to mean the large and good quality fish. Hence in north Europe, Tocharian and Russian the "best quality fish" meaning has been retained by the word *lakso* etc. This is one of the several possibilities which can be conceived today after thousands of years, and it may or may not be true.

The *Labeo boga* (also called Red-Gill Violet Shark) and the other species of the genus *Labeo* are natives of Indian sub-continent and are famous for their "red-coloured" gills as the mark of good quality. The Vedic phrase *rohiṇī lakṣmaṇā* means "endowed with red (gills) as charecteristc of good quality" (of the *Labeo* fish). The colour of the gills of a fresh fish is like the colour of the lac resin. This is how the lac resin *lakṣā* may have acquired its name.

Another possibility too can be entertained. When the Indo-Europeans reached Europe and found the substrate language word *lohi* meaning "large fish", they adopted it and adapted it to *lākṣa* and reserved it for the salmon because it was more meaningful to the IE speakers (spotted skin of salmon). And thus the fish acquired its current Germanic "*lachs*" etc because it was highly spotted.

This explains how the Sanskrit name *lākṣā* was given to the lac resin which is red in colour. However, we have no clue as to how the related word *lakṣa* acquired the meaning "one hundred thousand". However the same *Yajur-Vedic* mantra mentions that one who gifts Indra thus (*i.e.* good quality fish), gets "three hundred and thirty three (units of wealth, ?fish)" in return (brackets added). The number three hundred and thirty three should be considered 'a very large number'.

Chapter 27

Smaller mammals, reptiles and birds

Domestic Mouse

Witzel (2001:54) claims that mouse and hedgehog are animals of the temperate climate:

> "Finally, it must be considered that, generally, the IE plants and animals are those of the temperate climate and include the **otter, beaver, wolf, bear, lynx, elk, red deer, hare, hedgehog, mouse**; ... most of them are not found in India and their designations have either been adapted (as is the case with the beaver > mongoose *babhru*), or they have simply not been used any longer." (emphasis added).

This claim is wrong. It has been found from the DNA studies that all the domestic mice and rats have come out fom India after the Last Glacial maximum (Tate 1936; Ferris 1982; Auffray 1990; Boursot 1993, 1996; Din 1996; Priyadarshi 2012). Mice and hedgehogs are found in India even today. Bones of mice and hedgehogs have been recovered from archaeological excavations in India (Misra 2001:507; U. Singh:114).

The domestic mouse and the house rat are two human commensal species which originated in India. The domestication of the two had occurred in India before they migrated out about 15,000 and 20,000 years back respectively. Their domestication and migration in India is evidence of farming having evolved first in India. It is held that these species migrated essentially with farming related human migrations. Recent excavations indicate that India (Ganga Valley) had developed the oldest farming in the world (Rakesh Tewar 2008i; Dikshit 2009; G.R. Sharma 1980a, 1980b, 1985).

The DNA analysis of the mice (*Mus musculus*) informs us that the *domesticus* subspecies left India, entered Iran, reached West Asia and from there Southeast Europe. The other sub-species *musculus musculus* entered Central Asia from India to disperse in the Russian steppe and further west. These routes of migration of commensal mice overlap the routes and times of human migration as deciphered more recently by human DNA studies. The route of the *musculus musculus* sub-species overlaps the migration route of R1a1a human Y-DNA through Central Asia and Russia to Europe (Underhill 2009; Boursot; Priyadarshi 2011; Priyadarshi 2012). The *domesticus* sub-species migrated with the J2b human Y-DNA through Iran and Fertile Crescent to South Europe (Priyadarshi 2011, 2012; Boursot 1996).

It was found earlier that male DNA lineage J2b (M12; M102), distributed from India to South Europe, was associated with the migration of Indo-European language and farming in West Asia and Southern Europe (King and Underhill). J2b samples were only lately studied in India (Sahoo 2006; Sengupta 2006). Data for age of this lineage in India, Iran, Anatolia and the Balkans, obtained from different published papers show that this lineage too originated in India and then migrated to Europe through Iran and West Asia.

Our study rules out Semino's claim of origin of this lineage in West Asia or North Africa, and notes that Semino (2004:1026 fig 2D) got his result wrong only because he had excluded DNA samples from South Asia east of Pakistan. We thus find that the mice and human Y-chromosomal lineages migrated out from India with farming and

Indo-European languages by two routes, one northern and the other southern, both meeting again in the Central and Western Europe.

Philology of mouse:

Nicholas Kazanas has noted the philological distribution and variation of *mus* which in fact correlate well with the archaeological findings (Kazanas 2009a:162-163, n29). He examines the cognates for 'mouse' in the Indo-European family of languages and notes that Celtic and Baltic languages do not have a cognate word for mus. He writes, as the most revealing case, the philology of the mouse. The cognate stem does not appear in Celtic and Baltic. This is clearly because the Celtic and Baltic were the last to be reached in the Indo-European migration out of India by two routes. Sanskrit *mūs*; Greek *mūs*; Latin *mūs*; Germanic *mus*; Slavic *myšū*; Albanian *mū* and Armenian *mu-kn* (see Priyadarshi 2012).

Shrew (*Suncus*)

Asian house Shrew (*Suncus murinus*) is an Indian animal, which migrated with human migrations to other parts of the world, particularly to Arabia, East African coast and Malagasy (Duplantier 2002:156). Pokorny did not include the animal's name in his list of the Indo-European words. However, many authors have included it in their lists (PIE **swor-* Starostin's Database). Many genera of the shrew occur in Europe in the wild (like *Sorex araneus*). The cognates are found in the Italic, Greek and Slavic branches, often with altered meanings to mouse etc. Hence most probably, it was the Asian domestic shrew which was known to the ancient Indo-European speakers, not the wild European shrews.

In Sanskrit the word is *śalyaka* with the original meaning the porcupine (one with thorns; also *śallaka*). However the word was also applied to the shrew, with the suffix *-vata* (*śalyaka-vata*, one which looks like a porcupine), because the faces of the two animals are similar. The cognate words are: Latin *sorex* (field-mouse, lately being used for the shrew Valpi:438)[28], Latv. *sussuris*; Russian *zverek* (shrew), Bulg *səsar*; O. Gk. *húraks* (mouse, shrew), *hyrax* (shrew); Albanian *iriq* (shrew). There are other words which have not so far been mentioned in any published literature as cognates of "sorex", yet are certainly cognates of "sorex": *e.g.* Russian *xorëk* (pronounced *khoryok*, polecat; c.f. *śalyaka*); French *souris* (mouse), Italian *sorcio* (mouse), Romanian *soarece* (mouse). Turner constructs the Proto-Indo-Aryan form as **śariyaka* (porcupine; CDIAL 12334).

Hedgehog

The hedgehog too is an Indian mammal. Many species are exclusive to South and Southeast Asia. The "Indian hedgehog" (*Paraechinus micropus*) is a species restricted exclusively to India, and is particularly known to the scientists because of the important role which the Indian Hedgehog Protein (IHHP) plays in the humans.

Etymology of the names of the hedgehog has been the most messed up topic in the Indo-European etymology. It has been claimed that **eĝhi-* (L. *anguis*, Gk. *ékhis*, Sanskrit *ahi*: snake) was applied as the name of the hedgehog (*echidna*), because the hedgehogs are the "snake-eaters" (**eĝhi-no-s*). This is a wrong hypothesis. The hedgehogs can never kill a snake, although they can eat dead animals including the snake as well. Adams considers this evidence "folkloristic" (1999:130). Further it was claimed by the linguists that the **-no-s* part (meaning "killer", *-ghna* in Sanskrit) of the hypothetical word (**eĝhi-no-s*) became silent and the **eĝhi* (originally meaning 'snake') stayed retaining the meaning 'hedgehog'.

On the basis of this hypothesis, they derived *eĝhi* > *ĝher-* > *pork̂o-s* meaning that the pig looks like a hedgehog hence pig was derived from *eĝhi* (snake) (Pokorny:445-446). This leads to a complete loss of credibility to the etymological derivations.

---

28 Pokorny (1049) wrongly thinks that the *sorex* is from PIE su̯er (to hiss).

Harper too disagrees with this etymology of *echinos* (see *echinos* hedgehog in Harper). The hedgehogs can hardly kill ants. He suggests that the words (*echidna* etc) belong to Latin *echinos* and Greek *ekhinos* (sea-urchin), because all of them have thorn-like points on the body. This suggestion seems more plausible for the words *echinos* and *echidna*, and other related ones.

It is possible that the modern spelling of the word "hedgehog" (read "he-dgehog") is a product of the fertile brains of the folk-etymologists from some original word esembling the Sanskrit *jahaka*. In Sanskrit, the hedgehog (as well as porcupine) is called *jahakā*, which has many cognates in European languages, although the meanings differ. Pokorny gives this list of cognates as: PIE **ĝ(h)eĝh-*, Sk. *jahakā* (hedgehog); Lith. *šẽškas* (weasel, polecat) (Pokorny:424). In this list, the Lithuanian *šẽškas* has been wrongly placed, because Pokorny himself gives another etymology for the same Lithianian word *šẽškas* in the same volume from PIE *keƙ* (**keƙ* > *šẽškas* 'polecat', Pokorny:543).

Thus, by this manipulation, he is able to finally give the meaning for the PIE **ĝ(h)eĝh-* as "polecat" or "ferret". We have noted that Pokorny also lists Lith. *šẽškas* as cognate of another Sanskrit word *kaśikā* (mongoose) as derived from PIE *keƙ* ("polecat"; p. 543). This shows the confusion in the Indo-Europeanists regarding the etymologies of the hedgehog and the weasel.

It is noteworthy that in spite of the claims by the Indo-Europeanists, there is no common word for the hedgehog in the various IE languages of Europe. Thus we have for the "hedgehog": Italian *riccio*, French *hérisson*, Spanish *erizo*; German *igel*; Lith *ežys* etc. These are not related to each other. Although the hedgehog has been found in Europe since the early Holocene, yet absence of any definite or any common name for the animal means the Indo-Europeans came to Europe from outside.

Porcupine

In Eurasia, porcupine is India, Iran, Southeast Asia and Europe. Its body is covered with spikes, just like the hedgehogs, and often same or similar words have been used to name both of them in the Indo-Aryan and European languages (CDIAL 12334).

In Sanskrit, we get the word *jahakā* (the laugher) meaning the porcupine, and also the 'hedgehog' (MWD; CDIAL). The speech of the porcupine is like human laughing sound, hence the name. For this word, we get the following material: Sanskrit *jahakā* (porcupine, hedgehog, 'laughing-man'); Croatian, Bosnian *jež* (hedgehog), Czech *ježek*, Slovac *ježovec* (porcupine), Polish *jeżozwierz* (porcupine, hedgehog); Persian *chizak* and *zhūzha* (porcupine, hedgehog). In Persian, the word was thrust on to the frog also: Persian *jazag̲h̲* frog.

Some of the Indo-Aryan names of porcupine are: Sanskrit *śalyaka*, *śallaka*, *sedhā* (porcupine; one with thorns). The shrew was named *śalyaka-vata* (Sk., one which is like a porcupine in looks), from which many of the European names of the shrew have been derived (*vide supra*). The cognates of *śalyaka* lost the meaning "shrew" in the Italian peninsula, and acquired the meaning of mouse and other rodents in the Italic languages. Yet we this is enough evidence for inferring that the PIE homeland had the porcupine and shrew both.

Pokorny does not show awareness of this lexical material, and gives only two cognate words *viz.* Sanskrit *jahakā* and Lith. *šẽškas* for the PIE **ĝ(h)eĝh-*. Going against the available evidence Pokorny gives 'polecat' as the meaning of Sanskrit word *jahakā*—a meaning which is found nowhere in Sanskrit literature. He gives "hedgehog" as the meaning of *jahaka* with a question mark, and omits the porcupine completely. This can only be called as atrocious.

Reptiles

Lizards, chamaeleons and snakes are cold-blooded or anisothermal animals. Hence they cannot survive in very cold climates. Lizards depend on insects for food. Hence they need a warm and humid region to live in. India is thus the best habitat for these reptiles in Asia. Snakes are very much the same as other reptiles, yet they eat small mammals like rats and mice. Philology demonstrates that these small animals lived in the PIE homeland and cognates have survived in India and Southern European languages. Examples are:

Latin *Chamaeleon*; Greek *khamaileon*; Sanskrit *hemala.*

Lizard (E.); Latin *lacertus*; Sanskrit *saraṭu.*

Sanskrit *sarpa,* Latin *serpens*, Greek *herpenton* and Alb. *gjarpën* are all related. However, this set of words has lost the meaning "snake" in the Germanic and other European languages. English "snake" or German *schenake* are not cognates of *serpens* but are the cognates of "snail" (mollusk), and were probably later inventions after reaching North Europe.

Birds

Papihā (CDIAL 8204; Old Awadhi borrowed into Hindi; an Indian bird, Brain-fever Bird; *Hierococcyx varius*; or *Cuculus melanolencos*): Sk *pippakā* (also *pippīka*), PIE PIE **pīp(p)-* (Pokorny:830).

In Europe: Latin *pīpilō*; Gk. πῖπος or *pipos* (young bird), πίπρα f. or *pipa* (a kind of woodpecker *Pipus*); Sloven. *pípa* (chicken); Alb. *bibë* (young water-fowl) etc. It has survived in Europe in many verb forms. German *piepen, pip(p)itüre, pīpulum* (to whimper), Osc. *pipatio* (clamor plorantis), Lith. *pӯpti* (whistle) etc (Pokorny: 830).

Pika (Sk. Indian cuckoo): In Europe: English "Pie" (old name of magpie, a bird of crow family); Latin *pica* (magpie, f. of *picus*), Latin *picus* (woodpecker); Umbrian *pieca*, German name *Specht* (woodpecker). (Pokorny: 999; Harper).

Tittir (a bird): Sk. *tittira* (partridge); In Europe: PIE **teter*; M.Ir. *tethra* (hooded-crow); Germanic *thidurr* (capercaillie bird); OCS *tetrevi* (pheasant), Rus *teterev* (capercaillie), Lith. *teterva* (capercaillie), Iranian *tadharv* (pheasant); Gk. *tetraon* (capercaille).

Śuka **(Sk. parrot):** Phylology tells us that parrot was known to the early Indo-Europeans. However, when the IE speakers reached Europe, the word *shuka* was applied indiscriminately to mean any bird in Europe. Arm. *sag* (goose); O.C.S. *sova* (owl); Celt. *cavannus* (cry); Lith. *šaukiù, šaũkti* (cry, loud call, shout, cry, name); Russ. *syčь* (small owl, sparrow-owl), Cz. *sūc* (owl). (Pokorny: 535-536; Starostin: 1475).

Chapter 28

The Carnivores and other forest mammals

Lion

Today Indian lion (*Panthera leo*) is found only in a small open forest Gir in Gujarat, which is a relatively drier and open forest adjoining the Thar Desert. It is not found in the denser Central Indian and Eastern Indian forests, which are the favourite abodes of the tiger. Thus tiger and lion are mutually exclusive, particularly because of the operation of the Gauss's Competitive Exclusion rule. No two top carnivores can live in the same ecological niche. Lions try to camouflage in the tall grasses, with lighter paler shade, while tiger works under the camouflage of the darker trees and shrubs, which are found in the wetter forests. Thus they have adopted different hunting practices to suite their respective habitats.

It is well attested that there is no mention of the tiger in the *Rig-Veda* although the lion has been mentioned quite often. Tiger however appears in the *Yajur-Veda*. On the other hand the Harappan seals depict tigers, but no lion at all. The historians have no clue why it was so. Instead of exercising their minds scientifically, they tried to explain these findings not on the basis of ecological differences but on the basis of 'presumed' recial biases and taboos of the respective cultures against the lion and tiger.

Was this owing to the respective taboos or religious superstitions of the *Rig-Vedic* and the Harappan people, or the climate played a part in this phenomenon? The scientific approach demands that we must accept that the Harappa culture was surrounded with the dense forests. Therefore there were no lions, although many tigers and other animals of the wet climate lived in those forests as depicted in the Harappan seals (Possehl 2002:9). This is because the Harappa Civilization pertains largely to the mid-Holocene Optimum which prevailed about 5000-3000 BC.

On the other hand the *Rig-Veda* pertained to a drier period when the same region would have grasslands and open forests in which the lions would be found but not the tigers. About 3000 BC was the wettest time of the Indus Valley region when the Harappa culture was flourishing at its peak. The period 8000 BC to 6000 BC was colder and drier with lots of open forests and savannah grasslands, but no dense closed forests. Early Mehrgarh as well as the *Rig-Veda* pertained to this period when the lions would be found in the region but not the tiger.

It was John Marshall who noted first that the Bronze Age Northwest India was much wetter and lion being an animal of the dry regions could not be expected there (Possehl 2002:15). He supported this with the evidence that the burnt-brick housed and the massive drains were in the Harappa as the result of the necessity to protect from the heavy rains.

Marshall noted that tigers, elephants, rhinoceros, buffalo are all depicted on the stamp seals of Harappa and are all animals which prefer a wet habitat. The lion, a dry-land animal is conspicuous in its absence from the Indus imagery (Possehl:9, 15). However, Possehl himself wrongly thought that the climate of the Indus Valley Civilization was more or less the same as today, when he said that the peacocks and the pandolins depicted in the Indus imagery were exotic animals and did not belong to the fauna of the region (p. 120). His view that lion must have been there in the Indus (p. 120) too is wrong, because lion lives in the dry climates in open forests which the Indus Valley Civilization was not at that time. However to the west and northwest of the Indus Valley lion lived about 3000 BC as depicted in seals from Nausharo etc (Jarrige, Didier and Quivron:14, 24). The climate is so well reflected in the regional fauna that as soon as the Harappa region becomes dry again and desert starts penetrating the region, we get at Sibri a lion on a cylinder seal on which a zebu and a scorpion too have been engraved (Santoni 1981:56) at about 2000 BC.

There was a global wet and warmer period during the mid-Holocene Optimum, which can be described from 5500 BC to 3000 BC. However Thamban's study based on the Arabian Sea sediments notes a wet climate from 7500 BC to 6,500 BC (Thamban 2007:1009). This he thinks was due to the strong Arabian Sea monsoon. However the increased sediments in the Arabian Sea between 7500 BC-6500 BC should be attributed to the increase glacial melting and thus increased flow in the river system of northwest India, and not because of the assumed increase of the Arabian Sea monsoon. In Thamban's study, a dry climate follows starting 6,500 to 6000 BC, which is followed by the wet period again from 4000 BC or 3500 BC. Sinha and Sarkar's study also shows that the Northwest India region had a wet period between 4000 BC and 3200 BC (Sinha and Sarkar:2).

Dry climate resulted in open forests and savannah. Lion flourished in the open forests, savannahs and semi-deserts, where they work in groups to attack the prey. However tigers are not found in such forests because they prefer dense forests where they act singly often attacking the prey from a camouflage of the dense forest. This is the reason why we do not get the mention of the tigers in the *Rig-Veda*. The period between 4000 BC and 3200 BC is the wettest period reported from all studies of the palaeoclimate of the region. This is the time when dense forest would grow in the region. This is the habitat favourable to the tigers and unfavourable to the lions. Thus we get the absence of lions and presence of the tigers in the Harappan seals.

There is philological support to the presence of the lion in the PIE homeland. Pokorny (1959: 520) shows that the Sanskrit *keśa* (hair, mane), from PIE **kais*, is cognate to Tocharian A *śiśäk* (lion), Tocharian B *ṣecake* (lion) and Lat. *caesariēs* (hair of the head) from which the Eastern Latin word *Caesar* (Emperor) and German *kaisar* (king) have been derived. Hence the Sanskrit word *keśarī* (lion, king) is derived from *keśa*. Lithuanian *šẽškas* (weasel, polecat) too must be considered a cognate here, because the polecat is like a miniature lion in colour and form. Pokorny is confused about its etymology (*vide supra*).

There are other cognate forms of the word not recorded by Pokorny: Sanskrit *kesara* (hair, of eye-brows; mane of lion and horse), *kaṣāya* (lion, saffron colour after the colour of lion, saffron flower filaments); *keśin* (lion); Hindi *khesāri* (grass pea, a pulse; Witzel 2009 Fulltext, see table); Avestan *geshu* (curly hair), Persian *qaisar* (Roman Emperor), *ḥaidar* (lion), *qasr* (violence, force), *qaṣr* (pain in neck). In Europe we get Old English, Old Norse and O.M.G. *keiser* (king), Old Saxon *kĕsur*, OHG *keisur*, Old Icelandic *keisari*; Old Slavic *tsesari* (from which *tsar*, *C-zar*, *czar*; emperor; see Lehmann: K1). It has been generally suggested that it is a loanword into the Germanic. Other related word may be Arabic *qasr* (castle, pain in neck) may have been a borrowing from Sanskrit or Persian.

This association rules out Witzel's speculation that *keśa* is a para-Munda/ substratum word borrowed into Sanskrit (2001:53). It also refutes Witzel's theory that all Sanskrit word starting with *ke-* prefix must have been borrowed from Munda/ substratum language. This he says when he knew the etymology of *keśara* (see Witzel –Fulltext 2010, table on page 38)!! He preferred to suppress the fact about the relationship among the words *keśa*, one fore lion and words meaning emperors of Germany and Rome.

Estonian *keisar, keiser* (emperor) and Finn *keisari* (male ruler) are loan-words into Finno-Ugric (Harper[29]). The Finnish word *keisari*, which

[29] Harpar: Online Etymology Dictionary, see under 'czar'.

certainly is not from the Latin *Cesar*, has the same configuration as Indo-Aryan *kesarī*, and possibly is a loan word into Finnish during some ancient contact between the Finno-Ugric speakers and the Indo-Iranians. It is intriguing why this word has been left out by Burrow (1978; Reprint 2001:25) from the list of the Sanskrit loan-words into Finno-Ugric. Inclusion of this word in his list clearly would have destroyed his whole hypothesis, and reversed the direction of migration of the Indo-Iranians, which he thinks is from Volga basin to South Asia.

In light of this philological evidence, it may be further surmised that Persian and Kurd *sher* (lion) is probably derived from Sanskrit *keshari* by a loss of initial '*ke*'. Chinese *shi* (lion) too may be a loanword from Persian. Persian *geshu* (hair) is a cognate, although Pokorny (585 &586) derives it from another root **kes-* or **ĝhes-* (to scratch).

simha: Another early IE word for lion was **singhos* (Mallory and Adams 2006: 142). However, it has survived only at two places: Arm. *inj*, *ink* (leopard) and Sanskrit *siṃha* lion. Starostin's PIE database notes Armenian "*inǯ*" meaning 'leopard' and Proto-Tocharian **ṣēnśäke* (lion). On the basis of these words he proposes **simha* as at PIE stage meaning lion. Hazda (Kohistani-IA) *seseme* (leopard) and *sê?sêmê* (lion); Bantu *samba* (lion; Sands:186 cited by Starostin:132) could be related, and may be a case of borrowing from India.

Hence we can conclude that the lion was known to the early IE speakers by at least two words *kesarī* and *simha* (or **singhos*). However Witzel (1999:66) tries to mislead by saying that the proposed root (he lists: **sengha/singha* > **sinj'ha*; ***s1engha*) is a substrate word from the south Siberian steppe or East Europe borrowed into Indo-Iranian.

Leo: It has been claimed that the word "lion" or *leo* has no Indo-Iranian cognate. However it is not correct and in the languages of the northwest of the Indian sub-continent, the cognates of the word lion have been retained. The cognates have been borrowed into the

Semitic too from Persian. Thus the complete list of cognates of the word "lion" are:

Hebrew *labi* (lion), Egyptian *labia, lawai* (lioness); English "lion"; Latin *leo*; German *Löwe* (lion); Anatolian *luwe* (lion); Lithuanian *lãpė* (wild cat); Tocharian-B *lu* (animal); Kohistani (northwest IA) *sin-lāhú, sin-lāhā* (otter; literally river-lion, *lāhú* = lion, *sin*=river or Indus, Zoller:399); Persian *laḥim* (lion, Steingass:1119), Pushto *sīnd-lāo* (otter, Zoller), Proto-Hazda **lalupai* (lion), Hazda *nǀálúpãi* (lion).

Possibly the cognate words were lost from most of the north Indian languages because the lion did not live in the north Indian forests after about 5,500 BC, and was surviving at the brink of extinction in the Thar region at that time. Elst and Gamkrelidze and Ivanov have made out that the word *leo* was possibly coined from the root for 'roar'. Lion (E. from Old French); *leo* and *leonem* (Latin, lion); *lÖwe* (German, brave); *lew* (Pol.), *lev* (Czech) brave; **reuk* (PIE, roar); *rav-* (Sk. roar); *in-rauhtjan* (Goethic, roar); *ariwc* (Armenian, lion); *raukn* (O. Icelandic, harness animal); *reoc* (O.E. wild); *ljutij zwer* (Russ. fierce beast) etc (Gamqrelize and Ivanov 1995:431).

Leopard and Panther (tiger)

In spite of Witzel's claim (1999:66) that Sanskrit *pṛdaku* is Para-Munda substrate word philology shows that leopard, a typical Indian animal, was present in the Indo-European homeland.

PIE (Starostin) **prd* or **perd* (leopard): Sanskrit *pṛdaku* (adj. *pārdaku*), Greek *pardos*, Old Greek *párdo-s, párdalo-s, párdali-s, Pardel*, (panther), Tajik-Iranian dialect Sogd *pwrδnk*, Pashto *pṛāng*, N. Pers. *palang* (panther). (References: WP II 49 f.; source Starostin's database). Lith. *parudavęs* (foxy) may be related. Leopard was not found in Lithuania hence the word got applied to the fox.

In fact Starostin's **perd* may be semantically related to Pokorny's **sp(h) erd(h)-* to rush, running, Slov. *prôdek*, alert, awake, smart; M.H.G. *sporte* tail (leopard is famous for its long tail) and Sanskrit *spárdha-* to fight, especially in contests (Pokorny: 995-996).

The word "panther" has been suggested to be a cognate of Sanskrit *puṇḍarīka*. Tiger is absent from the *Rig-Veda* where the lion is present. However the tiger comes in the *Yajur-Veda* where it has been mentioned as the wild beast along with the constrictor snake *ajagara* which is either python or *Boa constrictor* (*TS* 7.3.14.1). Lion has been mentioned only in the praise of the gods, whose powers have been metaphorically compared with that of the lions. This does not represent the real presence of the lion in the region but represents more of the folk memory of lion in the people living in the dense forests of the Indus-Sarasvati region. Lion must have however occurred in the drier Thar region during the mid-Holocene Optimum, as Thar had turned then into grassland.

Jackal

Jackal has a southern warmer distribution. Sanskrit *śṛgāla*; Pers. *shaghal*, Kurmanci Kurd *chacal* ; German *schakal*; Lith. *šaklas*; Latv. *šakālis*; Bulgarian *chakal* (чакал), Russian *shakal*, Polish *szakal*; French *chacal*, all mean 'jackal' indicating that the homeland was in the south. Turkish *çakal* is a loan. However these words may be the result of the Bronze Age migration of the Indians to the steppe as well as Middle East and South Europe.

Some other words which show larger phonetic variation are possibly the words carried along the original Indo-European out of India migration, and have lost the original meaning, yet retained the names. These words mean fox, wolf, devil etc. This list include: O.Ice. *skrǫggr* (fox), Norse *skrogg* (wolf), Ice. *skröggur* (graybeard), Swedish dial. *skragge* (devil), M.H.G. *schreckel* (demon, ghost), *schröuwel* (dilapidated), Norse dialect *schräkel* (deformed creature) etc.

Lopāśa (fox, jackal): Philology provides us with the evidence proving that the animal fox was found in the Indo-European homeland. Cognate words for Sanskrit *lopāśa* (fox, jackal) are well represented in European languages often with the meaning altered to wolf, and sometimes to other animals:

Sk *lopasha*, PIE *u̯l̥̥p-, *lup-*,*su̯ilkʷ- (fox, jackal, wolf); Avestan *urupis* (dog), *raopis* (fox/jackal), M.Pers. *rōpās*, Pers. *rōbāh* (fox), Arm. *aluēs* (fox); Lat. *volpēs* (fox), *lupus* (wolf); Bret. *louarn* (fox), Welsh *llywarn* (fox); Polish (**lues*) *lis* (fox); Gk. ἀλώπηξ and ἀλωπός (fox); Ltv. *lapsa* fox. Hence Starostin (Database) reconstructs a PIE stem **lup-* meaning both wolf and fox.

Wolf

Some phylologists have wrongly attributed the etymology of the word 'wolf' from PIE root **wlqwos* or **u̯l̥kʷ-os*. This root is the source of some other words including the Vedic word having the meaning 'wolf' but not the word 'wolf' itself. Its Sanskrit cognate *vṛka* (tearer, wolf) has been used in the sense of 'wolf' in the *Rig-Veda* (*RV* 1.42.2, 1.105.7).

Its cognates are found in Indian, Iranian, Greek, Albanian, Baltic, Greek, Celtic, Slavic (only O.C.S.) and Germanic (only Old Icelandic). Cognates are Hindi *bheṙia*; Avestan *vəhrka-*; Gk. λύκος (*lukos*); O.Ice. *ylgr*; Lith. *vil̃ kas*; Ltv. *vìlks*, O.Pruss. *wilkis*, O.C.S. *vlьkъ* ds.; Alb. *ulk*, *ulku*, *Ulkos* (human name); Illyr. *Ulcudius*, *Ulcirus*; O.Brit. PN *Ulcagnus* (all meaning 'wolf'); O.Ir. *Olcán*, *olc*, gen. *uilc* (mad, wicked, evil). It is because of this reason that Starostin (database) reconstructs a PIE word for these words: **wᵉlk-*, and adds Tocharian B *walkwe* (wolf) to the list.

Ethnoecology of the Indo-Europeans determined the later vocabulary. Wolf lives and hunts in groups known as 'packs'. That is why it requires open fields or thin open forests. They do not live in the dense forests and that is why we do not get them in Southeast Asia. The retention of the cognate words implies presence of the wolf throughout the way from India to Europe (or the other way round, whatever) at the time of the IE migration. That provides evidence for the absence of the dense forests at that time. Such time was the Early Holocene *i.e.* the time before the mid-Holocene Optimum. Hence on account of the presence of the cognate words for wolf in India, Iran, Greece etc, we can say that the Indo-European migration took place before 6000 BC.

Chapter 29

Mosquitoes and Flies

These two species are well represented in the southern European languages although absent from the languages of the northern colder areas. Cognates are: Sanskrit *maśaka, mācikā, makṣa, makṣikā* (house fly), *maśaka, maśa* (mosquito); Greek: μυῖα or *muia* (house fly); Latin *musca* (house fly); Albanian: *mize* (gnat); Persian *makh*[30] (wasp, bee), *mausa, mūsa* (bee) (see Steingass: 1191, 1345); PIE *mak̂o-, or *mok̂-o- (fly, Pokorny:699). It may be said with certainty that this Indo-European word *musca* must be from a humid tropical region. At least the flies are not famous for being inhabitants of northern colder regions.

Honey Bees

There are cognates words of Sanskrit *madhu* (honey) in several Indo-European languages: PIE **médhu* (Pokorny:707); Sanskrit *madhu* (honey, wine); Avestan *maδu* (honey); O. Irish *mid, medo*, Welsh *medd, medu* (honey); Greek μέθυ (wine); Lithuanian *medùs*, Latvian *mẹdus*, Old

[30] Persian ***makh*** has retained many of the semantic features of flies and mosquitoes. Its meanings "bee" and "wasp" have retained the feature "biting" characteristic of mosquitoes. However other meanings like "sticking, annihilated, reduced to nothing" are features of a house fly. The last two have been well expressed in William Blake's poem "The Fly" (Am I not a fly like thee?).

Prussian *meddo* (honey); English "mead", German *met* (a wine made of honey).

The Uralic word for the bee's wax has been loanword from Indian. In the Mordvin language (Moksha dialect) *sta* and (Erzya dialect) *ksta, sta*; in Mari language *siste*, and in Udmurt *śiś*-- all mean 'beeswax' from Sanskrit *śiṣṭa* (beeswax, polished, gentle, remains after the juice-thing has been extracted).

These and many such Uralic words have been borrowed not from the adjoining Russian, but derived from Indian (Parpola and Carpelan: 115-119). This means the Uralics learnt the honey business from the immigrant Indians possibly during the Bronze Age.

Clearly honey and therefore bee were known to the Indo-European people in their homeland. Honey bee *Apis mellifera* cannot survive in the extreme of aridity or cold. They also need flowering plants for their food (Winston 1991). Hence India, where bees probably originated (Winston:7), was the natural home of the hone bee, particularly during the glacial period and the early Holocene, and the steppe was not conducive to the survival of the bee those days. Today there is a locally adapted race of the bee in the Russian steppe (*A. m. acervorum*, Winston:11). However possibly before 6000 BC, they did not exist there.

Chapter 30

Domestic Animals

The Pig

It has been the received knowledge from philological studies that the pig had been domesticated/herded by the Indo-European speakers before their dispersal took off from the homeland. Earlier DNA studies of the wild and the domesticated pigs have shown that the domestication of the wild boar took place at several places in Eurasia, out of which India and Southeast Asia were the earliest (Larson 2005). Shuli Yang (2011) noted that the "Asian pig domestication appears to have occurred mainly in Northeastern India, the Mekong region, and the middle and downstream regions of the Yangtze River. Interestingly, the three centers of domestication are all near the Tibetan highlands."

Matisso-Smith (2012:149) too noted that the wild pig originated in Southeast Asia and from there went across India to Near East. She suggested independent domestications in Southeast Asia (Sahul), India, China and Near East and Europe. However other DNA reports certainly suggest and older domestication in India (see DNA family tree in Larson 2005:Fig 1).

The most recent of the all mtDNA studies of the pigs shows that the family tree of the wild pig starts from Indonesia; thereafter chronologically located are the Indian pigs, whose descendants migrated to Iran and from there to the Near East. Then the descendants of the latter reached Europe (Meiri 2013:3, Fig 2).

Another graphic in the same article shows that the Indian domestic pig lineages were present in the Near Eastern and European domestic pig samples; however no Near Eastern pig DNA lineage could be traced in India (Fig. S1, S2; "Supplementary Information" of Meiri *et al* 2013). This data effectively rules out any Indian pig domestication under West Asian influence, and suggests that the West Asian pig domestication took place under the Indian influence.

To locate the precise place of domestication of the pig within the Eastern Asian pool (India and SEA), mitochondrial DNAs of the wild and domestic swine from Bhutan, Laos, Cambodia, Myanmar and Vietnam were compared under a high resolution technology (Tanaka 2008). No Indian sample had been included in the study, and the Bhutanese sample can be considered a proxy for the Indian ones. The results showed that only the South Asian (Bhutanese) samples had local domestication of the pigs. All other areas (Laos, Cambodia, Myanmar, Vietnam) had imported pig populations, implying that South Asia was the only place where the domestication had taken place.

The concept of the domestication of the wild boar reached Europe when the first domesticated pig entered Europe through the West Asian route. After this event, the pig soon reached the Paris basin by the fourth millennium BCE (DNA study, Larson 2007). The older swine bones recovered from the Bug-Dneister culture (6,500-5,000 BCE) were all wild except a few which all had been imported (Zvelebil and Lillie:74).

In the subsequent *Linearbandkeramik* (LBK) culture (Central Europe, 5400-4500 BCE) too pigs were rare (Milisauskas and Kruk 1989, quoted by Thorpe:29). The pig was absent from the Pontic-Caspian steppe as we move away from the forest margins of the East Europe even until 2000 years later. For example at Novoselovka (Donetskaya culture),

"There are equal quotes of individuals of cattle, ovicarpids, while horses are 2.5 times less frequent. Remains of pig are not known here" (Kotova:14).

In spite of the archaeological findings of the stray presence of some pigs only peripherally to the western fringes of the steppe, and no representation in the steppe proper, the DNA evidence confirms that the North Pontic-Caspian steppe has not contributed to the domestic pig population of the world at all (Larson 2005:figure 1). This completely rules out the domestication of the pig in the steppe. From linguistics, we know that the Aryan homeland had domesticated pigs. Hence the steppe could not have been the homeland of the Indo-Europeans because it made no contribution to the domestic pig population.

The Indo-Europeans did not evolve at the steppe. This we can say because the philological evidence strongly suggests that the homeland had the domestic pig before dispersal. Seven branches of the Indo-European have cognates for the swine (PIE *sūs* 'swine', Pokorny:1038-1039). However, most of the European cognates have lost the meaning 'swine' and they have acquired semantically related but actually much different meanings (*e.g.* porcupine, ploughshare, dirt or 'to sow' etc).

Lexical Material: Sanskrit *sūkara* (pig); Av. *hu* (pig, from **huvō*), Persian *sukar* (hedgehog, porcupine), M. Pers. *xūk* (swine), Pahlavi *xūg* (swine), *xūkar*[31] (hedgehog); Greek *us*, *uos* (boar), *ΰaina* (hyena, wildcat), *sufos* (dirty place); Gaul. **su-tegis* (dirty place); O.H.G and O.E. *sū* (to sow); Toch. B *suwo* (swine); Proto-Celt. **sukko-* (ploughshare, swine reconstructed from O. Irish name *Socc* 'swine'), Welsh *swch* (ploughshare); Ltv. *suvẽns, sivẽns*, O.Pruss. *seweynis* (dirty place), Ltv. *svīns* (smudges); Old Church Slavic *svinъ ds.* (dirt, smudges; Pokorny:1038-1039). The Slavic word *svinija* meaning 'swine' (O.C.S.) is not a naturally occurring word, but is an artificially created or substantivized form from **svīnī* (fem. to

31 Persian ***sukar***, Pahlavi ***xūg*** (swine) and ***xūkar*** of this list are not in the Pokorny's.

O.C.S. *svinъ*) reshaped (Pokorny:1038-1039; Starostin G.:3037). Although the scholars have not considered the Germanic word 'hog' as cognate of these, it is clearly derivable from the Sanskrit *sūkara* by the general rules of such conversions.

We can see that the cognate words acquire the alternative meanings like 'hedgehog' and 'porcupine' as soon as the IE language comes out of India and reaches Iran. When the IE language reaches Greece alternative meanings 'hyena' and 'wildcat' appear (in Greek). It is possible that the ancient Europeans consumed the meat of the small carnivores like hyena and the wild cat before the Neolithic had reached there. There is a tendency of loss of the meaning 'pig' in the Celtic and Germanic, and the words acquire meanings relating to 'digging', 'sowing' etc, which have semantic association with the behaviour of the wild boar, not with the domestic ones.

This happened because with the first wave of the Indo-European migrations linguistic dispersal took place, but not the technological like domestication. The greater they moved away from the homeland, the greater was the loss of elements of the farming culture and then the associated loss of the original meanings. Thus the Baltic and Slavic branches have completely lost the meaning 'swine', and have retained the meaning 'dirty place'. Domestic pigs are still kept in dirty places in the more primitive societies. This signifies the absence of the pig from the ancient steppe.

Sheep

It is the received information from philology that the sheep had been domesticated at the Indo-European homeland before dispersal. The wild sheep *Ovis orientalis* is the source of the domestic sheep. The common names "urial" and "mouflon" are often arbitrarily used for the wild sheep, yet these names do not denote the species or sub-species. The wild sheep is widely found in Northwest India (Lydekker 1898:169-171; Schaller 1977; Schaller and Mirza 1974; Edge and Oslon-Edge 1987;

Frisina 2001; IUCN Report 2008). However, this fact has been overlooked by all workers in the field of the animal DNA studies. The distribution of the *Ovis orientalis* is from India to the Balkans and India harbours four out of the total eight sub-species *viz. O. o. bocharensis* (Pamir and Laddakh), *O. o. cycloceros* (North-West Frontier Province, Indus valley, Baluchistan, Sind), *O. o. vignei* (Laddakh, Indus Valley, Kunarl, Chitral and Gigit River Valleys) and *O. o. punjabiensis* (Indus and Jhelum rivers to the Himalayan foothills). Other regions of the world have only one or two of the subspecies.

"Wild sheep" found on the Mediterranean islands are generally recognized to have been introduced by humans (Shackleton 1997, Wilson and Reeder 2005, cited in Valdez 2008), and genetic and archaeozoological studies suggest that they are feral populations of ancient domestic stocks (e.g., Groves 1989, Vigne 1994, Hiendleder *et al.* 1998, Manceau *et al.* 1999, Kahila bar-Gal *et al.* 2002, cited by Valdez 2008). Consequently, such taxa are excluded from the real "wild sheep" species the *Ovis orientalis* (as proposed by Gentry *et al.* 1996, Gentry *et al.* 2004, and Gippoliti and Amori 2004, cited by Valdez 2008).

The very presence of the largest number of subspecies is enough evidence for considering northwest India as the home of the sheep. This along with the oldest archaeological catche of the domesticate sheep bones from the Indian subcontinent dating back to 14,000 BCE constitutes solid evidence in favour of the first sheep domestication in India. So far the DNA researchers have not generally included the Indian wild sheep samples in their studies, and have also feigned ignorance of the works of the archaeologists like Zeder, Possehl, Meadow, Jarige, Allchin, G.R. Sharma, Rakesh Tewari etc.

Some authors have by very obvious manipulation even tried to prove that the domestication of animals took place in India about 5,000 BCE or after but not before that (Fuller 2006), and had started only after the domestic cattle and sheep had been brought into India from Central Europe (Kivisild 2011; Romero *et al* 2011). So who brought them? The

Aryans coming in 5500 BC? Everyone wishes to take the subject for a ride!

The studies conducted on the sheep DNAs revealed that no sheep was domesticated in Europe, steppe or Central Asia, and all the domestic sheep in these regions had been imported. It was also revealed in one of the studies Tarim Basin in Central Asia, as well as the Tajik and Kazakh sheep had been imported from India but not from China. On the other hand the Xinjiang province had received domestic sheep from both India and China. It is relevant to note that the sheep appeas in the Central Asian archeology in the Bronze, when a lot of trade and some migration from India did take

The sheep from India were not included in most of the studies. However, the studies which had included the Indian sheep mitochondtial DNAs showed the evidence for the first domestication of that DNA-lineage of the sheep which is the most widespread of all sheep lineages in the word.

Meadows *et al* (2007:1372) found five DNA lineages of the domestic sheep worldwide, none of which had been domesticated in the steppe or Europe. Only two lineages A and B are present in the steppe today and they show very "recent" expansion time (*i.e.* arrival) in the region (Tapio 2006:1781). Tapio *et al* have not clarified the meaning of the word "recent". However, the meaning of the word must be less than 3,500 years—the claimed date of the Indo-Aryan migration to India. This means the sheep was not present in the steppe when the Indo-Aryans started their claimed journey at the alleged 1500 BC.

Tapio noted about the current status of the sheep lineages in the various areas as: "Four (A, B, C, and D) highly diverged sheep lineages were observed in Caucasus, 3 (A, B and C) in Central Asia, and 2 (A and B) in the eastern fringe of Europe, which included the area north and west of the Black Sea and the Ural Mountains." (Abstract). Clearly the last noted (*i.e.* the same location as the claimed Aryan homeland) had the least number of lineages, ruling it out from being the place of domestication of the sheep, particularly in view of the above noted fact that the sheep found in the steppe were of recent introduction in that locality. Thus the steppe did not have the domestic sheep at 4,000 BCE or the putative date of Indo-European origin.

Recent DNA study revealed that the A lineage of the sheep which is the most widespread in the world was domesticated in India (S. Singh 2013). Another study by Pardeshi showed that the lineage A had been domesticated in India and no outside gene had intogressed into the three brees studied (Pardeshi 2007:5,6). Thus there is genetic evidence that the Indian domestic sheep (*i.e.* lineage A) has dispersed widely to all the part of the world, just like the Indian mice have spread to all over world. About the other lineages, work is goind on and it is possible that the B too was domesticated in the western part of Indian sub-continenet. No sheep had been domesticated in Europe, Central Asia and steppe. Study by Sulaiman revealed that the Tarim Basin sheep population had no genetic relationship with the sheep of Xinjiang region (Northwest China), but had strong genetic relationship with Indian sheep breeds Garole and Bonpala which had too been studied by the team (Sulaiman 2011: 77). Many of the Xinjiang sheep had too relationship with the Garole and Bonpala, indicating that the Northwest Chinese breeds had originated from many sources one of which was India. But the sheep of Tarim Basin showed genetic relationship only with the sheep of India, Tajikistan and Kazakhstan. This hints at the sheep migration from India to Tajikistan, Tarim Basin and Kazakhstan.

Europe does not have the wild sheep and the seemingly wild ones are actually feral[32] (Meadows 2011:706). Hence domestication of the sheep was not possible there. Central Asia's wild sheep (*Ovis vigne* or urial, and *Ovis ammon* or argali) were found not to have given birth to any domestic sheep in the world (Meadows 2011:702-3; Hiendleder 2002, 1998), although Central Asia has three lineages of the domestic sheep out of five. Clearly Central Asia got them from India and China, and

32 Feral=Run away from the domesticated stock.

possibly from the Near East (Blackburn 2006:first page of the advance PDF web release).

Another DNA study by Sun (2010) showed that the Central Asian domestic sheep consisted of two DNA populations--the sheep of India-Southeast Asia and the sheep of Mongolia-Tibet ancestry. No domestic sheep of Central Asia showed arrival from Europe, West Asia or the steppe, or even evolution from the local Central Asian wild sheep population. The sheep of India-Southeast Asia ancestry must have entered Central Asia from India and not through Tibet otherwise they too must have been counted within the Tibetan gene pool. Thus the DNA evidence strongly favours entry of the domestic sheep into Central Asia from India. Our proposed time for this event is during the Indus Valley Civilization (*vide infra*).

Archaeology of Sheep domestication:

Wild sheep/goat were hunted since long in the steppe (6,500 BCE, Dolukhanov 2005:1450) and Central Asia (e.g. 8,000 BCE, Dani and Masson 1999:115), yet no steppe or Central Asian wild sheep was ever domesticated (DNA evidence). It should be recollected that the steppe and Central Asia had better rainfall at those times, and had developed some forest ecosystem. In the Indian subcontinent, the sheep had already been domesticated from the local wild stock before Mehrgarh (8,000 BCE; Meadow, quoted by Possehl 2002:27). Meadow (1996:403, quoted by Possehl 2002:27) also provided evidence for goat domestication at the same layer.[33] The horse cave of Aq Kupruk had the domestic sheep and goat at 10,000 BCE (Possehl 2002:24).

Sheep bones have been found from the 14,000 BCE Hindu Kush Valley (Aq Kupruk) where the continuing presence of quantities of sheep bones into the Neolithic period has been surmised by the Allchins to

33 "To judge from the occurrence of five kids in each of two burials, however, goats are likely to have been domesticated already in the first levels of Period IA dating to early seventh or late eighth millennium."

be the evidence of some form of "exploitation" of the animal ultimately leading to the domestication before 8,000 BCE (Allchin and Allchin 1982:97; Perkins 1972). By the word "exploitation" we can understand animal-herding and animal husbandry.

Mahagara (10,000 to 8,000 BCE), Chopani Mando (older than 17,800 BCE in Upper Paleolithic) etc in Central India (G.R. Sharma 1985, 1980a, 1980b) had domestic sheep and goat. Rissman supported the Upper Palaeolithic domestication of sheep and goat in India with the following argument: "These species were hundreds of miles from their natural range in the foothills and peaks of Baluchistan and the Himalayas (Possehl and Rissmann). If removal of a species from its natural habitat is accepted as evidence of domestication (as claimed by Bokonyi 1969:219), then sheep and goat were arguably domesticated by the Upper Paleolithic in India" (Rissman 1989:16).

With time the supporters of West Asian origin of the domestic sheep and goat have changed their earlier view that West Asia was the oldest and exclusive place of domestication of the sheep and goat. Zeder, the doyen of the subject who had earlier proposed the goat domestication in the Zagros (2000), had to finally accept that the domestic goat of India ("East Pakistan" in his article) was indigenous, and as old, if not older, as West Asia (2006:148). It may be noted that for the Indian recoveries of sheep and goat, much more stringent criteria for domestication have been applied *e.g.* shortening of the body-size, shortening of horn etc. Bias in studies becomes obvious when we note that such criteria have not been applied to the goat bones recovered from the West Asia (8,000 BCE, Zeder 2005, 2006), Europe or the steppe.

The Indian recoveries of the sheep and goat bones, which were clearly domesticated as judged from the contexts of recovery, were dubbed undomesticated only because no shortening (or only minor shortening) of the bones and horns could be demonstrated. Again, Fuller created a unique criterion, created only for the occasion and applied only to India: the percentage of the purely wild texa in the assemblage.

Fuller considers the status as "herding" until the purely wild texa are reduced to less than 20 percent at Mehrgarh by 5000 BCE (Fuller 2006:26). Contrasting this, the sheep/goat bones looking exactly the same as wild have been considered domesticated in West Asia, and their percentage too has not been taken into account (Zeder 2005, 2000). If we remove such double standards of treatment, the date of Indian domestication of sheep and goat will go back to much older dates if we trust the more learned archaeologists like Possehl, Allchin or even the very much pro-West Asia archaeologist Meadow etc.

Zeder accepts the problem with the Fertile Crescent samples, and even challenges the various criteria for domestication. She writes: "Thus neither modern male nor female domestic goats in the Zagros sample are distinguishable from the wild goats on the basis of the breadth and depth measurements. Nor can female domesticates be distinguished from wild females on the basis of length measurements" (Zeder 2005:128).

In fact even the oldest of the sheep/goat bones at Mehrgarh show signs of domestication. On the basis of such evidence, Possehl asserted that they must have been brought from some other (older) centre of domestication from within India (Possehl 2002:29). This becomes more remarkable in view of the much older presence of sheep in Central Asia. Arrival of the domesticated goat from West Asia to Mehrgarh was ruled out by archaeological evidence (Meadow quoted in Possehl 2002:26-27).

In the West Asian Neolithic domesticated sheep, goat, cattle etc. appear as readymade, not as locally domesticated under the due process of domestication. There was no evidence of the local evolution or progression of the process of domestication in the Near East. This was considered by many as evidence for the arrival of the Neolithic and farming culture from India to West Asia (Kivisild 2005).

DNA studies can provide precise data for the date of domestication of animal and plant species. By such data, India comes to be the oldest place of domestication. Zeder (2005) puts it in the following words: "The geographic location of origin can be inferred from the geographic distribution of certain alleles or lineages as follows. In all livestock species, including goats, cattle, buffalo, pigs and sheep, a divergent DNA lineage occurs *only* in Southern and Eastern Asia. This suggests a possible centre of animal domestication in Southern or Eastern Asia." (p. 300), [italicised emphasis added]. This datum in fact suggests India and China to be not the "possible centres", but actually the earliest centres.

Mitochondrial DNA variation is an index of the age of a lineage in any area. Zeder wrote "In goats, however, mtDNA variation is not higher in the Fertile Crescent region compared to most other continental region" (2005:300). That means in simple words that the Fertile Crescent was not an early centre of goat (and by implication) domestication—something which the scholars have dared not pronounce so far.

Philology:

The cognates of the IE names of sheep are absent from Anatolian (Hittite), Tocharian and Albanian. They are also absent from the languages of the steppe, and if at all present do not mean 'sheep'.

One of the IE words for sheep are PIE *moiso-s* or *maiso-s* (sheep, Pokorny: 747), with cognates in five branches of IE. *viz.* Indian, Iranian, Germanic, Baltic and Slavic. Only Indian and Iranian branches have retained the meaning "sheep". Others mean 'leatherwork, bag' etc:

Sanskrit *mēṣa* 'sheep'; Av. *maēša-* 'sheep'; O. Ice. *meiss* 'basket', O.H.G. *meis(s)a* 'baggage', M.L.G. *mēse* 'barrel'; O.Bulg. *měchъ* 'hose', Russ. *měch* 'fell, fur, hose, sack, bag' etc.; Lith. *máišas, máiše* 'haying', Ltv. *máiss, máikss* 'sack, bag', O.Pruss. *moasis* 'bellows'. Some related words/ cognates are: Indo-Aryan *mes* (CDIAL 10343, skin-bag), Sanskrit *maisiya* 'ovine, skin-bag'; Russian *mekh* 'skin' *etc.* This refutes Witzel's (1999) claim that the Sanskrit *meṣa* is a loanword or substratal word from Burushaski *meṣ* 'bag'.[34]

Another word for sheep is English "ewe" 'sheep'. Cognates: PIE **óu̯i-s* 'sheep', Pokorny:784); Sanskrit *avi*; Greek *oia* and *ois*; O.H.G. *ouwi*, O.S. *evi*; Latin *ovis*; Welsh *ewig*; Lithuanian *avis*; O. Bulgarian *овь-са*, *овь-нъ* 'sheep'; Arm. *hov-iw* 'shepherd' etc. This word too is absent from the Slavic branch except the East European Bulgarian which is not a steppe nation. The cognates are also absent from Albanian, Hittite and Tocharian. Loss of the word or the meaning from the languages of the steppe implies absence of domestic sheep when the first founder wave of the Indo-European reached the steppe.

Goat

Archaeology of Goat Domestication

Goat was first domesticated in India sometime even before the growth of the Neolithic culture (discussed in the context of sheep). Based on the comparative anatomy, Lydekker (1898:242) had observed that "Goats are generally a southern species. The oldest archaeological specimens of goat belong to a species allied to the *markhor* from the foothills of the Himalayas.

Archaeology supports the first domestication of goat in India. Meadow (1996:403) found five kids of goats placed in a ritual way in two burials from about 8,000 BC Mehrgarh (Pakistan). He inferred that they must have been domesticated: "To judge from the occurrence of five kids in each of two burials, however, goats are likely to have been domesticated already in the first levels of Period IA dating to early seventh or late eighth millennium."

---

34 Witzel made this claim to neutralize the loss of meaning 'sheep' from the cognate words of ***mēṣa*** in the Germanic, Baltic and Slavic.

At Aq Kupruk (Hindu Kush Valley, Afghanistan) likely domesticated goat bones from 14,000 BC were recovered from human contexts (Perkins; Allchin and Allchin:97). Possehl (2002:24) mentions domesticated goat bones from 10,000 BC old Aq Kupruk site. Domesticated goat bones have been found from Mahagara, Chopani Mando etc in Central India dating back to 10,000 to 8,000 BC. Unfortunately, such archaeological findings have been completely ignored by many contemporary prehistorians primarily owing to their Eurocentric inclinations (*e.g.* Dorian fuller; Rubero *et al* etc).

For West Asia and Iran, domestication of the goat at 7,000 BC (or even earlier) is accepted even without any evidence of change in size of bones (Zeder 2005). Zeder notes that the 7000 BC (9000 BP) specimens of goat bones from Zagros (Ganj Dareh, West Iran) considered domesticated, do not show any shortening of size in comparison to the wild samples from the same time and place, nor any change in horn etc. Even thousand year later samples do not show much shortening. And, whatever shortening is noted, that is owing to the changing climate leading to the general shortening of the wild animals like gazelle etc in the region (Zeder 2005).

In fact this finding implies import in West Asia or Iran from outside rather than domestication from local wild animals. Some reduction in the body size of goats in the Zagros can be noted only after 6000 BC (Zeder 2005:133), which means that the older goat bones from Zagros are that of the wild animals, and really domesticated ones are found only after 6,000 BC.

Clearly the Indian domesticated goat even from Meadow's account is about 2000 years older than the West Asian domestication. This prompted Zeder (2005:126) to write "Similarly, the utility of body size reduction as a valid early, leading edge measure of initial animal domestication in the Near East remains an open question."

Clearly double standards of judgement should not have been applied for India and West Asia. If the same yardstick for the domestication of sheep is applied to both the regions, *i.e.* either 'shertening' or 'no-shortening' the Indian domestication of the goat is older from the West Asian one by at least 2000 years. In fact the degree of domesticatedness present in the oldest West Asian contextually human related gaot samples (of 6,000 BC) is the same as that of the Central Indian (17000 BC) and Aq Kupruk (14,000 BC) ones from similar contexts.

While domestication is accepted on circumstantial grounds for the Iran and Iraq sites at least 1000 years before any morphological feature appeared in the animal bones (Zeder 2006:141), similar circumstantial evidence presented for the Indian sites dating back to 14,000 BC (Possehl:24) are not accepted by the Eurocentric academic community.

G.R. Sharma dated the potentially domestic sheep/goat bones to the Upper Palaeolithic. The samples were dated 17,000 BC, but could be much older. This quite likely because because the goat-keeping hardly needs any skill, it can be easily over-powered and tied down. It could be kept in the huts, pit-dwellings and caves during the LGM. It can be restrained in the captive even with the help of an ordinary wooden fence. And it provided all: meat and milk for food, wool for dress or cover, leather for home-making and dress and horns to be used as weapons.

If that is accepted as the likely date of animal herding in India, the date of domestication for goat (Time since Most Recent Common Ancestor, TMRCA) derived from Joshi's study of goat DNA should be acceptable as the date of goat domestication in India. However, Joshi himself back-tracked from this results stating that the "Dravidian speakers probably entered about 10,000 years ago and Indo-Aryan speakers about 3,500 years ago ." (p. 461) He thought that the domesticated goats were brought to India by the invading tribes of the Dravidians who were farmers and that was followed by the Aryans who were pastorals.

Role of Goat in human prehistory

Goat and sheep were the first domesticated animals. Initially captured and kept for future needs of meat, leather and wool, the animal soon became a human live-stock. They provided material for making dress—both wool and leather during the long cold nights of the Last Glacial Maximum. Her utility in many spheres of life continued till historical times. Luikart (2006:294) notes, "Domestic goat skin was apparently the main material used for writing Biblical manuscripts ... Goat skin was also used by Roman military to construct hand-held battle shields and sandals. Goats and their skin were often used for tents, curtains, gift-offerings ...". Being smaller, goat and sheep are easier to capture, tame and manage than cow. They also do not require agriculture for food. Hence goats and sheep pastoralism without farming is the favourite way of living of many of the nomadic non-agricultural pastoral tribes surviving till today, and was an essential training required for man to encourage him to try taming the cattle.

DNA studies of goat domestication

Not many DNA studies of goat domestication have been dome so far. There are six mitochondrial DNA lineages of goats. Lineage A is the most widely distributed and most populous of all lineages in the world. Like everything else from the God's land, goat too was initially claimed to have been domesticated in West Asia. Luikart (2001) claimed West Asia to be the place of goat domestication particularly of the lineages A and C, and the dates given were 10,000 B.P. and 6,100 B.P. respectively.

However a Japanese study group found that there was a fourth lineage D also, which had been domesticated in Pakistan even before the lineage A (Sultana *et al* 2003:420). They also found that the wild goat *bezoar* of Pakistan, the *Sind Ibex* is closest genetically to the domestic goats of the world (Sultana:421). In other words, Pakistani wild goat *bezoar* known as the *Sind Ibex* is the source of the domestic goat populations of the world. However, because of ethnocentric prejudices in the Eurocentric scholars the report was just ignored after its publication.

Luikart's claims were soon proven wrong. MacHugh *et al* noted in the review of Luikart's article that the lineage C was actually not found in West Asia (2001:5384). The study of the ancient DNA obtained from the archaeological goat samples of South-west Europe conducted by Fernandez *et al* (2006) revealed that two lineages (later identified as A and C) had reached southern France before 7000 years back from today (or *c.* 5000 BC), a date older than Luikart's date of domestication for the lineage C. They wrote,

> "two highly divergent goat lineages coexisted in each of the two Early Neolithic layers of this site. This finding indicates that high mtDNA diversity was already present >7,000 years ago in European goats".

These two lineages were identified later as belonging to A and C. The mtDNA of these ancient goat samples proved that there were two independent and divergent domestications of goats, descendants of which were present at 7000 ybp in southwest Europe. Hence Fernandez completely destroyed Luikart's hypothesis. Fernandez's work also clarified that that the Southwest European goats (of 7000 BP) had divergent DNAs meaning that they had arrived there from two different routes, remaining in separate existence for thousands of years. This fits well with the model of two routes for Indo-European migration out of India, one along the Iranian coast and the other through Central Asia and the steppe.

Naderi *et al* (2007) conducted a large scale mitochondrial DNA study of goats, which was highly biased in favour of West Asia and was in effect designed to misguide. Normally India, Pakistan and Bhutan are parts of the region knwn as South Asia. Naderi split the goat DNA data for the region into three. Pakistan was clubbed along with Turkey, Syria, Jordan, Saudi Arabia, Iran and Iraq as the "Middle East" (Naderi 2007:Table 2 on pp 4-5). Bhutan was clubbed with China to constitute "East Asia". Another group of countries was arbitrarily named "West Asia" which included five countries namely India, Kyrgystan, Kazakhstan, Azarbaizan and Daghestan.

Obviously, the conclusions about the origin of the goats were going to be wrong. It is difficult to believe that all the nine authors who wrote this article had such appalling knowledge of geography. They should have clubbed India, Pakistan and Bhutan as a single "South Asia" region. As long as such biased and racist authors are there in the academics, no true history can come out.

However, if we ignore the conclusions made by the authors, and consider only the basic data generated by the study, it leads us to the conclusion that India-Pakistan were the source area of the lineage A too, and this view is consistent with Sultana's results.

The data contained in the Table 2 and Figure 2 of Naderi's study reveal the following facts if we re-examing them:

1. South Asia (India-Pakistan-Bhutan) carried maximum numbers of haplotypes: Total 267 haplotypes (India 207, Pakistan 55, Bhutan 5), of lineage A, B, C and D, out of total 465 individual goats examined.
2. Iran, Iraq, Jordan, Syria, Turkey and Saudi Arabian goats belonged only to mainly the A lineages, however lineage G occurred in Iran, Saudi Arabia and Turkey. Lineages B, C and D were absent from all these countries. That means perhaps the lineage G may have been domesticated locally in Iran after the arrival of domesticated lineage A from outside. G was also found in Egypt.
3. Haplogroup C is not present in any of these countries: Saudi Arabia, Syria, Jordan, Turkey, Iraq and Iran. These are the countries which were present on or adjoining the southern route out of India.
4. Haplogroup C is present in India, Pakistan, Mongolia, China, Slovenia, Switzerland, France, Portugal and Spain. This fact is supported by Othman (2012) too. But name of the very big

region China can mislead the readers. Chen (2005:808) further clarified that this lineage was present in only two region of the Modern Republic of China namely Xinjiang and Tibet which are in fact the eastern parts of Central Asia.

These two findings (1 & 2) taken together mean that the domestication of the haplogroup C took place in Pakistan, from where it was subsequently carried to Europe not through Turkey-Iran route but by the northern route out of India, remains of which are found today in Xinjiang and Tibet. It is also possible that this migration had take place in the 13th-12th millennium BC or earlier, before the Tardiglacial epoch of the Late Pleistocene.

5. Haplogroup or lineage D is found only in India, Pakistan, Kyrgystan, China and Austria (single example) in the Naderi's study. However Chen (2005) noted that in their study only a single goat from China and that too of Kashmiri origin (Laoning Cashmere breed) was found to belong to the haplogroup D. Hence China and Austria cannot be considered as source. In fact we need to accept Chen's finding that "lineage D is rare and only observed in Pakistani and Indian local goats." (Chen 2005:805). Sultana too had asserted that it originated in Pakistan.
6. Haplogroup or lineage B was found in India, Pakistan, Laos, Malaysia, China, Mongolia, Azarbaizan, South Africa, Namibia (Africa) and Greece in Naderi's study. It was not found in Europe except Greece, and also not found in the entire Middle East. Thus this haplogroup too appears to have originated in India-Pakistan. In Chen's study, "Lineage B is confined to eastern and southern Asia, including Mongolia, Laos, Malaysia, Pakistan, and India." (Chen 2005:805). Othman (2012) too supports this.
7. Haplogroup A was found in all the countries and regions studied. More data will be needed to fix its place of origin.

Naderi (2008:17662) found that the lineage C was the most common lineage in the wild goats (*bezoar*) of Fars, Yazd and Kerman Provinces of East Central Iran. These provinces are nearer to Pakistan and Afghanistan than to Turkey. But as the lineage C of goats in not found in Iran and West Asia, this finding only means that the wild bezoars of Iran are genetically close to the bezoars of Pakistan, the likely place of domestication of the goat of the lineage C.

The date of domestication/dispersal of this lineage suggested by Naderi (2008) too was 4600-7000 years before present, which would be inconsistent with the same being found in archaeological samples from France dated 7000 years before present (Naderi 2007:8 of advanced web publication). In nutshell, Naderi (2008) is confused, cannot synthesize the DNA data available about the domestication of goats, and cannot be relied.

Philological Examination

The first Indo-European migrants reached Europe, leaving their livestock. They adopted the European hunter-gatherer-fisher mode of life. Then the secondary waves came with goat and sheep, pure pastorals without agriculture. And it was still later that the proper farmers with cows arrived into Europe as the tertiary waves.

In India, there was no fusion or confusion of goat and cow. Yet when the cows reached Europe with the third wave of migration, the settled Indo-European speakers of Europe thought they were just larger goats. Hence the words used for goat were applied to the cows too in those countries.

A goat, being a milch-animal, was like a little cow. The Proto-Altaic word for 'goat' **baku* means 'small cattle'. That is why the words for cow in some languages are same as words for goat in some other languages.

In Sanskrit, we get cognates of quite a few PIE words meaning the goat, *e.g. bukka*, *aja* and **kapṛ* (see below; L. *capra*). Out of these three only two (*bucca* and *hafra* from *capra*) are represented in the Germanic. Latin has only one *capra*. Greek has words only from *aiĝ*. Overall, the languages of Europe are deficient in Indo-European words for the goat.

Meka (goat)

Sanskrit *mēká* (he-goat); Arm. *mak"I* (sheep); M.H.G. *mecke* (he-goat); Alb. *mek-sh* (buffalo-calf). Greek, Latin and Baltic branches have retained the cognates meaning "bleat" but have lost the meaning "goat" (Pokorny: 715-716).

Bukka and *barkara*

These all cognates mean 'goat': PIE **bhŭ̄ĝo-s* or *bhukko-s* (goat); Sanskrit *bukkā* (he-goat), *barkara* (goat), Hindi *bakarā*, Bengali *boka* (*c.f.* Proto-Turkic *buka*, bull); Bihari *botu* (he-goat; c.f. Proto-Turkic *bota*, young camel), Gypsi *buzni* (goat, *c.f.* Iranian); Proto-Gmc. **bukka-*, O.Ice. *bukkr, bokkr, bokki*, O.N. *bokkr*, O.E. *bucca*, north English *buck* ('male deer' also), O.H.G., M.H.G., M.Dutch *boc* (all meaning goat), Ger. *Bock* (goat, in names only), Eng. ?Butcher; Av. *būza* (he-goat), Pahlavi *buz*, Pers. *buz, buj* (goat, he-goat), Pers. dial. *boča* (young goat); Arm. *buz* (lamb); M.Irish *bocc, pocc*, Ir. *boc, poc*, Welsh *bwch*, Corn. *boch*, Bret. *bouc"h* (he-goat), M.Ir. *boccānach* (ghost, bogeyman) (Pokorny:174).

Cognates of *bukka* are present only in the five branches (*viz.* Indic, Persian, Armenian, Celtic and Germanic), and are completely absent from the south European (Italic, Greek and Albanian) and West Asian (Hittite) IE languages. This evidence proves that the goat was probably not domesticated in Anatolia or West Asia, from where South Europe is not much away. It is found that many words meaning the cow in Europe sound similar to *bukka* (goat) hinting at the likely semantic identity between the cow and the goat in early Europe:

> O.Ir. *bó* (<*báo* < *báu*; cow), O.Welsh *buch*, Welsh *buwch*, O.Corn. *buch*, Bret. *buc"h* (cow), Old Irish family name Βοουίνδα (*Bouvinda*, "pastor"; *c.f.* Indian name *go-vinda* meaning cowboy); modern English name *Boyne*, O.Ir. *Bó(f)ind* (cowboy). These all have been derived from the Proto-Celtic word **boukkā* (cow; Pokorny:482-483; Starostin:1346). We can safely say that the Proto-Celtic **boukkā* (cow) is most likely a cognate of the Proto-Germanic **bucca* (goat) and Sanskrit *bukkā* (he-goat).

The word *bukka* has been borrowed into other distant languages, sometimes with altered meanings. Munda and Santhali *boda* (he-goat); Tagalog (Philippine) *baka* (cow; *c.f.* Bengali *boka* 'goat'); Turkic *bakana* (goat), Mongolian *bog* (goat). Basque *aker* (he-goat) may be related to *bakkar* (rural Hindi). Pavlavi *buz* and Swahili *buzi* and *mbuzi* may be mutually related indicating early goat migration from India (Sind province) through eastern Persian Gulf to Arabia and then to East Africa. The goat reached Iran, Arabia and East Africa as an earlier wave than the cows. Arabic *baqara* or *baqra* (cow) seems to be a loanword, which was probably used to mean the goat in the beginning, but when the cows arrived into the area, it was applied to the cows.

Capra (L.)

Latin does not have most of the IE words for goat, yet it has *capra* (goat, roe deer; PIE **kapro*; Pokorny: 529). Some of its cognates are: Alb. *kaproll* (roebuck); O. Irish *gabor*, Welsh *gafr* (goat); Old Norse *hafr*, Germanic **hafra*. Its Indic cognate, the Sanskrit word *kapṛtha* means Indra (*Rig-Veda* 10.101.12). Literally the word would mean "situated within or amongst the goats" *i.e.* "one who lives with goats" or "the master/ protecto-god of goats" (< **kapṛ* + *-tha*). Pokorny gives its meaning "penis". Although male goats are symbolic of masculinity, and thereby of penis, yet the 'master of the goats' is the forerunner form of the god 'master of the cattle' (or Harappan and Vedic *paśupati*). The Celtic

O.Ir. *Bó(f)ind* has the same semantic locus as *kapṛtha*. Capri is also the name of a dress, and was probably made of the goat-skin in prehistory.

Another set of cognates *kurp* (Low German, shoe), O. Prussian (Baltic) *kurpi* (shoe) etc. may be related to the word *capra* (goat). The cognates of these words are present in Indo-Aryan too. It has also been loaned to Dravidian. Eastern Hindi (Bihari etc) *kharpā* (wodden sandles with a leather strap); *ceruppu, sarpu, kerpu* (sandal, shoe, Dravidian; Burrow: 178, no. 1963).

chaga

For the Sanskrit words *chāga* (goat; CDIAL 4958) and *chāgala* (goat; CDIAL 4963), no Proto-Indo-European form has been suggested, and it is considered an isolated Indo-Aryan word which is not represented in any other branch of the Indo-European family. It is also found in the Finno-Ugric family of languages as loan-word. Following cognates have been mentioned by some authors to support this claim: Proto-Finno-Ugric **caka* (goat, Parpola and Carpelan 2005:199; Witzel 2005:387 n. 96), Mord *sava* (goat); Proto-Iranian **ćāgaḥ* etc (Parpola and Carpelan 2005).

However PIE root-word **kago-* (goat; Pokorny:517-518) should be considered the cognate of Sanskrit *chāga*. The cognates of **kago* are Middle Dutch *hoekijn*, Old English *hēcen* ; Latvian *kaza* and O.Bulg. *koza* (Pokorny). Thus we can say that the word in not at all a borrowing from any imaginary South Asian substrate language.

It has been claimed that the word *chāga* entered the Finno-Ugric languages when the Proto-Indo-Aryan people were living in the steppe, before arrival to India, in the neighbourhood of the original Finno-Ugric home located in Siberia (Parpola and Carpelan 2005). This claim has been given an out of proportion evidential value by many authors. The very hypothesis of the southern Siberian home of the

Finno-Ugric languages has been found to be wrong on the basis of DNA findings and other facts (see detailed bibliography in Niskanen 2002).

Hence the borrowing into the Finno-Ugric must have been from people migrating out of India quite early, and subsequent to donating words to the Finno-Ugric, the words were later lost from the Indo-European languages settling in Europe (ancestors of the Balto-Slavic and Germanic). This fact would remove the Indo-Aryan homeland location far away from Europe and the steppe region.

aja and *tikṣṇa*

Starostin combines three PIE roots *viz.* **digh*, **aiĝ*- and **ăĝ* all meaning "goat" into one as a principal root *deiĝh*- (to prick, tick; Pokorny:187-188; Starostin:544, 251 Note). While the two (**aiĝ*- and **ăĝ*) are clearly arbitrary divisions of the same PIE root, the root **digh* is possibly not related with the other two and should be considered an independent root. On the other hand Pokorny's two different roots **digh* (goat, bitch) and *deiĝh* (to prick) are actually related on deeper semantic analysis.

The cognates of **digh* ('goat' Pokorny:222) are mainly from the Germanic branch of IE: PIE **digh*; O.H.G. *ziga* (goat), *zickī*, *zickīn* (young goat), O.E. *ticcen* (young goat), Nor. dial. *tikka* (sheep), Swe. dial. *takka*, (sheep), *tiksa* (sheep, bitch), *tikla* (young sheep or cow), as well as O.N. *tīk* (bitch), M.L.G. *tīke* (bitch); Arm. *tik* (hose from animal skin). Pokorny adds to the list one Thrac. (a dialect related to Gk.) word *diza*, with obscure meaning, and may be ignored. Thus the root **digh* has cognates in the Germanic and Armenian (also ?Greek) branches.

Starostin (2007:40n) thinks that the root **digh* meaning 'goat' derived from the root **deiĝh*- meaning 'sharp'. This supports our view. Although not noticed so far, the latter root too is present in Sanskrit as *tīkṣṇa* (sharp) and the derived words are present in Indo-Aryan often meaning goat, again not so far noted by any philologist:

> *tīkṣṇa* (Sk. 'sharp'), *tikkha* (Pali 'sharp'), *tīkhā* (Hindi, Punjabi 'sharp'), *tis* (Pashai-Dardic 'two year old he-goat'), *tic* (Khowar-Dardic 'he-goat') etc. (CDIAL 5839).

This goes well with the finding Starostin's finding that the root **digh* is derived from PIE root **deiĝh-* (to prick; 2007:765n, 40n), which has the same semantic field as the Sanskrit *tīkṣṇa* (sharp). Goat got this name having the meaning "sharp" because of its sharp horn, which is much sharper than that of sheep. And the Germanic bitch too got the name *tiksa* etc because of their sharp teeth. Females of all of them must have been used to provide milk during the pre-historic times, and that led to the fusion of the four animals cow, bitch, goat and sheep in the Germanic speaking areas.

The roots **aiĝ-* (goat, Pokorny:13) and (goat, Pokorny:6-7) are in fact one and the division made by Pokorny is arbitrary and was unnecessary. We will club the cognates together here for our study:

Gk. αἴξ (*aiks*), -γός (nanny goat); Arm. *aic* (nanny goat); Sanskrit *aja* (he-goat), *ajā* (goat); zero grade Av. *izaēna-* ("made from leather", actually "made from goatskin"), M. Persian *azak* (goat), Pers. *azg* (goat); Alb. *dhí* (goat), O. Alb. *edha* (goat, sheep; *c.f.* Arabic *adha-ha* sheep); Lith *ožkà* (goat), *ožys* (he-goat), O. Pruss. âzê (goat), *âzuks* (he-goat); Church Slavic *(j)azno* <**azьno* (skin, leather)

Sure enough Hebrew *ez* (goat) is borrowing of Sanskrit *ajā* (goat). Tamil *acham* (goat) is also from the Sanskrit *ajā*. These all indicate a very early trading of goats during prehistoric days.

Cattle (*Bos indicus*)

Bull: Original Indo-European cattle was humped (zebu). This is obvious from philological examination, which shows that the very word "bull" comes from the presence of a hump, indicating that the first cattle known to the Indo-Europeans were humped:

O.E. *bȳle*, M.H.G. *biule* swelling, blister; O.N. *beyla* hump (Starostin 2007:297); O.S. *bulde, bolde, byld* hump; O. Ice. *boli* bull; OE *bulluc, bula* young bull (Starostin 2007:365); Dan. *bulk* hump, nodules (Pokorny:98-102, 120-122).

The humped cattle (zebu) are found in India, Africa, Central Asia, China, Southeast Asia and also Europe. It has been determined after DNA studies that all these zebu cattle are of an exclusive Indian origin, wherever they live today, and had been domesticated in India before their transportation to the other countries (S. Chen 2009).

Cow: When the South Asians reached East and North Europe by the northern route, they could not take the hot-adapted zebu cows with them in the first outward wave in the Early Holocene. Hence the words meaning 'cow' or their meanings were lost from the northern countries of Europe. This led to the application of the words meaning cow to some other animals (usually game animals) in north Europe and sometimes in other regions too. Examples are:

> PIE **agh* (plough animal, ox); Sanskrit *ahī* (cow), Hindi *ahīr* (a cow-keeping caste); Avestan *azī* (pregnant); Arm. *ezn* (bovine animal); Middle Irish **aglo-* and **ag-* stem (bovine animal, cow), M. Irish *ag allaid* (deer, actually 'wild ox'), *ál* (brood, throw), Welsh *ael* (abundance, fertility), M.Welsh *aelaw* (abundance, fertility), *eilion* <**agliones* (fallow deer, horses). (Pokorny:7; Starostin 2007:21).

Thus the meaning cow has been retained only in Indian, Celtic (only partly) and Armenian branches. This is enough to indicate that the steppe people could not have had any cow in the beginning. Otherwise they should have retained the meaning in any language of the northern route. Another Sanskrit word *vasā* (cow) has survived only in Latin as *vacca* and has been lost from everywhere else in Europe (Pokorny:1111).

Cognates are: PIE $*g^{w}ou$- (cow); Sanskrit *go, gava, gau, gavī* (cow) etc; Persian *gav, gāv*, Avestan *gāuš* (cow); Tocharian *ko* (cow); Albanian *kau* (ox); Armenian *kov* (cow); English "cow". These are the only true surviving cognates where the meaning has been retained.

The claimed cognates of *go* in some languages like Latin *bōs* and *bovis*, Old Welsh *buch*, Old Irish *bo* all meaning 'cow' etc are not convincing to the common sense and could in fact be related with the word *bukka* (he-goat). When the Indo-Europeans left India and reached South Europe from the southern route, they continued to keep goat although left their cows. It was difficult to keep cows alive in the dry climate of Iran during early Holocene. However goats survived. Because the goat now performed nearly all the functions of cow it became the only "cattle" of the South Europeans when the Indo-Europeans first settled in Europe. It is only later that the cattle proper too was brought to Europe through when Anatolians domesticated then after Indian influence. This real cattle was now too thrust the name which goat had so far in South Europe. Thus the Latin *bos* and Celtic *boukka, buch, bo* etc mean cow today.

The claimed German cognate *Kuh* (used only in personal name as compound words like *Kuhkäse, Kuhstal* etc) is in fact an obsolete word and is never used independently to mean the 'cow'. In the usage the actual word meaning cow in German is *rind*, derived from a word meaning "deer". Cognates of *rind* are: O.H.G. *(h)rind*, O.E. *hrīðer, hrȳðer* (horned animal), O.E. *hrün, hran* (roedeer), German *Hirsch* (deer), O.N. *hrūtr* (ram), Dutch *rund* (cattle).

Another German word for cattle *rother* too seems to be a cognate of these (*c.f. hrīðer*). Thus Ger. *rind* (cow) < O.H.G. *(h)rin* (deer; *c.f.*) < Old Indian *hariṇa* (deer). This discussion leads to inference that the north European areas were originally devoid of the domesticated cows, and the wild *aurochs* of Europe were labelled "deer" etc they were humpless horned game animals, and could not be considered 'cow' at the first sight. In the Slavic O.C.S. *gu-mьno* means the 'threshing floor' and the meaning 'cow' has been completely lost. Cognates are lost from Hittite.

We cannot ignore the fact that the commonest words meaning cow in the Balto-Slavic and the Germanic languages are derived from the words meaning a "stag" or "deer". This means that the people of the Eastern and northern Europe had only a late acquaintance with the domesticated "cow", while the PIE speakers knew the cow and the bull well from the beginning. This shows a loss of the domesticated cow and the pastoral life once the first emigrants left India.

> PIE (Pokorny:574-77) **k̂ erəu̯o-s, k̂ r̥̄u̯o-s* (deer); Sanskrit *śarabha* (deer); Latin *cervus* (deer); Welsh *carw* (deer).
>
> But Lithuanian *kárvė* (cow), Czech *Karvina* (cow), Russian Church Slavonic *krava* (cow), O. Polish *karw* (cow), Polish *krowa* (cow), O. Prussian *curwis* (cow).

Another word *hiraṇa* which meant "deer" in PIE and Sanskrit was too applied to mean 'cow' in the Germanic, for the same reasons. Its cognates are:

> Sk. *hiraṇa*; O.E. *hrün*, O.N. *hreinn* (all meaning 'deer'); O.H.G. *hiruz*, O.S. *hirot*, O.E. *heorot*, O.N. *hjǫrtr*, Ger. family name *Hirsch* (all meaning 'ram'); O.H.G. *(h)rind*, O.E. *hrīðer*, in name *Horntier*, O.E. *hrȳðer* ds., Dutch *rund*, German *rother* (all mean 'cow' or 'cattle').

Rimantiene on the basis of archaeological findings noted that the first arriving bands of IE speakers had become hunter-gatherers by the time they reached Prussia (Germany) and the Baltic region (see "Conclusion" in Rimantiene 1998). When the domesticated cow arrived in Europe with subsequent waves of Indo-European migration, this cow was identified as some variety of deer and named after the names of the deer, because the cognates of "cow" had been lost. However how does the lone Germanic word word "cow" (English) retain its original meaning is not known to us.

Chapter 31

Camel (*uṣṭra*)

The history of camel too was vitiated by the Euro-racist authors writing in the field of the Indo-European history. This subject should have been left to the domain of the scientists and archaeologists. However everyone jumped into it writing one's lay conjectures as history of the camel. The result is that these historians said: *a*) India did not have any 'one-humped' camel before the first millennium BC. *b*) The one-humped dromedary camel was domesticated in Arabia, because this camel lives in desert and Arabia is a desert. *c*) The Aryans domesticated the two-humped camel in the steppe at Andronove about 1500 BC or earlier, from where the Chinese people too got their domestic camels. *d*) The Aryans brought the two-humped Bactrian camel to Iran and India in about 1500 BC, when they came to India through Central Asia and Iran. All these views need examination under the light of evidence.

Rissman commented after examining the concrete evidence of camel in the Harappa Civilization: "The absence of camel depictions on seals led some investigators to conclude that the camels were unknown to the Harapans, but these scattered finds suggest that some other explanation must be sought."

Thus Kuz'mina and Mallory think:. "In the second half of the 2nd millennium BC camel-breeding was known in Eurasia apart from Andronovans only among Central Asian tribes (Itina 1977: 138, 185-190; Kuz'mina 1980: 30)." (Kuz'mina and Mallory 2007:149). They do not present any argument or evidence in support of their view. The conclusion has been based on the presence of camel bones in the Andronovo region dating about 1500 BC and the general assumption that the Aryan people moved from the north to south at that time taking horse and camel with them from steppe to India.

However these camel bones found from the steppe are not older than the camel bones recovered from Harappa culture and Iran. The Andronovan camel bones must have been those of the imported domestic camels or from the meat of the hunted camels. Possibly prejudiced by such propaganda, archaeologist Catherine Jarrige also wrote, "In particular, ... the activity area of Pirak allowed us to bring to the light existence of a veritable agricultural revolution in early post Harappan times marked by ... and appearance of the camel, horse and donkey." (1995:53).

The time-frame of the events does not support the earliest domestication of the camel in the steppe. This period of time, the second half of the second millennium BC (i.e. between 1500-1000 BC) dated for the Andronovo culture and their camels too, is much later than the archaeological evidence of the presence of the domestic Bactrian camel in southeast Iran adjoining Indian boarders in the third millennium BC, and the presence of the dromedary camel in the Indus Valley and Central India in the fouth millennium BC. Hence the Central Asian and the Andronovo domestic camels must be considered inspired from the Iranian and Indian camel domestication, which had reached north from the south, not the *vice-versa*.

Parpola thinks that the Indian camel of the *Rig-Vedic* period was Bactrian camel not dromedary, which had been brought to India by the Aryans after 1500 BC. The *Rig-Vedic* camel could be the Bactrian ones, provided we accept the time of the *Rig-Veda* between 8,000 and

6,000 BC, when many Bactrian camels must have lived in India. The Bactrian camel is extremely well cold adapted animal and cannot live in the hot climates. If the date of the *Rig-Veda* is kept at 1500 BC to 1300 BC, survival of the Bactrian camel would not be possible in India. Because by this time the climate had become very hot. Bactrian camel must have become extinct from the wild existence in northwest India after 5,000 BC when the region became warm and well forested. However, the species might have survived in the colder districts of the Indian sub-continent in the northwest like Afghanistan and Kashmir up to 2000 BC. In fact the Laddakh district of Kashmir has Bactrian camels living in the freezing temperatures even toady, althoug in domestic form. In fact no Bactrian camel has been found from any southern country like Iran after 2000 BC when the climate became very hot, and we cannot expect this species to have survived in the Indus Valley too after 2000 BC.

Borrowing of the Indian name of camel into the Finno-Ugric and Turkic languages has been well documented (Kuz'mina 1963, also Bogolyubsky 1929: 14, 15; both cited by Kuz'mina and Mallory 2007:109). This means some linguistic migration out of India which could have taken place at the time of the R1a1a migration at about 8,000 BC or later during the Bronze Age.

Archaeology of Camel

India was the older home of camel than Arabia. The oldest *Camelus* fossils from Asia have been found from India (Miocene, Shivalik Hills) and have been described as the *Camelus sivalensis* (Falconer and Cautley 1845-49:112-117), from which the modern Indian camel *Camelus dromedarius* evolved in India (Rissman:15; Falconer and Cautley:120-121). However, the Eurocentric historians' group has always denied this fact (e.g. Kuzmina and Mallory; Parpola; David Anthony).

The oldest camelid evolved in North America (early Pleistocene) and migrated through the Ice-Age land bridge on the Bering Strait to northeast Asia (Bornstein 1990:232), and thence to Central Asia, China, India then to further west. The differentiation between *dromedarius* and the *bactrianus* must have taken place only after sexual sexial isolation of the two to the south of and to the the north of the Himalayas respectively long begore the period we are discussing. This India is the original home of the *Camelus dromedarius*. The Arabian origin of the *dromedarius* camel can at best be the ingnorant layman's guess.

North India was a desert between 35,000 BC and 16,000 BC and also between 13,000 and 8,000 BC when ostrich, camel and giraffe found it the perfect place to live in, and they wandered there particularly in Central and northwest India happily (Petraglia 2009:Fig 2). Between 8,000 BC and 6,000 BC North India was semi-desert grassland with open forests.

It is no more acceptable by the zoologists that the first camel (Bactrian) was originally domesticated in the steppe, or Central Asia or Bactria or Iran. The molecular analysis reveals that the Bactrian camel was domesticated in the Chinese cold desert about 5000-6000 years back (or, 3000-4000 BC), near the bend of the Yellow River (Ji 2009:381). Potts commented "Zoological opinion nowadays tends to favour the idea that *C. bactrianus* and *dromedarius* are descendants of two different sub-species of *C. ferus* (Peters and von den Driesch 1997:652) and there is no evidence to suggest that the original range of *C. ferus* included those parts of Central Asia and Iran where some of the earliest Bactrian camel's remains have been found" (Potts 2004a:145). In spite of the zoological findings going to the contrary, some historians have not stopped their efforts to propagate the false claims. For example, Kuz'mina and Mallory, on the basis of some anonymous falk-lore claim that the Chinese got their domestic Bactrian camels from the Aryans of Andronova of the steppe who had first domesticated the Bactrian camel in their view. (Kuz'mina and Mallory 2007:109).

No objective evidence supporting any old domestication of the dromedary camel in Arabia before 1000 BC exists (Wapnish 1981:105). However some 200 camel bones seemingly domesticated and dating back to 2700 BC have been discovered from a small island Umm an-Nar located off the coast of Trucial Oman in the Persian Gulf (Wapnish 1981:105). However there is no evidence that these domesticated camels exerted any impact on the domestication of the camel in the Arabian Peninsula even until 1000 BC (Wapnish 1981:105).

What was the use of the camels in a small island 'Umm an-Nar' in 2700 BC? Clearly this was a stationing point between Oman and India for the sea traders. These traders coming from the Indus Valley probably also traded in cattle and camels. It seems, the wild camels were captured from Arabia and then kept in the island for as long as required to tame them. Then they were traded in the Indus Valley. Otherwise bringing the camels to the island was a worthless effort for no good and no goal.

This is just a hypothesis. Yet the truth within it can be appreciated if we realize that a small island is the best location for taming the wild camels. Because the wild camels in the captive always try to escape in the beginning. If not located in an island, such domestication centres would require very high walled fences to prevent the camels from escaping.

Bringing camels live to a small island must have required robust shipping skills, which was then available with only the Harappans in the region. The island was a port city with exhibits all the features of the Harappa culture—in pottery, figurines, artefacts, fortified buildings etc. Still later we find Indus type seals in plenty by 2050 BC at the Eastern Arabian coastal cities like Dilmun (Laursen 2010). Thus the movement of the culture was from the island to the Arabian coast. Tosi (1974) presents evidence of active interaction of the island-city Umm an-Nar with southeast Iran region which was generally traversed by the Indian traders too before they crossed the narrowest part of the Persian Gulf.

In Arabia the camel domestication took place after 1000 BC, or slightly earlier than this date (Zarins 1978; Western 1979; Wapnish 1981:105; Peregrine 2002:254, 257; Sapir-Hen and Ben-Yoseph 2013:277-278). Older camel bones recovered from Arabia are all of wild camels. A recent archaeological finding fixes the date of the first entry of the domestic dromedary camel into the Levant (Aravah Valley, Israel) at 940 BC (Sapir-Hen and Ben-Yoseph 2013).

However we get the evidence of the domestic camels in the Middle East region since much earlier times, and all these skeletal and atrefactual samples belong to the Bactrian variety. Cuniform inscriptions of the Neo-Assyrian kings dating 11th century BC mention the two humped Bactrian camels (A. Salonen 1956, cited by Wapnish 1981:106 fn23). A much older, early second millennium BC cylinder seal and some other artefacts from the same period have been found from the same region of the Middlae East, all depicting the two-humped camel (many references for this, cited by Wapnish 1981:106 fnn 21 and 22; also Titus Kennedy 2010).

Kuzmina and Mallory write: "In the documents of Tiglath-pileser I (1116-1077 BC), Assur-bel-kal (1074-1057 BC) and Ashurnasirpal I (1050-1032 BC) they speak of a two-humped camel and from Salmanasar II, we find that camels are brought from the east (Luckenbill 1927; Yankovskaya 1956)." (Kuzmina and Mallory:109). This east was eastern Iran and Indo-Iranian boarder region which must have been a centre of commercial camel breeding at that time (Tosi 1974).

Clearly the Arabian Peninsula was not the source of the camel for the adjoining Assyria in these reports, indicating the complete absence of domestication of the camel from the Arabian Peninsula until about 1000 BC. The oldest domesticated camel depicted in an artefact (cylinder seal) of West Asia is a Bactrian one with a rider and has been made in the Old Syrian style dated 1750-1700 BC. It is available in the Walters Art Gallary of Iraq (Gordon 1939: Pl. 7.55; Collon 2000: Fig. 8; both cited by Daniel Potts 2004b:150; also Potts 2004a).

Clearly the domestic Bactrian camel had reached Mesopotamia about a thousand years before the domestic dromedary camle reached there. This means the domestication of the dromedary in Arabia was inspired from the arrival of domestic Bactrian camel. On the other hand we have archaeological evidence of domestication of the dromedary in India from much older dates (*vide infra*). The Egyptians became familiar with dromedary camel in the third millennium before the Arabs domesticated them (Zeuner 1963:342).

Tosi made persuasive argument for the domestication of the *Camelus bactrianus* in Iran in the third millennium BC from wild Bactrian camels, which he thought lived in Iran. He mentions the presence of the Bactrian camel at Ulug Depe (2500 BC) and Anau (3000 BC) in southern Turkmenistan (Tosi 1974:162), and Eastern Iran adjoining India (*ibid*:162-3). He finds the Omani culture growing under the Eastern Iranian influence (*ibid*:163), which would have ultimately resulted in the transfer of camel domestication technology to Arabia. Potts (1993) reported a Bactrian decorated comb from Arabia dating back to 2100 BC meaning thereby that there was intense cultural interaction between northwest Indian frontiers and Arabia during the Bronze Age, and this could have inspired the domestication of the camel in Arabia. Zarins too supported the Iranian origin of the domestic Bactrian camel and suggested that this species may have been imported into Arabia later.

The oldest archaeological evidence of the domestication of the two-humped Bacrtian camel (*Camelus bactrianus*) is based on the "woven wool" kept along with camel bone and camel dung found preserved in a jar at *Shahr-i-sokhta* (in Balochistan, southeast Iran at Afghano-Iran boarder) dating 2,700-2,500 BCE (Zeder 2006:146; Compagnoni and Tosi 1978:95-99; Wapnish 1981:106). *Shahr-i-sokhta* is located at the point where the boarders of Afghanistan, Iran and the former British India met.

No doubt *Shahr-i-sokhta* is located within Iran today, but during the Bronze Age it was part of the larger Harappan or South Asian Civilization. It is located 400 miles to the west of Mehrgarh. This as well as the nearby Mundigak archaeological complex from Kandahar (Afghanistan) share a series of artefacts which are exactly of the same kind or are similar to the ones from Harappa (Cortesi 2008). Thus the evidence of the domestic camel from *Shahr-i-Sokhta* belongs actually to the Harappa Civilization, where we get many more findings of the camel.

Quite a few camel bones had been recovered at Harappa and Mohenjo-Daro excavations (Sewell and Guha 1931:660; B. Prashad 1936:58-59; Bhola Nath 1969:106). These all were one-humped camels (*Camelus dromedarius*). Possehl too mentions the camel remains found from the Indus Civilization. He expresses the possibility that these could have been domesticated in the mature Harappa phase (Possehl 2002:63).

Sir John Marshall found a dromedary camel (*Camelus dromedarius*) scapula at the depth of 15 feet at Mohenjo-Daro excavation (Marshall 1931:660, 667). That depth is below the oldest Harappa period, before the urbanization period. Hence it should be dated sometime between 3500 and 4000 BC or even earlier. Clearly this camel must have been captured or domesticated from the nearby Thar (then grassland). This is consistent with the mention of this animal in the *Yajur-Veda*, which is a mid-Holcene (i.e. wet and not arid) period text (*Yajurveda* 13.50; *Rig-Veda* 8.5.37).

Another camel bone lying below the proto-historic or Harappan period was found by Carlleyle from Choya Nadi site near Indore in Madhya Pradesh (K.A.R. Kennedy 2000:41-2). This was never dated properly but from the contexts we can say it must be older than 3500 BC. In the fourth millennium B.C. the camel could have lived in the Madhya Pradesh either as domesticated animal brought from the Thar, or as wild animal living in the Central India desert-grassland. This we can think because the Madhya Pradesh had become desert-like owing to the shift of the Bay of Bengal monsoon to the Arabian Sea at that time.

In 1983-84 exploration of Rajasthan, camel bones were found from Gyaneshwar from contexts pertaining to the Pre-Harappa and the Copper Age periods and were judged to be under the process of domestication, (Rao 1986:72). Although the radiocarbon dates are not available so far, from the contexts we can date it to 4000 BC.

Camel was an important domesticated animal at Mehrgarh at least in the later period in the fourth millennium BC (Schaffer and Thapar 1992:247). At Khurab (Bampur Valley, Baluchistan of Iran) a metal-axe decorated with a seated camel dating to Bronze Age (2600 BC) had been found by Sir Aurel Stein during the excavation (Zeuner 1955; Lamberg-Karlovsky 1969; Maxwell-Hyslop 1955). Only one hump was visible in the artefact (Kuz'mina and Mair 2008:68). This camel could in fact be considered the dromedary one. An uncalibrated date 2200 BC (or 2700 BC if calibration done) for the camel at Bampur has been suggested (C. Jarrige, *Mehrgarh:Field Report* 1995:253).

Upinder Singh (2008:85) and also Sahu (1988:109) mention that the *Camelus dromedarius* constituted the normal wild fauna of Kanewal (Gujarat) during the Mesolithic period (5000-2000 BCE). However camel bones have been found from Shortughai and Kanewal of Gujarat within such human contexts as to indicating domestic status (Upinder Singh:157,165,169). At that time no domestic camel existed in Arabia, although wild camel herds were roaming in Oman. The Bactrian camel being a cold adapted and heat intolerant animal could not have survived at Kanewal in Gujarat at about 2,500 BC. Hence we can say with confidence that the camel bone found there must belong to the dromedary camel.

Shaffer and Thaper find that camel may have been domesticated at Mehrgarh especially during the later period. (1992:248). They also mention a camel burial discovered from KD phase or Early Harappa phase of the Indus Valley Civilization, which comes to before 3000 BC in the corrected/calibrated dates (*ibid*:273). They postulate that the Harappan people could not have made so much successful long distance trade relations with Middle East unless they had the camel.

Other archaeologists or their reports noting the dromedary camel in the early Indian archaeology include A.K. Sharma (Surkotada,

1990:380), Shah (Kanewal, in Mehta 1980:75), IAR (Kalibangan, 1964-65:38) and Stack-Kane (Rojdi, 1989:183). These all are from Harappa period or older. In the Arabian archaeology the domestic camel appears only about 1000 BC or later (Uerpman 2002; Beech 2009:17; Sauer and Blakely:10, 105-6), much before which the domestic dromedary camel had appeared in the Indian antiquity. However, this fact about India being the probable source of the dromedary camel has been subjected to denial and manipulation by the committed historians.

Other references to camel remains from Bronze Age India are: Mohenjo-Daro and Harappa (Fentress: 364, Table 2; Spassov and Stoytchev 2004:156) and Kalibangan (Meadow 1984, quoted by Crabtree and Champman 1989:18-19; Chatterji 2005:198). Kalibangan is earlier than Harappa. Camel burial has also been found from the Kot Diji Phase of Mohenjo-Daro (contemporary with Mehrgarh VII, 2800-2600 BC uncalibrated) which on calibratin would date to the fourth millennium BC (Dani and Masson 1999:271; Meadow 1984, cited in Dani and Masson:273). Dani and Masson noted "The Mehrgarh excavations indicate that ... the important (domestic) animals were cattle, sheep, goat, water buffalo and possibly camel (in the later periods)." (p. 248).

At Zagheh and Tepe Ghabristan (Qabrestan) on the Qazvin plain (west of Tehran in Iran), only *C. dromedarius* seems to have been present in the fourth millennium BCE (Mashkour, Fontugne and Hatte 1999:71, Table 2; Mashkour 2002:Table2 both cited by Potts 2004a). That means *dromedarius* had a widespred presence in the southern regions like Central India, Thar, Baluchistan, Iran and Arabia in early fourth millennium BC, and we do not get samples of the Bactrian camel from southern regions dating to such early periods as the fourth millennium. Bactrian camel appears only about 2000-2500 BC in Indus and East Iran region.

M. Ghosh (1976:162) reported the skeleton of a Bactrian camel found from Kausambi near Allahabad in north-Central India. In the absence of accurate dating he only noted that the site was more than 2000 years old. However from the other excavations too we know that the

Kausambi site is very old. Over and above that the Bactrian camel is a cold adapted animal and could not have lived in Kausambi after 6,000 BC. Thus radiocarbon study of the camel bone itself is desirable.

From Pirak of the Kachi plain, camel bones as well as its terracotta figurines have been found from dates which on calibration yield the date 1800 BC (Allchin and Allchin 1982:233). The double-humped charecter of these camels have led to suggestions about Central Asian influence. However, neighbouring *shahr-i-sokhta* had the Bactrian camel since long back--we have noted above. This was not the natural habitat of the Bactrian camel. Hence import of the domesticated Bactrian camel to Pirak can be thought of either from the Balochistan and Siestan region adjoining the Indus Valley area, or from Laddakh which was a natural habitat of the wild Bactrian camel.

Pirak (Indus Valley) artefact depicting the domestic Bactrian camel (1800 BC) is older or at least as old as the oldest West Asian artefact depicting the domestic camel (Santoni 1979: 177-179). Meadow too found Bactrian camel bones at Pirak (Meadow 1993:67,70). The evidence of the dromedary camel in West Asia is much later, and does not predate 1200 BC even by the most liberal assumptions. However there is artefactual evidence of the domestic dromedary camel from Egypt dating back to before 2200 BC. That could mean an earlier then Arabian domestication of the dromedary camels in India and Egypt.

It is interesting that the only type of camel present in modern Iran today is *C. dromedarius*, though *C. bactrianus* was well-established there until very recent times. Bones of *C. bactrianus* have been unearthed at Shah Tepe in Northern Iran in strata dating to 3000 B.C (Sapir-Hen and Ben-Yoseph 2013).

Some archaeologists feign ignorance of the older camel bones from Harappa and some give funny explanations. Kenoyer only accepts the presence of the camel from the Late Harappan period (Kenoyer 2005:26). McIntosh accepts the single humped (dromedary) camel bones found from Harappa (McIntosh 2008:132), but he gives unique explanation. McIntosh thinks that the meat of the wild camel from Arabia might have been imported by the Harappans, and the bones recovered are of the same meat (McIntosh:132).

It is a unique explanation. However such a wild conclusion is the result of the dogmatic and false belief that the dromedary could not have been domesticated in India *circa* 2000 BCE or 2500 BC and earlier. The imported meat hypothesis is clearly impractical, because there was no refrigeration and fast transport facility at that time, and such long distance importation of meat at a time which was hotter than today was not possible without causing severe rotting and food-poisoning. Such thinking is certainly absurd. Moreover, if anyone fancied camel's meat, and there had been no local camel, an import of the live Bactrian camel from northwest (like Bactria) was more pragmatic. Clearly the presence of the dromedary camel bones in Harappa indicates domestication or at least the widespread presence of the *Camelus dromedarius* in the region.

The most important fact to note in this context is that the archaeological evidence for the Indian domestic dromedary camel is much older than all of these dates. As the Arabian domestication of the dromedary camel took place only about 1000 BC, this camel could not have been transported to India in the third or the fourth millennium BC, and we will have to accept an earlier and independent domestication of the dromedary camel in India from the indigenous *Camelus dromedarius* of the Thar desert.

Camel occurs in the *Rig-Veda, Yajur-Veda* and *Atharva-Veda* (*RV* 1.138.2; 8.46.22, 28,36; *TS* 5.6.21.1; *AV* 20.127.2). The *Rig-Veda* mentions large herds of both the wild and the domestic camels. At one place, the *Rig-Veda* describes a large herd of running wild camels which disperses after being chased (*RV* 1.132.2). As the *Rig-Veda* and the *Atharva-Veda* belong to the dry periods, we can expect the camel to have lived in the wild existence in northwest India during these periods. During the *Rig-Veda*'s times, it was cold desert like condition during the

Early Holocene and the Bactrian camel must have entered the Indus-Sarasvati region from Afghanistan and possibly Laddakh.

However the climate was entirely different in the *Yajur-Vedic* times. Most of it was the wet forest ecosystem in northwest India, not suitable for the camel's survival. Therefore we cannot expect the wild existence of camel in this region during that mid-Holocene Optimum. We can get camel in a wet forest region only as domesticated animal living under the shelter and protection of man. In fact we find that the camel had been domesticated in India much earlier, say, about the Early Holocene, which was a dry period and many camels must have roamed in north India then.

After 3000 BC the northwest Indian aridity starts building up which becomes maximal at about 2150 BC (4.2 K event). This is the time when any camel could have lived independently in the wild in this region. And that is why we get today camel bones from Harappa, Surkotada, Kanewal, Kalibangan and perhaps Rojdi, which date to about 2200-2000 BC (U. Singh:85, 165, 167; McIntosh:131). Sortughai and Kalibangan have yielded camel figurines (McIntosh:131).

In the western Central Asia, a cold adapted and long-haired breed of the dromedary camel is found even today (Harris 2011:18). In fact many Central Asian, South Siberian and steppe petroglyphs depict single humped camels (Dani and Masson:103), and most probably there was a cold adapted type of the dromedary which existed in the Thar region of India as well as in Iran during the Early Holocene. Although Tibet and the Indian district Laddakh are ecologically natural habitats of the Bactrian camels today, they actually arrived into Central Asia and northern Iran only during the Bronze Age much later than they had been domesticated in East China about 4000-5000 BC.

In Central India, we get depiction of camel from Bhimbetka (Mathpal 1984:122). This place is hundreds of miles away from the natural habitat of camels today. Therefore we may surmise that this depiction dates back to a drier period. This could have been the Late Pleistocene or the Early Holocene when the ostrich too lived there.

Some DNA studies of the Arabian camels too have been done. Abdulaziz noted about their DNA results: "This indicated that the Saudi camels are closely related with low genetic variation and differentiation that were observed, confirming known historic information that the populations derived from a single origin." (2009:638). Such findings mean a later domestication. Mehta, in his DNA study of the Indian camel breeds found that all the Indian breeds are related. They also have geographical structuring (2006:77). These findings indicate local early origin and domestication event.

Karima (2011:2643-2644) gives comparative data of allele variability between the Indian, Arabian and Sudanese dromedary camels. The data reflects highest allelic variations or number of alleles in the Indian camels and lowest in the Arabian camels. That means the Arabian camels have been domesticated not only later than the Indian dromedary ones, but also possibly could have derived from the Indian stock.

Banerjee (2012) made comparative DNA study of Indian and African camels. It showed that the Indian mountain breed Malavi was the oldest of all breeds from India and Africa. The data indicate that from Western coasts of India, domestic camel entered into East Africa, from where they have gone to the other countries. This is consistent with similar conclusions about domestic cow (Zebu), which entered East Africa from India as the result of the active sea trade of Indian cattle at about 3000 BC (Freeman 2006; Priyadarshi 2011). Freeman *et al* (2006) found that *Bos indicus* was introduced into Africa by sea route and not through Suez/ Sinai land route. Zeder (2006:146) too supports this view.

Although vehemently denied by the Eurocentrics, linguistically there is strong evidence in favour of the presence of the dromedary camel in the Indo-European homeland. This fact has been always suppressed by the philologists who claim that the words for camel were picked up by the Indo-Aryans from the substrate langugage of Bactria while they were crrossing the region to reach India.

Etymologies of the Indo-European names of Camel

The philological material on the basis of which we can infer that the camel was present in the Indo-European homeland includes the following words:

drŏmas

Sanskrit *dhūmra* (camel; MacDonnell and Keith:402; MWD; *TS* 1.8.21.1); Portugese *dromedario* (camel), Latin *drŏmas* (a swift camel; Valpi:130) and *dromedarius* (camel-rider) point to the fact. Other words related to these are Greek *dromikos* (a place to run); Latin *dromic* (relating to racecourse); Old Norse *tramr* (demon, ghost).

The other Sanskrit word is *uṣṭra* which is well represented in the Indo-Aryan, Iranian, and less well so in the Armenian and Slavic branches of Indo-European, and also appears as loan word in the Semitic (or Afro-Asiatic) family.

uṣṭra

Indo-Aryan: Sankrit *uṣṭra, uṣṭi*, Hindi *ūṭ*, Kohistani *úx, ūṭ* (camel);

Iranian: Avestan *ushtra, ushthra*, Persian *ustur* (Steinegass:63), *shutur, 'utul, us, usturak* (camel), *ustara* (hair-shaving razor), *ushtār, ishtār* (haste), *sutur* (any quadruped beast of burden), *ustur-murg* (ostrich),

Pahlawi *uštar, uštur*, Pashto *ūkkha, ūśh, ūśbah, shutur, u<u>sh</u>tur* (dromedary camel), Baluchi *wštyr* (camel), Pashtoon *ukkh, uksh* (camel).

Slavic: Slovak *odrazník lode* (camel; from *udra* < *uṣṭra*).

Armenian: Armenian *owght* (camel).

In other languages, the Indian word *uṣṭra* has lost the original meaning and acquired the meaning "camel-bird" i.e. ostrich. It is noteworthy how close "ostrich" and Persian *usturak* (camel) are phonetically. Mallory and Adams present the views of many scholars which suggest that the European word *aurochs* (wild cow of Europe) too was a cognate word of Sanskrit *uṣṭra* (1997:135-136). This sounds plausible. However Mallory and Adams have identified the direction of migration wrongly.

Portugese and Spanish *struz* (camel, in compound word *ave-struz*, camel-bird); Middle Low German *strus* (ostrich, camel), German *Strutz* (ostrich), *strauss* (ostrich); Russian *straus* (ostrich). Other possible cognates may be 'stork',

Ostrich was well known to Europeans in the third millennium BC. They imported the ostrich egg-shells from North Africa (McIntosh 2009:173), and were aware of the bird as the camel-bird as is obvious from the Portugese name of the bird (*ave-struz*).

The Indo-Iranian word *uštra* was borrowed by the Akkadian language of West Asia during the Bronze Age where *uduru* and *udru* mean 'camel' (Black 2000:418; Mallory and Adams 1997:135). The Arabic word *usharā* (she-camel with ten months old baby) too seems to be a borrowing from the North Indian language. Bronze Age Anatolian Hurrian word *uḷtu* (camel) too is a borrowing (*ibid*). The word also enterd Southeast Asia and percolated the Austronesian and other languages: Javanese, Krama, Malay and Indonesian languages *unta, onta* (camel; c.f. Hindi *ūnt* camel); Thai *u:ut, ut* (camel). There is DNA evidence that Indians migrated to the Southeast Asia too during the Bronze Age. Thus the

Indian words for camel spread in all directions during the Bronze Age. Hence Anthony's speculation that this group of words originated in the language of the Bactria-Margiana region (BMAC) cannot be supported (Anthony 2010).

Hence it has been wrongly claimed that the names of the camel in the Indo-Iranian languages (Sanskrit *uṣṭra* and its cognates) are not Indo-European in origin and that they are from the local Indian substrate language (like Munda) or from some extinct language of the BMAC (Witzel 1999a:24 and 65 pdf). These authors also suggest that the camel was brought to India by the Aryan invadors in about 1500 BC. Witzel noted "Book 8 also knows of camels (*ushtra* 8.4.21-24, 31, 46-48, O. Iran. *uštra*, as in *Zaraθ-uštra*), that are first attested archaeologically in S. Asia in the Bolån area, at Pirak, c.1700 BCE." But the migration of the Indian substrate language word *uṣṭra* and its various forms to the steppe and subsequent borrowing into the Finno-Ugric could have been possible only if the direction of the migration was from the south to north and not the vice-versa. This fact too supports the northward movement of the domestication of camel and people from India.

Parpola claims that this set of words (*uṣṭra* etc) means the two-humped Bactrian camel. However this conjecture is wrong and without any evidence. In fact the word, *uṣṭra* in its various forms in the various languages has been generally used for the single humped camel, i.e. *Camelus dromedarius.*

The Sanskrit word for camel *uṣṭra* may be expanded as *ut+stra.* Here *ut-* signifies 'tallness'. The main stem is **stra* which is a fossilized form of Sanskrit words like *sthūra, sthūla* etc and carries the same semantic sense as Sanskrit *sthūra* (bull), English stor, stallion and steed, Greek *taurus* etc. (see PIE **ster* Pokorny:1022-27). Thus the complete semantic connotation of *uṣṭra* is "tall and large animal". This much of discussion is enough to prove that Sanskrit *uṣṭra* (camel) is a word of Indo-European origin.

Although its case was never examined philologically in the past, we can now examine other words/roots with phonetic and semantic resemblance:

> PIE **ster-* strong, stiff, rigid; Sanskrit *sthūrin, sthūlin* (camel), *sthūra* (thick, bull); Avestan *staora* (large cattle); Old English *stĕor* (castrated male cattle), Old English *steort* (tail, rump), English *steer* (ox), Gothic *stiur* (calf); Latin *Taurus* (bull); Greek *tauros* (bull) etc. Proto-Gmc. **star* (be rigid), O.H.G. *starah* (strong, big, large), O.H.G. *storren-* (to stand out, project), O.E. *stearc* (stiff, strong); Lith *storas* (thick). O.H.G. *staren* to stare, German *starren*, English verb "stare". Proto-Gmc. **strakjanan*, O.H.G. *strecchan* (to stretch), German *aus-strecken* (to stretch oneself out), O.E. *streccan.*

sthava

The early Holocene of Northwest India was arid and must have had both types of camels, the dromedary and the Bactrian—first one in the warmer Gujarat, Thar and Sind provinces and the other in the colder Laddakh, Kashmir, Afghanistan and the adjoining plains. In fact at 8000 BC, the climate was quite arid and camels must have been present in India, Iran and Central Asia. Hence we cannot vizualize any difficulty in transmission of the names of camel.

Many authors have been cited by Kuz'mina and Mallory, Bogolyubsky etc, stating that the Finno-Ugric and Turkic languages borrowed the Indo-Aryan words for the camel. I failed to get a reading of those articles even after extensive search. Nor have these authors mentioned which Indo-Aryan word for camel was borrowed into Finno-Ugric and what those words are. Hence I had to work out the whole thing afresh for this issue.

Finno-Ugric words meaning 'camel' are:

> Udmurt *dooe, du-e* (camel), Hungarian *teve* (camel)

Turkic (Altaic) all meaning 'camel'are:

> Turkish *deve, teve, tebe*, Mongol *teme-gen*, Old Turkic *tebe* (Orkh.), *teve* (Old Uygh.), Karakhanid *teve (tevej)*, Tatar *dŭ jä*, Middle Turkic *deve, teve,* Uzbek *tuja*, Uighur *toga*, Sary-Yughur *te, ti*, Azerbaidzhan *devä*, Khakassian *tibe*, Oyrat *tȭ, tebe etc* .

Kott/Asan (Yeniseian language) *tabat* (camel)
Sakha (Yakut) language (from Mongolic) *tebien* (camel)

Thus the common root is *tava, teve* or *deve.* Similar words from Indo-European which mean 'camel' are:

> Selice Romani Gypsi *ošteve-* or *števe-* as in the compound word *púpošteve* (*púp-ošteve* camel; Elšík 2009:296;
>
> Albanian *deve;*
> Serbian *deva*, Croation *deva*, Slovak *t'ava*, Bosnian *deva*, all meaning 'camel'.

The Gypsi word may suggest that the European name "Steve" might have the same origin. Harper mentions words like English "stevedore" and Spanish *estibador* (wool-packer, one who loads cargo). They could be related. The nearest match in Sanskrit for these words is *sthava.*

The Sanskrit word *sthava*, has acquired the meaning 'he-goat'. However its oldest meaning must, during the Early Holocene, have included the camel. In Persian the word exists as *ushtāv* and *ishtāv* (haste, despatch). There is a great functional resemblance between the he-goat and the camel, particularly during the early Holocene. Both provide wool, leather, milk and meat.

Another semantic resemblance comes from the saliva. Whitney mentions the word *ṣṭhīv* (spit, spew large quantities of saliva, Whitney 1885:181-2), which just describes one feature of these animals. Whitney also noted that the words with *shthū* and *stha* are just the two forms of the same root (Whitney:194-5). Thus its cognate words would include: Sanskrit *sthava* (he-goat), *sthavi* (weaver, sac, bag), *sthaviṣṭha* (very strong, tallest, largest; *TS* 2.5.5.2), *sthavira* (strong; *TS* 4.6.4.2) *sthavimat* (broad, thick side; *TS* 6.4.1.1).

The principal root in all these is *sthu* (Sk.; stout, strong, solid, big animal). In *sthava* (Sk. he-goat) the suffix *-va* (*q.v.* in MWD) adds relationship with cloth, wool, cover. Thus *sthava* is 'stout and strong animal which provides wool'. In Indian plains, when the Bactrian camel became extinct, the word *sthava* got applied to the 'he-goat' which provided the wool. Once upon a time the '*sthavi*' meant the 'camel' is clear from the Sanskrit word *sthaviṣṭha*. This word etymologically means *sthavi+ṣṭha i.e.* "sitting on the *sthavi*" and the derived dictionary meaning is "tallest, largest" (MWD)--a meaning which is not possible if the meaning of *sthavi* is 'he-goat'. For becoming highest one needed to sit on the back of a 'camel'. The cognates of this word travelled to Itan, then to Central Asia and Albanian. In Central Asia onwards it was borrowed by Altaic and Uralic languages where they continue to mean the camel. From this we get *teve, deve* etc (*vide supra*).

Ostrich:

There is abundant archaeological evidence favouring the existence of ostrich in Indian past up to the Early Holocene. In 1910, Bidwell reported the ostrich eggshells found in India and named this particular ostrich species as the *Struthio indicus*. Andrews (1910) too reported ostrich eggshells from north India. In fact, the ostrich bones had been reported from the Sivalik fossil deposits also. But the finding was difficult to digest the excavator Mr Lydekkar (1885) who rejected it. There are now thousands of such finds by now. However the fact has not been generally digested by the historians, prehistorians and archaeologists.

Ostrich beads and eggshells have been found from Batadombalena (Sri Lanka) and Patne (Maharashtra, India) dating back to 26,500 and 23,000 BC respectively (Deraniyagala; Sali 1985). A late Upper Paleolithic burial at Bhimbetka contains two ostrich-eggshell beads found near the neck of the man (Bednarik 1993). The discovery of more than one thousand ostrich eggshells at over 40 sites in Rajasthan, Madhya Pradesh and Maharashtra, several of them dated by radiocarbon 14C, as well as depiction of the bird in the rock art at Bazar Cave (Pachmarhi) and some other places, shows that ostrich, a bird adapted to the arid climates, was widely distributed in central and western India during the later part of the Upper Palaeolithic and the early Holocene (U. Singh:79; Sali 1985:144 in Misra and Bellwood; Harrison cited by Sali 1985; G. Kumar 1988).

Sali noted that the ostrich eggshells were absent from the Mesolithic layers at Patne (Maharashtra, near Goa and Belgaum). Mesolithic culture took off late at Patne. Wakankar (1985:176), while working in the same region noted that the Mesolithic culture was represented by fowl (chicken), bison, tiger and rhinoceros in that region. These are the features of very wet climate. Thus the Patne Mesolithic, when ostrich became extinct, was wet. Such climate was a feature of the mid-Holocene Optimum in the region. That means the ostrich disappeared from Patne once the mid-Holocene Optimum had arrived, roughly about 5500 BC.

Hence the ostrich lived in Central India up to a time before the onset of the wet period about 6000-5500 BC. Before this time it was a semi-arid/arid period. Radiocarbon dates indicated that the ostrich eggshells from Patne (Maharashtra) pertained to the Upper Paleolithic which was up to about 6000 BC for that part of the region (Kennedy 2000:165; James 2007:216).

In fact the Phase IIE of Patne, from which one ostrich eggshell was found covers up to 8000 BC (Sali 1985:144-5). Some Ostrich eggshells were also found from the Raichbal Valley, Gulberga, dating to the Mesolithic period of these areas (Rao 1986:40). Gulberga is drier than Patne even today and is located in Maharashtra between Solapur and Hyderabad. In this region the Neolithic starts about 4000 BC, before which the period is Mesolithic. This region was quite dry even during the mid-Holocene Optimum.

Thus we can say that the time when ostrich lived in India overlaps with our dates for the *Rig-Veda*. S.K. Tiwari presents review of evidence in favour of the presence of the ostrich in India during the Late Pleistocene period (2000:230-238). Other important works on Bhimbetka's dating, where ostrich was found, are by Mathpal (1984, 1985). The review oll such literature makes it clear that the latest date of ostrich in India corresponds to the Mesolithic times of the some Central Indian sites, which can be dated 8,000 BC to 6,000 BC. This consistent with the generally accepted date of extinction of ostrich from India (Chakravarty and Bednarik 1997:54).

Linguistics of ostrich

Ostrich has been often known by the same name as camel in many civilizations only a word meaning 'bird' added after the word for camel. Some of the examples are: Tamil *oṭṭaka-paṭci* ('camel-bird');

Farsi *ustur murgh* and *shutur murgh* camel-brd), Turkish *devekusu* (*deve*= camel, *kushu*= bird) etc all prove the thing.

Hebrew word for ostrich is: *ˀštwrmwrg* (a borrowing from the Persian *shutur-murg*, camel-bird). The words *shutur* (Sanskrit *uṣṭra*) and *murg* (Sanskrit *mṛga*) are Indo-Iranian, and not Semitic in origin, indicating that the Semitic people came to know of this bird through the Indo-Iranian speakers. This could happen only when the people were migrating from east to west.

Indo-European cognates of "ostrich": Russian страус **or** *straoos* (a reverse of oos-stra or *uṣṭra*); OE *austridge*; Old French *ostruce*, Late Latin *struthio*; Greek *strouthos* (ostrich), *strouthio-kamilos* (ostrich which looks like a camel).

There are other cognates too where the meaning has been changed to some large bird: PIE *storos*, *stornos*, *stṛ̥nos*? (a kind of bird; Pokorny: 1036); Lat. *sturnus* (star); O.E. *stearn* (tern or sterna birds); O.Pruss. *starnite* (seagull); compare also Cz. *strnad*, Russ. *strenátka* (yellowhammer bird); O.H.G. *star(a)*, Ger. *Star*, O.Ice. *stari*, O.E. *stær* all meaning the starling bird; Proto-Germanic **sturkaz*, German *storch*, English "stork".

Identifying the ostrich in the *Rig-Veda*

In our study, there is a chronological overlap of the *Rig-Veda* with the Early Holocene which was the arid/ semi-desert period for northwest India and when the ostrich definitely lived there. If our dating of the *Rig-Veda* is correct we must be able to find or identify the ostrich in the *Rig-Veda Samhita*.

The *Rig-Veda* mentions large, running birds, which had beautiful feathers, often red in colour, which were comparable to the ox, and which could be ridden. These birds looked like a deer without teeth. These birds never had the nest. They ran over the high plateau. This description matches the ostrich. As a hind-sight we can now say that these birds were the ostrich. We can see these references to ostrich as given in the Veda in detail below.

The *Rig-Veda* (1.182.7) mentions the "*parnā-mṛga*" (deer with feathers). Sanskrit word *parnā* means 'feather, pinion, plumage, leaf' (see MWD, p. 828). The *mṛga* is a terrestrial animal. Thus the word "*parnā-mṛga*" meant nothing but a flightless bird which had rich plumage. This was indeed the ostrich. (see MWD:828). Ostrich is a flightless bird and for that reason it comes within the semantic field of a *mṛga*. This Sanskrit word *mṛga* has survived in the Persian compound-word '*shutur-murg*' which means the ostrich. Adoption of the word *mṛga* to mean not a deer or antelope but birds in the Persian language was caused by the dry ecological condition of Iran during the Early Holocene where no antelope or deer lived at that time, although the flightless bird ostrich ran about in the highlands.

Although the ostrich has rudimentary wings, they are quite unnoticeable. The attractive feature in the bird is the luxurious handsome feathers which are often red. This knowledge about the ostrich helps us understand the meaning of another *Rig-Vedic* expression *suparṇā*. The word *suparṇā* meant 'one with beautiful feathers'. Not only cstrich but any beautifully feathered bird can be called *suparṇā*. It could also mean a tree with beautiful leaves.

However there is one instance in the *Rig*-Veda where the word *suparṇā* could have only meant the ostrich. This is the expression "*suparṇā vṛṣaṇa*" (*RV* 10.114.3). The expression means 'the bull which is richly feathered'. Amongst the birds, we can say, only the ostrich can be compared with the bull in strength, size or running speed. The meaning is obvious.

Again at one place, the *Rig-Veda* mentions a *parṇī mahiṣa i.e.* the feathered buffalo or the mighty bird. (*RV* 9.82.3). The meaning of *mahiṣa* is generally taken as the buffalo. However when it has feathers, plumage, the meaning is 'the bird which is large and mighty like a buffalo'. And that means the ostrich.

The same mantra further adds about the abode of the bird. It lives in the mountains located at the centre of the country or *nābhā pṛthivī*. This expression means Central India, which was traditionally considered the centre of the world, and later the zero longitude of Indian astronomy was passed through Ujjain in Central India. One hundred and fifty miles to the east of Ujjain in the same region, is located Bhimbetka within the mountains of the Vindhyachal range. From its rock shelters large number of ostrich eggs have been recovered dating back to the Mesolithic period of the region (about 8000 BC).

Another possible *Rig-Vedic* reference to the ostrich is: *suparṇo dhāvate divi*. The meaning is "the 'beautifully feathered one' runs fast on the high plane" (*RV* 1.105.1). This is the reference to the ostrich running fast on a high land.

One example of the use of the word for ostrich is *śakmanā śāko aruṇaḥ suparṇā* (the mighty bird with red and beautiful feathers) which 'never lived in a nest' (*RV* 10.55.6). Being flightless bird, the ostrich never lives in a nest and lays eggs on the ground itself. [*śakman* = power; *śāko*=might].

The *Rig-Veda* (6.75.11) says "*suparṇaṃ vaste mṛgo asyādanto gobhiḥ saṃnaddhā patati prasūtā*". This on re-syntaxing gives: "*vaste* (in the cover of) *suparnṇaṃ* (beautiful feathers) *adanto* (toothless) *mṛgo* (land-animal) *vasate* (lives) *asya* (whose) *saṃnaddha* (fastened) *gobhiḥ* (skin, feather) *apatati* (moults) *prasūtā* (born)". Thus the meaning is "the land-animal which is toothless, and is covered in the beautiful feathers, which are deeply fastened in skin, yet the feathers fall and spring out again".

These all can be dubbed by the Vedic scholars as the 'mystical', 'spiritual' or 'symbolic' phrases. However the literal meaning clearly means the ostrich. If the literal meaning is consistent with a particular ecological context from the pre-history of India, such meanings should apply. Thus we conclude that the ostrich was known to the *Rig-Vedic* people in the Early Holocene when the bird lived in India.

Giraffe (*Giraffa camelopardalis*)

Giraffe's habitat consists of savannah (grassland with widely-spaced trees), Sahel (transition zone between desert and savannah) and dry open woodlands, especially those regions which have the abundance of *Acacia*. Giraffe eats leaves of the trees, hence long and rising neck. They cannot survive in the dense and closed forests because their neck would get entangled by the branches of the trees. Once they get obstruction in escaping, they can be hunted down by the carnivore predators.

In Bhimbetka, many drawings pertain to the dromedary camel and at least one to the giraffe (Mathpal 1984:122, Fig. 27). Giraffe has been depicted in rock paintings in a large number of sites from Central India *e.g.* Pachmarhi, Adamgarh, Brihaspati Kund and many others which date back to the Late Pleistocene and early Holocene (Mathpal 1984:122). The drawings often depict hunting of this animal by a group of people (Mathpal 1984:53, 102, 17, 66). However some of these pictures depict, along with the giraffe, the animals of the wetter climate, like the rhinoceros etc indicating that the giraffe survived in Central India up to the early part of the mid-Holocene optimum, say 5000 BC or so.

"About 4,800 to 5,000 b.c. the historic times begin, when an entirely new race of people came in and founded the First Egyptian Dynasty. The Professor showed pictures of various utensils of this time, whereon, easily recognizable, were carved such animals as the **giraffe, lion, leopard, ibex,** and others, which have for long ages been extinct in the land." (emphasis added; Petrie 1902). We do not know wherefrom these artisans who made the utensils had arrived. But the faunal description matches the region spreading from modern Pakistan to Turkey going through Iran. The description shows that the giraffe was surviving in this region at least up to 5000 BC.

South and Central India had open ecosystems for long periods before mid-Holocene. It is possible that when the mid-Holocene optimum or the wet period arrived after 6000 BC, many of the giraffes which normally lived in dry climates did not die suddenly but met a slow extinction over some time and continued for some time in Central India even when the climate had become wet in the early part of the mid-Holocene. During this period the Bay of Bengal monsoon shifted to the Arabian Sea side and the eastern India became quite dry. Thus Central India became the transition zone between the wet western and the dry eastern India. Probably this is the reason why we get the depiction of giraffe along with the rhinoceros. The wet mid-Holocene coincides with our dating of the *Yajur-Veda*. We can say on the basis of archaeology and ecology, that the giraffe was certainly present in the early Holocene, the period of grasslands and open forests of northwest or rather whole of India, which is also our proposed date for the *Rig-Veda*.

Many authors have often dubbed these pictures found from India as "unidentified animal" or "the giraffe-like animal", which is not the fair description of these artefacts. Just as a spade is a spade, call a giraffe a giraffe. It has also been claimed by many that they represent depiction of some giraffe which might have been imported from Africa during the prehistoric times. These all are wild conjectures and reflect racist influence on historiography. Majority of the bones recovered from the Indian prehistory have never been identified, and no one can guarantee that no giraffe bone was actually present in those heaps of unidentified bones. If such bones have not been disposed with then it is desirable to have their DNAs extracted and tested.

India is home to the first two species of the genus *Giraffa viz. Giraffa priscilla* and *Giraffa punjabebsis* (Mitchell G. and Skinner: Abstrac; also p., 60). It entered East Africa from India through the then existing Indo-African land-bridge (*ibid*: Abstract). Therefore presence of giraffe in India should not be seen with any scepticism.

Falconer found two giraffe fossils from the Himalayas, which although resembled the modern *Giraffa camelopardalis*, yet were labelled the *Giraffa sivalensis*, because of the then prevailing custom of naming all the genera found from the Himalayas as "*sivalensis*" whether they be horse, or camel or the giraffe (Falconer 1868; Falconer and Cautley 1945-9).

One of the giraffes found in the Himalayas was exactly like the modern giraffe, except that it was only two-thirds the size of an adult: "a true well-marked species of giraffe closely resembling the existing species in form, but one-third less in height, and with a neck proportionately more slender" (Falconer and Cautley, cited by Mitchell and Skinner:60). It is clearly a description of a child or adolescent of the modern giraffe (Mitchell and Skinner: 60).

The second fossil was "all but indistinguishable from . . . the Nubian giraffe" (*ibid*). Nubian giraffe is a racial breed of the modern *Giraffa camelopardalis*, and is not at all a distinct species. Thus both the giraffes found by Falconer were modern, and should have been named *Giraffa camelopardalis*. But it is never too late and we should rename them as *Giraffa camelopardalis*.

The suggested date Early Pleistocene (*ibid*: 60) for these modern giraffe skeletons was not based on any physical or scientific method of dating but on the context of being found in the Himalayas. And everything found in the Himalayas was considered very old as per the then prevailing norm in the field of archaeology.

In 1846, when Falconer and Cautley published their report, no scientific method of dating was available. While doing the excavation Cautley reported that the fossils were all mixed up in heaps and jumbles in the Pinjaur (Pinjore) Valley, and the fossils were not excavated in true sense of the word, but searched out from the mess lying on the surface (Cautley 1835:586). Clearly there had been floods from the melting glaciers in past, land upheavals and earthquakes too, leading to turning up the fossils topsy-turvy. In a scientific study of the Pleistocene fauna of the Narmada Valley, Badam (1986) noted that there were often delayed burials of the bones secondary to some geological or climatic event.

Clearly the dates suggested for the fossils cannot be relied on. It is a shame that nobody worked on this issue, no radiocarbon dating has so far been done and no more efforts to search more fossils was ever done since the British left India. Only accusing the British will hot help, present day Indians themselves need to take spade and do the unfinished work. Thus it is not at all appropriate to accept those arbitrary dates fixed two centuries back. It is highly objectionable that these dates are accepted and applied to Indian prehistory and archaeology, without further investigation and examination.

In contrast to whatever dating was done by the nineteenth century British paleotologists working in India, it has been recently shown that the Pinjore surface, over which these fossils were found lying, had been formed as late as about 7,000 BC (Malik and Nakata 2003). The Sivalik fossils must have either been formed from the animals living there and dying in the Pinjore Dun itself, or much older fossils could have been brought there from the upstream as the washed down debris after 7000 BC from higher locations. However expecting such faunas in the still higher reaches of the Himalayas seems a bit far-fetched, and it is appropriate that we accept the date of these giraffes in the millennium following 7000 BC.

Finding of the extreme-cold adapted species like woolly mammoth along with the leaf-browser species giraffe side by side should have raised suspicion about the chronological mix up of the findings. Giraffe and woolly mammoth cannot live side by side. Moreover, the two giraffe samples, if they belonged to 500,000 BC, must have shown some difference from the modern giraffe skeleton, and not so much resemblance. Besides these facts, the savannah and the Sahel types of habitat with the sparse tall trees in wide grasslands without any snow cover existed in the Pinjaur Valley only as late as the Holocene, and the giraffe skeletons nust belong to that time. The fossils must always be examined and dated with great caution considering the food habits and the climatic requirements of the animals under consideration.

Insistence by some of the archaeologist for bone-recovery as a pre-condition for accepting the presence of any animal, even though pictures or other evidence abounds, is not fair. At least one thousand eggshells of ostrich have been found in India, but not a single definite ostrich bone. The ancient India giraffe, camel and horse were unfortunate not to have laid eggs, and it is only because of this reason that our archaeologists have so much difficulty in accepting their Early Holocene presence in India.

We must therefore accept that the giraffe was present in India up to the Early Holocene. In our examination, it is noted that the *Rig-Veda's* oldest portions pertain to this time and we also know that the riding of horse had started in India during the Mesolithic itself (Bhimbetka paintings and the *Rig-Vedic* literature). Hence the presence of a horse with a rider and a giraffe together in a rock-art is perfectly consistent finding.

Identification of the giraffe in the Vedic texts has not been done so far. We get descriptions of a bizarre animal in the *Rig-Veda* and *Yajur-Veda* which we cannot identify today. The animal has become extinct by this time and therefore has been considered fabulous by the scholars and translators of the Vedas today. We do not know which animal these references mean, but they could have meant the giraffe because we we know that the giraffe was present in India in the Early Holocene.

The *pṛṣatī* ('spotted one') and *pṛṣadaśva* ('spotted horse') of the *Rig-Veda* (1.37.2; 5.57.3; 5.58.6; 7.40.3; 8.7.28) describe an animal which is fierce, strong-bright (*vī□u-pavi*) and is the 'steed' or vehicle of the powerful wind-god *Marut*. Association with the wind-god is symbolic reference to the running-speed of the animal. Thus speed and strength and the spotted skin indicates that it was the giraffe.

At another place the *Rig-Veda* (5.55.6) mentions the name of this animal which is the vehicle of the god *Marut* as *bhrāja-dṛṣṭayaḥ* (ones with brilliant eyes) and *rukma-vakṣasaḥ* (the golden breasted ones). The giraffe has golden prominent chest.

At another place, the *Rig-Veda* (1.169.6) mentions this animal as the *pṛthubudhna*, which means one which has broad base (?sole of feet). These features described for this animal resemble the giraffe, not the 'spotted deer' that was suggested by Griffith. The animal *pṛṣatī* has been mention in the *White Yajuveda* as a divine vehicle-beast of the wind God *Maruta* (*White YV* 25.44). It is important to note that this animal was present in the *Rig-Veda* as well as in the white *Yajur-Veda*. This is consistent with giraffe's depiction along with the rhinoceros in some rock paintings.

Etymology: Sanskrit *pṛṣatī* (dictionary meaning: shaking cow, spotted antelope), *pṛṣant* (dappled, spotted), *pharās* (Vajjika-Bihari, an extinct animal), *ghor- pharās* (Vajjika, an animal which is in between a horse and a *pharās, Boselaphus tragocamelus*); Lith. *pur̃slas, pur̃sla* (flattery, froth of the salivary gland, saliva); *pur̃ kšti* (cat's snort of laughter, snaring); Latvian *pārsla* (blob of foam), Slav **parsa-* (dust, powder), [Pokorny: 823]; Pashto *parša* (cliff, rock, Pokorny:807).

The academic community has failed to accept the archaeological findings of the camels, ostriches and giraffes from the Rock Art of India, and have dubbed them as camel-like and giraffe-like animals. Clearly dubbing of these specimens as unidentified is evasion of responsibility and has been done on the basis of the present ecological description of India. However geo-climatic studies have revealed that the past ecology was very different and desert or semi-desert ecological situations prevailed in north India for a very long time.

Abbreviations

AD, *Anno Domino*, Common Era

API, *The Ayurvedic Pharmacopoea of India*, Part 1, Vol 1, A. Rajasekaran for Government of India, Dept of Ayush, Delhi, pdf edition.

AV, *Atharva-Veda*

BC, Before Common Era

CDIAL, *A Comparative Dictionary of the Indo-Aryan Languages* by Turner, R.L., OUP, London, 1962-1966.

CEDNL, *A Comparative and Etymological Dictionary of the Nepali Language*, Turner, R.L., Paul, Trench and Trubner, 1931.

CUP, Cambridge University Press

DED *Dravidian Etymology Dictionary* by Burrow, T.A., Clarendon Press, 1984 (2nd Ed.).

FAO, Food and Agriculture Organization.

GED, *A Goethic Etymology Dictionary*, by Lehmann, W.P., BRILL 1986.

H. Hindi

IAR *Indian Archaeology Review*.

IUCN (International Union for Conservation of Nature and Natural Resources) 2008, see under Valdez in Bibliography.

MHG, Middle High German

MWD, Monier-Williams Dictionary

O.E., Old English

OED, Oxford Etymology Dictionary

OHG, Old High German,

OUP, Oxford University Press

RCS, Royal Church Slavonic

RV, *Rig-Veda*

Sk., Sanskrit

SV, *Sama-Veda*

TS, *Taittiriya Samhita*, also known as the *Krishna* (Black) *Yajur-Veda*

VS, *Vajasaney Samhita*, also known as the *Shukla* (white) *Yajur-Veda*

YV, *Yajur-Veda*

Bibliography

A.A., 1940, Excavations at Harappa, *Current Science*, 1940, 9(10):473; book review of M.S. Vats 1940, *op. cit.* The author of the review preferred the AA initials to his name.

Abdulaziz, M. A-S. *et al*, 2009, Evaluation of the genetic variability of microsatellite markers in Saudi Arabian camels, *Journal of Food, Agriculture & Environment*, 7(2):636-639.

Abramovic, H. *et al*, 2012, Antioxidant and antimicrobial activity of extracts obtained from rosemary (*Rosmarinus officinalis*) and vine (*Vitis vinifera*) leaves, *Croat. J. Food Sci. Technol.*, 4(1):1-8.

Achar, B.N.N., 2000, On the astronomical basis of the date of *Satapatha Brahmana*, *Indian Journal of History of Science*, 35:1-19.

Achilli, A. *et al*, 2011, Mitochondrial genomes from modern horses reveal the major haplogroups that underwent domestication, *PNAS*, Early Ed. 1111637109.

Adams, D.Q., 1999, *A Dictionary of Tocharian B*, Rodopi.

Adams, R.P., 2014 (4th Edition), *Junipers of the World*, Trafford Publishing, USA.

Agrawal, D.P. *et al*, 1963, Tata Institute Radiocarbon Date List I, *Radiocarbon*, 5:273-282.

--------, *et al*, 1965, Tata Institute Radiocarbon Date List III, *Radiocarbon*, 7:291-295.

Ahmadi, M.T. *et al*, 2011, Rainfall Redistribution by an Oriental Beech (*Fagus orientalis* Lipsky) Forest Canopy in the Caspian Forest North of Iran, *J. Agr. Sci. Tech.*, 13:1105-1120.

Akhani, Hossein *et al*, 2010, Plant biodiversity of Hyrcanian relict forests, N. Iran: An overview of the flora, vegetation, palaeoecology and conservation, *Pak. J. Bot.*, Special Issue (S.I. Ali Festschrift) 42: 231-258.

Alba, Elenita, 1994, Archaeological evidences of animals as trade goods: A preliminary survey, *National Museum Papers*, 4(2):1-66.

Allaby, R.G. *et al*, 2005, Evidence of the domestication history of flax (*Linum usitatissimum* L.) from genetic diversity of sad2 locus, *Theoretical and Applied Genetics*, 112:58-65.

Allchin, B. and Allchin, R., 1982, *The Rise of Civilization in India and Pakistan*, Cambridge University Press.

Allchin, F.R. and Joshi, J.P., 1995, *Excavations at Malvan: Report of the Archaeological Survey of India and Cambridge University in 1970 on the Gujarat plan,* Archaeological Survey of India, New Delhi.

Allevato, E. *et al*, 2011, "Holocene environmental reconstruction in Southern Calabria (Italy): an integrated anthracological and pedological approach", Pedo-anthracology and Pre-Quaternary charcoal, SAGVNTVM Extra II, 5th International Meeting of Charcoal Analysis, Velencia, Spain, Sept. 5th-9th, 2011.

Ammerman, A.J. and Cavalli-Sforza, L.L., 1984, *The Neolithic Transition and the Genetics of Populations in Europe, Princeton University,* Press, Princeton, N.J.

Anderson, R.S. *et al.*, 2011, Postglacial history of alpine vegetation, fire, and climate from Laguna de Río Seco, Sierra Nevada, southern Spain, *Quaternary Science Reviews*, 30:1615-1629.

Andrews, C.W., 1910, Note on some Fragments of the Fossil Egg-shell of a large Struthious Bird from Southern Algeria with some Remarks on some Pieces of the Eggshell of an Ostrich from Northern India, *Internat. Ornith. Kongr*, Berlin, pp. 169-174.

Anekonda, S.M., 2006, Resveratrol—A boon for treating Alzheimer's disease? *Brain Research Reviews*, 52(2):316-326.

Anonymus, 1846, *The Magazine of Science*, Volume 7, Caled Turner Hackney Press, Church Street, London.

Anthony, D.W. and Brown, D., 1989, "Looking a gift horse in the mouth: identification of the earliest bitted equids and the microscopic analysis of bit wear," in Crabtree, P. *et al* (Eds.), *Animal domestication and its cultural context: Essays in honor of Dexter Perkins and Pat Dal*, Philadelphia, pp. 99–116.

Anthony, D. and Brown, D., 1991, The origins of horseback riding, *Antiquity* 65(246):22-38.

Anthony, D. and Brown, D., *2000*, Eneolithic horse exploitation in the Eurasian steppes: diet, ritual and riding, *Antiquity* 74: 75-86. The Dereivka horse claim was retracted in this article.

Anthony, D., 1997, Current thoughts on the domestication of the horse in Asia, *South Asian Studies*, 13:315-318; republished in part as Anthony 2005.

Anthony, D., 2005, "The Domestication of the Horse in Asia", in Trautmann, T.R. (Ed), *The Aryan Debate*, OUP, 2005/ 2007, pp. 251-253.

Anthony, D., 2009, *The horse, The Wheel and Language: How the Bronze Age riders from the Eurasian steppe shaped the modern world*, Princeton University Press.

Arnold, E.V., 1901, The *Rig Veda* and *Atharva Veda*, *Journal of the American Oriental Society*, 22:309-320.

Aruz, J. *et al* 2003, *Art of the First Cities: The Third Millennium B.C. from the Mediterranean to the Indus*, Metropolitan Museum of Art, New York.

Athar, M. *et al.*, 2007, Resveratrol: a review of preclinical studies for human cancer prevention, *Toxicol. Appl. Pharmacol.* 224(3):274–83.

Atharva-Veda Samhita, test and translations used included ones by Sri Ram Sharma Acharya, Haridwar; Bloomfield; Griffith.

Auffray J.C. *et al* 1990, The house mouse progression in Eurasia: a palaeontological and archaeozoological approach, *Biol. J. Linn. Soc.*, 41:13ñ25.

Ayurvedic Pharmacopoeia of India, Part I, Volume VI, First Edition, 2008, Government of India, New Delhi.

Azzarili, Augusto, 1975, Two Proto-historic Horse Skeletons from Swāt, Pakistan, *East and West*, 25(3/4):353-357.

Azzaroli, Augusto, 1985, *An Early History of Horsemanship*, BRILL.

B. N. Narahari Achar, 2000, On the Astronomical Basis for the date of Satapatha Brahmana: A Re-examination of Dikshit's theory, *Ind. Jour. Hist. Sci.* 35:1-10.

Badam, G.L. *et al*, 1986, Preliminary taphonomical studies of some Pleistocene fauna from the Central Narmada Valley, Madhya Pradesh, India, *Palaeogeography, Palaeoclimatology, Palaeoecology*, 53(2-4):335-348.

Badam, G.L., 1985, "The Late Quaternary Fauna of Imamgaon", in Misra, V.N. and Bellwood, P. (Eds.), *Recent Advances in the Indo-Pacific Prehistory: Proceedings of the International Symposium Held at Poona, December 19-21, 1978*, BRILL.

Banerjee, P. *et al*, 2012, Population Differentiation in Dromedarian Camel: A Comparative Study of Camel Inhabiting Extremes of Geographical Distribution, *International Journal of Animal and Veterinary Advances*, 4(2):84-92.

Bankoff, Greg, 2004, Bestia Incognita: The horse and its history in the Philippines 1880–1930, *Anthrozoös*, 17(1):3-25.

Barger, J.L. *et al.*, 2008, A Low Dose of Dietary Resveratrol Partially Mimics Caloric Restriction and Retards Aging Parameters in Mice, *PLoS ONE*, 3(6):e2264. doi:10.1371/journal.pone.0002264

Battarbee, R.W. and Binney, H.A., 2009, *Natural Climate Variability and Global Warming: A Holocene Perspective*, John Wiley and Sons.

Beck, Hans T., 2005, "Caffeine, Alcohol, and Sweeteners", in Prance, G. and Nesbitt, M. (Eds.), *The Cultural History of Plants*, Routledge, New York/London.

Bedigian, D. and Harlan, J.H., 1986, Evidence for the cultivation of sesame in the ancient world, *Economic Botany*, 40(2):137-154.

Bednarik, R., 1993, About Palaeolithic ostrich eggshell in India, *Indo-Pacific Prehistory Association Bulletin*, 13:34-43.

Bednarik, R., 2003, The earliest evidence of palaeoart, *Rock Art Research*, 20:89–135.

Beech, M. *et al*, 2009, Prehistoric camels in south-eastern Arabia: the discovery of a new site in Abu Dhabi's Western Region, United Arab Emirates, *Proceedings of the Seminar for Arabian Studies*, 39:17–30.

Bellow, H.W., *A Dictionary of the Pukkhto Or Pukshto Language*, 1867.

Bellwood, P., and Renfrew, Colin (Eds.), 2002, *Examining The Farming/language Dispersal Hypothesis*, McDonald Institute for Archaeological Research, Cambridge.

--------, *et al.*, 2005, *First Farmers: The Origins of Agricultural Societies*, Wiley-Blackwell, Oxford.

--------, and Oxenham, Marc, 2008, "The expansion of farming societies and the role of Neolithic Demographic transition", in Jean-Pierre, Bocquet-Appel and Ofer Bar-Yosef (Eds.), *The Neolithic Demographic Transition and its Consequences*, Springer, Netherland.

Bengston, J.D. and Ruhlen, M., 1994, "Global Etymologies", in Ruhlen, Merritt (Eds.); *On the Origin of Languages: Studies in Linguistic Taxonomy*, Stanford University Press, Stanford, pp. 277-336.

Bennett, Casey and Kaestle, Frederika A., 2010, Investigation of Ancient DNA from Western Siberia and the Sargat Culture, *Human Biology*, 82(2):143-156.

Benniamin, A, 2011, Medicinal ferns of northestern India with special reference to Arunachal Pradesh, *Indian Journal of Traditional Knowledge*, 10(3): 516-522.

Bhargava, M.L., 1964, *The Geography of Rig Vedic India*, Upper India publishing house, Lucknow.

Bhatnagar, S.P. and Moitra, Alok, 1996, *Gymnosperms*, New Age International.

Bhattacharyya, A., 1991, Ethnobotanical observations in the Ladakh region of northern Jammu and Kashmir state, India, *Economic Botany*, 45(3): 305-308.

Bidwell, E., 1910, Remarks on some fragments of Egg-shell of a fossil Ostrich from India, *Bull. Brit. Orn. Club.*, 759-761, cited in Kálmám, Lambrecht, *Bibliographia palaeo-ornithologica usque ad annum* 1916.

Bjune, A.E. *et al*, 2004, Holocene vegetation and climate history on a continental–oceanic transect in northern Fennoscandia based on pollen and plant macrofossils, *Boreas*, 33:211-223.

Black, Jeremy *at al*, 2000, *A Concise Dictionary of Akkadian*, Otto Harrassowitz Verlag.

--------, 2006, *The Literature of Ancient Sumer*, Oxford University Press.

Blackburn, H.D. *et al*, 2006, Genetic diversity of *Ovis aries* populations near domestication centres and in the New World, *Genetica*, 126(1-2):Online publication.

Bloch, Jules, 1936, *La Charrue védique*, *Bulletin of the School of Oriental Studies, University of London*, 8(2/3): 411-418. Indian and Iranian Studies: Presented to George Abraham Grierson on His Eighty-Fifth Birthday.

Bloomfield, M., 1897, *Hymns of the Atharva-Veda together with extracts from the ritual books and the commentaries translated by Maurice Bloomfield*, Sacred Books of the East, Volume 42.

Blyakharchuk, T.A. *et al* 2004, Late Glacial and Holocene vegetational changes on the Ulagan high-mountain plateau, Altai Mountains, southern Siberia, *Palaeogeography, Palaeoclimatology, Palaeoecology*, 209:259–279.

Blyakharchuk, T.A. *et al*, 2007, Late Glacial and Holocene vegetational history of the Altai Mountains (southwestern Tuva Republic, Siberia), *Palaeogeography, Palaeoclimatology, Palaeoecology*, 245:518–534.

Bokonyi, S., 1969, "Archaeological Problems and Methods of Recognising Animal Domestication", in Ucko, P. and Dimbleby, G. (Eds.), *The Domestication and Exploitation of Plants and Animals*, Duckworth, London, pp. 219-232.

-------, 2005, "Horse Remains from Surkotada", in Trautmann, T.R. (Ed), *The Aryan Debate*, Oxford, OUP, reprinted 2007, pp. 237-242. Originally published 1997 in *South Asian Studies*, 13:308-315.

Bolte, A. *et al*, 2007, The north-eastern distribution range of European beech--a review, *Forestry*, 80(4):413-429.

Bömcke, E. *et al*, 2010, Genetic variability in the Skyros pony and its relationship with other Greek and foreign horse breeds, *Genetics and Molecular Biology*, advance online pdf version, *Sociedade Brasileira de Genética*. Later published as *ibid*, 2011, 34(1):68-76.

Boon, H. and Smith, M., 2004, *The Complete Natural Medicine Guide to the 50 Most Common Medicinal Herbs*, Robert Rose.

Bornstein, S., 1990, The ship of the desert. The dromedary camel *(Camelus dromedarius)*, a domesticated animal species well adapted to extreme conditions of aridness and heat, *Rangifer*, Special Issue (3): 231-236.

Bouby, L. *et al*, 2013, Bioarchaeological Insights into the Process of Domestication of Grapevine (*Vitis vinifera* L.) during Roman Times in Southern France, *PLoS ONE* 8(5):e63195. doi:10.1371/journal.pone.0063195.

Bouckaert, R. *et al*, 2012, Mapping the Origins and Expansion of the Indo-European Language Family, Science, 337(6097):957-960.

Boursot, P. *et al* 1993, Evolution of House Mice, *Annual Review of Ecology and Systematics* 24:119-152.

--------, 1996, Origin and radiation of the house mouse: mitochondrial DNA phylogeny, *Journal of Evolutionary Biology*, 9:391-415.

Bowling, A.T. *et al*, 2003, Genetic variation in Przewalski's horses, with special focus on the last wild caught mare, 231 Orlitza III, *Cytogenet Genome Res*, 101: 226–234.

Bramanti, B. *et al*, 2009, Genetic discontinuity between local hunter-gatherers and Central Europe's first farmers, *Science* 326:137-140.

Breitmaier, E., 2006, *Terpenes: Flavors, Fragrances, Pharmaca, Pheromones*, John Wiley and Sons.

Briggs, Keith (transliterator), 2010, *Rig Veda, a metrically restored text*, by van Nooten, Barend A. and Holland, Gary B., Harvard Oriental Series, Harvard Oriental, vol. 50.

Brittain, W., Paterson, Row and Turner, Caled (Editors and Printers), 1846, *The Magazine of Science and School of Arts*, Vol 7, London.

Brown, T.A. *et al*, 2008, The complex origins of domesticated crops in the Fertile Crescent, Trends in Ecology and Evolution, 30(10):Advance web release.

Bryant, Edwin, 2001, *Quest for the Original Vedic Culture*, Oxford, OUP.

Burrow, T., 1947, Dravidian Studies VI: The loss of initial c/s in South Dravidian, *Bulletin of School of Oriental and African Studies*, 12:132-147.

--------, 1948, Dravidian Studies VII: Further Dravidian words in Sanskrit, *Bulletin of School of Oriental and African Studies*, 12:365-396.

Buxton, Richard, 1849, *A Botanical Guide to Flowering Plants Ferns, Mosses, and Algæ, Found Indigenous Within Sixteen Miles of Manchester: With Some Information as to Their Agricultural, Medicinal, and Other Uses*, Longman and Company.

Cai, D. *et al*, 2009, Ancient DNA provides new insights into the origin of the Chinese domestic horse, *Journal of Archaeological Science* 36:835–842.

Cambridge, University of, 2014, News, Decline of Bronze Age 'megacities' linked to climate change, 27 February 2014.

Carpenter, C.D. *et al*, 2012, Anti-mycobacterial natural products from the Canadian medicinal plant Juniperus communis, *J Ethnopharmacology*, 43(2):695-700.

Carroll, F.A., *et al*, 2012, Holocene climate change, vegetation history and human impact in the Central Mediterranean: evidence from the Maltese Islands, *Quaternary Science Reviews*, 52:24-40.

Cautley, P.T., 1835, "Extract of the private letter from Captain Cautley to the Secretary" in the *Proceedings of the Asiatic Society, Wednesday Evening, the 4th November, 1835*, published in the *Journal of the Asiatic Society of Bengal*, 4:586-7.

Cermak, Jan *et al*, 2005, "Isolated Mountain Forests in Central Asian Deserts: A Case Study from the Govi Altay, Mongolia," in Broll, G. and Keplin, B. (Eds.), *Mountain Ecosystems: Studies in Treeline Ecology*, Springer, pp. 253-273.

Chakrabarti, D.K., 1999, *India: An Archaeological History*, N Delhi, OUP.

Chakravarty, K.K. and Bednarik, R.G., 1997, *Indian Rock Art and its Global Context*, Motilal Banarsidass, Delhi.

Champion, H.G. and Seth, S.K., 1968, *A revised survey of the forest types of India*, Manager of Publications, Delhi, India.

Chatterji, L., 2005, *Heritage of Harappa*, Volume 1, Global Vision Pub House.

Chauhan, M.S., 1995, Origin and history of tropical deciduous Sal (*Shorea robusta* Gaertn.) forests in Madhya Pradesh, India, *Palaeobotanist*, 43(1):89-101.

--------, and Quamar, M.F., 2012, Mid-Holocene vegetation *vis-à-vis* climate change in southwestern Madhya Pradesh, India, *Current Science*, 103(12): 1455-1461.

Chen, F. *et al*, 2009, Holocene climate variability in Arid Asia: Nature and mechanism (Editorial), *Quaternary International*, 194:1-5.

Chen, S. *et al*, 2009, Zebu cattle are an exclusive legacy of the South Asian Neolithic, *Molecular Biology and Evolution*, 0:msp213v1-msp213.

Chen, S.-Y. *et al*, 2005, Mitochondrial diversity and phylogeographic structure of Chinese domestic goats, *Molecular Phylogenetics and Evolution*, 37:804-814.

Chen, W., Wang, W.M., Dai, X.R., 2009, Holocene vegetation history with implication of human impact in the lake Chaohu area, Anhui Province, East China, *Vegetation History and Archaeobotany,* 18:137e146.

Chunxiang Li *et al*, 2010, Evidence that a West-East admixed population lived in the Tarim Basin as early as the early Bronze Age, *BMC Biology* 2010, **8:**15doi:10.1186/1741-7007-8-15.

Cieslak, M., 2010, Origin and history of mitochondrial DNA lineages in domestic horses, *PLOS*, 5(22):e15311.

Clark, E.L. *et al* (compilers and editors), 2006, *Summary Conservation Action Plans for Mongolian Mammals: Regional Red List Series Vol. 2.* Zoological Society of London (In English and Mongolian).

Clift, P.D. *et al*, 2012, U-Pb zircon dating evidence for a Pleistocene Saraswati River and capture of the Yamuna River, *Geology*, 40:211-214; DOI 10.1130/G32840.1.

Compagnoni, B., and M. Tosi. 1978, "The camel: Its distribution and state of domestication in the Middle East during the third millennium B.C. in light of finds from Shahr-i Sokhta", in Meadow, R.H. and Zeder, M.A. (Eds.), *Approaches to faunal analysis in the Middle East*, pp. 91-103, Peabody Museum Bulletin 2, Cambridge.

Comrie, Bernard, 2002, "Farming dispersal in Europe and the spread of the Indo-European language family", in Bellwood, P. and Renfraw, C. (Eds.), *Examining The Farming/language Dispersal Hypothesis*, McDonald Institute for Archaeological Research, University of Cambridge.

Conner, S.E., 2006, *A Promethean Legacy: Late Quaternary Vegetation History of Southern Georgia, Caucasus*, Ph. D. Thesis submitted to the School of Anthropology, Geography and Environmental Studies, and School of Art History, Cinema, Classics and Archaeology, University of Melbourne.

Cortesi, E. *et al*, 2008, Cultural Relationships beyond the Iranian Plateau: The Helmand Civilization, Baluchistan and the Indus Valley in the 3rd Millennium BCE, *Paléorient*, 34(2):5-35.

Costantini L. and Lentini A. 2000. "Studies in the Vegetation History of Central Baluchistan, Pakistan: Palynological Investigations of a Neolithic Sequence at Mehrgarh", in Taddei, M. and De Marco, G. (Eds.), *South Asian Archaeology 1997*, pp. 133-159, *Istituto Italiano per l'Africa e l'Oriente*, Rome.

Costantini, Lorenzo, 2008, The first farmers in western Pakistan: the evidence of the Neolithic Agro-Pastoral settlement of the Mehrgarh, *Pragdhara*, 18:166-178.

Costantini, Lorenzo, *The Archaeology of Agro-Biodiversity*, Food and Agriculture Organization of the United Nations, on the net, accessed 18 May 2014.

Crabtree, P.J. and Champana, D.V., 1989, "The contributions of Dexter Perkins, Jr. and Patricia Daly to zooarchaeological studies and their implications for contemporary faunal research", Crabtree, P.J. *et al* (Eds.), *Early Animal Domestication and Its Cultural context: Dedicated to the Memory of Dexter Perkins, Jr. and Patricia Daly*, pp. 5-13, UPenn Museum of Archaeology.

Crellin, J.K., 1994, *Home Medicine: Newfoundland experience*, McGill-Queen's Press– MQUP.

Crooke, W., 1906, *Things Indian: Being Discursive Notes on Various Subjects Connected with India*, John Murray, London.

Crystal, David, 1987, 1992 (reprint), *The Cambridge Encyclopedia of Language*, Cambridge University Press.

Culpeper, Nicholas, republished 1816 (original 1653), *Culpeper's complete herbal*, Richard Evans, London.

Dandekar, R. N., 1947, "The Antecedents and the Early Beginnings of the Vedic Period", *Indian History Congress Proceedings of the 10th session.*

Dani, A.H. and Masson, V.M., 1999, *History of Civilizations of Central Asia*, Vol 1, Delhi, Motilal Banarsidas.

Davis, B.A.S., 1994, *Palaeolimnology and Holocene Environmental Change from Endoreic Lakesin the Ebro Basin, Morth-East Spain*, Ph D Thesis, the University of Newcastle Upon Tyne.

Dennel, Robin and Porr, Martin, 2014, *Southern Asia, Australia and the Search for Human Origins*, Cambridge University Press.

Deotare, B.C. *et al*, 2004a, Late Quaternary geomorphology, palynology and magnetic susceptibility of playas in western margin of the Indian Thar Desert, *J. Geophys. Union*, 8(1):15-25.

--------, *et al*, 2004b, Palaeoenvironmental history of Bap-Malar and Kanod playas of western Rajasthan, Thar desert, *Journal of Earth System Science*, 113(3):403-425.

Deraniyagala, S.U., 1992, *The prehistory of Sri Lanka: An ecological perspective*, Department of the Archaeological Survey, Government of Sri Lanka. Colombo.

Devi, K.M. and Ghosh, S.K., 2013, Molecular phylogeny of Indian horse breeds with special reference to Manipuri pony based on mitochondrial D-loop, *Mol. Bio. Rep.*, 40(10):5861-7.

Dhavalikar, M.K., 1984, Toward an ecological model for Chalcolithic Cultures of Central and Western India, *Journal of Anthropological Archaeology*, 3:133-158.

Digerfeldt, G. *et al*, 2007, Reconstruction of Holocene lake-level changes in Lake Xinias, central Greece, *The Holocene*, 17(3):361-367.

Dikshit, K.N. and Mani, B.R., 2013, The origin of Indian civilization buried under the sands of 'Lost' River Saraswati, *Dialogue*, 15(1):47-59.

Dikshit, K.N., 1938, Lectures on the Prehistoric Civilization of the Indus Valley, Madras.

Dikshit, K.N., 2009, *Jhusi*, Indian Archaeological Society, New Delhi.

Din, W. *et al*, 1996, Origin and radiation of the house mouse: clues from nuclear genes, *Journal of Evolutionary Biology*, 9-5:519-539.

Dixit, Y. *et al*, 2014, Abrupt weakening of the summer monsoon, in northwest India~4100 years ago, *Geology*, doi:10.1130/G35236.1.

Djamali, M. *et al*, 2009, A late Holocene pollen record from Lake Almalou in NW Iran: evidence for changing land-use in relation to some historical events during the last 3700 years, *Journal of Archaeological Science*, 36:1364–1375.

Dogette, H., 1991, "Sorghum history in relation to Ethiopia", in Engels, J.M.M. *et al* (Eds.), *Plant Genetic Resources of Ethiopia*, Cambridge University Press.

Doherty, Colin, 2012, *Ficus religiosa - New Crop Summary & Recommendations*, New crop report, Horticultural Science 5051: Plant Production II, University of Minnesota.

Dolukhanov, P. *et al*, 2005, The chronology of Neolithic dispersal in Central and Eastern Europe, *Journal of Archaeological Science*, 32:1441-1458.

--------, *et al*, 2010, Early pottery makers in Eastern Europe: Centres of origins, subsistence and dispersal in Jordan, P. and Zvelebil (Eds.), *Ceramics before farming: The dispersal of pottery among prehistoric Eurasian*, California, Left Coast Press.

Drews, Robert, 2004, *Early Riders*, Routledge, London/New York.

Duerst, J.U., 1908, "Animal remains from the excavation at Anau in its relation to the history and to the races of domesticated horse" in Pumpelly, R. (Ed.), *Explorations in Turkestan, Expedition of 1904*, Carnegie Institute of Washington, Washington D.C., pp. 341-442.

Dunn, M. *et al*, 2011, Evolved structure of language shows lineage-specific trends in word-order universals, *Nature*, 473:79-82.

Duplantier, J-M. *et al* 2002, Evidence for a mitochondrial lineage originating from the Arabian peninsula in the Madagascar house mouse (*Mus musculus*), *Heredity* 89: 154-158.

Dyer, J., 2013, *Wild Horses and Other Stories*, eBookIt.com.

Dymoc, W., Warden, C.J.H. and Hooper, D., 1892, *Pharmacographia Indica: A history of the principal drugs of vegetable origin met with in British India*, Part V, Kegan Paul, Trench Trubner and Co. Ltd, London.

Edge, W. D. and Oslon-Edge, S. L., 1987, *'Ecology of wild goats and urial in Kirthar National Park, Pakistan', Final report*, Montana Cooperative Wildlife Research Unit, University of Montana, USA.

Eggeling, Julius (translator), 1900, *The Satapatha Brahmana: according to the text of the Madhyandina School, Part V*, being the Volume XLIV of Muller, Max F. (Series Editor), *The Sacred Books of the East: translated by various oriental scholars*, Oxford at Clarendon Press.

Elina, G. A. *et al*, 2010, *Late Glacial and Holocene palaeovegetation and palaeogeography of Eastern Fennoscandia, Finnish Environment 4*, Finnish Environment Institute, Helsinki.

Elšík, Viktor, 2009, "Loanwords in Selice Romani, an Indo-Aryan language of Slovakia", in Haspelmath, M. and Tadmor, U. (Eds.), *Loanwords in the World's Languages: A comparative handbook*, Walter de Gruyter, pp. 260-303.

Engels, J.M.M. and Hawkes, J.G., 1991, "The Ethiopian gene centre and its genetic diversity", in Engels, J.M.M., Hawks, J.G. and Worede, M. (Eds.), *Plant Genetic Resources of Ethiopia*, Cambridge University Press, pp. 23-41.

Enzel, Y. *et al*, 1999, High-Resolution Holocene Environmental Changes in the Thar Desert, Northwestern India, *Science*, 284:125-128.

Epstein, H. and Mason, I.L., 1971, *The origin of the domestic animals of Africa*, African Pub Corp.

Erkan, P. *et al*, 2011, Analysis of airborne pollen grains in Kırklareli, *Turk J Bot*, 35:57-65.

Evans, L.T., 1996, *Crop Evolution, Adaptation and Yield*, Cambridge University Press.

Ewart, J.C., 1909, The possible ancestors of the horses living under domestication, *Proceedings of the Royal Society of London Series B: Containing papers of a biological character*, 81:392-397; also published in *Science* 1909 by the American Society for the Advancement of Science.

--------, 1911, "Animal Remains", in Curle, James (Ed.), *A Roman Frontier Post and its People*, Appendix II, Society for Antiquaries of Scotland, Glasgow.

Falconer, H., 1868, (edited Murchison, Charles), *Palaeontological Memoirs and Notes of the late Hugh Falconer: With a Biographical Sketch of the Author Compiled and edited by Charles Murchison*, Robert Hardwicke, London.

Fallon, S.W.A., 1879, *A New Hindustani-English Dictionary with illustrations from Hindustani literature and folk-lore*, Turbner and Co., London-Benaras.

Farjon A., 2010, *A handbook of the World's conifers*, BRILL, Leiden.

Farooqui, A. *et al*, 2013, Climate, Vegetation and Ecology during Harappan Period: Excavations at Kanjetar and Kaj, Mid-Saurashtra coast, Gujarat, *J. Archaeol. Sci.*, 40(6): 2631-2647.

Fentress, Marcia, 1985, "Water resources and double cropping in Harappa food production", in Misra, V.N. and Bellwood, P. (Eds.), *Recent Advances in the Indo-Pacific Prehistory: Proceedings of the International Symposium Held at Poona, December 19-21, 1978*, BRILL.

Fernandez, H. *et al*, 2006, Divergent mtDNA lineages of goats in an Early Neolithic site, far from the initial domestication areas, *PNAS*, 103(42): 15375–15379.

Fernández, Santiago *et al*, 2007, The Holocene and Upper Pleistocene pollen sequence of Carihuela Cave, southern Spain, *Geobios*, 40(1):75–90.

Ferris, S.D. *et al* 1983, Mitochondrial DNA evolution in mice, *Genetics*, 105-3:681-721.

Feurdean, A., 2001, A Paleoecological reconstruction of the late glacial and Holocene based on multi-disciplinary studies Steregoiu site (Gutai Mts., NW Romania), *Geologia*, 46:125-140

Fineschi, S. *et al*, 2002, Chloroplast DNA variation of white oaks in Italy, *Forest Ecology and Management*,156:103–114.

Finsinger, W. *et al*, 2006, The expansion of hazel (*Corylus avellana* L.) in the southern Alps: a key for understanding its early Holocene history in Europe? *Quaternary Science Reviews* 25:612–631.

--------, *et al*, 2010, Early to mid-Holocene climate change at Lago dell'Accesa (central Italy): climate signal or anthropogenic bias? *Journal of Quaternary Science*, 25(8):1239–1247

Firouz, L.L., 1998, "The original ancestors of the Turkoman Caspian horses", presented at the first international Conference on Turkoman Horses, Ashgabat, Turkmenistan, May 1998.

Forsten, A. and Sharapov, S., 2000, Fossil Equids (Mammalia, Equidae) from the Neogene and Pleistocene of Tadzhikistan, *Geodiversitas*, 22(2):293-314.

Frachetti, M. and Benecke, N., 2009, From sheep to (some) horses:4500 years of herd structure at the pastoralist settlement of Begash (south-eastern Kazakhstan), *Antiquity*, 83: 1023–1037.

--------, 2012, Multiregional Emergence of Mobile Pastoralism and Non-uniform Institutional Complexity across Eurasia, *Current Anthropology*, 53(1):1-38.

Francfort, P.H., 1992, Evidence for Harappan irrigation system, *Eastern Anthropologist*, 45:87-103.

Freeman A. R., *et al*, 2006, Combination of multiple microsatellite data sets to investigate genetic diversity and admixture of domestic cattle, *Anim. Genet.*, 37 (1):1-9.

Frisina, M.R., 2001, Status of the Punjab urial (*Ovis orientalis [vignei] punjabiensis*) population in the Kalabagh Salt Range of Punjab Province, Pakistan, IUCN Report.

Fuller, D.Q. and Boivin, N., 2009, Crops, cattle and commensals across the Indian Ocean Current and Potential Archaeobiological Evidence, *Etudes Ocean indien*, 42-43:2-24.

-------, 2008, "The spread of textile production and textile crops in India beyond the Harappan zone: an aspect of the emergence of craft specialization and systematic trade", in Osada, Toshiki and Uesugi, Akinori (Eds.), *Linguistics, Archaeology and Human Past*, Indus Project, Kyoto, Japan, pp. 1-26.

--------, and Harvey, E.L., 2006, The archaeobotany of Indian pulses: identification, processing and evidence for cultivation, *Environmental Ecology*, 11(2):219-246.

--------, and Madella, M., 2002, "Issues in Harappan archaeobotany: Retrospect and Prospect", in Settar, S. and Korisettar, R. (Eds.), *Indian Archaeology in Retrospect: Protohistory: archaeology of the Harrappan civilization*, Volume 2, Indian Council of Historical Research, New Delhi.

--------, 2006, Agricultural Origins and Frontiers in South Asia: A Working Synthesis, *J World Prehist*, 20:1–86.

Fussi, B. *et al*, 2010, Phylogeography of *Populus alba* (L.) and *Populus tremula* (L.) in Central Europe: secondary contact and hybridization during recolonization from disconnected refugia, Tree Genetics and Genomics, 6:439-450.

Gaillard, M.-J., 2010, Holocene land-cover reconstructions for studies on land cover-climate feedbacks, *Clim. Past*, 6:483–499.

Gamqrelize, T and Ivanov, V. V., 1995, *Indo-European and the Indo-Europeans. A Reconstruction and Historical Analysis of a Proto-Language and a Proto-Culture*, Vol 2, M. de Gruyter.

Garzilli, E., 2003, The Flowers of *Ṛg-Veda* hymns: Lotus in V.78.7, X.184.2, X.107.10, VI.16.13 and VII.33.11, VI.61.2, VIII.1.33, X.142.8, *Indo-Iranian Journal*, 46(4):293-314.

George, R., 2003a, *The Wines of South of France*, Hachette, UK.

--------, 2003b, "Drinking Wine", in Sandler, M. and Oinder, R. (Eds.), *Wine: A Scientific Exploration*, CRC Press.

Ghosh, A., 1990, *An Encyclopaedia of Indian Archaeology*, Leiden, BRILL.

Ghosh, M., 1976, Record of the prehistoric remains of two humped Asiatic camel (*Camelus bactrianus* Linn) from Kausambi, Uttar Pradesh, India, *Science and Culture*, 42: 161-162.

Giardini, M. *et al*, 2013, Archaeobotanical investigations and human impact at the Imperial Harbour of Rome, *Ann. Bot. (Roma)*, 3:199-205.

Giesecke, T. *et al*, 2007, Towards an understanding of the Holocene distribution of *Fagus sylvatica* L. *J. Biogeogr.*, 34:118-131.

--------, *et al*, 2012, Exploring Holocene Changes in Palynological Richness in Northern Europe – Did Postglacial Immigration Matter? *PLoS ONE*, 7(12): e51624. doi:10.1371/journal.pone.0051624.

Gimbutas, M., *The Prehistory of Eastern Europe, Part 1*, 1956.

Giosan, L. *et al*, 2012, Fluvial landscapes of the Harappan civilization, *PNAS* 109(26): E1688-E1694.

Gopal, Lallanji, 2008, "Technique and Process of Agriculture in Early Mieval India (c. AD 700-1200)", in Gopal, Lallanji (Ed.), *History of Agriculture in India, Up to C. 1200 A.D.*, Concept Publishing Company.

Gordon, C.H., 1939, Western Asiatic seals in the Walters Art Gallery, *Iraq*, 6(1):3-34.

Goyal, P. *et al*, 2013, Subsistence system, palaeoecology, and 14C chronology at Kanmer, A Harappan site in Gujarat, India, *Radiocarbon*, 55(1):141–150.

Gray, R. D. and Atkinson, Q. D., 2003, Language-tree divergence times support the Anatolian theory of Indo-European origin, *Nature*, 426: 435-439.

Griffith, Ralph (Translator), 1896, *The Hymns of the Rig-Veda*, E.J. Lazarus and Co., Benares.

Groves, Colin P., 1995, "Domesticated and Commensal Mammals of Austronesia and Their Histories", in Bellwood, P., Fox, J. and Tryon, D., *The Austronesians: Historical and Comparative Perspectives*, republished ANU E Press, 2006.

Gupta, Anil K., 2004, Origin of agriculture and domestication of plants and animals linked to early Holocene climate amelioration, *Current Science*, 87(1):59.

Gupta, S.P., 2001, River Saraswati in History, Archaeology, and Geology, *Puratattva*, 31: 30-38.

-------, 2005, "The Indus-Sarasvati Civilization", in Trautmann, T.R. (Ed), *The Aryan Debate*, OUP, 2005. Reprinted as Oxford India Paperbacks, 2007, pp. 156-204.

Haak, W. *et al*, 2005, Ancient DNA from the first European farmers in 7500-year-old Neolithic sites, *Science*, 310:1016-1018.

--------, *et al*, 2010, Ancient DNA from European Early Neolithic Farmers Reveals Their Near Eastern Affinities, *PLoS Biology*, 8(11): e1000536. doi:10.1371/journal.pbio.1000536

Haddad Junior, V. *et al*, 2006, Venomous mollusks: the risks of human accidents by *Conus* snails (Gastropoda: Conidae) in Brazil, *Revista da Sociedade Brasileira de Medicina Tropical*, 39(5):498-500.

Hammond, N., 2008, *Wtg Trees*, New Holland Publishers.

Harlan, J.R. *et al*, 1970, Origin and distribution of the Seleucidus race of *Cynodon dactylon* (L.) Pers. var Dactylon, Graminae, *Euphytica* 19:465-469.

Harman, B.J., 2010, *Kimberly's Song*, Author House.

Harper, Douglas, *Online Etymology Dictionary*, web site etymonline.com. Accessed 6 June 2011.

Harris, D.R., 2011 (reprint of 2010), *Origins of Agriculture in Western Central Asia: An Environmental-Archaeological Study*, University of Pennsylvania Press.

Hawkins, B.W., 1866, *The Artistic Anatomy of the Horse*, Winsor and Newton.

Hellar, C.A. and Beniwits, N.L., 2000, Adverse cardiovascular and central nervous system events associated with dietary supplements containing ephedra alkaloids, *New England Journal of Medicine*, 343(25):1833-8.

Hellenthal,, G. *et al*, 2014, A Genetic Atlas of Human Admixture History, *Science*, 343:747-751.

Hemphill, B.E., 1999a, Biological affinities and adaptations of Bronze Age Bactrians: IV. A craniometric investigation of Bactrian origins, *Am. J. Phys. Anthropol.*, 108(2):173-192.

--------, 1999b, Foreign elites from the Oxus civilization? A craniometric study of anomalous burials from Bronze Age Tepe Hissar, *Am J Phys Anthropology*, 110(4):421-34.

---------, and Mallory, J.P., 2004, Horse-mounted invaders from the Russo-Kazakh steppe or agricultural colonists from Western Central Asia? A craniometric investigation of the Bronze Age settlement of Xinjiang, *American Journal of Physical Anthropology*, 125: 199-222.

Hendricks, B.L., 1995, *International Encyclopedia of Horse Breeds*, University of Oklahoma Press, Oklahoma.

Herzschuh, U. *et al*, 2004, Holocene vegetation and climate of the Alashan Plateau, NW China, reconstructed from pollen data, *Palaeogeography, Palaeoclimatology, Palaeoecology* 211:1– 17.

Hiendleder, S. *et al*, 1998, Analysis of Mitochondrial DNA Indicates that Domestic Sheep are derived from two different ancestral maternal sources: No Evidence for Contributions From Urial and Argali Sheep, *Journal of Heredity*, 89:113–120.

--------, *et al*, 2002, Molecular analysis of wild and domestic sheep questions current nomenclature and provides evidence for domestication from two different subspecies, *Proc Biol Sc*, 269(1494):893-904.

Higgins, G., 2012, *Horse Anatomy for Performance*, David and Charles.

Hijma, M.P. and Cohen, K.M., 2010, Timing and magnitude of the sea-level jump preluding the 8200 yr event, *Geology*, 38:275-278.

Hook. f. (Hooker, Joseph Dalton), and Thomson, Thomas (and Ex Author Brandis, E.), "*Juniperus wallichiana* Hook. f. & Thomson ex E. Brandis ", in *The forest flora of North-West and Central India*, 1874.

Hussein, K.M., 2006, Climatic characteristics of the Late Pleistocene and Holocene continental deposits from southwestern Syria based on palynological data, *Darwiniana*, 44-2:329-340.

Hytteborn, H., 2005, "Boreal Forests of Eurasia", in Andersson, F.A. (Ed.) *Cuniform Forests*, Vol. 6 of *Ecosystems of the World*, Elsavier.

Indian Archaeology Review (IAR), Burzahom 1960–1961:11; 1961–1962:17–21; 1962–1963: 9–10; 1964–1965:13; 1965–1966:19; 1968–1969:10; 1971–1972: 24; Kaw 1989) and Gufkral (*IAR* 1981–1982, pp 19–25). quoted by Misra 2001, *q.v.*

Isaksson, S., 2009, Vessels of Change: A long-term perspective on prehistoric pottery use in southern and eastern middle Sweden based on lipid residue analyses, *Current Swedish Archaeology*, 17:131-149.

Issar, A.S., 2003, *Climate Changes during the Holocene and their Impact on Hydrological Systems*, Cambridge University Press/ UNESCO.

James, E.O., 1966, *The Tree of Life: An archaeological study*, BRILL.

James, H.A.V., 2007, "The emergence of modern human behaviour in South Asia: A review of the current evidence and discussion of its possible implications", in Petraglia, M.D. and Allchin, B.,

The Evolution and History of Human Populations in South Asia: Inter-disciplinary Studies in Archaeology, Biological Anthropology, Linguistics and Genetics, Springer.

Jang, J.H. *et al.*, 2003, Protective effect of resveratrol on beta-amyloid-induced oxidative PC12 cell death, *Free Radic. Biol. Med.* 34:1100-10.

Jansen, T. *et al*, 2002, Mitochondrial DNA and the origins of the domestic horse, *PNAS*, 99(16):10905-10910.

Jarrige, Catherine, 1995, *Mehrgarh: field reports 1974-1985, from Neolithic times to the Indus civilization*, Deptt. of Culture and Tourism, Govt. of Sind, Pakistan.

Jarrige, J.-F., 2008, Mehrgarh Neolithic, *Pragdhara* 18:135-154.

---------, Didier, A. and Quivron, G., 2011, Shahr-I-Sokhta and the Chronology of the Indo-Iranian Regions, *Paléorient*, 37(2):7-34.

Jeffreys, D., 2008, *Aspirin: The remarkable story of a wonder drug*, Bloomsbury Publishing.

Jha, N. and Jha, B.K., 2006, *The Ekashringa Ashwa Varaha: Iconography-Migration & the Horse Seal*, web publication.

Ji, R. *et al*, 2009, Monophyletic origin of domestic bactrian camel (*Camelus bactrianus*) and its evolutionary relationship with the extant wild camel (*Camelus bactrianus ferus*), *Animal Genetics*, 40:377–382.

Jiang, W.Y. *et al*, 2006, Reconstruction of climate and vegetation changes of the lake Bayanchagan (Inner Mongolia): Holocene variability of the East Asian monsoon, *Quaternary Research*, 65:411–420.

Jigna, P. and Sumitra, C., 2006, In-vitro antimicrobial activities of extracts of *Launaea procumbns* Roxb. (Labiateae), *Vitis vinifera* L. (Vitaceae) and *Cyperus rotundus* L. (Cyperaceae), *Afri. J. Biomed. Res.*, 9(2):89-93.

Jones, M. *et al*, 1998, Wheat domestication, *Science*, 279:302-303.

--------, and Brown, T., 2000, Agricultural origins: the evidence of modern and ancient DNA, *The Holocene*, 10:769-776.

Jones-Bley, K. and Zdanovich, D.G., 2002, *Complex Societies of Central Eurasia from the 3rd to the 1st Millennium BC: Ethnos, language, culture*, Institute for the Study of Man, 2002.

Joshi, M.B. *et al*, 2004, Phylogeography and Origin of Indian Domestic Goats, *Mol. Biol. Evol.* 21(3):454-462.

Kaiser, K *et al*, 2009, Charcoal and fossil wood from palaeosols, sediments and artificial structures indicating Late Holocene woodland decline in southern Tibet (China), *Quaternary Science Reviews*, 28:1539-1554.

Kak, S., 1993, Astronomy of the *Satapatha Brahmana*, *Indian Journal of History of Science*, 28-1:15-34.

Kandemir, G. and Kaya, Z., 2009, Oriental Beech *Fagus orientalis*, *European Technical Guidelines for Genetic Conservation and Use*, European Forest Genetic Resources Programme, Biodiversity International, Maccarese, Italy.

Kantanen, J. *et al*, 2009, mtDNA and Y chromosomes of Eurasian cattle, *Heredity*, 103(5):404-15.

Karafet, T.M. *et al*, 2005, Balinese Y-Chromosome Perspective on the Peopling of Indonesia: Genetic Contributions from Pre-Neolithic Hunter-Gatherers, Austronesian Farmers, and Indian Traders, *Human Biology*, 77(1):93–113.

Karima, F.M. *et al*, 2011, Genetic variations between camel breeds using microsatellite markers and RAPD techniques, *Journal of Applied Biosciences*, 39:2626-2634.

Kavar, T. and Dovc, P., 2008, Domestication of the horse: Genetic relationship between domestic and wild horses, *Livestock Science*, 116(1-3):1-14.

Kazanas, Nicholas, 1999, The *Rigveda* and Indoeuropeans, *Annals of Bhandarakar Research Institute*, 80:15-42.

--------, 2009, *Indo-Aryan Origins and other Vedic Issues*, Aditya Prakashan, New Delhi.

--------, 2012, Vedic and Avestan, *Vedic Venues*, 1:183-229.

--------, 2013, The Collapse of the AIT and the prevalence of Indigenism: *archaeological, genetic, linguistic and literary evidences*, Prof. Yogendra Mishra Memorial Lecture, April 2013, Magadh Mahila College, Patna University.

Kearsley, Graeme R., 2010, *Asian Origins of African Culture*, Yelsraek Publishing, London.

Kehl, M., 2009, Quaternary climate change in Iran - The state of knowledge, *Erdkunde*, 63(1):1-17.

Kennedy, K.A.R., 2000, *God-apes and Fossil Men: Paleoanthropology of South Asia*, University of Michigan Press, USA.

Kennedy, Titus, 2010, The Domestication of the Camel in the Ancient Near East, *Bible and Spade*, 23(4).

Kenoyer, J.M. and Vidale, M., 1992, "A new look at stone drills of the Indus Valley tradition", in Vandiver, P.B. *et al* (Eds.), *Material Issue in Art and Archaeology*, Material Research Society Symposium Proceedings, Vol 267, Symposium held Apr 27-May 1, 1992, San Fransisco, USA.

--------, 1998, *Ancient Cities of the Indus Valley Civilization*, Oxford University Press.

--------, 2000, Early Developments of Art, Symbol and Technology in the Indus Valley Tradition, *INDO-KOKO-KENKYU, Indian Archaeological Studies*, 22:1-18.

---------, 2001, "Bead technologies at Harappa, 3300-1900 BC: A comparative study", in Jarrige, C. and Levefre, V. (Eds.), *South Asian Archaeology*, Paris, pp.157-170.

---------, 2005a, "Culture change during the Late Harappan period at Harappa", in Bryant, E.F. and Patton, L.L. (Eds.), *The Indo-Aryan Controversy: Evidence and inference in Indian history*, Routledge, pp.21-49.Kenoyer, J.M. and Heuston, Kimberley B., 2005b, *The Ancient South Asian World*, Oxford University Press.

--------, *et al*, 2013, A new approach to tracking connections between the Indus Valley and Mesopotamia: initial results of strontium isotope analyses from Harappa and Ur, *J. Archaeological Science*, 40(5):2286-2297.

Keyser-Tracqui, C. *et al*, 2005, Mitochondrial DNA analysis of horses recovered from a frozen tomb (Berel site, Kazakhstan, 3rd Century BC), *Animal Genetics*, 36:203–209.

Khare, C.P., 2007, *Indian Medicinal Plants: an illustrated dictionary*, Springer, Verlag-Berlin/ Heidelberg.

King, R.J and Underhill, P.A., 2002, Congruent distribution of Neolithic painted pottery and ceramic figurines with Y-chromosome lineages, 76(293):707-714.

--------, *et al*, 2008, Differential Y-chromosome Anatolian Influences on the Greek and Cretan Neolithic, *Annals of Human Genetics*, 72:205-214.

Kittler, R. *et al*, 2003, Molecular evolution of *Pediculus humanus* and the origin of clothing, *Current Biol*, 13(16):1414-7.

Kivisild, Thomas R., 2005, "Comment" on James and Petraglia, Modern Human Origins and the Evolution of Behavior in the Later Pleistocene Record of South Asia, *Current Anthropology*, 46(Supplement):S18.

--------, 2011, Personal communication by email in response to some queries made by me to him in his capacity of the "corresponding editor" of the article by Romero *et al* 2011.

Koivulehto, J., 2001, "The earliest contacts between Indo-European and Uralic speakers in the light of lexical loans", in Carpolan, C. (Ed.), *Early Contacts between Uralic and Indo-European: Linguistic and Archaeological Considerations* (*Mémoires de la Société Finno-Ougrienne*, 242), Helsinki, pp. 235-263.

Konow, Sten, 2001, Bashgali Dictionary: An Analysis of Colonel J. Davidson's Notes on the Bashgali Language, Asian Educational Service.

Koryakova, L. and Epimakhov, A., 2007, *The Urals and Western Siberia in the Bronze and Iron Ages*, Cambridge University Press.

Kotova, N.S., 2003, *Neolithization in Ukraine*,British Archaeological Reports, J. and E. Hedges (Publishers), Oxford.

Kremenetski, K. and Velichko, A., 2007, *Lateglacial-Holocene Environment History, Kazakhstan*, American Geophysical Union.

Kumar G, *et al.*, 1988, Engraved ostritch egg shell objects: new evidence in Upper Palaeolithic art in India, *Rock Art Res.*, 5: 43–52.

Kumar, Satish *et al*, 2007, Phylogeography and domestication of Indian river buffalo, *BMC Evolutionary Biology*, 7:186.

Kuz'mina, E.E. and Mallory, J.P., 2007, *The Origin of the Indo-Iranians*, Leiden, BRILL.

Kuz'mina, E.E. and Mair, V.H., 2008, *The Prehistory of the Silk Road*, University of Pennsylvania Press.

Kvavadze, E. *et al*, 2009, 30,000-Year-Old Wild Flax Fibers, *Science*, 325(5946):1359.

Lahiri, N., 2009, "Archaeology and some aspects of the social history of early India", in Chattopadhyaya, B.D. (Ed.), Chattopadhyaya, D.P. (Gen. Ed.), *A Social History of Early India*, Vol II, Part 5, Pearson Longman/ Centre for Studies in Civilization, Delhi.

Lal, B.B., 1998, Rigvedic Aryans: The Debate Must Go On, *East and West*, 48(3-4):439-448.

---------, 2005a, "The true horse clears the hurdle", in Trautmann, T.R. (Ed), *The Aryan Debate*, OUP, 2005, Reprinted as Oxford India Paperbacks, 2007, pp. 230-233.

---------, 2005b, "Aryan invasion of India: perpetuation of a myth", in Bryant, E. and Patton, L.L. (Eds.), *The Indo-Aryan Controversy*, Routledge, Oxon

Lalueza-Fox, C. *et al*, 2004, Unraveling Migrations in the Steppe: Mitochondrial DNA Sequences from Ancient Central Asians, *Proc. Royal. Soc. of London B*, 271:941-947.

Lamberg-Karlovsky, C.C., 1969, Further notes on the shaft-hole pick-axe from Khurab, Makran, *Iran*, 7:163-168.

-----------, 2005, "Archaeology and Language: The case of the Bronze Age Indo-Iranaians", in Bryant, Edwin (Ed.), *Indo-Aryan controversy: Evidence and inference in Indian history*, London/New York, Routledge, pp. 142-177.

Larson, Gregor *et al*, 2005, Worldwide phylogeny of wild boar reveals multiple centres of domestication, *Science*, 307:1618-1621.

---------, *et al*, 2007, Ancient DNA, pig domestication, and the spread of the Neolithic into Europe, *PNAS*, 104 (39):15276-15281.

Lau, A.N. *et al*, 2009, Horse Domestication and Conservation Genetics of Przewalski's Horse Inferred from Sex Chromosomal and Autosomal Sequences, *Mol. Biol. Evol.* 26(1):199–208.

Laursen, S.T., 2010, The westward transmission of Indus Valley sealing technology: origin and development of the 'Gulf Type' seal and other administrative technologies in Early Dilmun, c.2100–2000 BC, *Arab. arch. epig.*, 21: 96-134.

Law, R.W., 2008, *Inter-regional interaction and urbanism in the ancient Indus Valley: A geological provenience study of Harappa's rock and mineral assemblage*, Ph. D. Thesis, University of Wisconsin, Madison.

Lawler, Andrew, 2012, 'Rethinking the thundering', *Archaeology*, May-June 2012:42-47.

Lehmann, W.P., Hewitt, H.J. and Feist, S., 1986, *A Goethic Etymology Dictionary*, BRILL.

Lindgren, G. *et al*, 2004, Limited number of patrilines in horse domestication, *Nature Genetics*, 36(4):335-336.

Lippold, S. *et al*, 2011a, Whole mitochondrial genome sequencing of domestic horses reveals incorporation of extensive wild horse diversity during domestication, *BMC Evolutionary Biology*, 11:328.

--------, *et al*, 2011b, Discovery of lost diversities of the paternal horse lineages using ancient DNA, *Nature Communications*, 2, Article no:450.

Lira, J. *et al*, 2010, Ancient DNA reveals traces of Iberian Neolithic and Bronze Age lineages in modern Iberian horses, *Molecular Biology*, 19:64-78.

Liya, Jin *et al*, 2012, Causes of early Holocene desertification in arid central Asia, *Climate Dynamics*, 38(7-8):1577-1591.

Lo-Johansson, I., 1991, *Only a Mother*, University of Nebraska Press.

Loon, Gabriel Van, 2003, *Charaka Samhita: Handbook on Ayurveda*, Vol I, Durham Centre for Ayurveda, Durham.

Louppe, D. (Ed.), 2008, *Plant Resources of Tropical Africa: Timbers* / Sub-Volume 1; Volume 7; PROTA.

Lubotsky, Alexander, 2001, "The Indo-Iranian substratum", in Carpelan, C., Parpola, A., and Koskikallio, P. (Eds.), *Mémoires de la Société Finno-ougrienne* 242, Helsinki, pp. 301-317. Originally appeared in: *Early Contacts between Uralic and Indo-European: Linguistic and Archaeological Considerations. Papers presented at an international symposium held at the Tvärminne Research Station of the University of Helsinki 8-10 January 1999.*

Luikart, G. *et al*, 2001, Multiple maternal origins and weak phylogeographic structure in domestic goats, *PNAS*, 98(10):5927-5932.

--------, *et al*, 2006, "Origins and Diffusion of Domestic Goats Inferred from DNA Markers: Example Analyses of mtDNA, Y Chromosome, and Microsatellites", in Zeder, M.A. *et al*, *Documenting Domestication: New Genetic and Archaeological Paradigms*, pp. 294-305, University of California Press.

Lydekkar, S., 1885, Notes on some siwalik bones erroneously referred to a Struthioid, *Geol. Mag.* pp. 237-238.

--------, 1887, The fossil vertebrata of India, *Records of the Geological Survey of India*, Volumes 20(2):51-80.

--------, 1898, *Wild oxen, sheep and goats of all lands: living and extinct*, London, Rowland Ward Limited.

Macdonell, A.A. and Keith, A. B., 1967, *Vedic Index of Names and Subjects*, (volumes 1 and 2), Motilal Banarsidass, New Delhi; First Ed 1912, London.

Mackay, Ernest, 1940, "Games and Toys", in Vats, M.S., *op.cit.*, pp. 549-561.

Mackay, E.J.A., 1943, *Chanhu-Daro Excavations 1935-36*, American Oriental Society, New Haven Connecticut; also, Kraus Reprint Corporation.

MacKenzie, M.A., 1998, *Androgynous Objects: string bags and gender in Central New Guinea*, Routledge.

Mackie, D.V., 1911, Extracted notes from the report of the Agricultural Inspector of the Philippines, *The Philippine Agricultural Review*, 4(6-12):476-77, published by Bureau of Agriculture, Department of Agriculture and Natural Resources, Philippines.

Madella, M. and Fuller, D.Q., 2006, Palaeoecology and the Harappan Civilisation of South Asia: a reconsideration, *Quaternary Science Reviews*, 25:1283-1301.

Madhuri, K. *et al*, 2012, *Saussurea lappa* (Kuth root): review of its traditional uses, phytochemistry and pharmacology, *Orient Pharm Exp Med*, 12(1):1-9.

Magri, D., 2008, "Patterns of post-glacial spread and the extent of glacial refugia of European beech (*Fagus sylvatica*)", *Journal of Biogeography*, 35:450-63.

Mahdi, Waruno, "Linguistic and philological data towards a chronology of Austronesian activity in India and Sri Lanka" in Blench, Roger (Ed.), *Language change and cultural transformation*, Routledge, 1999.

Mahindale, M.A., 2005, Indo-Aryans, Indo-Iranians and Indo-Europeans, in Trautmann, T.R. (Ed.), *The Aryan Debate*, OUP, Reprinted as Oxford India Paperbacks, 2007, pp. 42-61.

Malik, J.N. and Nakata, T., 2003, Active faults and related Late Quaternary deformation along the Northwestern Himalayan Frontal Zone, India, *Annals of Geophysics*, 46(5):917-936.

Mallory, J.P., 1989, *In search of the Indo-Europeans: Language, archaeology and myth*, Thames and Hudson, London.

--------, and Adams, D.Q., 1997, *Encyclopaedia of Indo-European Culture*, Taylor and Francis.

--------, and Adams, D.Q., 2006, *The Oxford introduction to Proto-Indo-European and the Proto-Indo-European world*, Oxford University Press.

Mallowan, M.E.L. and Rose, J.C., 1935, *Prehistoric Assyria: The Excavations at Tall Arpachiyah, 1933*, Oxford University Press

Manandhar, N.P., 2002, *Plants and People of Nepal*, Timber Press, Portland, Oregon.

Manansala, P.K., 2006, *Quest of the Dragon and Bird Clan*, Lulu (an internet based publishing house).

Mani, B.R., 2013, No Dark Age in Indian History: Archaeological Evidence, *Dialogue*, 15(1):40-46.

Mannam, M.M. *et al*, 2008, *Ethnobotanical Leaflets* 12: 281-285.

Mannan, A. *et al.*, 2010, Survey of artemisinin production by diverse Artemisia species in northern Pakistan, *Malaria Journal*, 9:310.

Marshall, Sir John, 1996 (re-published version of the original of 1931), *Mohenjo-Daro and the Indus Civilization: being an official account of the archaeological excavations at Mohenjo-daro carried out by the Government of India between years 1922 and 1927*, Vols. I and II, originally published Arthur Probsthain, London; republication in 1996 by Asian Educational Service.

Marvie Mohadjer, M. R., 1983, The structure of Iranian Oak-forests (*Quercus castaneifolia* C. A. Mey.) in the eastern part of the caspian forests, *Iran. J. Nat. Res.*, 37:41-55 (In Persian).

Mashkour, M. *et al*, 1999, Investigations on the evolution of subsistence economy in the Qazvin Plain (Iran) from the Neolithic to the Iron Age, *Antiquity* 73:65-76.

--------, 2002, *Chasse et elevage au nord du Plateau central iranien entre le Neolithique et l'Age du Fer. Paléorient*, 28: 27-42.

Masson, V.M., 1988, *Altyn Depe*, UPenn University of Archaeology.

Mathpal, Y., 1984, *Prehistoric Rock Paintings of Bhimbetka, Central India*, Abhinav Publications.

--------, 1985, "The hunter-Gatherer way of life depicted in the Mesolithic Rock Paintings of Central India", in Misra, V.N. and Bellwood, P.S. (Eds.), *Recent Advances in Indo-Pacific Prehistory: Proceedings of the International Symposium Held at Poona, December 19-21, 1978*, BRILL.

Matisoo-Smith, E. *et al*, 2012, DNA for Archaeologists, Left Coast Press.

Matthews, R., 2002, Zebu: harbingers of doom in Bronze Age western Asia?, *Antiquity* 76:438-46.

Matveeva, N.P., 2000, *Sotsialno-Ekonomicheskie Strukturi Naceleniya Zapadnoy Sibiri v Rannem Zheleznom Veke* (Socio-Economic Structure of the Population of Western Siberia in the Early Iron Age), Russian Academy of Sciences-Siberian Division and Nauka, Novosibirsk.

Max Muller, F., 2004 (original ed. 1897), *Hymns of the Atharva Veda: The Sacred Books of the East Part 42*, Kessinger Publications.

Maxwell-Hyslop, K.R., 1955, Note on a shaft-hole axe-pick from Khurab, Makran, *Iraq*, 17(2):161.

Mayewski, P.A. *et al*, 2004, Holocene climate variability, *Quaternary Research* 62(3): 243–255.

McIntosh, Jane R., 2008, *Ancient Indus Valley: New Perspectives*, ABC-CLIO, Understanding Ancient Civilizations Series.

McIntosh, Jane, 2009, *Handbook to Life in Prehistoric Europe*, Oxford University Press.

Meadow, R.H., 1981, "Notes on the Faunal Remains from Mehrgarh, with a focus on cattle (*Bos.*)", in Allchin, B. (Ed.), *South Asian Archaeology*, pp. 34-40.

--------, 1984, "Animal domestication in the Middle East: A view from the eastern margin", in Clutton-Brock, J. and Grigson, C. (Eds.), *Animals and Archaeology: 3. Early herders and their flocks*, British Archaeological Reports, International Series, No. 202, Oxford, pp. 309-337.

--------, 1989, "Pre-historic wild sheep and sheep domestication on the eastern margins of the middle East", in Crabtree, P.J. *et al*, *Early Animal Domestication and Its Cultural Context: Dedicated to the Memory of Dexter Perkins, Jr. and Patricia Daly*, UPenn Museum of Archaeology.

--------, 1993, "Animal Domestication in the *Middle East*: A Revised View from the Eastern Margin" in Possehl G.L. (Ed.), *Harappa Civilization*, Oxford & IBH, New Delhi, pp. 295-320.

--------, 1993, Continuity and change in the agriculture of the Greater Indus Valley, *International Association for the Study of the Cultures of Central Asia: Information Bulletin* 19:63-77.

---------, 1998a, Pre- and proto-historic Agricultural and pastoral transformation in northwestern South Asia, *Review of Archaeology*, 19(2):12-21.

--------, and Patel, Ajita, 1998b, A comment on 'Horse Remains from Surkotada' by Sandor Bokonyi, *South Asian Studies*, 13:308-315.

Meadows, J.R.S. *et al*, 2007, Five ovine mitochondrial lineages identified from sheep breeds of the near East, *Genetics*, 175:1371-1379.

Meadows, J.R.S. *et al*, 2011, Haplogroup relationships between domestic and wild sheep resolved using a mitogenome panel, *Heredity*, 106:700-706.

Mehendale, M.A., 2005, "Indo-Aryans, Indo-Iranians and Indo-Europeans", in Trautmann, T.R. (Ed.), *The Aryan Debate*, Oxford University Press, New Delhi.

Mehrgarh: Field Reports 1974-1985, from Neolithic Times to the Indus Civilization, Department of Culture and Tourism, Government of Sindh in collaboration with the French Ministry of Foreign Affairs, Balochistan, 1995.

Mehta, R.N. *et al*, 1980, Excavation at Kanewal., *Maharaja Sayajirao University, Archaeology Series*, no. 17, Vadodara.

Mehta, S.C. *et al*, 2006, Genetic differentiation of Indian camel (*Camelus dromedarius*) breeds using random oligonucleotide primers, *AGRI*, 39: 77-88, FAO.

Meiri, M. *et al*, 2013, Ancient DNA and Population Turnover in Southern Levantine Pigs- Signature of the Sea Peoples Migration? *Nature: Scientific Reports*, 3:3035, doi: 10.1038/srep03035.

Meuller-Schwarze, Dietland D. and Sun, L., 2003, *The Beaver: Natural History of a Wetlands Engineer*, Cornell University Press.

Miehe, G. *et al*, 2007, Mountain forest islands and Holocene environmental changes in Central Asia: A case study from the southern Gobi Altay, Mongolia, *Palaeogeography, Palaeoclimatology, Palaeoecology*, 250:150–166.

Miller, L.H. and Su, Xinzhuan, 2011, Artemisinin: Discovery from the Chinese Herbal Garden, *Cell*, 146(6):855-858.

Misra, V.D., 2008, "Beginning of agriculture in the Vindhyas (North-Central India)" in Gopal, L. (Ed.), *History of Agriculture in India, Up to C. 1200 A.D.*, Concept Publishing Company.

Misra, V.N., 2001, Pre-historic human colonization of India, *J Biosc*, 26(4) supplement: 491-532.

Mitchell, G. and Skinner, J.D., 2003, On the origin, evolution and phylogeny of giraffes *Giraffa camelopardalis*, *Trans. Roy. Soc. S. Afr.*, 58 (1):51–73.

Mitchell, P., 2005, *African Connections: Archaeological Perspectives on Africa and the Wider World*, Rowman Altamira.

Mithen, S., 2006, *After the Ice: A Global Human History 20,000-5,000 BC*, Harvard University Press.

Monier-Williams, Sir Monier, 1899, *Sanskrit English Dictionary*, online version by uni-koeln.de.

Montemayor, M.R.,1954, "Half Century of Progress in Livestock raising", in *Proceedings of the 8th Pacific Science Congress of the Pacific Science Association Held at the University of the Philippines, Diliman, Quezon City, 16th to 28th November 1953: A. Botany: symposium on medicinal plants*, National Research Council of the Philippines.

Montserrat, J.M. 1992, *Evolución glaciar y postglaciar del clima y la vegetación en la vertiente sur del Pirineo: Estudio Palinolögico, Consejo superior de Investigaciones Cientfficas, Monograffas del Instituto Pirenaico de Ecologfa*, No. 6, ISBN 84-600-8069-2

Moore, K.M. *et al*, 2003, "Animal herding, hunting and the history of animal domestication at Anau Depe", in Hiebert, F. *et al* (Eds.), *A Central Asian Village at the Dawn of Civilization: Excavations at Anau, Turkmenistan*, University of Pennsylvania Press, pp. 154-159.

Motuzaite-Matuzeviciute, G. *et al*, 2013, The earliest evidence of domesticated wheat in the Crimea at Chalcolithic Ardych-Burun, *Journal of Field Archaeology*, 38(2):120-128.

Moulherat, C. *et al*, 2002, First Evidence of Cotton at Neolithic Mehrgarh, Pakistan: Analysis of Mineralized Fibres from a Copper Bead, *J Archaeological Sc.*, 29(12):1393-1401.

Murray, J., *Arabian Horses*, ABDO, 2010.

Naderi, S. *et al*, 2007, Large-scale mitochondrial DNA analysis of the domestic goat reveals six maternal lineages with high haplotype diversity. *PLoS ONE* 10:e1012.

--------, *et al*, 2008, The goat domestication process inferred from large-scale mitochondrial DNA analysis of wild and domestic individuals, *PNAS*, 105(46): 17659–17664.

Nair, P.K.R., 1993, *An Introduction to Agroforestry*, Springer.

Nambiar, G.R. and Raveendran, K., 2008, Indigenous Medicinal Plants Scripted in *Amarakosam*, *American-Eurasian Journal of Botany*, 1(3): 68-72.

Nath, Bhola, 1969, The role of animal remains in the early prehistoric cultures of India, *Indian Museum Bulletin*, 4(1):102-110.

Newton, J.R., 2011, *Ancient Mitochondrial DNA From Pre-historic Southeastern Europe: The Presence of East Eurasian Haplogroups Provides Evidence of Interactions with South Siberians Across the Central Asian Steppe Belt*, *Masters Theses.* Paper 5, Grand Valley State University.

Nikitin, A.G. *et al*, 2010, Comprehensive Site Chronology and Ancient Mitochondrial DNA Analysis from Verteba Cave–a Trypillian Culture Site of Eneolithic Ukraine, *Interdisciplinaria Archaeologica*, 1(2):9-18.

--------, *et al*, 2012, Mitochondrial haplogroup C in ancient mitochondrial DNA from Ukraine extends the presence of East Eurasian genetic lineages in Neolithic Central and Eastern Europe, *J. Hum. Genet.*, 57(9):610-2.

Niskanen, Markku, 2002, The Origin of the Baltic-Finns from the physical anthropological point of view, *The Mankind Quarterly*, 43(2):122-123.

Ntutela, S. *et al*, 2009, Efficacy of *Artemisia afra* phytotherapy in experimental tuberculosis, *Tuberculosis* (Edin), 89(Suppl 1): S33–S40, doi:10.1016/S1472-9792(09)70009-5.

Nuwer, R., 2012, An Ancient Civilization, Upended by Climate Change, *The New York Times*, May 29, accessed 14 March 2014.

Oakenfull, E.A. *et al*, 2000, A survey of equid mitochondrial DNA: implications for the evolution, genetic diversity and conservation of *Equus*, *Conservation Genetics*, 1:341-255.

Orwa, C. *et al*, 2009a, Agroforestree Database:a tree reference and selection guide, version 4.0 http://www.worldagroforestry.org/treedb2/AFTPDFS/Ficus_religiosa.pdf

-------, *et al*, 2009b, Agroforestree Database: a tree reference and selection guide, version 4.0; http://www.worldagroforestry.org/treedb/AFTPDFS/Commiphora_wightii.pdf

Osborn, H.F., 1915, "Review of the Pleistocene of Europe, Asia and Northern Africa", in Hovey, E.O. (Ed.), *Annals of the New York Academy of Sciences*, 26(1):215-315.

Othman, O.E, 2012, Mitochondrial DNA as a marker for genetic diversity and evolution, *Advances in Genet Eng Biotechnol*, 1:1.

Outram, A.K., 2009, The earliest horse harnessing and milking, *Science*, 323(5919):1332-1335.

Owen, D.I., 1991, The first equestrian: an Ur III glyptic scene, *Acta Sumerologica* 13:259–73.

Ozturk, M., 2013, An overview of the atmospheric pollen in Turkey and the northern Cyprus, *Pak. J. Bot.*, 45(S1): 191-195.

Pardeshi, V.C. *et al*, 2007, Mitochondrial haplotypes reveal a strong genetic structure for three Indian sheep breeds, *Animal Genetics*, doi:10.1111/j.1365-2052.2007.01636.x

Parpola, A and Carpelan, C., 2005, "The Cultural Counterparts to Proto-Indo-European, Proto-Uralic and Proto-Aryan", in Bryant, Edwin F. and Patton, Laurie L. (Eds.), *The Indo-Aryan Controversy: Evidence and inference in history*, Routledge, pp. 115-119.

Paterno, Judith, 1981, The Indigenous Horse, *Filipinas Journal of Science and Culture*, volume 4.

Pelle, T. *et al*, 2013, Reconstruction of Holocene environmental changes in two archaeological sites of Calabria (Southern Italy) using an integrated pedological and anthracological approach, *Quaternary International*, 288:206-214.

Pellecchia, M. *et al*, 2007, The mystery of Etruscan origins: novel clues from *Bos taurus* mitochondrial DNA, *Proc R Sc B*, 274:1175-1159.

Pennacchio, M., Jefferson, L. and Havens, K., 2010, *Uses and Abuses of Plant-Derived Smoke: Its Ethnobotany as Hallucinogen, Perfume, Incense, and Medicine*, Oxford University Press.

Pennigton, R.T. and Ratter, J.A., 2010, *Neotropical Savannas and Seasonally Dry Forests: Plant Diversity, Biogeography, and Conservation*, CRC Press.

Peregrine, P.N. (Ed.), 2002, *Encyclopedia of Prehistory,* Volume 8: South and Southwest Asia, Springer.

Perkins, D. Jr., 1972, "The fauna of the Aq Kupruk caves: A brief note", in Dupree, L., *Transactions of the American Philosophical Society,* 62(4):73.

Petit, R.J. *et al*, 2002, Identification of refugia and post-glacial colonisation routes of European white oaks based on chloroplast DNA and fossil pollen evidence, *Forest Ecology and Management,* 156:49–74.

Petraglia, M. *et al*, 2009, Population increase and environmental deterioration correspond with microlithic innovations in South Asia ca. 35,000 years ago, *PNAS,* 106(30):12261-12266.

Petrie, Flinders, 1902, "Excavating in Egypt and its Results", in *Abstract of Papers read before the Society together with the Annual Report for the year ending June 11th, 1902,* Natural History and Philosophical Society, pp. 5-8.

Peyron, O. *et al*, 2013, Contrasting patterns of climatic changes during the Holocene across the Italian Peninsula reconstructed from pollen data, *Clim. Past*, 9:1233–1252.

Pimenoff, Ville N., 2008, *Living on the Edge: Population genetics of Finno-Ugric-speaking humans in North Eurasia*, Academic Dissertation, Department of Forensic Medicine, University of Helsinki, Finland.

Platts, John T., 1884, *A Dictionary of Urdu, Classical Hindi and English*, W.H. Allen and Co., London.

Pohle, P., 1990, *Useful plants of Manang District: A contribution to the ethnobotany of of the Nepal-Himalaya*, Stuttgart, Germany.

Pokharia, Anil K., 2008, Palaeoethnobotanical record of cultivated crops and associated weeds and wild taxa from Neolithic site, Tokwa, Uttar Pradesh, India, *Current Science*, 94(2):248-255.

Pokorny, J., 1959, *Indogernanische Etymologisches Worterbuch*. The English translation by Starostin was generally consulted, however occasionally the original German was also consulted. Citations pertain to the original. The meanings of the German words verified from the Collins German-English Dictionary.

Polanski, S. *et al*, 2012, Simulation and Comparison Between Mid-Holocene and Preindustrial Indian Summer Monsoon Circulation Using a Regional Climate Model, *The Open Atmospheric Science Journal*, 6:42-48.

Porcher, F.P., 1863, *Southern Fields and Forests: Medical, Economic and Agricultural, A medical botany of the Confederate States*, Surgeon-General Richmond VA, Charleston.

Possehl, G. *et al*, 1989, *Harappan Civilization and Rojdi*, BRILL Archive.

Possehl, G., 1997, "Climate and the eclipse of the ancient cities of the Indus", in Dalfes, H.N. *et al* (Eds.), *Third Millennium BC Climate Change and Old World Collapse*, NATO ASI Series 49, Springer-Verlag, Berlin Heidelberg, pp. 193–244.

Possehl, G. and Gullapalli, P., 1999, "The Early Iron Age in South Asia" in Pigott, V. (Ed.), *The Archaeometallurgy of the Asian Old World*, **MASCA Research Papers in Science and Archaeology, Volume 16, MASCA,**The University Museum, Philadelphia, pp. 153-175.

Possehl, G.L., 2002, *The Indus Civilization*, Rowman Altamira.

Possehl, G.L., 2007a, "The Indus Civilization", in Hinnells, J.R. (Ed.), *A Handbook of Ancient Religions*, Cambridge University Press.

Possehl, G.L., 2007b, The Middle Asian interaction sphere: Trade and contact in the 3rd millennium BC, *Expedition*, 49(1):40-42.

Potts, Daniel T., 1993, A new Bactrian find from southeastern Arabia, *Antiquity*, 67:591-6.

-------, 1997, *Mesosopotamian civilization. The material foundations,* Athlone Press, London.

--------, 2004a, "Bactrian Camel and Bactrian-Dromedary Hybrids", Lecture delivered for the Inner Asia/Silkroad Study Group (IASSG) and co-sponsored by the Silkroad Foundation and the Stanford University Center for East Asian Studies, 21 October 2004.

--------, 2004b, Camel hybridization and the role of *Camelus bactrianus* in the ancient Near East, *Journal of the Economic and Social History of the Orient*, 47(2):143-165.

Powell, E.J., 1938 (1912-), *A lexicon to Herodotus*, CUP, Cambridge.

Prasad, M., Chauhan, M.S. and Shah, M.P., 2002, Morphotaxonomic study on fossil leaves of *Ficus* from late Holocene sediments of Sirmur District Himachal Pradesh, India and their significance in assessment of past climate, *Phytomorphology* 52: 45-53.

Prasad, M. *et al*, 2008, Existence of the genus *Shorea* in the Himalayan foot-hills of India since 5600 year B.P., *The Palaeobotanist*, 57(3): 497-501.

Prasad, Vandana *et al*, 2013, Mid–late Holocene monsoonal variations from mainland Gujarat, India: A multiproxy study for evaluating climate culture relationship, *Palaeogeography, Palaeoclimatology, Palaeoecology,* Advance web publication by Elsevier: http://dx.doi.org/10.1016/j.palaeo.2013.05.025

Prashad, B., 1936 Animal remains from Harappa, *Memoirs of the Archaeological Survey of India*, 51(61).

Priyadarshi, P., 2011, *The First Civilization of the World*, Siddhartha Publications, Delhi.

---------, 2012, *Of Mice and Men:* DNA, Archaeological and Linguistic correlation of the two linked journeys of mice and men, *Vedic Venues*, 1:316-352.

--------, 2013, Some Domestic Animals of the Indo-European Homeland and their dispersal, *Vedic Venues*, 2:200-247.

Pugach, I. *et al*, 2013, Genome-wide data substantiate Holocene gene flow from India to Australia, *PNAS*, doi 10.1073/pnas.1211927110.

Puhvel, Jaan, 1964, The Indo-European and Indo-Aryan Plough: A Linguistic Study of Technological Diffusion, *Technology and Culture*, 5(2):176-190.

Pundir, R.K., 2004, Characterization of Spiti Horses of India, *Animal Genetic Resources Information* FAO, 34:75-81.

Purkayastha, S. *et al*, 2012, Evaluation of antimicrobial and phytochemical screening of Funnel, Juniper and Kalonji essential oils against multi-drug-resistant clinical isolates, *Asian Pacific Journal of Pacific Biomedicine*, 2(3 supplement):S1625-S1629.

Ranhotra, P.S. and Bhattacharya, A., 2011, Modern vegetational distribution and pollen dispersal study within Gangotri valley, Garhwal Himalaya, *IGBP PAGES PHAROS Workshop: Land-cover reconstructions in the monsoon affected Tropical world - pollen modeling approach and data synthesis*, January 2011.

Rao, Nagaraja M.S. (Ed.), 1986, *Indian Archaeology 1983-84--A Review*, Archaeological Survey of India, Government of India, New Delhi.

Rashid, H. *et al*, 2011, Late Glacial to Holocene Indian Summer Monsoon Variability Based upon Sediment Records Taken from the Bay of Bengal, *Terr. Atmos. Ocean. Sci.*, 22(2):215-228.

Raverty, H.G., 1867, *A Dictionary of the Puk'hto, Pus'hto or Language of the Afghans: with remarks on the originality of the language, and its affinity to other oriental tongues*, Williams and Norgate, London.

Rédei, Károly, 1986b, "*Zu den indogermanisch-uralischen Sprachkontakten*", *Sitzungberichte der Österreichischen Akademie der Wissenschaften, philosophisch-historische Klasse* 468.

Renfrew, C., 1987 (1990), *Archaeology and Language: The Puzzle of Indo-European Origins*, Jonathan Cape, London, republished in 1990 by CUP Archives.

Riddiford, N.G. *et al*, 2012, Holocene palaeoenvironmental change and the impact of prehistoric salt production in the Seille Valley, eastern France, *The Holocene*, 22(8):831-845.

Ridgeway, W., 1905, *The Origin and Influence of the Thoroughbred Horse*, CUP Archives, Cambridge.

Rig-Veda Samhita

Rimantiene, Rimute, 1998, "The first Narva Culture farmers in Lithuania", in Zvelebil, M. (Ed.) *Harvesting the sea, farming the forest: the emergence of Neolithic societies in the Baltic Region*, Continuum International Publishing Group.

Rissman, P., 1989, "The status of research on animal domestication in India and its cultural context", in Crabtree, P.J. *et al* (Eds.), *Early Animal Domestication and Its Cultural Context: Dedicated to the Memory of Dexter Perkins, Jr. and Patricia Daly*, UPenn Museum of Archaeology.

Roberts, N. *et al*, 2011, Climatic, vegetation and cultural change in the eastern Mediterranean during the mid-Holocene environmental transition, *The Holocene*, 21(1):147 –162.

Romero, I.G. *et al*, 2011, Herders of Indian and European cattle share their predominant allele for lactase persistence, *Molecular Biology and Evolution*, Advance Access Published August 11, 2011.

Roth, S.A., 2001, *Taylor's Guide to Trees: The Definitive, Easy-To-Use Guide to 200 of the Garden's Most Important Plants*, Houghton Mifflin Harcourt.

Roy, B.P., 2008, "*vrksayurveda* in Ancient India", in Gopal, Lallnji (Ed.), *History of Agriculture in India, Up to C. 1200 A.D.*, Concept Publishing Company.

Rubino, Carl, 2013, Reduplication, Feature 27-27A, in Dryer, M.S. and Haspelmath, M. (Eds.), *The World Atlas of Language Structure Online*, Max Planck Institute for Evolutionary Anthropology, Leipzig; Available online at http://wals.info/chapter/27, Accessed on 9 Jan 2014.

Rudenko, S.I., 1970, *Frozen Tombs of Siberia: The Pazyryk Burials of Iron Age Horsemen*, University of California Press.

Sahoo, Sanghmitra *et al*; "A prehistory of Indian Y chromosomes: Evaluating demic diffusion scenarios", in *PNAS* 2006 Jan., 103(4): 843-848.

Sahu, B.P., 1988, *From Hunters to Breeders: Faunal background of Early India*, Anamika Publ. and Distributiors.

Sali, S.A., 1985, "The Upper Palaeolithic Culture at Patna, District Jalgaon, Maharashtra", in Misra, V.N. and Bellwood, Peter (Eds.), *Recent Advances in Indo-Pacific Pre-history: Proceedings of the International Symposium*, BRILL, pp. 137-146.

--------, 1989, *The Upper Palaeolithic and Mesolithic cultures of Maharashtra*, Deccan College Post-Graduate and Research Institute, Pune.

Sanchez, M.D., 2000, World Distribution and Utilization of Mulberry, Potential for Animal Feeding, *Food and Agriculture Organization document, FAO Electronic Conference on Mulberry for Animal Production.*

Santoni, M., 1979, "*Les objets*", in Jarrige, J.-F. and Santoni, M., *Fouilles de Pirak*, vol. 1, Boccard, Paris, pp. 167-232.

--------, 1981, "Sibri and the South Cemetery of Mehrgarh: third millennium connections between northern Kachi Plain (Pakistan) and Central Asia", in Allchin, B. (Ed.), *South Asian Archaeology 1981*, Cambridge University Press, London.

Sapir-Hen, L. and Ben-Yoseph, E., 2013, The Introduction of Domestic Camels to the Southern Levant: Evidence from the Aravah Valley, *Tel Aviv*, 40:277-285.

Sarianidi, V., 1986, *Die Kunst des alten Afghanistan*, Leipzig.

Sastri, K.N., 1957, *New Light on the Indus Civilization*, Atma Ram (Publishers).

Sauer, J.A. and Blakely, J.A., 1988, "Archaeology along the spice route of Yemen" in Potts, D.T. (Ed.), *Araby the Blest: Studies in Arabian Archaeology*, Museum Tusculanum Press.

Sayers, M.R., 2008, *Feeding the Ancestors: Ancestor Worship in Ancient Hinduism and Buddhism*, Ph. D. Dissertation Presented to the Faculty of the Graduate School of The University of Texas at Austin.

Schaffer, J.G. and Thapar, B.K., 1992, "Pre-Indus and Early Indus cultures of Pakistan and India", in Dani, A.H. and Masson, V.M. (Eds.), *History of Civilizations of Central Asia, Volume 5*, UNESCO.

Schaller, G. B., and Mirza, Z. B., 1974, 'On the behaviour of Punjab urial *(Ovis orientalis punjabiensis)*' in *The behaviour of ungulates and its relation to Management vol* (1), IUCN, Morges, Switzerland, pp. 306- 12.

--------, 1977, *Mountain Monarchs-Wild Sheep and Goats of the Himalaya*, Univ. Of Chicago Press.

Schmidt, A.R. *et al*, 2011, Holocene settlement shifts and palaeoenvironments on the Central Iranian Plateau: Investigating linked systems, *The Holocene*, 21(4):583-595.

Schug, G.R. *et al*, 2013, Infection, Disease, and Biosocial Processes at the End of the Indus Civilization, *PLoS ONE*, 8(12): e84814. doi:10.1371/journal.pone.0084814.

Schurr, Theodore G., 2001, Tracking Genes Across the Globe: A review of *Genes, Peoples, and Languuages* by Luigi Luca Cavalli-Sforza, *American Scientist*, 89(1). http://www.americanscientist.org/bookshelf/pub/tracking-genes-across-the-globe, accessed 1 June 2014.

Schwarz, A.S. *et al*, 2013, "Anthracological analysis from a mining site in the eastern Alps to evaluate woodland uses during the Bronze Age", in Damblon, Freddy (Ed.), *Proceeding of: Fourth International Meeting of Anthracology, Brussels, 8-13 September 2008*, BAR International Series 2486.

Semino, O. *et al*, 2004, Origin, Diffusion, and Differentiation of Y-Chromosome Haplogroups E and J: Inferences on the Neolithization of Europe and Later Migratory Events in the Mediterranean Area, *Am. J. Hum. Genet.* 74:1023–1034.

Sengupta, S. *et al*, 2006, Polarity and Temporality of High-Resolution Y-Chromosome Distributions in India Identify Both Indigenous and Exogenous Expansions and Reveal Minor Genetic Influence of Central Asian Pastoralists, *Am J Hum Genet.*, 78(2): 202–221.

Sewell, R. B . and Guha, B. S., 1931, "Zoological Remains", in Marshall, Sir John, *Mohenjo-daro and the Indus Civilization*, in 3 volumes, Vol II, pp. 649-672, A. Probsthain, London.

Sfetcu, Nicolae, 2014, *Health & Drugs: Disease, Prescription & Medication*, Google eBook. Accessed 14 June 2014.

Shaffer, J.G. and Thapar, B.K., 1992, "Pre-Indus and Early Indus cultures of Pakistan and India", in Dani and Masson (Eds.), *History of Civilizations of Central Asia*, Vol 1, UNESCO, pp. 247-282.

Shah, N.C. and Joshi, M.C., 1971, An ethnobotanical study of the Kumaon region of India, *Economic Botany*, 25(4):414-423.

Sharma, A. K., 1990, "Animal Bone Remains" in Joshi, J.P. (Ed.), *Excavation at Surkotada 1971-72 and Exploration in Kutch*, New Delhi, pp. 372-83.

Sharma, B.D., 2008, "The origin and history of wheat in Indian agriculture", in Gopal, L. (Ed.), *History of Agriculture in India, Up to C. 1200 A.D.*, Concept Publishing Company.

Sharma, G.R., 1980a, *Beginnings of agriculture: from hunting and food gathering to domestication of plants and animals: Epi-Palaeolithic to Neolithic : excavations at Chopani-Mando, Mahadaha, and Mahagara*, Abinash Publication.

--------, 1980b, *History to Protohistory: Archaeology of the Vindhyas and the Ganga Valley*, Allahabad University, Allahabad.

---------, 1985, "From hunting and food gathering to domestication of plants and animals in the Belan and Ganga Valleys", in Misra, V.N. and Bellwood, P. (Eds)., *Recent Advances in Indo-Pacific Pre-history: Proceedings of the International Symposium Held at Poona, December 19-21, 1978*, BRILL, pp. 359-368.

Sharma, R.S., 1996, *Looking for the Aryans*, Orient Longman, Hyderabad.

Shinde, V. *et al*, 2008, "Exploration in the Ghaggar Basin and excavations at Girawad, Farmana (Rohtak District) and Mitathal (Bhiwani District), Haryana, India" in Osada, T. and Uesugi, A. (Eds.), *Linguistics, Archaeology and the Human Past*, Occassional Paper 3, Indus Project, Research Institute for Humanity and Nature, Kyoto, Japan. Also published later as: *Current Studies on the Indus Civilization*, Manohar, 2010.

Shirwalkar, P. and Shinde, V., 2008, Early farming cultures of Saurashtra: Their contribution to the development of the regional Harappa culture, *Pragdhara*, 18: 215-227.

Singh, B. and Bhatt, B.P., 2008, Provenance variation in pod, seed and seedling traits of *Dalbergia sissoo* Roxb., Central Himalaya, India, *Tropical Agricultural Research and Extension* 11:39-44.

Singh, B. *et al*, 1996, An ethnobotanical study of Indus Valley (Ladakh), *Journal of Economic and Taxonomic Botany, Additional Series*, 12:92-101.

Singh, Bhagwan, 1987, *Harappa Sabhyata and Vaidik Sahitya* (in Hindi), vol 1, Radhakrishna Prakashan Pvt. Ltd., pp. 77-99.

Singh, G.S., 2000, "Ethnobotanical Study of useful plants of Kullu District in northwestern Himalaya India", in Maheshwari, J.K. (Ed.), *Ethnobotany and medicinal plants of Indian sub-continent*, Scientific Publishers, Jodhpur, India.

Singh, K.N. and Lal, B., 2006, Notes on Traditional Uses of Khair (*Acacia catechu* Willd.) by Inhabitants of Shivalik Range in Western Himalaya, *Ethnobotanical Leaflets* 10: 109-112.

Singh, Purushottam, 2008, "History of millet cultivation in India", in Gopal, Lallanji (Ed.), *History of Agriculture in India, Up to C. 1200 A.D.*, Concept Publishing Company.

Singh, R.P., 2008, "Agricultural background of the Chalcolithic cultures of Central India and Deccan", in Gopal, L (Ed.), *History of Agriculture in India, Up to C. 1200 A.D.*, Concept Publishing Company.

Singh, S. *et al*, 2013, Extensive Variation and Sub-Structuring in Lineage A mtDNA in Indian Sheep: Genetic Evidence for Domestication of Sheep in India, *PLoS ONE*, 8(11): e77858. doi:10.1371/journal.pone.0077858.

Singh, Upinder, 2008, *A History of Ancient and Early Medieval India: From the Stone Age to the 12th century*, Pearson Education India.

Sinha, R. and Sarkar, S., 2009, Climate-induced variability in the Late Pleistocene–Holocene fluvial and fluvio-deltaic successions in the Ganga plains, India: A synthesis, *Geomorphology*, Advance web release.doi:10.1016/j.geomorph2009.03.011

Solis, A. *et al*, 2005, Genetic diversity within and among four South European native horse breeds based on microsatellite DNA analysis: implications for conservation, *Journal of Heredity*, 96(6):670-678.

Sonakia, A. and Biswas, S., 1998, Antiquity of the Narmada *Homo erectus*, the early man of India, *Current Science* 75(4):391-393.

Sood, S.K. *et al*, 2001, *Ethnobotany of the cold-desert tribes of Lahoul-Spiti (N. W. Himalaya)*, Deep Publication, Delhi.

Southworth, F. C., 2005, *Linguistic archaeology of South Asia*, Routledge Curzon, London & New York.

Spassov, N. and Stoytchev, T., 2004, The dromedary domestication problem: 3000 BC rock art evidence for the existence of wild One-humped camel in Central Arabia, *Historia naturalis bulgarica*, 16:151-158.

Stack-Kane, V., 1989, "Animal Remains from Rojdi", in Possehl G.L. and Raval, M.H. (Eds.), *Harappan Civilization and Rojdi*, Brill Academic Publisher.

Starkel, L., 1999, 8500-8000 yrs BP Humid Phase—Global or Regional? *Science Reports of Tohoku University*, 7th Series (Geography), 49(2 Special Issue on GLOCOPH '98):105-133.

Starostin, Georgiy Sergeevich (Translator and Editor), 2007, *Proto-Indo-European Dictionary*, A revised edition of Julius Pokorny's *Indogermanisches Worterbuch*, DNGHU Assoqiation.

Starostin, Sergei, *Database*, on the web. starling.rinet.ru. Accessed 10 July, 2012.

Staublei, K., 1995, Radiocarbon dates of the earliest Neolithic in Central Europe, *Proceedings of the 15th International 14C Conference*, Coop, G. T. *et al* (Eds.), *Radiocarbon* 37(2): 227-237.

Staubwasser, M. and Weiss, H., 2006, Holocene climate and cultural evolution in late prehistoric–early historic West Asia, *Quaternary Research*, 66:371.

--------, *et al*, 2003, Climate change the 4.2 ka BP termination of the Indus valley civilization and Holocene south Asian monsoon variability, *Geophysical Research Letters*, 30:1425, doi:10.1029/2002GL016822.

Steingass, F.J., 1892, *A Comprehensive Persian-English Dictionary*, Routledge and K. Paul, London.

Stevens, L.R. *et al*, 2001, Proposed changes in seasonality of climate during the Late glacial and Holocene at Lake Zeribar, Iran, *The Holocene*, 11(6):747-755.

Stewart, R., 1869, *The American Farmer's Horse Book*, C. F. Vent, Cincinnati.

Sudhakar, M. *et al*, 2006, Evaluation of antimicrobial activity of *Cleome viscosa* and *Gmelina asiatica*, *Fitoterapia*, 77(1):47-9.

Sulaiman, Y. *et al*, 2011, Phylogeny of 19 indigenous sheep populations in northwestern China inferred from mitochondrial DNA control region, *Asian Journal of Animal and Veterinary Advances*, 6(1):71-79.

Sultana, S. *et al*, 2003, Mitochondrial DNA diversity of Pakistani goats, *Animal Genetics*, 34:417–421.

Sun, W. *et al*, 2010, The phylogeographic system survey of native sheep breeds in the eastern and southern Central Asia, *J Anim Breed Genet*, 127(4):308-317.

Sushruta-Samhita, *Uttaratantra*

Suttie, M., *Morus Alba L.*, FAO document, accessed 1 June 2014.

Tanaka, K. *et al*, 2008, Mitochondrial diversity of native pigs in the mainland South and South-east Asian countries and its relationships between local wild boars, *Animal Science Journal*, 79(4):417-434.

Tapio, M. *et al*, 2006, Sheep Mitochondrial DNA variation in European, Caucasian and Central Asian Areas, *Mol Biol Evol*, 23(9):1776-1783.

Tate, G.H.H, 1936, Some Muridae of the Indo-Australian Region, *Bulletin of the American Museum of Natural History* 72-6:501-728.

Tawrell, Paul (Author and Publisher), 2006 (2nd Ed), *Camping & Wilderness Survival:* The Ultimate Outdoors Book, Canada.

Tengberg, M., 1999, Crop husbandry at Miri Qalat, SW Pakistan (4000-2000 BC), *Veg Archaeobotany*, 8(1-2):3-12.

--------, *et al*, 2008, The golden leaves of Ur, *Antiquity*, 82:925-36.

Tewari, Rakesh *et al*, 2008, Early Farming at Lahuradewa, *Pragdhara* 18:347-373.

Thamban, M., 2007, Indian Summer Monsoon Variability during the Holocene as Recorded in Sediments of the Arabian Sea: Timing and Implications, *Journal of Oceanography*, 63:1009-1020.

Thiebault, S., 1988, Palaeoenvironment and ancient vegetation of Baluchistan based on charcoal analysis of archaeological sites, *Proc. Ind. National Science Academy*, 54A(3):501-509.

Thi'ebault, S., 1992, "Complementary results in anthracological analysis from sites in Baluchistan", in Jarrige, C. (Ed.), *South Asian Archaeology 1989: papers from the 10th international conference of South Asian Archaeologists in Western Europe, 3-7 July 1989, Paris* (Monographs in World Archaeology 14): 274. Madison (WI): Prehistory Press.

Thieme, Paul, 1951, *Der Lachs in Indien, Kuhn's Zeitschrift fur vergleichende Sprachforschung* 69:209-216. [in German].

Thomas, Ken, 1999, "Getting a life: stability and change in social and subsistence systems on the North-West Frontier Pakistan in later pre-history", in Godsen, C. and Hather, J.G. (Eds.), *The Prehistory of Food: Appetites for Change*, Routledge/One World Archaeology, London.

Thomas, Ken, 1999, Archaeology on the North-West Frontier: the Bannu Project, Pakistan, *Archaeology International*, 3:39-42; DOI: http://dx.doi.org 10.5334/ai.0313.

Thomas, P.K and Joglekar, P.P., 1995, Faunal studies in archaeology, *Memoires of the Geological Society of India*, 32:496-514.

Thompson, J.A., 1922, *The Outline of Science: A four volume overview of the different sciences*, Volume Four, Wiseside Press, LLC. "The story of domesticated animals" (pp. 1105-1130) is a chapter in the book.

Thomson, Karen and Slocum, Jonathan, Introduction to the online electronic version of the Van Nooten and Holland's book, *Rig Veda: a Metrically Restored Text.* Accessed 8 June 2014.

--------- and ---------, *Ancient Sanskrit online*, Lesson 9, accessed 8 June 2014.

Thorpe, I.J., 1996, *The Origins of Agriculture in Europe*, Routledge, London/ New York, The citations in our book pertain to the 1999 paperback version.

Tickoo, J.L. *et al*, 2005, Lentil (*Lens culinaris*) in India: Present status and future perspectives, *Indian Journal of Agricultural Science* 75(9):539-562.

Tiwari, S.K., 2000, *Riddles of Indian Rockshelter Paintings*, Sarup and Sons.

Tonkov, S., 2005, Vegetation and climate changes in the high mountains on the Balkan peninsula (Southeast Europe) in postglacial times, *PAGES second Open Science Meeting Proceedings*, Beijing, 10-12 August,2005.

Tosi, M., 1974, "Some Data for the Study of Prehistoric Cultural Areas on the Persian Gulf", in *Proceedings of the seminar for Arabian Studies IV*, held at the Middle East Centre, Cambridge, 28-29 June, 1973, pp. 145-171, Archaeopress. IV, 1974.

Toups, Melissa A. *et al*, 2011, Origin of clothing lice indicates Early clothing use by anatomically modern humans in Africa, *Mol. Biol. Evol.*, 28(1):29-32.

Trautmann, T.R. (Ed), *The Aryan Debate*, OUP, 2005, Reprinted as Oxford India Paperbacks, 2007.

Tripathi, V., 2008, "Agriculture in the Gangetic plain in the first millennium BC", Gopal, Lallanji, *History of Agriculture in India, Up to C. 1200 A.D.*, Concept Publishing Company.

Trivedi, A. and Chauhan, M.S., 2009, Holocene Vegetation and Climate Fluctuations in Northwest Himalaya, Based on Pollen Evidence from Surinsar Lake, Jammu Region, India, *Journal of Geological Society of India*, 74:402-412.

Turner Nepali, see Turner, Ralph, 1961.

Turner, Ralph, Lilley 1961 (original 1931), *A Comparative and Etymological Dictionary of the Nepali Language*, Routledge.

--------, 1962-66, *A Comparative Dictionary of Indo-Aryan Language*, Oxford University Press, London.

Uerpmann, H. –P. and Uerpmann, M., 2002, The Appearance of the Domestic Camel in South-east Arabia *The Journal of Oman Studies,* 12: 235–260.

Underhill, P.A., 2002, "Inference of Neolithic population histories using Y-chromosome haplotypes", in Bellwood, P. and Renfrew, P. (Eds.), *Examining the farming/language dispersal hypothesis*, McDonald Institute for Archaeological Research, Cambridge, pp. 65–78.

--------, *et al*, 2009/2010, Separating the post-Glacial coancestry of European and Asian Y-chromosomes within haplogroup R1a, *European Journal of Human Genetics* 2009, 4 November, advance internet publication; later published *EJHG* 2010, 18:479-484.

United States Bureau of Animal Industry, 1912, Annual Report of the Bureau of Animal Industry (for the year 1910), Washington Government Printing Office (27th Report).

Vaisey-Genser, Marion and Morris, Diane H., 2003, "History of the cultivation and uses of the flaxseed", in Alister, D.M. and Westcot, N.D. (Eds.), *Flax: The genus Linum*, CRC Press.

Valdez, R. 2008, *Ovis orientalis*, in, IUCN 2013. IUCN Red List of Threatened Species. Version 2013.2. <www.iucnredlist.org>. accessed 24 May 2014.

Valdiya, K.S., 2013, The River Saraswati was a Himalayan-born river, *Current Science*, 104(1):42-54.

Valpi, F.E.J., 1828, *An Etymological Dictionary of the Latin Language*, Printed by A. J. Valpi, 1828, London.

Van Nooten, Barend and Holland, Gary, 1995, *Rig Veda: A Metrically Restored Text With an Introduction and Notes*, (Harvard Oriental Series 50), Harvard University Department of Sanskrit and Indian Studies.

Vanessa, G. and Jean, B., 2005, First Discovery of Black Mulberry (*Morus nigra* L.) Pollen in a Late Bronze Age Well at Sint-Gillis-Waas (Flanders, Belgium): Contamination or *in situ* Deposition? *Environmental Archaeology*, 10(1):91-96.

Vardhan, R., 2006, *Floristic plants of the world Vol III*, Sarup and Sons, New Delhi.

Vats, M.S., 1940, *Excavations at Harappa*, Two Volumes, Govt of India-Manager of Publications, Delhi.

Vavilov, N.I. (translated into English by Doris L□ve), 1992, *Origin and Geography of Cultivated Plants*, Cambridge University Press.

Vila, Carles *et al*, 2001, Widespread origins of domesticated horse lineages, *Science*, 291(5503): 474-477.

Villems, R. *et al*, 1998, 1998, "Reconstruction of maternal lineages of Finno-Ugric speaking people and some remarks on their paternal inheritance", in Julku, K., and Wiik, K. (Eds.), *The Roots of Peoples and Languages of Northern Eurasia I*, Jyvaskyla, Finland, pp. 180-200.

--------, *et al*, 2002, "Archaeogenetics of Finno-Ugric speaking populations", in Julku, K. and Gummerus, O.Y. (Eds.), *The Roots of Peoples and Languages of the Northern Eurasia IV*", Jyväskylä, Finland, pp. 271-284.

Vishnu-Mittre, 1974, "Palaeobotanical evidence in India", in Hutchison, J. (Ed.), *Evolutionary Studies in World Crops*, Cambridge University Press.

---------, 1978, Palaeoecology of the Rajasthan desert during the last 10,000 years, *The Palaeobotanist*, 25:549-558.

Vogel, J.C. and Waterbolk, H.T., 1963, Groningen Radiocarbon Dates, *Radiocarbon*, 5:163-2021.

Wade, C.M. *et al*, 2009, Genome sequence, comparative analysis, and population genetics of the domestic horse, *Science*, 326: 865–867.

Wakankar, V.S., 1985, "Bhimbetka: The stone tool industries and rock paintings", in Misra, V.N. and Bellwood, Peter (Eds.), *Recent Advances in Indo-Pacific Pre-history: Proceedings of the International Symposium*, BRILL, pp. 175-6.

Waly, N.M., 2009, Verifying the Scientific Name of Costus [*Saussurea lappa* ((Decne.) C.B.Clarke.) – Asteraceae], *JKAU*: Sci., 21(2):327-334.

Wapnish, P., 1981, Camel Caravans and Camel Pastoralists at Tell Jemmeh, *Journal of the Ancient Near East Society*, 13:101-121.

Warmuth, V. *et al*, 2011, European domestic horses originated in two Holocene refugia, *PLoS One*, 6(3): e18194.

---------, *et al*, 2012a, Reconstructing the origin and spread of horse domestication in the Eurasian steppe, *PNAS*, Early edition on the web posted 7 May 2012. doi:10.1073/pnas.1111122109

--------, *et al*, 2012b, Autosomal genetic diversity in non-breed horses from eastern Eurasia provides insights into historical population movements, *Animal Genetics*, online advanced publication, DOI: 10.1111/j.1365-2052.2012.02371.x

Watt, G., 1908, *A Dictionary of the Economic Products of India*, London.

Weninger, B., *et al*, 2006, Climate Forcing due to the 8200 cal BP event observed at Early Neolithic sites in the Eastern Mediterranean, *Quaternary Research*, 66(3):401-420.

Western, Rob W., 1979, Controversy over the Domestication of the camel, (Notes on correspondence submitted to "*Antiquity*"), *Bulletin*, 8:24-25.

Whitney, W.D., 1885, *The Roots, Verb-Forms and the Primary Derivatives of the Sanskrit language*, Leipz, Brietkopf and Hartel, and Trubner and Co., London.

Wick, L. *et al*, 2003, Evidence of Late glacial and Holocene climatic change and human impact in eastern Anatolia: high-resolution pollen, charcoal, isotopic and geochemical records from the laminated sediments of Lake Van, Turkey, *The Holocene*, 13(5):665-675.

Winston, M.L., 1991, *The Biology of the Honey Bee*, Harward University Press.

Witas, H.W. *et al*, 2013, mtDNA from the Early Bronze Age to the Roman Period Suggests a Genetic Link between the Indian Subcontinent and Mesopotamian Cradle of Civilization, *PLoS ONE*, 8(9): e73682. doi:10.1371/journal.pone.0073682.

Withering, William, 1776, *A Botanical Arrangement of all the Vegetables Naturally Growing in Great Britain*, Cadel and Elmsley.

Witzel, M., 1999, Early Sources for South Asian Substrate Languages, *Mother Tongue* special issue, Oct. 1999.

---------, 2001, Autochthonous Aryans? The Evidence from Old Indian and Iranian Texts. Electronic Journal of Vedic Studies *EJVS*, 7(3):1-115.

---------, 2003, Sintashta, BMAC and the Indo-Iranians: A query, an internet publication by Witzel.

--------, 2005, "Indocentricism: autochthonous visions of ancient India", in Bryant, E.F. and Patton, L.L. (Eds.), *The Indo-Aryan Controversy: Evidence and inference in Indian history*, Routledge, London & New York, pp. 341-404.

Wright, H.E. *et al*, 2003, "Late-Glacial and Early-Holocene Dry Climates from the Balkans Peninsula to Southern Siberia" in Tonkov, S. (Ed.), *Aspects of Palynology and Palaeoecology*, Pensoft Publishers, Sofia, Moscow, pp. 127-136.

Yang, Shuli *et al*, 2011, The Local Origin of the Tibetan Pig and Additional Insights into the Origin of Asian Pigs, *PLoS ONE* 6(12): e28215. doi:10.1371/journal.pone.0028215.

Yasuda, Y. and Tabata, H., 1988, Vegetation and Climatic Changes in Nepal Himalayas II. A preliminary study of the Holocene vegitational history in the Lake Rara National Park area West Nepal, *Proceedings of Indian National Science Academy*, 54A(4):538-548.

Yonebayashi, C., Minaki, M., 1997, Late Quaternary vegetation and climatic history of eastern Nepal, *Journal of Biogeography*, 24-6:837-843.

Yule, Henry, Sir 1903, *Hobson-Jobson: A glossary of colloquial Anglo-Indian words and phrases, and of kindred terms, etymological, historical, geographical and discursive.* New ed. edited by William Crooke, B.A. London: J. Murray, 1903.

Zarins, J., 1978, The Camel in Ancient Arabia: a Further Note, *Antiquity*, 52:44-46.

Zavaleta, A.N., 2012, *Medicinal Plants of the Borderlands: A Bilingual Resource Guide*, Author-House.

Zeder, Melinda A. and Hesse, B., 2000, The initial domestication of goats (*Capra hircus*) in the Zagros mountains 10,000 years ago, *Science*, 287:2254-2257.

--------, 2005, "A View from the Zagros: new perspectives on livestock domestication in the Fertile Crescent", in Vigne, J.-D. *et al* (Eds), *First Steps of Animal Domestication: New archaeozoological approaches*, Oxbow Books, Oxford.

--------, *et al*, 2006, Documenting domestication: the intersection of genetics and archeology, *Trends in Genetics* (Genetics, Archeology and the Origins of Domestication; Elsevier) 2006, 22(3):139-155.

Zeuner, F.E., 1955, The identity of the camel on the Khurab pick, *Iraq*, 17:162-163.

Zenuer, F.E., 1963, *A History of Domesticated Animals*, Harper and Row/ Hutchinson, London.

Zhao, Y. *et al*, 2008. Sensitive response of desert vegetation to moisture change based on a near-annual resolution pollen record from Gahai Lake in the Qaidam Basin, northwest China. Global and Planetary Change 62:107–114.

---------, *et al*, 2009, Vegetation response to Holocene climate change in monsoon-influenced region of China, *Earth Science Review*, 97:242-256.

Zimmer, S., 2003, The Problem of Proto-Indo-European Glottogenesis, appeared in *General Linguistcs* 39/1-4, 2002: 25-55 (1999), recte. 2003:25-55. Corrected by the author himself and republished on the net. Accessed 1 June 2014, (original in German 1991).

Zoller, C.P., 2005, *A Grammar and Dictionary of Indus Kohistani*, Walter de Gruyter.

Zvelebil, Marek and Lillie, Malcom, 2000, "Transition to agriculture in Eastern Europe", in Price, Douglas (Ed.), *Europeis First Farmers*, Cambridge University Press, Cambridge.

Index

oak 177; absence from Italy 228; arrival in N. Europe 198; distribution in past 215; Early Holocene 212; expansion in Europe 219; habitat 220
oak savannah Iran 216; Indus Valley 216; Jammu 216; Nepal 217; Iran 217
oak, names in European 202-3; no common name 202
olive (philology) 285
opium 279-280
Oriental horse, origin of 122
orja (Arya) 103
oṣadhi 70
Osborn 123; on *sivalensis* 146
ostrich 375, linguistics of 376-7; *RV* 379
otter 297-8
Outram 160
oyster 291-2
Padova, horse burial at 127
pain, willow for 174
palāla (millet) 64
Pamir 106,107,108,164
Panicum, dactylon 65; *frumentaceum* 62, 64; *italicum* 62; *miliaceum* 63; *miliare* 64; *sumatrens* 64
panther 323
Panthera leo, see lion.
Paraechinus 312
Parjanya RV 266
parkaṭī 203; abundance 265; Austronesian cognates 206; European meanings 264; philology of 206,263; thunder-God 264-5
parṇa 246,261
parṇā-mṛga RV 378
parrot in Harappa 137
pastoral 66; economy 113
pastoralism 21
patella 292
patolaka 291
pearl 292
perkwu-s (PIE) 203, chimera word 203
Petrovka 114
phagos applied to beech 215; philology 210
Philippines Agricultural Review 149
Philippines, *sivalensis* horse in 147
Phoenix species 75
Phragmites 181; *P. karaka* 92
pig 328-31; Europe 329; absent from Balto-Slavic 331
Pindos horse 163
pine 239; -forest Early Holocene 186; in Iran 244; philology 186
Pinus in India 242
pinus-steppe 243-243
pipal, Goddess in 240
Piper longum 77
pipīlikā, ant *AV*, 259; absent in *RV* 260
pippakā 315
pippala (trembling) cognates of 258; IE philology of 250
pippala (tree) 69,70,72; leaves 72; transfer of name 260
pippali, pippalī 77,257
Pirak, horse 113; horse figurines 140; camel figurine 365
Pistachio 205
Pistacia 205
pit-dwelling 43-4
plāk- cognates meaning garment 270; meaning shape of pipal leaf 269-270
plākṣa 74
plākṣa and *parkati* 267; and plexus 267; and wood 269; cognates meaning flickering 270; fluttering 271
playa 33; Thar 81